Fundamentals of Medical Practice Investigation

Fundamentals of

Medical Practice Investigation

Jeffrey D. Lane

CRC Press
Taylor & Francis Group
Boca Raton London New York

CRC Press is an imprint of the
Taylor & Francis Group, an **informa** business

CRC Press
Taylor & Francis Group
6000 Broken Sound Parkway NW, Suite 300
Boca Raton, FL 33487-2742

First issued in paperback 2020

ISBN-13: 978-1-4987-5628-0 (hbk)
ISBN-13: 978-0-367-59627-9 (pbk)

Library of Congress Cataloging-in-Publication Data

Names: Lane, Jeffrey D., author.
Title: Fundamentals of medical practice investigation / Jeffrey D. Lane.
Description: Boca Raton, FL : CRC Press, 2017. | Includes bibliographical references and index.
Identifiers: LCCN 2016004702 | ISBN 9781498756280 (alk. paper)
Subjects: LCSH: Medical laws and legislation--United States. | Physicians--Malpractice--United States. | Medical care--Law and legislation--United States. | Medical care--United States--Evaluation.
Classification: LCC KF2905 .L357 2017 | DDC 344.7304/11--dc23
LC record available at http://lccn.loc.gov/2016004702

Visit the Taylor & Francis Web site at
http://www.taylorandfrancis.com

and the CRC Press Web site at
http://www.crcpress.com

This work is dedicated to my mother, Sally G. Lane and to the memory of my father, the late Chester C. Lane, Jr.
Thank you for raising me right.

Contents

Preface

The state agencies that are charged with regulating the practice of medicine, commonly referred to as *state medical boards*, are faced with a daunting task. Their mandate is to protect the public by enforcing the laws and rules related to the practice of medicine. These laws are commonly referred to as *medical practice acts*. State medical boards must ensure that a physician is properly educated, trained, and competent to practice medicine safely prior to issuing a license to practice as well as to discipline a physician when laws and rules are violated.

The boards would not be able to adequately carry out this mission without benefit of thorough, quality investigations. A thorough and quality investigation begins and ends with the investigator. A well trained, knowledgeable, and experienced investigator is perhaps one of the most important members of the medical board team in terms of the board's ability to regulate the practice of medicine.

Medical practice investigation occupies a very specialized niche in criminal justice and regulatory arenas. These investigations can be extremely tedious, complex, and often deal with a plethora of esoteric terms and concepts. The education and training required to be a successful medical investigator will not come exclusively from the basic law enforcement police academy or from courses provided in college curricula.

During my tenure as the Director of Investigations for the Georgia Composite Medical Board, specialized training in medical investigations was difficult to find. As a Georgia Peace Officer Standards and Training Council (POST) certified instructor, I often found myself having to develop training courses for the board's investigators attempting to focus more on the specific medical-related aspects of investigation.

These comments are certainly not meant to disparage any training agency or its programs. The majority of investigative training programs are designed to reach a much broader audience and the programs I have encountered over the years have been excellent. Training agencies often lack resources to develop such topic-specific programs designed for the relatively small specialized medical investigation entities. In light of the sparsity of specific medical investigation training, I seek to develop this text as a resource for medical investigators. The investigative fundamentals presented in the text may also be applied to investigations concerning an array of other healthcare practitioners to include physician assistants, nurses, dentists, physical therapists, psychologists, etc.

This book is in no way intended to be the absolute final authority on medical investigation. Even though medical investigators share a common goal, that is to find the truth, we often get there via different routes. Each board in every state has a similar mandate as described above, and each state has its own laws and regulations, many similar to other states and many not so similar, all affecting the course of investigation. The book is designed to be a guide assisting the investigator along the way.

It is fully respected and appreciated that the investigative principles and methods contained in the book may or may not apply to all state boards and it is fully understood that each state board has its own way of carrying out its duties as they must comply with the laws and procedures of their state. It is hoped that the information contained herein will benefit new, inexperienced investigators, experienced investigators as a refresher, and perhaps benefit law enforcement officers, as they encounter medical investigators in joint investigations or find themselves confronted with a medical practice issue in their jurisdiction.

A final thought before forging ahead. When I was appointed as an investigator for the Georgia Secretary of State's Office in 1981, I had no concept of medical investigation. The only knowledge I had regarding medicine and medical practice was from an occasional visit to the doctor. Shortly after my appointment, I and my fellow investigators attended an agency-wide meeting to hear a presentation given by G. Douglas Talbott, MD. The late Dr. Talbott was the founder of Talbott Recovery Campus (TRC) in Atlanta, Georgia. TRC is an addiction/substance abuse treatment facility and developed one of the early treatment programs focusing on medical professionals. He and some of his staff came to the Georgia Medical Board to discuss the programs offered by TRC and develop a relationship with the board as the board dealt with practitioners suffering from substance abuse issues.

At one point during the presentation, Dr. Talbott turned the program over to a petite, middle-aged female. She identified herself as a practicing physician recovering from years of substance abuse and addiction (I'll call her Dr. Smith). Dr. Smith talked of the hardships she placed on her family, her practice partners, and the potential of harming her patients. She began to cry. As a cocky 25-year-old former police officer, even I was touched by her story. I thought to myself, how does such a highly educated and successful person fall into drug addiction? I was so naïve to think that addiction was only for the impoverished, the disenfranchised, the lowest levels of society. Her story caused me to realize that addiction can affect anyone on any social stratum.

As Dr. Smith continued her story of treatment at TRC and her continuous recovery, she proudly announced that she has been sober for 8 years. Applause broke out. She turned to one of the senior investigators sitting next to me (I'll call her Jane) and with tears in her eyes she said, "Jane, thank you for saving my life." Jane proceeded to rise from her seat and the two embraced.

At first blush, I thought this was quite unusual. I asked myself, aren't we as investigators supposed to be tough, distant from those whom we investigate? After the meeting I went to Jane's office and asked her to share her story with me about Dr. Smith. The board received information that Dr. Smith arrived at the emergency department of a local hospital for her shift as the ED physician and smelled of alcohol. The ED nurses were concerned because Dr. Smith was unsteady on her feet and was slurring her speech. The case was assigned to Jane for investigation. Jane walked me through her investigation; the witness interviews, collection of evidence (pharmacy data, forged prescriptions, medical records, failed urine drug screen report), and her subsequent meeting with Dr. Smith.

During the meeting with Dr. Smith, Jane presented the evidence developed during the investigation. Dr. Smith vehemently denied having a substance abuse problem. Jane remained steadfast and continued to encourage the doctor as she reviewed the evidence. After some time, Dr. Smith realized that Jane was not going away. Dr. Smith turned and stared out of the window of her office for several minutes. Jane remained quiet and patient. Dr. Smith turned back to Jane and quietly asked, "Where can I get help?" "Am I going to lose my license?" Jane gave Dr. Smith a list of treatment facilities approved and acknowledged by the board and encouraged her to contact one of them sooner rather than later. As to Dr. Smith's medical license, Jane told her that she could not control how the board would respond to this case, but told Dr. Smith that she would make it very clear in her report that Dr. Smith was cooperative, contrite, and expressed a desire to seek treatment.

Dr. Smith entered in-patient treatment at TRC and was discharged 3 months later. She then participated in an aftercare program for the following 5 years and has remained sober since. During Dr. Smith's in-patient treatment, the medical board allowed her to place her license in abeyance until such time that she was able to demonstrate that she was safe to practice. Six months after her discharge from in-patient treatment, the medical board allowed her to return to the practice of medicine.

Why do I share the story of Jane and Dr. Smith? I share the story to simply illustrate that we, as investigators, who come into contact with a variety of people and situations, may never know to what extent our words and actions affect others. Jane was merely doing her job investigating a suspected impaired physician; something she had done many times. The Smith case was just one of many cases assigned to her. Jane had no conscious intention to impact Dr. Smith's life or anyone else's. The investigation was well-worked, possessing all of the necessary evidence. Jane's presentation of the evidence, her interview skills, and her patience with Dr. Smith proved crucial in Dr. Smith's decision to seek treatment. Jane conducted the Smith investigation 8 years prior to the meeting with TRC and it was not until Dr. Smith expressed her thanks that Jane learned of her impact on Dr. Smith's life.

Disclaimer

Throughout the course of the text, various topics concerning constitutional law, case law, federal law, and federal rules and regulations are discussed as they pertain to certain topics to include interviews, respondent or subject interviews, evidence, subpoena authority, search and seizure, and criminal and administrative procedure. The discussions pertaining to these laws, rules, cases, and procedures are NOT intended to be all inclusive or to provide expert direction or guidance and are not discussed in their full context as to their application to investigations and criminal and/or administrative prosecutions. They are intended to provide a basic framework and starting point for the readers' further study. The author does not purport to be an expert on constitutional law, case law, the federal law/rules, the laws and rules of the states, or criminal and administrative procedure. The reader should become knowledgeable of the laws and regulations of their specific state as they pertain to evidence, interrogation, search and seizure, and the like.

When wealth is lost, nothing is lost.
When health is lost, something is lost.
When character is lost, everything is lost.

Reverend Billy Graham

Acknowledgments

As I worked on the manuscript for this project, I recalled many instances throughout my career that were indispensable to the creation of this book. I have had several mentors who helped shape me as the investigator, manager, and leader I am today. They instilled in me a sense of pride in my work as a public servant and a dedication to professionalism I would not have had otherwise. They made me better. I would like to acknowledge these individuals without whom this book would not have been possible.

Upon my appointment as an investigator with the Georgia Secretary of State's Office in 1981, I arrived with an excitement and eagerness typical of an impressionable 24-year old. I was very fortunate that two senior investigators took me under their wing and taught me the ins and outs of medical investigation. As I wrote the chapters relating to the various investigative protocols, I recalled many of their teachings. I owe much to Cheri Crowley, retired group supervisor, U.S. Drug Enforcement Administration, and David Procter, retired special agent, Georgia Bureau of Investigation. Cheri and David, thank you.

In 1991, I was unexpectedly promoted to the position of Director of Investigations (DOI) at the Georgia Secretary of State's Office. The DOI reported directly to the division director responsible for several state licensing boards. My division director was William G. (Bill) Miller, Jr. It was on his recommendation that I was appointed as the DOI. Bill was instrumental in my success at this point in my career. Many obstacles came against me early on during my tenure as DOI and I knew that I could always count on Bill to listen and offer his sage advice and friendship. Bill, thank you.

The Georgia General Assembly voted to remove the Georgia Composite Medical Board (GCMB) from the Secretary of State's Office in late 1999. The GCMB became an independent state agency and I transferred there as the DOI. A short time later, LaSharn Hughes was named executive director (now retired) for the board and, as a result, I became a direct report to her. LaSharn taught me how to effectively deal with people and be more of a team player. She helped me to become a more effective manager resulting in a more efficient and productive investigative section. LaSharn is a consummate leader, bringing the Georgia Medical Board to new levels of competency and respect throughout the country. LaSharn and I developed a close professional relationship, and I deeply value her knowledge, her skill, and her friendship. LaSharn, thank you.

During my research for this book, I was extremely fortunate to have been able to interview four extremely intelligent and highly knowledgeable professionals. Each provided invaluable expertise to the subject matter and I am deeply grateful to them. Susan Darnell, RN, and Alena Brookshire, RN, were very giving of their time during our interviews and provided much-needed detail and essential features for the chapter on medical records. Susan and Alena, thank you. I relied heavily on Janet Wray, Senior Assistant Attorney General, Georgia Attorney General's Office, and Gary Kelley, Inspector General, Georgia Department of Agriculture, for their input and knowledge concerning the trial and hearing process and how to provide effective testimony. Both have spent their entire careers in the courtroom or administrative hearings. Both Janet and Gary have extensive experience in preparing cases for trial and eliciting effective testimony. Each provided me unlimited access for my interviews. Janet and Gary, thank you.

I would be remiss if I did not also acknowledge Curt Ellis, Director of Investigations (retired), North Carolina Medical Board. Curt spent untold hours reviewing and editing the early draft of the manuscript providing sound advice and suggestions. Curt has probably forgotten more about medical investigations than I will ever know. Curt was a trusted colleague for many years and I consider him a great friend. Curt, thank you.

I wish to also acknowledge and thank the many individuals and organizations who granted permission for me to use their material.

The last and most important person to whom I owe a tremendous debt of gratitude is my wife, Laurie. Almost daily, for the duration of this project, she would be bombarded with my thoughts and ideas. She would listen patiently and offer her suggestions. She proofread several chapters and offered advice and suggestions. Often I became discouraged with the book and she never failed to build me up and give me the encouragement needed to press on. She often told me, "If you don't write it, who's going to?" She always left me with something to think about that would inspire me to keep moving forward. When I received word that CRC Press agreed to publish the book, I think that she was more excited than I was. Thank you, L^2.

Author

Jeffrey D. Lane began his medical investigative career in 1981 as an agent for the Georgia Office of Secretary of State. He was appointed Director of Investigations for the Georgia Secretary of State's Office in 1991 and served in this position until 2000 when he was appointed Director of Investigations for the Georgia Composite Medical Board. He served in this position until his retirement in 2012 after 31 years of service. During his career in public service, he also served as an adjunct faculty member in the Department of Criminal Justice, Georgia State University for 16 years. Lane is a life member of the Georgia Association of Chiefs of Police and was an active member of the Peace Officers Association of Georgia, the National Association of Drug Diversion Investigators, and the Georgia State University Criminal Justice Alumni Association.

Lane is a 1978 graduate of the University of Mississippi with a bachelor of public administration degree in criminal justice. He is a 1994 graduate of Georgia State University with a master's in criminal justice where he was awarded the Graduate Academic Honor Award. In 2004, he was awarded the Distinguished Alumni Service Award by the Department of Criminal Justice for his contributions to Georgia State University and the criminal justice community. He has published in several criminal justice journals and periodicals that include the *Academy of Criminal Justice Sciences*, *Georgia State Criminal Justice Review*, and the *FBI Law Enforcement Bulletin*.

chapter one

Medicine and the investigation thereof

The purpose of this book is to introduce the reader to basic investigative fundamentals when called upon to investigate a medical practitioner. The relevance of the book is based on one simple premise: medical practitioners not only figuratively, but literally, touch our lives. When medical mistakes are made, or when a patient is abused by their practitioner, the effects can be devastating. The affected patient/victim deserves a thorough intelligently conducted investigation. Author Paul Starr in his Pulitzer Prize winning work, *The Social Transformation of American Medicine*, eloquently describes the physician/patient relationship: "Even among the sciences, medicine occupies a special position. Its practitioners come into direct and intimate contact with people in their daily lives; they are present at the critical transitional moments of existence. They serve as intermediaries between science and private experience, interpreting personal troubles in the abstract language of scientific knowledge. For many people, they are the only contact with a world that otherwise stands a forbidding distance. Physicians offer a kind of individualized objectivity, a personal relationship as well as authoritative counsel. The very circumstances of sickness promote acceptance of their judgment. Often in pain, fearful of death, the sick have a special thirst for reassurance and vulnerability to belief."[1]

What is meant when we speak of *fundamentals*? My thoughts immediately go to the word basic, the foundation on which more complex intricate processes are built. In medicine, one would think that certain fundamentals should be mastered before moving on to more complex procedures. One would be concerned if they were about to undergo a coronary artery bypass procedure if their physician had not mastered the fundamentals of anatomy, chemistry, biology, etc., learned in medical school. It is said in the world of sports, fundamentals win games. In the game of baseball, the fundamentals consist of pitch, catch, throw, and hit. When these fundamentals are mastered and carried out on the field of play, the odds of winning increase.

The conduct of medical investigations is not much different in that mastering the fundamentals of investigation greatly increases the likelihood of a well thought out, thoroughly conducted investigation. In sports, the goal is to perform at our best, implementing sound fundamentals and hopefully win the game. In the conduct of medical investigations, the goal is to implement sound fundamental investigative techniques resulting in a thorough investigation obtaining the necessary facts to determine if some form of sanction is warranted.

This book seeks to guide the reader through several areas of common physician misconduct and other medical-related areas of concern. The chapters provide the basics in terms of carrying out a fundamentally sound investigation. Throughout one's career, as skills and knowledge develop, more complex investigations will be confronted; however, regardless of the complexity of the case, the investigator will be able to rely on the central fundamental basics. During my tenure as the Director of Investigations for the Georgia Composite Medical Board, I attempted to instill in the investigative staff the importance of adhering to the fundamentals. When a case was turned in to me for review, it was closely scrutinized to ensure that "all of the bases were covered." If not, the case was returned to the investigator for completion.

As we continue the discussion of medical practice investigation, it is important to draw some distinctions. The concept of medical practice investigation should not be confused with medical malpractice investigation. The two are in no way synonymous; however, they are certainly interrelated. As used in this book, the term "medical practice investigation" refers to the investigation of a medical practitioner for alleged violations of laws, rules, and regulations pertaining to the practice of medicine. For example, a medical practice investigation may examine allegations of sexual boundary violations, inappropriate excessive prescribing of controlled substances or physical or mental impairment.

Medical malpractice investigation refers to allegations of a breach of the standard of care whereby the medical practitioner is alleged to have practiced medicine negligently causing an injury to the patient. A medical malpractice investigation is another example of a medical practice investigation. More will be discussed on malpractice investigations in Chapter 8.

Definition

It would be presumptuous to assume that the definition of the "practice of medicine" is understood by all who may read this work. Undoubtedly all of us have been exposed to this term at one time or another just as I am certain that all of us have had an occasion to visit a physician for some type of illness, injury, surgery, etc. It is important to develop a working definition of the "practice of medicine" otherwise the remaining chapters may have little import.

There is no single all-encompassing definition. An examination of the definition of the practice of medicine in the state codes reveals that all states use various combinations of the following: (1) diagnosing, preventing, treating, and curing disease; (2) holding oneself out to the public as able to perform the foregoing; (3) intending to receive a gift, fee, or compensation for the above; (4) attaching such titles as "M.D." to one's name; (5) maintaining an office for reception, examination, and treatment; (6) performing surgery; and (7) using, administering, or prescribing drugs or medicinal preparations.[2] States use myriad variations of these terms in their definitions. States typically utilize words such as *diagnosis, treatment, prevention, cure, advise, and prescribe*. These words are usually accompanied by *disease, injury, deformity, and mental or physical condition*.[2]

The definition in the medical practice statutes of four randomly chosen states from four regions of the United States was reviewed for similarities. The states are Michigan (northern region), Alabama (southern region), Delaware (eastern region), and Oregon (western region).

Michigan Public Health Code 333.17001(1)(f)

> "Practice of medicine" means the *diagnosis, treatment, prevention, cure,* or relieving of a *human disease,* ailment, *defect,* complaint, or other *physical or mental condition,* by attendance, advice, device, *diagnostic* test, or other means, or offering, undertaking, attempting to do, or *holding oneself out* as able to do, any of these acts.[3]

Alabama Code Section 34-24-50

> The "practice of medicine or osteopathy" means: (1) To *diagnose, treat,* correct, advise, or *prescribe* for any *human disease,* ailment, injury, infirmity, *deformity, pain,* or other *condition, physical or mental,* real or imaginary, by any means or instrumentality; (2) To maintain an office or place of business for the purpose of doing acts described in subdivision (1), whether for compensation or not; (3) To use, in the conduct of any occupation or profession pertaining to the *diagnosis or treatment* of *human disease* or *conditions,* the designation *"doctor," "doctor of medicine," "doctor of osteopathy," "physician," "surgeon," "physician* and *surgeon," "Dr.," "M.D.,"* or any combination thereof unless such a designation additionally contains the description of another branch of the healing arts for which a person has a license.[4]

24 Delaware Code, Chapter 17, Subchapter 1, § 1702(9)

> "Practice of medicine" or "practice medicine" includes: (a) Advertising, *holding out to the public*, or representing in any manner that one is authorized to practice medicine in this State; (b) Offering or undertaking to *prescribe*, order, give, or administer any drug or medicine for the use of another person; (c) Offering or undertaking to *prevent* or to *diagnose*, correct, and/or *treat* in any manner or by any means, methods, or devices a *disease*, illness, *pain*, wound, fracture, infirmity, *defect*, or abnormal *physical or mental condition* of another person, including the management of pregnancy and parturition; (d) Offering or undertaking to perform a *surgical* operation upon another person; (e) Rendering a written or otherwise documented medical opinion concerning the *diagnosis* or *treatment* of a person or the actual rendering of *treatment* to a person within the State by a *physician* located outside the State as a result of transmission of the person's medical data by electronic or other means from within the State to the physician or to the physician's agent; (f) Rendering a determination of medical necessity or a decision affecting or modifying the *diagnosis* and/or *treatment* of a person; (g) Using the designation *Doctor, Doctor of Medicine, Doctor of Osteopathy, physician, surgeon, physician* and *surgeon, Dr., M.D.*, or *D.O.*, or a similar designation, or any combination thereof, in the conduct of an occupation or profession pertaining to the *prevention, diagnosis*, or *treatment* of *human disease* or *condition*, unless the designation additionally contains the description of another branch of the healing arts for which one holds a valid license in the State.[5]

Oregon Revised Statutes, Chapter 677.085

> A person is practicing medicine if the person does one or more of the following: (1) Advertise, *hold out to the public* or represent in any manner that the person is authorized to practice medicine in this state; (2) For compensation directly or indirectly received or to be received, offer or undertake to *prescribe*, give or administer any drug or medicine for the use of any other person; (3) Offer or undertake to perform

> any *surgical* operation upon any person. (4) Offer or undertake *to diagnose, cure* or *treat* in any manner, or by any means, methods, devices or instrumentalities, any *disease,* illness, *pain,* wound, fracture, infirmity, *deformity, defect* or abnormal *physical or mental condition* of any person. (5) Except as provided in ORS 677.060, append the letters *"M.D."* or *"D.O."* to the name of the person, or use the words *"Doctor," "Physician," "Surgeon,"* or any abbreviation or combination thereof, or any letters or words of similar import in connection with the name of the person, or any trade name in which the person is interested, in the conduct of any occupation or profession pertaining to the *diagnosis* or *treatment* of *human diseases* or *conditions* mentioned in this section.[6]

As one can see by the italicized terms and phrases, the four definitions cited, while significantly different in their wording and structure, utilize many of the same terms and phrases. It will be important for the medical investigator to become familiar with the statutes of their particular state and to learn from prior case history the medical board's and the courts' interpretation of the statutes and definitions.

This is particularly important in that there are several other health professions that diagnose and treat certain conditions. These professions are generally regulated by their own licensing board, that is, dentistry, nursing, chiropractic, podiatry, etc. Another potential quagmire is the advent of numerous "alternative" therapies that are not subject to any government regulation establishing standards of care, practitioner training, and education. Several of these holistic practices include chelation therapy, homeopathy, aroma therapy, and reflexology to name a few. A more thorough discussion of these modalities will be discussed in Chapter 14.

The standard of care

The *standard of care,* also referred to as the minimum standard of acceptable and prevailing medical practice, is viewed as the measure by which a physician's care and treatment of patients is evaluated. The medical practice acts of all U.S. states, District of Columbia, and U.S. territories contain language essentially stating that the practice of medicine below the standard of care or practice that fails to conform the acceptable and prevailing practice of medicine is considered unprofessional conduct and is sanctionable.

How is the standard of care defined? Federal, state, and local laws help frame the definition as do the rules and regulations of state medical boards and medical specialty boards, that is, boards recognized by the American Board of Medical Specialties. It is interesting to note that there exists no universally accepted medical definition, however, *standard of care* is steadfastly established in law.[7] It is defined as "the caution that a reasonable person in similar circumstances would exercise in providing care to a patient."[7] In other words, a physician has a duty to exercise the degree of care expected of a minimally competent physician in the same specialty and under the same circumstances.[7]

In 1860, the Supreme Court of Illinois issued its first decision on what constitutes standard of care.[7] The lawsuit alleged that a physician was negligent in that he improperly applied a plaster cast. The court stated, "When a person assumes the profession of physician and surgeon, he must…be held to employ a reasonable amount of skill and care."[8]

Two broad approaches to medicine

In the United States, there exist two broad approaches to the practice of medicine; *allopathic* medicine and *osteopathic* medicine.

Allopathic medicine

Allopathic medicine is a system of medicine that aims to combat disease by use of remedies producing effects different from those produced by the disease being treated.[9] Allopathic medicine is often referred to as conventional medicine, and practiced by physicians with an MD degree. Remedies referred to in the definition include medications and surgery.

Osteopathic medicine

Osteopathic medicine is a distinctive form of medical care that takes a "whole person" approach to health care. Osteopathic physicians tend to concentrate on treating the patient as a whole as opposed to just treating specific symptoms. Osteopathic physicians recognize that all body systems are interrelated and dependent upon one another for good health. Illness is treated in the context of the whole body.[10]

Osteopathic physicians use all of the tools available through modern medicine including prescription medicine and surgery. They also incorporate osteopathic manipulative medicine (OMM) into their regimen of patient care when appropriate. OMM is a set of hands-on medicine techniques that may be used to diagnose, treat, and prevent illness and injury and relieve pain.[10]

Physicians licensed as Doctors of Osteopathic Medicine (DOs), like their allopathic counterparts (MDs), must pass a national or state medical board examination in order to obtain a license to practice medicine. DOs provide comprehensive medical care to patients in all 50 states and the District of Columbia.[11]

The medical board of most states license and regulate both allopathic and osteopathic physicians. Fourteen states have both a medical board that licenses and regulates allopathic physicians (MDs) and a separate osteopathic medical board licensing and regulating osteopathic physicians (DOs). A survey of the medical practice act and the rules and regulations of the 14 states that have both boards reveal that their laws, rules, and regulations closely parallel each other and in some states they are identical.

Investigation

The practice of medicine is a centuries old, time-honored profession. Over time, the practice of medicine has become extremely complex due to many factors to include, but not limited to, significant advancements in medical research and technology resulting in an array of medical specialties, a more complicated tangled social environment, emergence of the information age, and greater scrutiny by government agencies. No doubt the existence of specialists and subspecialists greatly enhance patient care, however, when care becomes fragmented among several practitioners, effective communication may be negatively affected, thus having a negative effect on patient care.

The world we live in today is complicated. Society seems to have become more egocentric. If someone does not obtain a desired result, anger and frustration can easily manifest. Blame is then meted out to others who may or may not be deserving of such. When it comes to physicians, often on the receiving end of this anger and frustration is the state medical board; the state government agency charged with regulating the practice of medicine. Complaints filed with the state medical board can be highly charged. Patients who believe that they were injured by their doctor, or a patient's family member who believes the same, tend to develop certain expectations of what they think the board should do to the physician in terms of discipline and sanctions. When the board dismisses the complaint and enters no sanction or takes a lesser action than what was expected, the patient or family member can become incensed.

Over the past several years, the practice of medicine has come under much more scrutiny by government agencies. Consumer complaints and certain consumer organizations have helped to bring this about. This is not necessarily a bad thing. What it means is that physicians and medical organizations are now being held more accountable, not only by consumers, but by government as well. Consumers are more readily willing to vent their frustration and disagreement with medical board decisions. Consumer watchdog groups, the press, and higher levels of government, to include the governor's office and the state legislature, are placing medical boards under greater scrutiny as well. In difficult economic times, state legislatures are looking at state medical boards, as well as other agencies, in terms of their effectiveness and justification of their existence.

The process of investigation plays a significant role with regard to these issues. A thorough investigation enables the board to do its job; that is to ensure that physicians are safe to practice and to impose sanctions on those who practice substandard, hopefully helping them to become better physicians. The investigation should be fair and balanced as it pertains to both complainant and the accused physician. If a need exists to take a disciplinary or corrective action against the physician, it must be supported by facts derived from a thorough investigation. There is a big difference between a good physician who had a bad day and an incompetent bad physician.

What makes medical practice investigations different from other types of investigations? Medical practice investigations follow basic established investigative protocols. However, the laws governing the practice of medicine can be intricate and somewhat complicated. Most state medical boards are empowered by the state legislature to adopt rules and regulations to augment the law; to help clarify or define certain aspects of the law. These rules and regulations can be voluminous and complicated as well.

The practice of medicine is a unique profession rife with esoteric terms, abbreviations, acronyms, and symbols. Interviews of patients and other witnesses will likely concern medical procedures, medications, and complications. The interview with the physician will likely concern similar matters to include medical decision making, rationale for the particular procedure or treatment regimen, and the physician's education and training. Cases involving sexual assault or boundary issues can also be tricky. When does the physical exam become an assault or a boundary violation?

Evidence sought by the medical investigator can also be very unique such as certain documents to include the medial record, pharmacy data, medical instruments, and medications to name a few. The medical record is perhaps the most fundamental piece of evidence in this type of investigation. Review of the patient's medical record can be a very daunting task. (More will be discussed regarding the medical record in Chapter 6.) Pharmacy prescribing data is unique requiring knowledge of medications, effects, contraindications, dosing, etc.

As one can see, medical investigations, although following basic investigative protocols, do pose unique hurdles to overcome in bringing about a successful investigation. A successful investigation does not necessarily equate to discipline or imposed sanctions. The purpose of the investigation is to determine the facts. The investigator's role is to conduct a thorough investigation of the facts, not to acquit or convict. An investigation that is conducted ethically, and seeks to obtain all necessary testimony and evidence to uncover the facts would be considered an effectual investigation. It should be stressed that each case is unique and should be approached as such. It should also be stressed that the investigative techniques and approaches presented in this text are intended to provide a basic fundamental approach and are not mutually exclusive of other investigative techniques and approaches. Each case should be evaluated on its own merit and the appropriate investigative approach chosen with an understanding that as the investigation progresses, the initial investigative approach may require modification as information is gathered and leads developed.

References

1. Starr, P. 1982. *The Social Transformation of American Medicine.* New York: Basic Books, pp. 4–5.
2. Bacigalupi, J. 2012. *A Uniform Approach to the Unlicensed Practice of Medicine.* JD dissertation, William S. Boyd School of Law, University of Nevada, Las Vegas.
3. Michigan Medical Practice Act. Accessed March 5, 2013. http://www.legislature.mi.gov/(S(er5g23izh0orchbsgukvdtdq))/mileg.aspx?page=GetObject&objectname=mcl-333-17001
4. Alabama Medical Practice Act. Accessed March 5, 2013. http://alisondb.legislature.state.al.us/acas/CodeOfAlabama/1975/150994.htm
5. Delaware Medical Practice Act. Accessed March 5, 2013. http://www.dpr.delaware.gov/boards/medicalpractice/index.shtml
6. Oregon Medical Practice Act. Accessed March 5, 2013. http://www.oregon.gov/OMB/STATUTESRULES/.aspx
7. Strauss, D. and J. M. Thomas. 2008. What does the medical profession mean by "Standard of Care?" *American Society of Clinical Oncology,* 27(32): 192–193.
8. *Illinois Lawsuit, Richie v. West.* 1860. 23 Ill. 329.
9. Webster's Medical Desk Dictionary. 1986. *Webster's Medical Desk Dictionary.* Springfield, MA: Merriam-Webster, Inc. Publishers.
10. American Osteopathic Association. *About Osteopathic Medicine.* Accessed September 10, 2015. http://www.osteopathic.org/osteopathic-health/about-dos/about-osteopathic-medicine/Pages/default.aspx
11. American Association of Colleges of Osteopathic Medicine. *Osteopathic Medicine.* Accessed August 25, 2015. www.aacom.org/become-a-doctor/about-om

chapter two

Professional ethics

For decades sociological and criminological theorists have researched the causes of deviant behavior. Medical professionals are, by no means, immune from engaging in deviant behavior. Medical practitioners are, after all, human beings, and subject to the same temptations, frustrations, and desires as the rest of us. It is impossible to derive one definitive explanation as to why human beings engage in deviant behavior. Physicians have long been held in very high esteem in society and when a physician falls from this lofty position, it does not go unnoticed.

Hippocratic Oath

Hippocrates, long noted to be the "father" of western medicine, was revered for his commitment to professionalism and discipline.[1] The Hippocratic Oath is perhaps one of the most influential documents in the history of medical ethics. The oath is the foundation on which the pillars of medical ethics stand. The oath:

"I swear by Apollo the physician, and Asclepius, and Hygieia and Panacea and all the gods and goddesses as my witnesses, that, according to my ability and judgment, I will keep this Oath and this contract:

To hold him who taught me this art equally dear to me as my parents, to be a partner in life with him, and to fulfill his needs when required; to look upon his offspring as equals to my own siblings, and to teach them this art, if they shall wish to learn it, without fee or contract; and that by the set rules, lectures, and every other mode of instruction, I will impart a knowledge of the art to my own sons, and those of my teachers, and to students bound by this contract and having sworn this Oath to the law of medicine, but to no others.

I will use those dietary regimens which will benefit my patients according to my greatest ability and judgment, and I will do no harm or injustice to them.

I will not give a lethal drug to anyone if I am asked, nor will I advise such a plan; and similarly I will not give a woman a pessary to cause an abortion.

In purity and according to divine law will I carry out my life and my art.

I will not use the knife, even upon those suffering from stones, but I will leave this to those who are trained in this craft.

Into whatever homes I go, I will enter them for the benefit of the sick, avoiding any voluntary act of impropriety or corruption, including the seduction of women or men, whether they are free men or slaves.

Whatever I see or hear in the lives of my patients, whether in connection with my professional practice or not, which ought not to be spoken of outside, I will keep secret, as considering all such things to be private.

So long as I maintain this Oath faithfully and without corruption, may it be granted to me to partake of life fully and the practice of my art, gaining the respect of all men for all time. However, should I transgress this Oath and violate it, may the opposite be my fate."[2]

Professional ethics

A discussion of professional ethics is helpful to gain some insight as to what is considered professional medical practice and conversely what is not. Prior to forging ahead, it may be beneficial to examine the nature of a profession and the concept of ethics separately; then meld the two.

Profession

There are common characteristics found in all professions. Sociologist Eliot Freidson put forth the idea that a profession is a specific occupation, performing work with special characteristics while competing for economic, social, and political rewards.[3] A profession tends to have a certain amount of autonomy that comes from the nature of the work performed and from its relationship to external institutions. The concept of a profession, however, goes beyond this rather narrow view to include consideration of the moral or social value of the work.[4] Professions are expected to serve as guardians of social values and to articulate and hold those values publicly, thereby the profession becomes a way of life with a moral value; the profession becomes a calling, not just an occupation.[3,4]

Perhaps one of the most essential concepts to be woven into the "fabric" of a profession is the concept of trust. This is especially true with regard to the practice of medicine. Public trust in physicians depends on the integrity of both individual physicians and the profession itself.[5] Swick[3] asserts that medical professionalism must be grounded in what physicians actually do and how they act individually and collectively. These behaviors demonstrate that physicians are worthy (or unworthy) of trust given by patients and society as a whole.[3] Several key behaviors and commitments emerge from the Swick[3] study and the Physician Charter proposed by the American Board of Internal Medicine Foundation et al., which are considered necessary in establishing a level of public trust and individual patient trust.[3,5] The following are several of the behaviors and commitments emerging from the above-mentioned articles:

- Primacy of patient welfare
- Patient autonomy
- Promote social justice in the healthcare system
- Commitment to maintaining competence
- Commitment to honesty with patients
- Patient confidentiality
- Maintaining appropriate boundaries with patients
- Improvement of quality of care
- Improving access to care
- Maintain trust by managing conflicts of interest
- Respond to societal needs
- Exercise caring, compassion, altruism, empathy, respect
- Exercise accountability
- Reflection on their actions and decisions[3,5]

Ethics

The concept of ethics refers to moral principles and values relating to human conduct; whether the conduct is right or wrong, good or bad in terms of motive for the conduct and the end result of the conduct. The profession puts forth what is considered ethical and professional behavior and when these tenets are violated, the profession should fairly and swiftly deal with those who exhibit unethical behavior.[3,5]

The Four Principles Approach

To further examine some of the ethical issues in medicine, the *four principles approach* will be used.[6]

The four principles are:

- Respect for autonomy
- Beneficence
- Nonmaleficence
- Justice

Autonomy

The concept of autonomy refers to "self-rule;" having the ability to make our own decisions. Autonomy requires the respecting of decisions of all those involved in the therapeutic process, to include the physician and patient. Respecting the patient's autonomy requires their permission before the physician engages in treatment, in other words, the physician must obtain informed consent from the patient prior to initiating treatment.[6]

Respecting autonomy also requires the practitioner to maintain the confidentiality of the patient's protected health information. Without the promise of confidentiality, patients will likely be hesitant to provide the practitioner very private and personal information necessary to develop a proper treatment plan. Ergo, the confidential maintenance of private patient information, respects the patients' autonomy and increases the practitioner's ability to treat the condition.[6]

Respect for autonomy also requires a physician/patient relationship based on honesty. Patient autonomy is breached if the patient feels they are being deceived especially as it pertains to their diagnosis. In this same vein, good communication skills are essential to maintaining autonomy. Good communication requires good listening skills and clearly communicating the necessary information to allow the patient to make informed decisions regarding their health care.[6]

Beneficence and nonmaleficence

When a physician undertakes to treat a patient's malady, the unavoidable risk of harm is manifest. If a "no harm" principle is applied, therapeutic decisions should be based on an analysis of the potential risks and benefits. No effective therapy comes without potential risk. Does the therapy under consideration have benefits that outweigh the risks or vice versa? The question then becomes… to what extent is the recommended therapy beneficent (beneficial) as compared to the potential maleficence (harm)? Thorough research and clinical trials help to determine the risks and benefits of therapies and medications.[6]

The concepts of beneficence and nonmaleficence must also consider harm posed by malpractice and incompetence. From an ethical standpoint, it would seem to be fundamentally imperative that professional standards be developed and embraced by medical providers so as to minimize the potential for harming a patient. Diagnosing and providing medical treatment presumes that the physician possesses a certain level of training and competence.[6]

Justice

Justice is often considered synonymous with fairness. In the context of health care, justice can be examined from three different perspectives: fair distribution of scarce resources, respect for peoples' rights, and respect for the law.[6] When examining justice as it relates to the allocation of resources, several concerns emerge, to include:

- Providing sufficient health care to meet the needs of all who need it. When this cannot be accomplished, to distribute resources in proportion to the extent of peoples' needs for health care.
- Providing equal access to health care.
- Allowing patients to exercise autonomy in selecting their health care.
- Maximizing the benefits derived from available resources.[6]

Examining the decision-making process as it pertains to the above-listed concerns reveals four prima facie decision-making principles. First, the physician should not make decisions based on facts that have no moral basis or justification, disallowing the physician's own self-interests to affect his/her decisions as they relate to patient care and healthcare resources. In other words, if the physician's beliefs, values, morals, etc. are in conflict with those of the patient, such prejudices or bias should not interfere with patient care.[6]

The second of the decision-making principles concerns the cost-efficient use of healthcare resources available to the physician. When looking at the fair distribution of scarce resources, the physician should make efforts to be a good steward of such resources. If a less expensive drug is available and will effectively treat the patient's condition, the less expensive drug should be prescribed. However, if the patient's malady is best treated with a more expensive drug, then the more expensive drug should be prescribed. Here, once again, the concept of beneficence and nonmaleficence must be considered.[6]

The third decision-making principle concerns respect for patients' rights. In the United States, we as citizens enjoy certain rights, many of which are enumerated in the "Bill of Rights," the first 10 amendments to the U.S. Constitution. The first amendment provides for our right of free speech and freedom of expression. A physician's refusal to treat a patient due to the physician's disapproval of the patient's lifestyle would be morally unacceptable justification to refuse treatment. For example, if the physician is adamantly opposed to smoking tobacco he/she is not morally justified to withhold treatment from a patient who smokes.[6]

The fourth principle concerns obedience of morally acceptable laws. An example here would concern confidentiality of the patient's protected health information. One of the tenets of medical practice is to maintain patient confidentiality. Many states have enacted laws requiring a physician to report to government agencies certain infectious diseases, suspected child abuse, etc. The physician is now placed in a situation whereby he/she wishes to maintain patient confidentiality, however, the law requires him/her to divulge certain protected information. If the law was enacted through a democratic legislative system, respecting conflicting views, and based on certain common moral values, then the law would be considered morally acceptable and subject to obedience.[6]

Influencers of unethical behavior

What are seen as some of the influences that cause certain physicians to engage in unethical behavior? How is medicine changing? Many see significant changes in the practice of medicine in recent years. The rise of patient autonomy, or self-determination, is viewed as a significant shift. Patients today see their physician as more of an advisor. Accordingly, the center of patient care is no longer necessarily in the physician's office or the hospital, rather where the patient lives and works. Patients more often are making daily choices that affect their health. This can be tricky for physicians in that a patient's decisions regarding their health care should be of utmost importance, the physician must be sure that those decisions are within ethical standards of care and do not lead to inappropriate care.[5,7]

Another significant change in medicine is the commercialization of health care. This challenge can often lead to additional frustrations when dealing with time constraints and third-party payers. Healthcare employers are requiring physicians to see more patients in less time and many encourage a "cook book" format. The result is a rushed examination leading to misdiagnosis, medical errors, and diminished communication between the physician and patient.[7]

Is health care seeing an erosion of professional ethics and an emergence of an "ethics of trade?" Evidence of this is demonstrated by the rise of "boutique" medicine involving body enhancement procedures such as the use of onabotulinumtoxinA, dermal fillers, body sculpting, liposuction, the marketing of nonbeneficial treatments, and to name a few. While many of these treatments are legitimate and often beneficial, such practices can easily become money driven rather than being driven by what is best for the patient.[7]

As stated earlier, physicians are human beings and are affected by the world in which they live and work. All of us have certain "drives" that influence our decision making and physicians are no different. There are certain drives that can have dramatic influence on professional decision making. These drives include the drive for power and influence, the drive for prestige, the drive for position, and the drive for money.[7] These drives are not inherently bad however. There is nothing wrong with striving for influence or position in one's career. The drive for prestige and money are not inherently bad either. When a physician allows him/herself to be blinded by these drives at the expense of quality and ethical medical practice, they can easily find themselves crossing the line into unethical, and perhaps, even criminal behavior.

The ethical investigator

Much of this chapter has dealt with ethics and professionalism as they relate to physicians and medical practice. It should be noted that ethics and professionalism is no less important as they relate to the medical investigator. As investigators, our stock in trade is not only competency but also our credibility. Our credibility is measured by our adherence to the highest standards of ethical conduct and professionalism. When we fail in this, our credibility as investigators is damaged as is the reputation of the state medical board itself. Much of what was discussed earlier in this chapter relating to the medical "profession" can be overlaid onto the investigative/law enforcement profession. As stated earlier, professions are expected to serve as guardians of social values and to articulate and hold those values publicly, thereby the profession becomes a way of life with a moral value; the profession becomes a calling, not just an occupation.[3,4] This is also true of the investigative/law enforcement profession.

Investigators are and should be held to a higher standard of conduct. One might ask why there should be a different standard of conduct for law enforcement and investigators. Simply stated, law enforcement and public agency investigative personnel are keepers of the public's trust. Said personnel are endowed with certain powers and authority to adversely affect one's rights, privileges, and livelihood. One's ethical base derives from our values; not only our personal values but societal values as well. Our values are those ideas, behaviors, and actions that are important to us.[8] Our values strongly influence the decisions we make. Our values form the basis of our understanding of ethics.[8]

Societal values are those ideals that are esteemed by a culture or group and such values are from where we derive an understanding of ethics and ethical behavior.[8] Examples include integrity, honesty, hard work, kindness, empathy, sympathy, justice, and to name a few.[8]

Ethics can now be interpreted as "doing the right thing." The "right thing" is based on our societal values and the notion that "right is right" and "wrong is wrong."[8] It is important that as medical investigators we must be able to do the following:

- Readily recognize an ethical dilemma
- Identify one's options to address the dilemma
- Make a rational and ethically sound choice of which option to choose
- Take expeditious action based on that choice
- Accept responsibility for the outcome[9]

It should also be stressed that we, as public officers, cannot merely think ethically, we must act ethically. Furthermore, ethics considers not only the action taken, but also the motivation for the action. In other words, doing the right thing for the wrong reason is considered unethical.[9] It may be easier to think ethically but it takes a certain amount of courage to act ethically. Courage may be considered the quality of mind or spirit that enables us to face difficulty, danger, pain, etc., without fear. Courage also refers to one's beliefs and convictions, to act in accordance with our beliefs, especially in spite of criticism.

Let's briefly consider the word integrity. Integrity is held to be a strong unyielding adherence to a code of moral uprightness.[10] As public servants, it is important to identify our own "code of moral uprightness." In other words, to what extent am I willing to bend or "give in" to the pressures exerted by others?

A final look at ethics will include a brief discussion of the concepts of nonfeasance, misfeasance, and malfeasance.

- *Nonfeasance* describes a failure to act that results in harm or injury to another.[11] Example: The investigator is provided irrefutable information from the state's physician health program (PHP) that Dr. Doe has undergone an evaluation for substance abuse and is unsafe to practice medicine as he refuses to enter treatment. The medical record clearly indicates Dr. Doe's admission to forging prescriptions to feed his addiction. The investigator takes the PHP's report and does nothing with it; fails to bring it to the supervisor's attention or see to it that the information is presented to the board for emergency action. The failure of the investigator to act in this instance could be considered nonfeasance.
- *Misfeasance* describes the wrongful performance of a normally lawful act or the wrongful and injurious exercise of lawful authority.[11] Example: The investigator is investigating a case of illegal prescribing of controlled substances to known drug traffickers by a physician who happens to be a surgeon. The case results in a warrant for the doctor's arrest. The arrest is effected and the investigator applies handcuffs to the physician's wrists. The handcuffs are inappropriately applied causing neurological damage to the physician's wrist resulting in him no longer able to perform surgery. The wrongful performance (inappropriately applied restraining device) of a lawful act (applying restraining device while under arrest) could be considered misfeasance.
- *Malfeasance* describes a legally unjustified act causing harm to another to include an act in violation of the public trust.[11] Example: The investigator is called to testify at a hearing against a physician charged with unprofessional conduct. Under oath, the investigator

gives false testimony and commits perjury. The perjured testimony resulted in the revocation of the physician's license. The investigator willingly committed a legally unjustified act (perjury) causing an injury (revocation of the respondent's license).

Ethical decision making

There are a few well-known "tests" that can help when faced with an ethical dilemma.

- The Critical Thinking Test
  This test is a simple series of "yes" or "no" questions. When asked in succession the answers should help guide the investigator toward making the appropriate choice.
  - Is my action legal?
  - Will the end result be good?
  - Will it work?
  - Is there a better, less harmful way to achieve the same goal?
  - Will my decision undermine or contradict another equally important principle?
  - Even if the end results are good, do the means violate an ethical principle?
  - Can my decision be justified if it is made public?[8]
- Media Test
  This test requires the answer to one simple question. How will I feel if my decision is on the 6 o'clock news or the front page of the local newspaper? Often perception becomes reality in the eyes of the public. Even though your actions may be legal and justified, they may give rise to questionable practices.[8]
- Gut Test
  The gut test relies on the premise that we are able to intuit the right decision. The test relies on the principle that if it feels wrong it probably is wrong.[8]

What are some basic attributes or characteristics necessary for the medical investigator from an ethics standpoint? What are some factors that influence how the medical investigator is perceived? The professional medical investigator should be trustworthy and honest. Respectful, competent, persistent, rational, creative thinkers, detail oriented, assertive, and a good listener are all important qualities.[12] The medical investigator should also exhibit calm and reasonable behavior, unbiased conduct, and attempt to always project a professional objective attitude. How medical investigators are perceived by others is affected by others' perception of their integrity, competency, and credibility. The medical investigator should never compromise on their ethics and integrity. To do so would be catastrophic.

References

1. Garrison, F. H. 1966. *History of Medicine*. Philadelphia: W.B. Saunders Company.
2. North, M., trans. 2002. *Hippocratic Oath*. National Library of Medicine. Accessed June 10, 2015. www.nlm.nih.gov/hmd/greek/greek_oath.html
3. Swick, H. 2000. Toward a normative definition of medical professionalism. *Academic Medicine*, 75: 612–616.
4. Wynia, M. K., S. R. Latham, A. C. Kao, J. W. Berg, and L. L. Emanuel. 1999. Medical professionalism in society. *New England Journal of Medicine*, 341: 1612–1616.
5. American Board of Internal Medicine Foundation, American College of Physicians-American Society of Internal Medicine Foundation, European Federation of Internal Medicine. 2002. Medical professionalism in the new millennium: A physician charter. *Annals of Internal Medicine* 136: 243–246.
6. Gillon, R. 1994. Medical ethics: Four principles plus attention to scope. *British Journal of Medicine*, 309: 184–188.
7. Barnet, R. J. 2007. Physician ethics and professional conduct. Presentation given at Administrators *in Medicine (AIM) Investigator Training Conference*, Orlando, Florida, June.
8. Criminology Careers. 2015. Ethics in Law Enforcement and Policing. Accessed September 17, 2015. http://criminologycareers.about.com/od/Career_Trends/a/Ethics-In-Law-Enforcement.htm
9. Gleason, T. 2006. Ethics training for police. *The Police Chief*, 73(11). http://www.policechiefmagazine.org/magazine/index.cfm?fuseaction=display_arch&article_id=1054&issue_id=112006
10. Klein, C. 2012. Police Ethics: The Creed-Integrity, Courage, and Allegiance Define a LEO. Accessed September 10, 2015. http://www.lawofficer.com/articles/2012/10/police-ethics-creed.html
11. Black, H. C. 1990. *Black's Law Dictionary*, 6th edition. St. Paul: West Publishing Company.
12. Hannah, T. 2007. Professionalism and ethics. Presentation given at *Administrators in Medicine (AIM) Investigator Training Conference*, Orlando, Florida, June.

chapter three

The regulation of the practice of medicine

Amendment 10 of the U.S. Constitution states:

> The powers not delegated to the United States by the Constitution, nor prohibited by it to the States, are reserved to the States respectively, or to the people.[1]

This amendment empowers the states to enact laws and regulations to protect the health, safety, and welfare of its citizens. The practice of medicine is not an inherent right of an individual, but a privilege granted by the people of a state acting through their elected representatives.[2] It is readily recognized that incompetent and unprofessional medical practice poses a significant threat to the safety of citizens seeking medical care. All 50 states, the District of Columbia, and the U.S. territories have enacted laws and regulations to oversee the practice of medicine to include the establishment of medical boards to enforce such regulations.[2] These statutes are commonly referred to as a *Medical Practice Act (MPA)*. Many state medical boards also license other healthcare professionals such as physician assistants.

In addition to licensing physicians, state medical boards investigate complaints, discipline licensees who violate the law or rules, conduct physician evaluations, and facilitate rehabilitation of physicians when appropriate. State medical boards also adopt policies and guidelines related to the practice of medicine designed to improve the overall quality of health care in the state.[2]

The structure and authority of medical boards vary from state to state. Some boards are independent and maintain all licensing and disciplinary powers, while others are part of a larger umbrella agency, such as a state department of health, exercising varied levels of responsibilities or functioning in an advisory capacity. State medical boards are typically made up of volunteer physicians and members of the public who are, in most cases, appointed by the governor. Most boards have at least one "consumer" member; a nonmedical individual serving to ensure consumer representation. An excellent source to locate a specific medical board, link to their website, research their laws and rules, and the composition of the various boards is the Federation of State Medical Boards (FSMB). The FSMB is a national organization that represents the 70 medical and osteopathic boards of the United States and its territories. The FSMB is somewhat of a clearinghouse for information and guidance concerning issues facing medical regulation to include policy statements, suggested language for legislation as well as a national voice on behalf of state medical boards.[3]

How physicians gain licensure

Obtaining a license to practice medicine in the United States is a rigorous process. Through licensing, state medical boards ensure that all practicing physicians have appropriate education and training, and that they abide by recognized standards of professional conduct while serving their patients.[2]

Those entering the profession must meet predetermined qualifications that include medical school graduation, postgraduate training, and passage of a comprehensive national medical licensing examination that tests their knowledge of health and disease management and effective patient care. Applicants must submit proof of their education and training and provide details about their work history. They also must reveal information that may affect their ability to practice, such as health status, malpractice, and criminal convictions. Only those who meet a state's qualifications are granted permission to practice medicine in that state.[2]

After physicians are licensed, they must renew their license periodically, usually every one or two years, to continue their active status. During this license renewal process, physicians must demonstrate that they have maintained acceptable standards of ethics and medical practice and have not engaged in improper conduct. In nearly all states, physicians must also show that they have participated in a program of continuing medical education.[2]

How state medical boards regulate physicians after licensing

The ongoing duty of a state medical board goes far beyond the licensing and re-registration of physicians. Boards also have the responsibility of determining when a physician's professional conduct or ability to practice medicine warrants modification, suspension, or revocation of a license to practice medicine.[2]

Boards review and investigate complaints and/or reports received from patients, other state medical boards, health professionals, government agencies, and healthcare organizations about physicians who may be incompetent or acting unprofessionally, and take appropriate action against a physician's license if the person is found to have violated the law. State laws require that boards assure fairness and due process to any physician under investigation.[2]

Board members devote much time and attention to overseeing the practice of physicians. When a board receives a complaint about a physician, the board has the power to investigate, hold hearings, and impose discipline, including suspension, probation or revocation of a physician's license, public reprimands, and fines.[2]

While medical boards find it necessary to suspend or revoke licenses when appropriate, some problems can be resolved with additional education or training in appropriate areas. Boards may place restrictions on a physician's license or put a physician on probation to protect the public while a physician receives special training or rehabilitation aimed at an existing issue.[2]

Difference between a medical board disciplinary action and malpractice

The differences between a disciplinary action taken by a medical board and a malpractice judgment or settlement against a physician are significant.

Board actions and malpractice claims are two different things. Board actions are issued against physicians after a formal process of complaint, investigation, and hearing. While an action taken by a medical board against a physician indicates that a violation of the Medical Practice Act has occurred, malpractice claims are not always reliable measures of a physician's competence or a violation of the law. Issues such as a physician's time in practice, the nature of his or her specialty, the types of patients treated, and geographic location can have a significant influence on the number and amounts of malpractice judgments and settlements.[2]

Malpractice settlements are sometimes handled by insurance companies who opt for settlement based on the terms of coverage, not the validity of the underlying claim. These terms may also authorize settlement of a claim without any consultation of the physician involved or an ultimate determination of fault. It is common practice for medical boards to use malpractice data as a tool to detect unprofessional conduct that may violate the Medical Practice Act. Some boards have built-in levels of malpractice that trigger investigations, such as a certain number of malpractice settlements in a certain span of time.[2]

Sharing of information

All state medical boards engage in an ongoing, cooperative effort to share licensure and disciplinary information with one another by regularly contributing data to the Federation of State Medical Board's Physician Data

Center—a comprehensive data repository that contains information about the more than 870,000 actively licensed physicians in the United States, as well as board disciplinary actions dating back to the early 1960s.[2]

Medical boards use the Physician Data Center in several ways. Boards query the Data Center when new applicants apply for licensure in a state. The Data Center alerts boards if an applicant has been disciplined in another jurisdiction. The Data Center's Disciplinary Alert Service proactively alerts all states in which a disciplined physician is licensed within 24 to 48 hours after a disciplinary action taken by one of those states has been reported to the Data Center. This service helps to prevent disciplined doctors from practicing undetected across state lines.[2]

How state medical boards serve the public

As they fulfill their role of overseeing the practice of medicine in a state, medical boards provide value for both patients and physicians. By following up on complaints and disciplining physicians when needed, medical boards ensure public trust in the basic standards of competence and ethical behavior in their physicians. By striving to ensure that physicians have been properly trained and are maintaining their professional skills, medical boards help protect the integrity of the medical profession.[2]

By defining the practice of medicine in a state, boards play an influential role in how medical care is delivered. A state's Medical Practice Act may contain many important regulations on the use of medical devices, the administering of certain kinds of drugs and the conditions under which medical care can be provided.[2]

One of the most important roles state medical boards play is serving as a repository of publicly available information about physicians. This information can be useful to consumers in helping them choose a physician when they need medical care. Boards provide a valuable service to consumers who are seeking information about physicians by disclosing if a physician is currently licensed in good standing, if disciplinary action has ever been imposed, or if formal disciplinary charges are pending.[2]

The public can also inquire if the board has other public information in a physician's record, such as criminal convictions, sanctions taken by hospitals, and malpractice judgments and settlements. Consumers, who believe that a physician has engaged in unprofessional conduct or that the quality of medical care they received is substandard, should contact their state medical board.[2]

State medical board physician profiles

State medical boards make available a variety of physician information on their individual state websites through online "physician profiles."

At a minimum, medical board profiles include licensure status and disciplinary history. More comprehensive profile systems may include full board orders of disciplinary actions, malpractice judgments, and criminal convictions.[2]

Some also provide information that creates important context to help consumers make decisions about their healthcare providers. For example, a profile including data on physician medical malpractice may include details about the length of a physician's time in practice, the nature of his or her specialty, the types of patients treated and geographic location, all of which can significantly influence the number and size of malpractice judgments, settlements, and awards.[2]

Much of this information may be available at your state medical board's website. The types of information available from your state board may include:

- Medical licenses (active or inactive)
- Final disciplinary orders or actions by regulatory boards or agencies, including other state medical boards, the U.S. Food and Drug Administration, the U.S. Drug Enforcement Administration and Medicare
- Final suspensions or revocations of hospital privileges
- Criminal convictions
- Malpractice payment information
- Medical schools attended and graduation dates
- Graduate medical training (residency) programs attended and completion dates
- Specialty board certifications
- Area(s) of practice[2]

Physician discipline statistics

Figure 3.1 is a compilation of disciplinary actions taken against physicians in 2012 based on the type of action taken.

Figure 3.2 shows the number of physicians with a board action by year 2008–2012.

Figure 3.3 shows the number of physicians disciplined by category of action, 2008 and 2012.

The Medical Practice Act

The state statutes governing the practice of medicine, commonly referred to as medical practice acts (MPAs), provide for certain duties, powers and authority, requirements for licensure, authority to take disciplinary action, definitions of conduct that may result in disciplinary action, procedural

KEY US STATISTICS - PHYSICIAN DISCIPLINE

STATE MEDICAL BOARD ACTIONS	2012
Total state medical board actions	9219
Board actions by category*	
License Restricted	1480
Reprimand	1224
Fine	995
Administrative Action	949
Probation	913
License Suspension	907
Continuing Medical Education Required	819
License Surrendered	511
Conditions Imposed	465
License Revoked	299
License Denied	170
Other	487
Reciprocal Actions Taken by State Boards	1306
Number of Physicians Disciplined	**4479**
Physicians placed on probation	857
Physicians with a license suspension	739
Physicians with a license revocation	275

* The total number of board actions is higher than the total number of disciplined physicians because physicians may have had more than one action taken against them.

Figure 3.1 State medical board actions for 2012. (From Federation of State Medical Boards.)

requirements, and to name a few. The MPA also provides authority for the board to promulgate rules and regulations to enable the board to carry out the law and to more clearly define certain aspects of the law. For example, the law provides for the board to take disciplinary action for unprofessional conduct. The rules of the board specifically define the various acts and behaviors considered to be unprofessional.

The board's primary mission is to protect the public. Public protection is accomplished in two rather broad ways: (1) to license competent physicians in accordance with the law and rules of the board ensuring that the physician meets all of the necessary requirements for licensure, and (2) to investigate complaints alleging violations of the law and/or rules of the board and take appropriate disciplinary or corrective action.

It is important to note that medical boards from state to state vary in composition, and scope of regulatory authority. Another variance existing

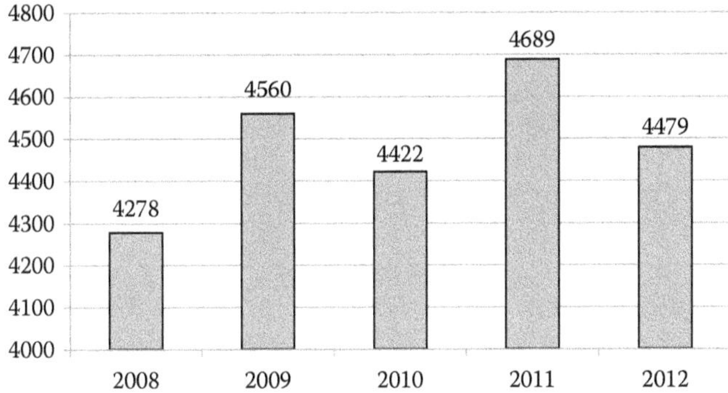

Figure 3.2 Number of physicians with a board action by year, 2008–2012. (Federation of State Medical Boards.)

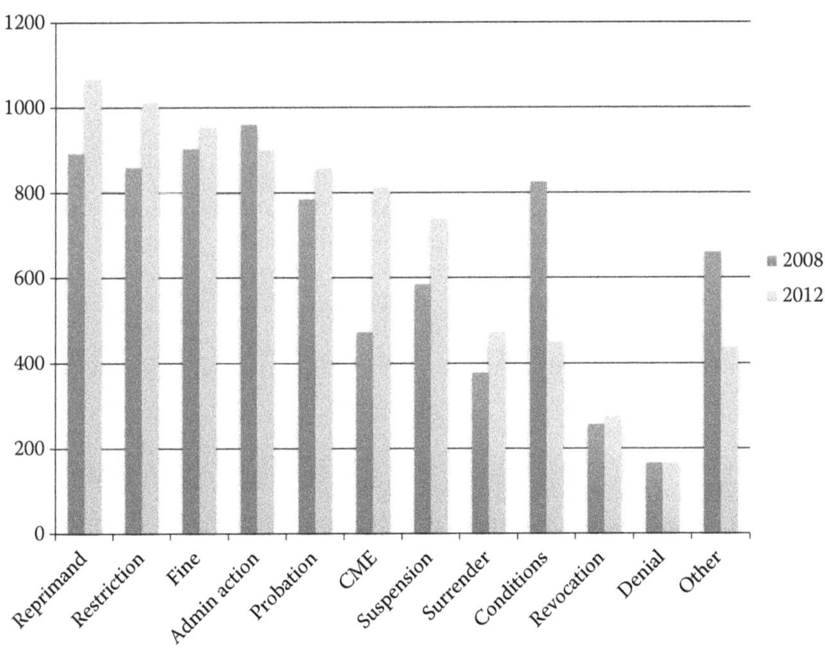

Figure 3.3 Number of physicians disciplined by category of action, 2008 and 2012. (Numbers in these categories represent total number of physicians who had actions taken against them. Numbers in the same categories in Figure 3.1 are higher because they include cases in which multiple actions were taken against an individual physician.) (From Federation of State Medical Boards.)

among the various boards across the country is the issue of amelioration of poor medical practice versus punishment. Given the fact that board members are political appointees and as individuals have their own attitudes, values, and beliefs, opinions and stances on how the board should proceed will vary. Obviously each case should be evaluated on its own merit. Some cases may warrant a more corrective approach to include education or treatment, whereas other cases may warrant outright discipline such as the unscrupulous reckless prescribing of controlled substances or sexual assault.

State medical boards, being an agency of state government, rely on an administrative staff to carry out the daily functions of the board. The staff typically includes an executive director who directs and oversees the daily operations. Certain management staff oversees the licensing function, investigations, support operations, etc. Boards typically employ legal staff, investigative staff, clerical staff, and other support staff to carry out its mission.

A complaint has been filed. The complaint has been thoroughly investigated. The findings of the investigation have been presented to the board. What are the potential outcomes? What actions are available to the board outlined in the MPA and rules? Keep in mind that such outcomes may vary from state to state. Possible outcomes are:

- Closure of the case with no action being taken
- Closure with a letter of concern (letters of concern may be private and not disclosed to the public or may be public)
- The case may be sent for an outside independent peer review to ascertain if the practice in question was within or below the minimum standard of care
- Referral to the board's legal personnel to pursue disciplinary action including
    - Public reprimand
    - Private reprimand
    - Fines
    - Additional medical education
    - Practice restrictions
    - Probation
    - Suspension of license
    - Revocation of license

State medical boards have a very serious undertaking. Their work also touches many lives to include patients, families of patients, future patients, victims, aspiring physicians, physicians, their reputation, their livelihood, hospital staff membership, ability to participate on insurance panels for reimbursement, and participation in Medicare/Medicaid programs. Integral to this undertaking is the investigation of complaints and alleged violations of the MPA. It has been said that, in terms of a medical board's effectiveness, "as investigations go, so goes the board."

References

1. United States Constitution, Amendment 10 National Constitution Center, http://constitutioncenter.org/interactive-constitution/amendments/. Accessed April 20, 2013.
2. Federation of State Medical Boards. 2014. US Medical Regulatory Trends and Actions. Accessed April 23, 2013. Used with permission. https://www.fsmb.org/Media/Default/PDF/FSMB/Publications/us_medical_regulatory_trends_actions.pdf
3. Federation of State Medical Boards. About the FSMB. Accessed April 24, 2013. Used with permission http://www.fsmb.org/about-fsmb/

chapter four

The investigative process

In this chapter, the basic process of investigation will be discussed.

Definition and purpose of an investigation

First, defining the term investigation will be helpful as we begin to develop a framework of the process. A rather simple straightforward definition of investigation is *the process of observing or inquiring in detail; to examine systematically.*[1] What is the purpose of an investigation? The purpose of conducting an investigation is to substantiate or refute certain allegations. Such is accomplished by identifying and thoroughly interviewing witnesses and victims, identifying and properly obtaining physical and/or documentary evidence, a well-thought out and well prepared interview of the respondent, and follow-up on developed information leading to additional witnesses and/or evidence.

When allegations of legal violations are made, the complainant and the subject of the allegations have an expectation that the investigation will be detailed and conducted in a systematic and logical manner. The investigator has a duty to conduct investigations in like manner; a duty to the citizens being served and to the agency for whom they work. By conducting the investigation in a systematic or organized fashion, there is less likelihood that important information and evidence will be overlooked. How can we define a "successful" investigation? Must the successful investigation result in some form of punitive action against the physician? Not necessarily. The findings of many investigations do not result in sanctions. Does that mean that the investigation was unsuccessful or improperly handled? No. A successful investigation is one wherein the investigator thoroughly interviews all pertinent witnesses and victims, properly obtains and handles evidence, conducts a thorough and probing interview with the respondent, and follows up on all developed leads.

Like many other processes, an investigation has a beginning, middle, and an end. In the context of a medical investigation, the following is a simple illustration of the basic process:

- Beginning
    - Initial complaint review

- Middle
    - Conduct all necessary interviews
    - Collect all necessary evidence
- End
    - Organize the case file chronologically
    - Prepare the report of investigation

As a novice investigator in 1981, I was handed my first case. I had had little to no training in the investigative process. I read the complaint and then asked myself, "now what?" A sound approach useful not only for the novice investigator, but also for the seasoned investigator as well, is the *investigative method*. The investigative method is akin to the scientific method and provides an organized framework in which to structure the investigation.[2] The scientific method consists of five parts:

1. State the problem
2. Form the hypothesis (a supposition or proposed explanation with limited information)
3. Observe and experiment
4. Interpret the data
5. Draw conclusions[2]

Let's examine a case involving allegations of excessive and inappropriate prescribing of controlled substances and apply the scientific method.

State the problem: Determine if the respondent is prescribing controlled substances in an excessive and/or inappropriate manner.

Form the hypothesis: Based on the limited prescribing information provided in the complaint, it would appear that the respondent is prescribing drugs in a questionable manner. At this point, the investigator should consider the respondent's motive which could be greed or perhaps fear of drug-dependent "patients" who threaten injury if the respondent ceases prescribing for them. Does the respondent have the means to commit the alleged violations? Yes. He is a physician licensed to practice medicine and has prescriptive authority.

Observe and experiment: What steps are to be taken next in the investigation? What observations need to be made to more fully and accurately reveal the respondent's prescribing practices? Perhaps a survey of the respondent's prescribing patterns from multiple pharmacies will shed light on the problem.

Interpret the data: Examine the prescribing data provided by the several pharmacies. What does the data tell us? What specific drugs are being prescribed? How often? At what dosages? Quantity? Are certain patients identified as receiving prescriptions over an extended period of time? Example: The pharmacy data reveals that 14 patients are receiving prescriptions for oxycodone 30 mg, 240 pills per prescription and have been receiving these prescriptions every two weeks for over two years. Continuing to interpret the data, the medical records of the 14 identified patients should be examined for legitimacy (or illegitimacy) of the respondent's prescribing. The records may also be referred to an expert for his/her opinion as to whether or not the prescribing fell below the standard of care.

Draw conclusions: Based on the interpretation of the data (pharmacy data and medical records) and an expert peer review opining that the treatment was below the minimum standard of care, it can be concluded that the respondent violated certain laws and rules pertaining to the proper prescribing of controlled substances.

Attributes of an effective investigator

A list of all of the essential traits attributing to the consummate investigator would be extensive, however, there are several traits that require mention. Self-discipline and self-motivation are extremely important. Investigators typically have large case-loads and are required to manage multiple tasks at once. A less than motivated investigator will be unable to stay current with their cases causing the process to slow allowing a potential problem practitioner to continue harming others. Self-discipline is crucial in that the investigator must be able to maintain control of their emotions and actions. The sheer nature of the job places the investigator in uncomfortable and stressful situations at times.

Open-mindedness and objectivity are also important traits.[3] The investigator must not go into an investigation with their mind already firmly made up as to the facts. Many times throughout my career, I conducted investigations that at the outset appeared to be atrocious allegations, however, once the investigation progressed, the facts revealed just the opposite. In today's society, the ability to be culturally adroit is essential.[3] The investigator should be skilled in interacting across gender, ethnic, generational, social, and political group lines.[3] Psychologically speaking, desirable attributes include emotional balance, intuitiveness, discernment, inquisitiveness, and perseverance.[3] Investigators should also be skilled in the use of inductive and deductive reasoning.[1] Inductive reasoning is a process whereby the facts are examined and a conclusion is reached. Specific facts are examined and based on this examination a logical explanation emerges. Deductive reasoning begins with a hypothesis as to what happened and this hypothesis (explanation) is tested against the emerging facts of the investigation.[1]

What are some specific abilities and skills that should be possessed of the investigator?

Abilities	Related skills
Recognize/identify physical evidence	Properly collect and preserve physical evidence[4]
Conduct probing interviews	Sound knowledge of interview techniques[4]
Develop and follow up leads	Identify additional witnesses, records, and other evidence[4]
Prepare quality written reports	Knowledge and skill with the English language, punctuation, grammar, sentence structure, etc.[4]
Assist the attorney in preparation of case	Understanding of the elements of the violations and the evidence necessary to prove the violations[4]
Testify in court/hearings	Exercise proper demeanor and be well prepared[4]

Survey of state medical practice acts

A survey was conducted of the medical practice act and rules/regulations of the 50 medical boards, 14 independent osteopathic medical boards, and the District of Columbia medical board, totaling 65 boards. The survey revealed much consistency and commonality with regard to the laws and rules as they pertain to licensing requirements and what constitutes unprofessional conduct and other grounds for sanctions. The most common sanctionable offenses among all boards are:

- Practicing medicine below the standard of care
- Inappropriate prescribing of controlled substances
- Sexual misconduct/boundary violations
- Chemical or physical impairment
- Criminal convictions
- Disciplinary actions taken by other state licensing boards
- The unlicensed practice of medicine or aiding in the unlicensed practice of medicine

The survey was conducted by going to each board's website and researching the laws and rules. In several instances, a law or rule could not be found specifically addressing several of these offenses. When these situations occurred, an email was submitted to the specific board requesting a citation or guidance as to where to locate the law or rule or if such a law or rule exists. In some instances, no responses were obtained. For example, 86% of all boards have a specific law or rule prohibiting sexual misconduct. An email was submitted to the seven boards wherein a specific law or rule prohibiting sexual misconduct could not be found. Neither of the seven responded to the email. It is highly likely that these seven boards do have a law or rule prohibiting sexual misconduct in their code or contained in a different set of rules, therefore this percentage is likely higher. The same is likely with regard to the other four offenses showing less than 100%.

As to the above seven offenses, the percentage of boards having a specific law or rule addressing the offense is as follows:

- Practicing medicine below the standard of care—100%
- Inappropriate prescribing of controlled substances—97% (2 boards did not respond)
- Sexual misconduct/boundary violations—86% (7 boards did not respond)
- Chemical or physical impairment—100%
- Criminal convictions—98% (1 board did not respond)
- Disciplinary actions taken by other state licensing boards—97% (2 boards did not respond)
- The unlicensed practice of medicine or aiding the unlicensed practice of medicine—94% (4 boards did not respond)

The survey also examined two very important tools that are an extremely valuable resource to boards as they investigate allegations of unprofessional conduct and other violations of the law and rules. One is the statutory authority to issue subpoenas to compel the production of medical records and other documents necessary to the investigation. The other is statutory authority to order a physician to undergo a mental and physical evaluation in cases concerning allegations of impairment due to substance abuse or physical infirmity that may render the physician unsafe to practice medicine.

The survey revealed that 90% of all boards have subpoena authority granted them in their respective medical practice act. Six boards did not respond to a request for this information. Ninety-two percent have statutory authority to order a physician to undergo a mental/physical evaluation concerning allegations of substance and/or physical infirmity. Five boards did not respond to a request for this information as well. As stated earlier, authorization for these powers may be contained in another part of these boards' statutes, ergo the percentage could be higher.

Initial complaint review

The initial case/complaint review is critical. At this stage, the investigator's approach to the investigation is conceptualized and formulated. The initial review should consider several points and questions. What are the specific allegations? A clear understanding of the specific allegations is important as you begin to develop your investigative strategy. What laws or rules are alleged to have been violated? Is this matter within the jurisdiction of the board? How should my investigation proceed to gather facts to prove or disprove the specific allegations? Who filed the complaint? Whether the complainant is a patient, patient's family, another healthcare practitioner, a government agency, etc. will determine your initial approach. Are there any potential witnesses mentioned in the complaint? The type of case will likely affect one's initial conceptualization of the case (your initial overall idea as to what happened).

The investigative approach will likely be affected as well. For example: A case of inappropriate prescribing of drugs will more than likely take one down a different path as opposed to a case of alleged sexual misconduct. Based on the nature of the complaint, are there likely to be witnesses to the event? Potential witnesses could include family members of the patient, nurses, staff, other practitioners, etc.

What potential evidence will be needed to prove or disprove the allegations? Again, necessary evidence will be dictated by the type of case being investigated. Examples of common types of evidence sought in a medical investigation will include patient medical records (physician office records and/or hospital records), prescribing records from pharmacies, hard-copy prescriptions, court records, hospital adverse action records, hospital incident reports, telephone records, drug screen records, mental/physical examination records, medications, pill bottles, photographs, audio/video interview recordings from other involved agencies, financial/billing records, insurance claim records, records/reports from other involved agencies (law enforcement, other licensing boards, etc.), and autopsy reports.

Keep in mind that this list is not all-inclusive. When documentary evidence is involved, efforts should always be made to obtain certified copies of the records. Certification of the records is the process of authenticating the documents as true and correct copies of the original. More on this point will be discussed in Chapter 6.

An excellent starting point is to develop a simple investigative outline. This is beneficial in that it provides a basic "road map" as to the conduct of the investigation and helps eliminate overlooking important aspects of the case. The outline provides a beginning, middle, and an end resulting in a more logical approach to the investigation. It can also assist in time management for the investigator who may be carrying a multiple case caseload. The outline brings organization to the investigation and will be a valuable tool to the investigator when it is time to prepare the report of investigation (Chapter 15).

A sample outline may resemble the following:

- Review complaint
    - Who filed the complaint?

    - What is the nature of the complaint? (complaint type)
    - Any potential witnesses identified?
    - Other potential witnesses not identified
- Interviews (Chapter 5)
    - Who needs to be interviewed?
        - In person or telephone?
    - Preparation for interviews
    - Interview complainant/victim
        - Obtain written statement
    - Interview witnesses
        - Obtain written statements
    - Prepare memoranda of interviews for case file
- Evidence
    - What evidence will be necessary?
    - From whom or what entity?
    - Prepare subpoenas or other request documents for documentary evidence.
- Interview of the subject physician (respondent)
    - After all necessary interviews are completed and necessary evidence gathered
    - Prepare for interview
    - Conduct the interview
    - Obtain written statement
- Prepare the report of investigation (Chapter 15)
    - Organize investigative notes, memoranda of interviews, evidence in chronological order.
    - Prepare the report in chronological order.

A well thought-out complaint analysis and an initial investigative outline will go a long way to ensure a thorough and efficient investigation.

References

1. Swanson, C., N. Chamelin, L. Territo, and R. Taylor. 2006. *Criminal Investigation*, 9th edition. New York: McGraw-Hill Higher Education.
2. Gilbert, J. 2007. *Criminal Investigation*, 7th edition. Upper Saddle River, NJ: Pearson Prentice Hall.
3. Bennett, W. and K. Hess. 2007. *Criminal Investigation*, 8th edition. Belmont, CA: Thomson Wadsworth.
4. Osterburg, J. and R. Ward. 1997. *Criminal Investigation*, 2nd edition. Cincinnati, OH: Anderson Publishing Co.

chapter five

Witness interviews and respondent interviews

It can be said that investigators perform three very broad basic tasks. They talk to people, listen to people, and write about it. Investigative work inherently involves interaction with other people. Information is vital to the success of an investigation and the investigator is responsible for amassing the information in a manner that is organized and easily understood. Those who possess this information are the victims, complainants, witnesses, and the subject of the investigation. Investigative work, whether criminal or regulatory, involves dealing with the unfortunate situations affecting others. Medical investigations are no exception. Medical investigators find themselves involved with patients who have been injured via negligent medical procedures, excessive prescribing of drugs, and even sexual assault by their medical practitioner.

The vast majority of an investigator's time is spent collecting information. The information must then be organized and ultimately evaluated to ascertain what the information tells us. Information, the crucial element of any investigation, comes from other people and the ability to extract information from others is vital.

Witness interview

Some definitions are in order as we continue to develop a framework of the investigative process. What/who is a witness? What is an interview? A *witness* is an individual that possesses distinct information as it relates to the allegations. The possession of said information is attributed to the witness being present during the alleged encounter.[1] The witness may have observed the alleged actions or heard or participated in conversations concerning the allegations. The witness may have been provided information by others and if so, these additional witnesses should be interviewed. In terms of medical investigations, a witness can be the victim, the complainant, a family member, other healthcare practitioners involved in the patient's care, someone who may have accompanied the patient to the physician's office to name a few.

For purposes of conducting an investigation, an *interview* is a purposeful and planned verbal interaction between the investigator and a witness.[2] The purpose of the interview is to obtain the information possessed by the witness. Ideally interviews should be conducted in person face-to-face, however, depending on the criticality of the witness a telephonic interview may be appropriate.

It is essential that detailed planning occur prior to the interview. Unlike many criminal investigations, rarely will there be spur-of-the-moment crime scene interviews conducted by a medical investigator. More on planning will be discussed later in this chapter. Interviewing witnesses is an essential means to obtain the information necessary for the investigation to proceed.

The interview is a good time to assess the witnesses' competency and credibility. Witness *competency* is concerned with basic qualifications to render testimony. Competency is often gauged in terms of age, intelligence, mental status, and the like. *Credibility* centers on a witness' believability.[3] Is the testimony believable, trustworthy, reliable? A simple example is a witness stating that he/she was present when the alleged event occurred, however, the witness was not present. The witness' testimony as to what occurred during the event would be considered not credible.

Interpersonal communication skills on the part of the investigator are an important factor affecting the witness' willingness to participate in the interview. Witnesses and victims may manifest many emotions to include agitation, distress, anger, and embarrassment. The investigator should be prepared to confront these emotions with a certain level of compassion and understanding. Conveying these emotions to the interviewee may help calm them and help them to open up.[3]

Time, location, and setting of the interview

Important aspects of the interview are time, location, and setting. When interviewing victims, complainants, and witnesses, it is important to have a setting that allows the witness to feel comfortable and less stressed. Privacy is another important aspect of the interview. There are times when the interviewee may wish to have another party present during the interview such as a spouse, other family member, friend, etc. Given that confidential information will be discussed, it is imperative that the interviewee understand this and is comfortable having the third party present. The investigator will have to decide if this is appropriate given the nature of the investigation and will also need to ensure that the third party is a noninterfering third party. Face-to-face interviews are best practices in that it allows for an opportunity for the investigator to evaluate the witness in terms of competency and credibility and to observe their nonverbal cues or "body language." Convenience, in terms of time and location, is also important; however, the investigator should not place themselves in a position to lose their psychological advantage or in an unsafe or questionable situation. State medical boards are agencies of state government; therefore, they have statewide jurisdiction. In many cases, the investigator has to go to the witness rather than the witness come to them.

The interview with the subject of the investigation, the physician, should be conducted with aplomb, imperturbability, and professionalism. Physicians are fellow professionals and live and work in an environment very different from most others. Obviously the medical investigator will encounter physicians who do not act professionally and this can prove to be a challenging situation. Some physicians may display an attitude of superiority and arrogance toward the investigator. Others may display attitudes of complacency and apathy toward the complaint while others may exhibit submission and fear. In any of these situations, the investigator should maintain composure and professionalism, "taking the high road." The investigator should not meet arrogance with arrogance. The interview with the physician is not a competition as to who is the most arrogant or who is superior. Nothing productive will come of such a situation.

Physicians are busy people. In most cases, setting an appointment to meet with the physician is desirable. This allows for adequate time to be set aside for a thorough discussion to ensue. It also allows time for the physician to retain counsel as is his/her right. Keep in mind, however, that there are circumstances when an unannounced visit to see the physician is warranted. Cases such as alleged impairment (substance abuse, mental impairment), unsanitary conditions, or allowing unlicensed individuals to perform medical duties/procedures would warrant and justify an unannounced visit.

Certain cases may warrant the interview to be conducted in a location other than the physician's office or hospital. The physician also may request the interview be conducted elsewhere. This would be acceptable depending on the location; however, the investigator should always be in a position to maintain control of the interview and should never place him/herself in an unsafe or questionable situation. If necessary, take another investigator to assist. Again, privacy is paramount. Be fully aware of all confidentiality statutes in your state's medical practice act. The physician will naturally want to know specific information about the complaint, and the specific information the investigator already knows and based on the law, this information may be restricted from disclosure.

Preparation for the interview

The interview process involves four basic steps. They are preparation, introduction, body, and conclusion.

Preparation

- Know the facts of the case. In terms of information, know what you have and what you need.[2]
- What is this witness' relation to the case?
- When and where should this interview take place?[2]
- Prepare a list of questions and topics to be discussed prior to the interview. This allows the investigator to stay on track and to not overlook questions that need asking. It will also be helpful when preparing the eventual report of investigation.

Introduction

- Establish rapport with the witness. Often this can be accomplished by initiating "small talk" about matters of mutual interest.[4]
- Explain the purpose of the interview. Explain to the witness why they are an important part of the investigation.

Body

- Ask the witnesses to relay what they know and/or observed in their own words.[5]
- Allow the witnesses to tell what they know without interruption.[2]
- Make notes so as to go back and ask questions to fill in any gaps.[5]
- Ask questions in a systematic and chronological order.[3]
- Use open-ended questions to keep the witness talking and thinking. Keep "yes" and "no" questions to a minimum and keep questions clear and uncomplicated.[3]
- Avoid complex multi-part questions.[3]
- Keep your talking to a minimum and listen.[2]

Conclusion

- Go over the information with the witness to ensure accuracy and completeness.
- Obtain all identifying and contact information from the witness.
- Be sure to thank the witnesses for their cooperation and leave open the opportunity to re-contact them if necessary.

Developing pertinent questions

As a young rookie police officer, I accompanied my field training officer (FTO) on a call concerning a theft. The FTO spent a significant amount of time interviewing several witnesses. After the call was completed and we returned to the police vehicle, I asked my FTO "you asked such good questions; how do you know what questions to ask?" My FTO simply replied "I just ask what I want to know." Simple but somewhat profound.

The principal tools of interviewing are questions. Therefore, it is important to develop skill in crafting and asking them as this will have a bearing on the amount and value of the information obtained from the witness.[2] Each witness will have a unique view or understanding of the event about which they are being interviewed. We must ask "what do I want or need from this witness?" "What is my goal in conducting this interview?" "What do I want to know?" Our questions must be relevant or pertinent to our goals; therefore, the first step is to define the goal(s) of the interview. When the goals are identified, they can be converted into specific points. The specific points can then be converted into questions. Example: You have been assigned to investigate a complaint of sexual boundary violations against a physician. The complainant is a female patient who alleges that she was inappropriately touched by the physician during an examination. As we have stated, the interview is a planned conversation between you the investigator and the witness. Let's plan for this interview.

First, let's establish the goal(s) for this interview. The overarching goal is to develop facts and information to either confirm or refute the allegations. Another goal could be to identify other witnesses or victims. What specific points can be identified to help us meet our goal? What do you want to know? It is important to reinforce here that sound knowledge of the elements of the offense will help guide the development of specific points that can be translated into questions.

Sexual misconduct has been defined as "behavior that exploits the physician/patient relationship in a sexual way."[6] The behavior may be verbal, physical…..that could be reasonably construed by the patient as sexual.[6] Our goal now takes on more focus. Did the physician take advantage of, or in some way abuse the patient during the visit? If so, how so? Now we can translate these points into relevant questions. What was the purpose of the patient's visit to see the physician? Was the patient touched by the physician? Ask the patient to describe the examination. In what manner was the patient touched? On what part(s) of the body was the patient touched? Was the touching sexual in nature? Was anything spoken by the physician? What did he/she say? Was what said sexual in nature? Did the patient say anything during the incident? Did the patient ask the physician to stop the touching? Did the patient interpret the touching and comments made by the physician as sexual? Were any witnesses present; medical assistant, nurse, etc.?

An effective approach to this is the journalistic technique. This technique seeks to determine the who, what, when, where, why, and how of an event. Who is the victim? Who is the patient? Who did it, who saw it, who heard it? What happened, what was seen, what was heard, what was done after the event? What was happening before the event? When did the event occur? When was the medical error discovered? When was it reported? When and where was follow-up care received? Where did the event occur? Where was the patient, where was the physician, where were the witnesses during the event? Why was the patient seeing the physician? Why did they wait to report the problem? How did the event occur?

Asking the question

The way a question is asked can have a significant impact on the interviewee's response. Was the question asked in a manner that was straightforward and not confusing? Are we communicating with the witness at a level the witness can understand and relate? Are we exhibiting any nonverbal cues that may inadvertently have a negative effect on the interviewee?

We are often taught to observe the witness' body language for nonverbal cues, however, we often fail to consider our own body language to wit, "what nonverbal message(s) am I sending to the witness?" It is important to be aware of our question delivery, eye contact (or lack thereof), our facial expressions, and tone of voice. All of these nonverbal cues can significantly affect the success of the interview.

If the interviewee feels intimidated, they may be reluctant to be as forthcoming as they might be otherwise. Lack of eye contact from the investigator may be perceived as a lack of interest on the part of the investigator resulting in the interviewee becoming less interested in assisting in the investigation. Tone of voice can also deliver certain messages, sometimes unintended. The tone of voice and voice inflection can indicate a number of emotions such as anger, irritation, frustration, doubt, joy, deceit, and to name a few. Investigators should always be cognizant of their body language and tone of voice. Introduction of unwanted nonverbal cues can have a negative impact on the success of the interview.

Listening and observing

A successful interview will rely heavily on the investigator's listening skills. Often in human interaction, we hear but we do not listen. It is crucial that the investigator actively listen to what the witness is saying and what they are not saying.[3] Active listening also requires close observance of the witness' body language. Through nonverbal cues, what is the witness communicating? How should the investigator respond to these cues?

An excellent technique for active listening is to allow the witness to relate their entire story while the investigator takes notes. Be careful to not get preoccupied in note-taking so as to appear to be ignoring the witness. After the witness has told their story, the investigator should retell the story paraphrasing and allow the witness to make corrections. This technique lets the witness know that you were listening and helps provide for more accurate information. The investigator can then ask specific questions to ensure accuracy and to probe for specific answers if necessary.

Some probing techniques include encouraging the witness in a supportive manner. The investigator may need to ask for an immediate elaboration or explanation. Paraphrasing is another probing technique as is the technique of confrontation. If the witness is telling you something that you know is blatantly false, polite professional confrontation may be in order.

Documenting the interview

There are several ways to document the interview. It is preferable to obtain a written statement from the witness. A written statement ties the witness to their story and provides a permanent record for the investigative file. The investigator should also prepare a memorandum of interview (MOI). The MOI is a document prepared by the investigator summarizing the content of the interview. The MOI should contain all contact and identifying information regarding the witness and should also include the date, time, and location of the interview and who was present. Many agencies audio and video record the interviews. This, too, is an excellent method in that what was said during the interview is captured and does not change.

Interview review

How often do we as investigators slow down and reflect on our work and skills? Probably not very often. Investigators usually carry large caseloads, travel across the state to conduct investigations, scheduling interviews, serving subpoenas or other documents, preparing reports of investigation, and other paperwork. It is important, however, that investigators take the time to assess their skills especially when it comes to conducting interviews. As stated earlier in this chapter, information from other people is perhaps the most important intelligence gained in the investigation. Therefore, strong interview skills are necessary.

A good way to improve one's interview skills is to reflect on the interview and ask: Was the time and location appropriate? Was I sufficiently prepared? Were my questions well developed and delivered? Did I obtain the information needed? This can be done in the car while traveling to another appointment, at the office, or whenever/wherever the investigator can find the time.

Respondent/subject interview

The term "respondent" or "subject" refers to the physician who is the focus or subject of the investigation. Interviews with respondents/subjects will often take on different approaches as opposed to witnesses. Basically when interviewing a witness, the investigator is attempting to *gain* information. Often, when interviewing the respondent, we are matching what we have learned from our investigation against the respondent's answers. By the time the investigator seeks an interview with the respondent, the investigation should be relatively complete. The investigator now knows what evidence exists to demonstrate the respondent's culpability.

For example, the respondent has been accused of writing drug prescriptions using the forged signature of his partner in the name of a fictitious patient and using the drugs for himself. The investigator has obtained the questionable prescriptions and presented them to the respondent's partner. The partner affirms that the signature on the prescriptions is not his signature. He further states that the patient named on the prescription does not exist. An interview with the pharmacist at the pharmacy where the prescriptions were tendered confirms that the respondent is the one who tendered the prescriptions and picked up the medication. When interviewing the respondent about the fraudulent prescriptions, the investigator will likely ask if the respondent is familiar with the particular patient, producing a negative response. The respondent might then be asked if he has ever prescribed medications for the patient, again producing a negative response. The investigator may then present the prescriptions to the respondent at which time the respondent denies that he wrote the prescriptions for the patient and points out that the prescriptions were signed by his partner. The investigator may then reveal the findings of his interviews with the partner and the pharmacist, placing the respondent in a rather problematic position. Here the investigator is tying the information that he/she acquired during the investigation to the respondent. In other words, do the evidence and witness statements point to the respondent?

The Miranda warning

The Fifth Amendment to the U.S. Constitution provides that ".....no person shall be compelled in a criminal case to be a witness against himself...."[7] The Sixth Amendment provides that "In all criminal prosecutions, the accused shall enjoy the right....... to have the assistance of counsel for his defence [sic]."[8] As such, a brief discussion of the Miranda warning is warranted. In 1966, the U.S. Supreme Court, upon its review of the case of Ernesto Miranda, overturned his conviction citing that he was not advised of his rights against self-incrimination under the 5th amendment to the U.S. Constitution and his right to counsel under the 6th amendment. In light of the Supreme Court's ruling, law enforcement officials must advise any person of their rights prior to conducting a *custodial interrogation* whereby incriminating responses to police questioning may be elicited. In essence, the Supreme Court asserted that a citizen cannot waive a right (or rights) that they do not know that they have.[9]

The advisement of these rights has become known as the Miranda Warning and the required warning is as follows:

- You have the right to remain silent;
- Anything you say can be used against you in a court of law;
- You have the right to consult with a lawyer and have that lawyer present during the interrogation;
- If you cannot afford a lawyer, one will be appointed to represent you;
- You can invoke your right to be silent before or during an interrogation, and if you do so, the interrogation must stop.
- You can invoke your right to have an attorney present, and until your attorney is present, the interrogation must stop.[10,11]

Two primary prerequisites must exist for the Miranda Warning to apply:

- The person is in *custody.*
- The person is *under interrogation* (questioning).[11]

What does it mean to be in custody? Custody can be defined as a limitation on an individual's freedom of action by virtue of a lawful process or authority. Custody is typically measured as to what extent a "reasonable person" would believe that the officer in some way suggested that they were not free to leave. As such, custody is not limited to formal arrest and constraint. Interrogation is defined as those words or actions by law enforcement officers that are likely to elicit incriminating responses to questioning.[11]

Black's Law Dictionary defines *custodial interrogation* as:

> ….questioning initiated by law enforcement officers after a person is taken into custody or otherwise deprived of his freedom in some significant way; *custody can occur without formal arrest and in areas other than the police station….*[12] (emphasis added by author)

Herein lays the conundrum that must be considered by medical board investigators. Consider the following scenario:

> Medical Board Investigator Smith is conducting an investigation of John Doe, MD concerning allegations that Dr. Doe issued prescriptions for certain controlled substances in fictitious patient names. He then filled the bogus prescriptions at multiple pharmacies and used the drugs for himself. Dr. Doe's actions (if true) would be considered the diversion of controlled substances in violation of certain criminal laws. Investigator Smith has conducted the investigation and is now ready to interview Dr. Doe.

Investigator Smith is not a sworn law enforcement officer and is not seeking to charge Dr. Doe with criminal violations; however, the questions he will be asking Dr. Doe may elicit incriminating responses. The interview will be conducted by Investigator Smith and fellow medical board investigator Jones. The interview will be conducted at Dr. Doe's medical office after the clinic is closed for the day.

Do Investigator Smith and/or Jones have a duty to advise Dr. Doe of his rights under the Miranda ruling? Is Dr. Doe in custody? Is an interrogation about to commence? In terms of being in custody, Dr. Doe has not been placed under arrest for a criminal violation. Have the investigators deprived Dr. Doe of his freedom in "some significant way?" Can the mere presence of the investigators create a belief or feeling that Dr. Doe is not free to leave or terminate the interview?

If the interview/interrogation commences without Dr. Doe being advised of his rights and he fully confesses to issuing fraudulent prescriptions and diverting controlled substances, will the confession withstand defense scrutiny in a potential administrative proceeding? The confession would likely withstand a defense challenge in such a forum in that it is not a criminal proceeding. Would the confession withstand defense scrutiny in a potential criminal proceeding? This could be open for debate as it is not unusual for a medical board to refer a case to local prosecutors for criminal prosecution. This matter can be further clouded if Investigators Smith and Jones are sworn law enforcement officers possessing the powers of arrest. When Smith and Jones present their case to the prosecutor, the first question the prosecutor is likely to ask will be if Dr. Doe was advised of his rights under Miranda prior to the interview? This could make a difference as to whether or not the prosecutor takes the case.

Under no circumstances, it is being suggested that every subject/respondent interview be preceded by the Miranda Warning; however, consideration of this issue and clarification via the board's legal counsel or local prosecutor would be the prudent thing to do. Once again, the author does not purport to be an expert on constitutional law and the Miranda rule. This matter is merely being presented for thoughtful consideration in the conduct of investigations that may involve potential criminal violations.

The respondent interview can be the most important aspect of the investigation. It offers the possibility of determining whether the respondent is culpable of committing the acts alleged in the complaint and offers an opportunity for the respondent to admit his/her actions.[1] As with any other interview, preparation is essential and closely follows the previous discussion for witness interviews. For the respondent interview, it is important to learn as much as possible about the following:

- The offense—knowledge of the elements of the alleged offense and a sound understanding of the information necessary to prove the allegations
- The victim—their background, nature of the victim's injury or loss
- The evidence—what evidence has been developed/obtained that points to the respondent?
- The respondent—obtain as much background information as possible, past complaints, disciplinary actions, etc. Did the respondent have the capability and opportunity to commit the alleged offense(s)? Gauge the respondent's attitude, level of hostility or cooperativeness.[3]

The respondent interview should be conducted in complete privacy devoid of distractions. The investigator should develop a list of topics and questions to cover during the interview. This will allow for thorough coverage of the specific details of the allegations and will assist in not overlooking important points. It is highly likely that answers to some questions will spawn other follow-up questions. The respondent interview should be conducted using questions that are clear and easily understood. In most cases, the respondent interview will begin by focusing on a relatively wide base of general information than narrowing the focus on more specific matters as the interview progresses.[3]

It should be made clear that there is no one specific approach to this type of interview. One's approach will be based on the nature of the allegations, the background and attitude of the subject, and the extent of the evidence developed. Two common approaches emerge and of course, may be intertwined as the interview progresses. The two approaches are the *logical* approach and the *emotional* approach.[3,4]

Logical approach

This approach is based on common sense and sound reasoning.[3,4] Example: A case involving an allegation of prescription forgery wherein the investigator has the original forged prescription in hand; a sworn statement from the physician who purportedly signed the prescription stating that it is not his signature and that he did not issue this prescription; and a statement from the pharmacist stating that it was the subject who tendered the prescription, the investigator can appeal to common sense.

Emotional approach

This approach appeals to the subject's sense of honor, morals, righteousness, fair play, justice religion, decency, etc.[3,4] Example: A case involving an allegation of drug diversion leading to addiction and impairment; the investigator may appeal to certain emotional factors such as the subject joining the medical profession to help those who suffer, placing his/her patients in jeopardy by being impaired, damaging the reputation of the medical profession, violating the Hippocratic oath, placing his/her family in jeopardy, etc.

Good preparation will help to determine which approach, or combination of approaches, to take.

Verbal and nonverbal responses

During the interview, the investigator should be aware of and take note of the subject's verbal and nonverbal responses to questions.

Truthful verbal responses

Truthful verbal responses tend to show no reluctance to use harsh, realistic words to describe the event. Truthful answers tend to be direct and spontaneous. Truthful responses tend not to introduce irrelevant matters and rarely require the question be repeated. They tend to be given in a distinct and clear tone of voice, and are rational. The truthful responder will demonstrate sincere seriousness and concern.[13]

Untruthful verbal responses

In contrast, untruthful responses tend to avoid the use of harsh realistic words when referring to the allegations. Denials tend to be confined to specific aspects of the offense and responses tend to be delayed, evasive, and vague. The untruthful responder may exhibit either a very poor memory or a remarkably good memory. Often the untruthful responder will have excellent memory regarding events leading up to and after the alleged offense; however, their memory becomes somewhat obscure when discussing the actual event itself.[13,14] Other characteristics of untruthful responses include:

- Requests for the questions to be repeated
- Mumbling or subdued tone of voice
- Over-politeness
- Laughter or other levity accompanying answers
- Changes in speech patterns (increased or decreased rate of speech)
- Timing of responses (delay in answering may indicate deception)
- Making excuses
- Invocation of oaths ("I swear to God," etc.)
- Answering with a question
- Feigned unconcern
- Lack of self-reference (uses less first person pronouns, avoids statements of ownership)
- Equivocation (expressions of uncertainty, weak modifiers, vague expressions)
- Avoidance of emotive words (use of euphemisms, i.e., avoids words such as "steal" and prefers to use the word "borrowed.")[14–16]

It should also be noted that when lying, certain physiological and biological processes occur. Such indicators of lying include sweating, flushing or paleness of the skin, pulse rate increase, dry mouth, excessive swallowing, licking of the lips, darting eye movements, and to name a few.[16,17]

Nonverbal responses

Research suggests that as much as 70% of communication among people occurs at the nonverbal level. Often, the true meaning of verbal communication is amplified or modified by nonverbal cues such as posture, gestures, facial expressions, and other body movements.[13]

The degree of eye contact maintained by the subject and the investigator is considered one of the most important transmitters of nonverbal behavior symptoms. Deceptive subjects generally do not look directly at the person conducting the interview. Truthful subjects are typically not defensive in their looks or actions and can easily maintain eye contact.[13]

Body posture is another potential indicator of truthfulness or deception. The truthful person will likely sit upright, positioned in front of the interviewer. They appear relaxed and posture changes will appear smooth and natural. The deceptive person will often exhibit full body motions (complete change of posture) when asked emotive questions. They will often slouch in the chair, and may also appear unnaturally rigid and stiff.[13,14] They tend to sit at an angle to the interviewer and will often have their arms crossed and locked in front of their chest.[13,14] The crossing and locking of the feet/ankles under the chair could be considered another indicator of deception.[14] Other potential nonverbal indicators of deception include the use of illustrators which are generally hand motions demonstrating points when talking. The rate of illustrator use may increase when asked threatening or emotive questions.[14] The use of manipulators is another indicator of deception. Manipulators are gestures or motions that are subconsciously used as displacement activities to reduce stress. Examples include grooming, picking lint from clothing, playing with objects such as pencils, etc.[14]

Behavior symptoms can be very useful in detecting deception but should not be considered definitive. It is critical to understand that no one behavior symptom in and of itself should be relied upon to distinguish truth from deception. All behavior symptoms should be evaluated collectively.[13]

The above discussion regarding verbal and nonverbal responses is by no means intended to be exhaustive. Much research has been conducted in this area and the reader is encouraged to examine the literature for a more thorough understanding of this area of study. Honing one's skills of recognizing and effectively evaluating certain behavior symptoms will only enhance the quality and quantity of information gleaned from your interviews.

References

1. Gilbert, J. 2007. *Criminal Investigation*, 7th edition. Upper Saddle River, NJ: Pearson Prentiss Hall.
2. Palmiotto, M. 1998. *Criminal Investigations*, 2nd edition. Bethesda, MD: Austin & Winfield.
3. Swanson, C., N. Chamelin, L. Territo, and R. Taylor. 2006. *Criminal Investigation*, 9th edition. New York: McGraw-Hill Higher Education.
4. Bennett, W. and K. Hess. 2007. *Criminal Investigation*, 8th edition. Belmont, CA: Thomson Wadsworth.
5. Weston, P., C. Lushbaugh, and K. Wells. 2000. *Criminal Investigation: Basic Perspectives*, 8th edition. Upper Saddle River, NJ: Prentiss Hall.
6. Federation of State Medical Boards of the United States, Inc. 2006. Addressing Sexual Boundaries: Guidelines for State Medical Boards. Accessed August 3, 2014. http://www.fsmb.org/Media/Default/PDF/FSMB/Advocacy/GRPOL_Sexual%20Boundaries.pdf
7. United States Constitution, Amendment 5.
8. Unites States Constitution, Amendment 6.
9. United States Supreme Court Ruling, *Miranda v. Arizona*, 384 U.S. 436, 1966.
10. Find Law. Miranda Warnings and Police Questioning. Accessed January 10, 2015. http://criminal.findlaw.com/criminal-rights/miranda-warnings-and-police-questioning.htmlrs

11. Tucker Law Group. When a Miranda Warning Is Required. Accessed September 17, 2015. http://www.tlgattorneys.com/2012/04/when-a-miranda-warning-is -required/
12. Black, H. C. 1990. *Black's Law Dictionary*, 6th edition. St. Paul: West Publishing Company.
13. Inbau, F., J. E. Reid, and J. P. Buckley. 1986. *Criminal Interrogation and Confessions*, 3rd edition. Baltimore: Williams & Wilkins.
14. Association of Certified Fraud Examiners, Inc. (ACFE). 2013. Beyond the Numbers: Professional Interviewing Techniques, Accessed September 17, 2015. http://www.acfe.com/uploadedFiles/Shared_Content/Products/Self-Study_CPE/Beyond%20the%20Numbers_2014_TOC(1).pdf
15. Clikeman, P., The 10 Tell-Tale Signs of Deception: The Words Reveal. *Fraud Magazine*, January/February 2012. Accessed September 3, 2015. http://www.fraud-magazine.com/article.aspx?id=4294971184
16. Adelson, R. Detecting deception. *Monitor on Psychology*, July/August 2004, 35(7). Accessed September 8, 2015. http://www.apa.org/monitor/julaug04/detecting.aspx
17. National Criminal Justice Reference Service. 1980. Nonverbal Communications in Interrogations. Accessed September 15, 2015. https://www.ncjrs.gov/App/publications/abstract.aspx?ID=73775

chapter six

The medical record

In Chapter 4, a list of potential evidence items was enumerated as they pertain to medical investigations. Each unique investigation will, of course, determine what evidence is necessary and as a result, various items of evidence may take on various levels of importance. Given the fact that medical investigations typically revolve around the medical care provided to patients, it can be asserted that perhaps the most important of evidentiary items is the patient's medical chart, also referred to as the medical record.

The information contained in this chapter comes directly from an actual medical record obtained via the patient's consent. Identifying information has either been changed to fictitious information or otherwise redacted. The elderly patient sustained a fall resulting in a fracture of the intertrochanteric section of the femur (fracture of the hip). The patient's course of treatment will be followed by examining the several parts of the medical record in hopes of gaining a better understanding of what information should be documented in the chart and what the chart tells us. It should also be noted that two legal registered nurse consultants were interviewed for their knowledge and insight as it pertains to the content of the medical record.

The medical chart and its purpose

The medical chart is a document that records knowledge, facts, and events as they pertain to a patient's course of treatment. Interactions between the patient and all healthcare providers are also documented. Most states have specific statutory requirements for physicians, hospitals, and other healthcare professionals and entities to create and maintain a medical record to document patients' courses of treatment.

The medical record is also used to record past medical care as well as future plans for treatment of specific medical complaints and conditions. In modern medicine, the patient is likely to see different treatment providers, to include various specialists, depending on their illness or condition. A patient's course during a hospital admission may involve interactions with a multitude of providers to include multiple physicians, nurses, medical assistants, technicians, therapists of varying types, dietary personnel, imaging, and laboratory personnel. For optimum patient care, all providers must be able to communicate accurately and efficiently. The medical record is a crucial element in the communication process. The chart tells other providers what treatments have been provided, medications administered, therapies performed, and communicates to others what actions/treatments are necessary moving forward.[1,2]

The medical chart should also contain and maintain all test results and the results of other diagnostic studies. Access to this data is important as the physician, and at times, other healthcare providers seek to formulate a diagnosis and plan of treatment. Information and data contained in the chart also provides the ability to follow the course of treatment so as to ascertain its effectiveness or lack thereof.

Especially with regard to physicians practicing outside of the hospital setting and seeing patients over long periods of time, the medical chart aids in identifying trends in patient behaviors such as progress toward treatment goals, side effects of medications or other treatment modalities, and changes in the patient's demeanor or affect.[3]

A well-documented chart should, at a minimum, contain the following:

- The patient's subjective complaints
- All discussions with the patient
- History and physical examinations
- Tests and results
- The physician's objective findings
- Evaluations and consultations
- Referrals
- Accurate details regarding drugs prescribed
- Information from prior or current treating physicians to include copies of their records
- Patient instructions regarding the treatment regimen
- Discussion of risks and benefits of the treatment plan
- Informed consent forms
- Plans for periodic review[3]

Medical board investigations, by their very nature, seek to determine if the physician practiced within or below the standard of care. Determining such will rely to a large degree on the physician's documentation. Via the physician's documentation, the medical board will assess the physician's level of awareness of risks involved with the prescribed treatment regimen and assess the physician's rationale for their treatment choices and the elements of their judgment.[3]

Obtaining a medical record

Medical records are protected from unauthorized disclosure under federal law as well as state law. The federal law applicable to the protection of medical record information is the Health Insurance Portability and Accountability Act of 1996, otherwise known as HIPAA (Public Law 104–191, 104th Congress). HIPAA is administered and enforced by the U.S. Department of Health and Human Services (US DHHS). This law protects all individually identifiable health information in any form; electronic, paper, or oral. HIPAA states that protected health information cannot be disclosed without a valid authorization (Appendix 1). HIPAA does provide some exceptions for agencies considered to be health oversight agencies which include state medical boards. US DHHS requires specific language to be used by state medical boards when requesting medical records from a physician, hospital, or other healthcare entity. Many state medical boards have statutory authority outlined in their state's medical practice act authorizing the medical board to obtain medical records pursuant to an official investigation. This authority may include subpoena authority or "orders to produce." The law will also contain provisions on dealing with a healthcare entity that refuses to release the records after receiving a valid authorization, subpoena, or other authorized request document.

The subpoena, order, or properly executed authorization, hereinafter referred to as "request document," may be served to the healthcare entity by hand or via certified mail. The method of service will be dictated by the type of investigation being conducted and the urgency with which the records are needed. The request document should contain specific identifying information regarding the patient so that the correct record is released, specificity as to the exact records being sought, the date of treatment or a specific time period for the records to cover, a date deadline for compliance and delivery of the records and where and to whom the records should be delivered.

Medical investigations rarely seek original medical records. In most cases, a *certified copy* of the chart will be sufficient. What is meant by a certified copy? In order for items of documentary evidence to be admissible in an administrative hearing and meet the exception to the rule against hearsay, the record must be certified. Certification is a written attestation by the custodian of the record that the copy provided is a true and correct copy of the original which is made in the usual and ordinary course of business.[4] The certification document should be signed by the custodian of the record in the presence of a notary or one who is otherwise authorized to administer oaths. This would be the case for any document that would be tendered as evidence in a hearing such as copies of pharmacy data, prescriptions, billing records, hospital records, hospital incident reports, to name a few.

Any item to be tendered as evidence can in no way be altered. When working with documentary evidence it is imperative that the certified copy not be altered in any way. Do not write in the margins, underline, or use a highlighter to mark certain information! An argument could be made that the record was altered subsequently barring the document from admission into evidence. If a working copy of the record is necessary simply copy the certified copy, then place the certified copy in the case file or other secure location.

It should also be noted that hospitals and many private practice offices are trending toward the use of electronic medical records or computerized record keeping. If the medical records are provided in electronic format (CD, external memory device, etc.) such should be treated as evidence and properly secured. A separate document should accompany the electronic records properly certifying the electronic records. Should a working copy of the record be necessary for other purposes, the records should be electronically copied into a separate file and the original electronic device must remain unaltered and properly secured.

Reviewing the medical record

Most state medical boards have on their staff or through a consulting contract medically trained personnel who conduct review of medical records from a clinical or standard of care perspective. There are times, however, when the investigator, who may not be medically trained, will be required to conduct a review of the chart. In such a case, the nonmedically trained investigator will not be reviewing the chart from a clinical or standard of care perspective; however, the investigator will be looking for nonclinical discrepancies in the documentation or performing comparative analysis or time line analysis.

Comparative table

Charts and tables are effective ways to compare and contrast certain information. A case of a patient presenting with hip pain can be examined by comparing and contrasting two approaches: the currently accepted standard of care approach and the approach taken by the physician under investigation. Table 6.1 shows a compare and contrast table depicting the two aforementioned approaches for a patient presenting to the emergency department (ED) with hip pain.

Time line

Another effective table is the time line. A time line provides a simple but effective way to highlight a sequence of events such as a patient's course of treatment in a hospital or in a physician's office practice. One approach to the time line is to simply list chronologically the dates and times of sentinel or otherwise pertinent events as the patient's course of treatment

Table 6.1 Compare and contrast table: Approaches to a patient with hip pain presenting to ED

Currently accepted approach to the evaluation of patient with hip pain	Dr. John Doe's approach to the evaluation of patient with hip pain
	Patient presents to ED with severe hip pain ×3 days; patient unable to ambule
Detailed history and interview patient regarding possible falls or other injurious events	Interviewed patient (minimal discussion of falls or injuries or other injurious events)
Perform complete physical examination	Performed cursory physical examination
Order imaging (X-ray, MRI)	No imaging ordered
Initial interpretation of images	
Order orthopedic consult	No orthopedic consult ordered
Based on ortho consult and imaging, admit patient for surgery[5]	Patient discharged with Ibuprofen 800mg., advised to see PCP if pain persists
	Patient ultimately discharged from ED with untreated intertrochanteric hip fracture

Source: Adapted from Steele, M. and Ellison, S. 2004. In *Emergency Medicine: A Comprehensive Study Guide*, 6th edition, 1718–1722. New York: McGraw Hill, Inc.

progresses. Table 6.2 shows a chronological listing of events concerning the evaluation of a patient with hip pain.

Another type of time line is the continuum time line. Table 6.3 shows a time line of events in the form of a continuum for a patient coming to the ED.

The medical record is a treasure trove of information and a thorough review of the chart could mean the difference in substantiating or refuting the allegations in the complaint. The documentation, or lack thereof, could be the only basis the medical board has to assess the physician's rationale for the treatment regimen and his/her decision making.[3]

Parts of the medical record

This section will examine the various parts of a medical record and what information is typically contained in them.

Ambulance call report or ambulance trip sheet (Appendix 2)

If the patient is brought to the ED via ambulance, the ambulance crew will prepare an ambulance call report (ACR). In some jurisdictions, this report may be referred to as the ambulance trip sheet. The ACR is an extremely

Table 6.2 Time line table with chronological listing of events

Evaluation of patient JP's hip pain in emergency department and subsequent admission		
5/3/15	19:01	Patient arrives at ED via ambulance
	19:20	Triage by ED triage nurse
	19:59	Seen by ED physician
	20:47	Patient to imaging
	21:55	Patient admitted
5/4/15	15:54	Patient undergoes surgery for right intertrochanteric femur fracture
5/5/15		Patient begins ambulating with walker
5/6/15		Patient begins physical therapy
	18:22	Nurse finds patient laying on floor next to bed; call to charge nurse for assistance
	18:23	Patient assisted back to bed; call to orthopedic service for stat consult
	18:52	Ortho consult; patient in severe pain (8/10); imaging ordered
	19:30	Patient taken to imaging
	20:10	Patient back in room; in bed
5/7/15	09:00	Ortho service, Dr. _______, meets with patient to discuss imaging findings; re-fracture of hip
	09:27	Patient re-scheduled for surgery
5/8/15	07:44	Patient undergoes 2nd surgery
5/15/15	14:03	Patient discharged to skilled nursing facility

Source: Adapted from Brookshire, A. K. 2015. Allen & McCain, P. C. Interview by author. Atlanta, GA, September 23; Darnell, S. A. 2015. Allen & McCain, P.C. Interview by author. Atlanta, GA, September 23.

Table 6.3 Continuum time line table

Evaluation of patient JP's hip pain in emergency department

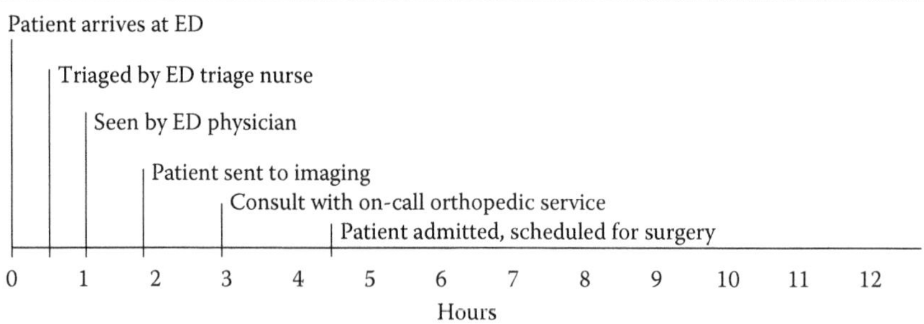

Source: Adapted from Brookshire, A. K. 2015. Allen & McCain, P. C. Interview by author. Atlanta, GA, September 23; Darnell, S. A. 2015. Allen & McCain, P.C. Interview by author. Atlanta, GA, September 23.

valuable document in that it documents the activities of the ambulance crew at the scene and their interaction with the patient. The ACR will also identify potential witnesses to include the ambulance crew, family members present, neighbors that might be present, etc.

As stated at the outset of this chapter, information used in this discussion comes directly from an actual medical record. We will refer to the patient as John Q. Patient or Mr. P. Let's examine Mr. P's ambulance call report.

Mr. P is an 81 y/o Caucasian male weighing 150 lb. The ambulance service was notified of the injury on 1/3/2015 at 18:22:42 and was dispatched at 18:25:14, arriving at the scene at 18:35:00. They departed the scene at 18:51:19 and arrived at the hospital at 19:01:16. The injury occurred at the patient's home and the patient was found lying on the floor upon the arrival of EMS. The ambulance crew's primary impression was a traumatic injury. The ACR provides a narrative prepared by the crew as to the events at the scene. A summary of the narrative indicates that the patient fell from a standing position as a result of losing his balance and had pain to the right upper leg and right arm. The ACR describes the patient's condition and indicates transfer to XYZ hospital. A cursory past medical history is provided, as well as the patient's current condition, injury onset (date/time), vital signs, ECG monitoring (if performed), procedures and treatments provided, intubation (if performed), medications administered, patient transport information, ambulance crew members, and response times. Other information contained in the ACR may include additional patient demographics, allergies, results of physical examination, consultations with ED physician, and any restraints, splints, or other modalities used.

Some medical investigations will require interviewing the ambulance crew. That is why the ACR is so important. If the care provided by the ED physician is in question, the ACR may provide vital information that will help the reviewing authority (the board) better understand the physician's approach to treatment and whether said approach was within the standard of care.

Emergency department record (Appendix 3)

The emergency department record (EDR) documents the interactions between the patient and members of the ED staff as well as others who may be accompanying the patient (family, friend, etc.). ED staff will include the physician(s), triage nurses, ED nurses, physician assistants, medical assistants, administrative personnel, and possibly others. When necessary, specialists may be called in to assess the patient.[1,2]

The patient will initially be seen by a triage nurse. The triage nurse determines the seriousness of the injury or condition and the immediacy in which the patient needs to be seen by the ED physician. The triage nurse obtains information as to the patient's complaint, and performs a cursory examination, takes vital signs, and places the patient into the queue of other patients waiting to be seen, again, based on the emergent nature of the patient's condition.[1,2]

After triage, the patient will be taken to an examination room. The ED nurse will likely be the next provider to see the patient. He/she will conduct a more extensive interview, to include medical history, with the patient and perform a more thorough physical examination. At this time, the ED nurse may suggest certain diagnostic tests to include blood work, ECG, x-rays, etc., again based on the patient's condition and hospital protocols. The extent to which a nurse may be able to order diagnostic tests will be determined by the scope of practice authorized under his/her licensure. For example, in most states a registered nurse (RN) is not authorized to order tests or prescribe medications. The RN typically carries out the order of the physician. However, advanced practice registered nurses (APRN) also referred to as nurse practitioners (NP) are authorized to order certain tests and prescribe certain medications. Again, the scope of practice for RNs and APRNs will be dictated by the laws and rules of their regulatory body.[1,2]

The patient will then be seen by the ED physician. He/she will perform a physical examination and evaluate the results of any diagnostic tests that have been completed or otherwise order diagnostic tests if indicated. An initial diagnosis will be made. Based on the diagnosis and present condition of the patient, emergency procedures will be initiated by the ED physician and in nonemergent situations, the patient may require admission for additional tests, surgery, etc.[1,2] Depending on the patient's complaint and emergent medical needs, the ED physician may call in a specialist for a consult. The consultant would be called in to assist in developing a diagnosis, or perform a procedure. When we further examine Mr. P's medical record a consult note is found for an orthopedic consult concerning right hip pain and suspicion of a fracture. The consultant physician will prepare a note to the ED record documenting findings, recommendations, and any treatment rendered or procedures performed. This is referred to as the consult note. The consult note will be discussed in more detail forthcoming. If the patient is to be admitted for further testing, surgery, or other treatment, the ED physician will consult with another physician (in this case, the orthopedic physician) or a hospitalist to accept the patient for admission.[1,2]

In looking at Mr. P's ED record, we find that the following information is included:

- History: Time of arrival, mode of arrival, time seen by ED physician
- Chief complaint (short narrative of circumstances surrounding the injury)

- Past medical history
- Past surgical history
- Family medical history
- Additional information (smoking status, etc.)
- Review of systems (HEENT [head, eyes, ears, neck, and throat], eyes, respiratory, cardiovascular, gastrointestinal, genitourinary, musculoskeletal, skin, neurological)
- Physical examination (vital signs, constitutional, head, eyes, ears, neck, cardiovascular, pulmonary/chest, abdomen, musculoskeletal, neurological, skin, psychiatric)
- ED course (procedures, screening assessments, stroke assessment, diagnoses/management options, allergies, previous medications)
- Medical decision making (vitals, pulse oximetry, review of past medical records)
- Physician orders (X-ray right hip 2 or more views, X-ray chest 1 view, CBC, metabolic panel, PT and PTT, urinalysis, inpatient consult with orthopedic surgery, admit to inpatient)
- Lab studies
- Imaging studies (result of X-rays)
- Progress notes
- Consult note

Face sheet (Appendix 4)

This document is generated at the time of a patient's admission to the hospital whether emergency or nonemergency. The face sheet will contain demographic information about the patient. Information in the face sheet should include the following:

- Patient name
- Social Security Number
- Medical record number
- Sex/Race
- Date of birth
- Address
- Phone number
- Employer/Employment Status
- Name and phone number of nearest relative
- Insurance information
- Admission information (arrival date/time, admission date/time, admission type, admission source, means of arrival, primary medical service, admitting physician, attending physician, referring physician, admission diagnosis)
- Discharge information
- Final diagnoses

- Procedures (closed reduction intertrochanteric fracture of femur, packed cell transfusion)

Admission note/history and physical (Appendix 5)

Upon admission to the hospital, the patient will undergo a comprehensive history and physical examination performed by a physician, physician assistant, or nurse practitioner. The admission note will document the reason for the patient's admission and treatment plan.[1,2] Mr. P's admission note contains the following information:

- Patient name, date of birth
- Providers conducting the history and physical
- Chief Complaint
  - Patient presents with leg pain; 81 y/o male to ED with ACEMS from home with complaint of right upper leg pain. Patient complains of 2/10 pain. The chief complaint is typically recorded as what is stated by the patient.
- History of Present Illness
  - A more thorough explanation of the chief complaint is provided. In this section, the provider probes the patient for additional details as to the injury, medications taking, and other medical issues.
- Review of Systems (ROS)
  - This part of the admission note records a screening of several major organ systems in the body. The systems commonly screened are:
    - Neurological
    - Psychological
    - Endocrine
    - Gastrointestinal
    - Respiratory
    - Cardiovascular
    - Rheumatological
    - Integument (skin, hair, nails)[2]
  - When Mr. P's review of systems is examined, we see that the following screenings were conducted:
    - General (fever, chills, appetite changes, perspiration, etc.)
    - Head
    - Eyes
    - Cardiovascular
    - Pulmonary
    - GI (gastrointestinal)
    - GU (genitourinary)
    - Musculoskeletal

  - Neurological
  - Skin
  - Psychological
- Past Medical History
  - This section will include information regarding past complaints, injuries, treatments, or surgeries and may also assist in the development of a proper diagnosis.
  - We can see that Mr. P's past medical history includes hypertension, hyperlipidemia (elevated lipids), coronary artery disease, carotid artery occlusion, GERD (gastroesophageal reflux disease), history of myocardial perfusion scan, pigmented basal cell carcinoma, and colon polyp. Past surgical history indicates a coronary artery bypass graft, esophagus surgery, upper gastrointestinal endoscopy, and colonoscopy.
- Current Medications
  - Current medications being taken by the patient, to include name of drug, dose, and interval, should be documented in this section. All over-the-counter medications, and any supplements should also be documented.
  - Upon review of Mr. P's record, we find that he is currently taking five medications:
    - Amlodipine 5 mg, 1 tab by mouth once daily
    - Aspirin 81 mg, 1 tab by mouth once daily
    - Atorvastatin 40 mg, 0.5 mg by mouth once daily
    - Fluoxetine 10 mg, 2 tabs by mouth once daily
    - Omeprazole 40 mg, 1 tab by mouth once daily
- Allergies
  - This section documents all allergies that the patient is aware of to include allergies to medications, foods, chemicals, etc.
  - Mr. P professes no known allergies.
- Family History
  - The family history section provides past medical information concerning the patient's relatives. Many diseases are hereditary and knowledge of the family medical history may aid in developing a diagnosis.
    - Mr. P indicated that his brother suffered from heart disease, however, his family history is negative for the other conditions listed.
- Social History
  - This section examines the patient's social history such as drug use, alcohol use, sexual history, employment history, etc.
  - By examining the record we learn that Mr. P is married and is a former 15-year smoker, smoking 1 pack/day, quitting in 1964. It appears that a rather brief social history was obtained.

- Physical Examination
  - The physical exam section documents the findings of a comprehensive physical examination and should include information on the following:
    - Vital signs
    - General appearance
    - Head
    - Eyes, ears, nose, and throat
    - Neck
    - Lungs
    - Chest
    - Breast (male and female)
    - Heart
    - Abdomen
    - Extremities
    - Psychological
    - Neurological
    - Vascular
    - Skin
- Laboratory Testing
  - Specific laboratory tests to be conducted will depend on the nature of the illness or injury. Upon review of Mr. P's chart, the following lab tests were conducted:
    - Complete Blood Count (CBC) with auto differential—this will include white blood count and hemoglobin
    - Comprehensive metabolic panel—this will include BUN (blood urea nitrogen) and creatinine
    - PT and PTT (prothrombin time and partial thromboplastin time)
    - Urinalysis
    - NT-PRO BNP (N-terminal of the prohormone brain natriuretic peptide; [screen for congestive heart failure])
    - Troponin
- Radiology
  - Again, depending on the patient's condition, certain imaging studies may be conducted to include X-rays, CT scan, or MRI. Mr. P appears to have had X-rays taken of his right hip indicating a nondisplaced right femoral intertrochanteric neck fracture. He also had a chest X-ray indicating an enlarged heart.
- Assessment
  - This section of the admission note documents the physician's assessment after evaluating the prior history, physical, labs, and

imaging. Is there a diagnosis? In Mr. P's case, the physician's assessment is a right femoral intertrochanteric fracture.

- Plan of Treatment
  - This section documents the plan of treatment subsequent to the diagnosis. Depending on the illness or injury and whether a solid diagnosis can be made, the plan may include further testing. The plan may also include therapeutic procedures, medications, specialty consults, and surgery.
  - The plan for Mr. P is to admit for surgery, regular diet, NPO (nothing by mouth) after midnight, orthopedic surgery consulted by ED physician, orthopedics to see patient in morning, pain management, IVF (intravenous fluids), EKG, and telemetry.

Radiology note (Appendix 6)

The radiology note describes the findings of imaging studies such as X-rays, CT scans, and MRIs. The radiology note is prepared by the radiologist who reads or interprets the images. The radiology note should contain the following information:

- Patient name and identifying information
- Name of the procedure or study ordered (X-ray hip right 2 or more views)
- Ordering physician/provider
- Date/time of procedure
- Brief narrative of findings/impression ("a nondisplaced right femoral intertrochanteric neck fracture is noted.")
- Date of report
- Notification of review of previous X-rays or other images
- Radiologist's signature

Consult note (Appendix 7)

Depending on the nature of the patient's condition, past medical history, or injury, the attending physician may feel compelled to seek an opinion from a specialist. The emergency physician is skilled in dealing with myriad medical issues; however, may not specialize in a particular field of medicine such as cardiology, obstetrics and gynecology, orthopedics, etc.[1,2] In the case of Mr. P, the ED physician was able to read and interpret the X-ray; however, he requested the input of an orthopedic specialist to confirm the diagnosis and develop the plan of treatment. The consulting physician will prepare the consult note which becomes a part of the hospital chart. In a private practice setting, the consultation note is often in the form of a letter from the specialist to the treating physician and becomes a part of the treating physician's office chart.

Upon review of Mr. P's chart, we find the consult note containing the following information:

- Name of the service consulted (cardiology, neurology, orthopedics, etc.)
- Name of physician ordering the consultation
- Reason for consultation
- Date of request for consult
- Date of consultation
- Chief complaint/History of illness/Hospital course summary
- Physical examination (S.O.A.P. format)
  - Subjective, objective, assessment, and plan
- Scheduled medications
- Labs
- Imaging study results
- Assessment or diagnosis
- Plan (in Mr. P's case the plan is for surgery)
- Signature of consulting physician

Informed consent (Appendix 8)

Informed consent is the method whereby a patient consents, or authorizes, the treatment or procedure to begin. Some form of informed consent is required by law in all 50 states. The statutes vary; however, there is some commonality between them. Generally, obtaining informed consent from the patient requires the disclosure of certain information. The patient must be informed of the diagnosis of their condition requiring the recommended treatment or procedure, the treatment or procedure to be implemented or performed, the recognized and accepted risks and/or complications that may result from the treatment or procedure, the likelihood of success of the recommended treatment or procedure, practical alternatives to the treatment or procedure, and the patient's prognosis if the treatment or procedure is declined.[1,2] In some states, the failure to obtain informed consent constitutes a battery (physical assault) committed upon the patient punishable as a criminal offense. The following requirements apply when obtaining informed consent:

- Consent must be given voluntarily by the patient.
- The patient must be an adult.
- The patient must have the ability, or power to act, to give consent. (A review of the informed consent law in the investigator's particular state will provide more detail in this area as well as requirements for informed consent for minors, and adults lacking the ability to provide consent.)

- Informed consent must be obtained prior to beginning the treatment or procedure.
- The informed consent document should be contained in the patient's medical record.[1,2]

In addition to the above, a review of Mr. P's informed consent document indicates the following:

- Date of consent
- Description of procedure
- An affirmation that the risks, potential complications, benefits, alternative treatments or procedures were fully explained to the patient or guardian
- Signature of the patient or guardian and date of signature
- Signature of the person witnessing the patient/guardian give consent
- Signature of an interpreter or translator if utilized[1,2]

Operative note or procedure note (Appendix 9)

Often referred to as the "op note," the operative or procedure note provides for a documented description of a procedure undergone by a patient. The procedure note is prepared by the physician performing the procedure. A review of the op note in Mr. P's chart reveals the following:

- Name of the physician performing the procedure and assistant
- The physician's service (in this case orthopedics)
- Time and date of the procedure
- Name of the procedure (closed reduction of right intertrochanteric femur fracture)
- Location of procedure (operating room [OR])
- Anesthesia to be used (general)
- Indication for procedure (reasons to perform the procedure)
- Patient's preop status (right intertrochanteric femur fracture)
- Informed consent obtained
- Technique used
- Equipment or hardware used (rod, locking screw, etc.)
- Detailed step-by-step narrative describing the procedure
- Status of patient postprocedure (to postanesthesia care unit [PACU] in stable condition)
- Physician/surgeon signature

Anesthesia note (Appendix 10)

The anesthesia note is an accounting of the procedures undertaken concerning the preparation and administration of anesthesia to the patient.

The note consists of several sections to include brief patient demographics, the name of the surgeon and the physician anesthesiologist, allergies, procedure summary, medical personnel (MD anesthesiologist, CRNAs, etc.), a minute-by-minute chronology of events, lines, drains, and airways, preoperative vitals, anesthesia history, surgical history, anesthesia medications, and anesthesia evaluation.[1,2]

As we examine the anesthesia note from Mr. P's chart, we learn that the procedure was conducted on 1/4/2015 and the anesthesia was begun at 14:13 and stopped at 16:14. The procedure is noted as an open reduction with internal fixation (ORIF) trochanteric/hip fracture (right hip). The anesthesia staff is identified, their role during the procedure, and the times each one began and ended their role. Next we see a minute-by-minute time line of events: 14:43 anesthesia start, 14:57 induction, 14:58 intubation, 15:21 procedure start, 16:00 procedure end, 16:14 handoff to PACU, 16:14 anesthesia stopped.

In the lines, drains, and airways section, we see that Mr. P was intubated with an LMA (laryngeal mask airway) placed at 14:58 and inserted by the anesthesiologist and removed at 16:04 by the CRNA. In the anesthesia medications section, we see that several medications were given, the dosage of each medication, route of administration, date/time of administration, and by whom the medications were administered. As we examine the anesthesia plan, we see that Mr. P is classified as ASA 3 which refers to a patient with severe systemic disease with some functional impairment.[1,2] This classification is likely due to the fact that Mr. P suffers from coronary artery disease resulting in a double bypass surgery in 2011. General anesthesia was used and the patient is on an NPO (nothing by mouth) protocol.

The anesthesia note should also include documentation of any unusual events such as difficulty in intubation, insertion of central lines, sudden drop in blood pressure, oxygenation, etc.[2]

Physician order sheet (Appendix 11)

The physician order sheet is a crucial mode of communication between the attending physician and/or surgeon and other healthcare providers such as nurses, other physicians, respiratory technicians, dietary, etc. This record documents the orders made by the attending physician. The physician order sheet will include medications ordered, dosage, route of administration, and frequency of administration. Orders may also include dietary restrictions, physical therapy (type and frequency), frequency of vital signs to be taken, orders to notify the physician under given situations/occurrences, specialty consults, etc. If a verbal order is given by the physician to a nurse, the order should be reduced to writing into the physician order sheet by the nurse and the specifics of the order, date, and time of the order should be recorded.[1,2]

Upon review of the physician order sheet from Mr. P's chart, we learn the following: Mr. P was ordered Morphine 4 mg. injection to be given every four hours as needed for pain, ondansetron 4 mg. injection to be given every six hours as needed for nausea, vital signs to be taken every four hours for twenty-four hours, notify physician if urinary output is less than 30 mL/kg/hr or no void within eight hours after Foley removed; heart rate less than 50 or greater than 120; systolic BP less than 90 or greater than 160; respiratory rate less than 10 or greater than 20; unable to maintain pulse oximeter equal or greater than 90. Other orders were given; however, at this juncture, discussion would be a bit redundant.

Progress note (Appendix 12)

The progress note documents the progress, or lack thereof, of the patient's response to the treatment and condition. Progress notes are usually prepared daily after the physician has seen the patient while making rounds at the hospital. The physician will review the nurses' notes and other information (vitals, test results, labs, etc.) and comment on the patient's progress and renew existing orders or issue new orders, depending on the patient's condition and needs.[1,2]

Progress notes are often written in the S. O. A. P. format. This is an acronym for Subjective, Objective, Assessment, and Plan. It should also be noted that many physicians in a private practice setting often utilize the S. O. A. P. format for their office charts.[1,2]

Subjective: Subjective findings are the problems complained of by the patient, for example, pain, inability to void, unable to sleep, dizziness, etc. Subjective findings are often documented based on what the patient states.[1,2]

Objective: Objective findings are based on conclusions made by medical processes to include physical examination, results of lab tests, radiology reports, etc.[1,2]

Assessment: Based on the objective findings, the physician will evaluate the patient's progress and document his/her findings. In other words, do the objective findings indicate improvement or a worsening condition? Should other diagnoses or treatments be considered?[1,2]

Plan: Based on the subjective and objective findings and the assessment, the physician will then determine a plan. For example, Does the patient need additional testing? If so, what? Is the patient progressing to the point that dietary changes are appropriate? Is the patient ready to get out of bed and begin ambulating?

A progress note taken from Mr. P's medical record indicates that the physician met with him on 1/6/2015 at 14:58 (postoperative day 2). Mr. P's primary complaint was pain. The objective findings indicate normal vital signs, alert, comfortable, wound clean and dry with no evidence of infection, no evidence of deep vein thrombosis (DVT), and right hip/leg neurovascularly intact. It appears that Mr. P's hemoglobin and hematocrit are a bit low. The physician's assessment reveals status post proximal IM nail right hip, physical therapy progress is good, no complications, and acute blood loss anemia—symptomatic—received blood through the night—feels better now. The plan is noted as partial weight bearing, continue current postop course, okay to transfer to SAR (subacute rehab) from ortho standpoint—will need to continue current PT and see in office for X-rays at four weeks postop (PO); will need suture removal 12–14 days PO per SAR staff.

Nursing notes (Appendix 13)

As one gains experience reviewing medical records, they will notice that nursing notes constitute a large part of the chart. Nursing notes are prepared by the nurses assigned to care for the patient. The notes document the date and time of nursing activity to include medications given, observations of the nurses, vital signs, and any other nursing function conducted with regard to the particular patient as well as the identity of the specific nurse performing the activity.[1,2] Nursing notes should contain the following information:

- Date and time of events and activities and by whom the note was written.
- Physical evaluation of the patient to include vital signs, and any other information or observations that other providers should know that can/will affect proper care.
- Results of physical examinations. (heart, lungs, abdomen, etc.)
- Examination of the skin. (Intact? Ulcers? Condition of sutures, wounds, dressings, etc.)
- Patient inputs and outputs to include nutritional assessment, height, weight, food and drink intake, urine output, etc.
- Documentation of any aberrant findings on physical exam, psychological assessment, or on observations of patient behaviors. Any aberrant findings should be immediately noted in the nursing notes and reported to the appropriate person; the nursing supervisor, the physician on call, or both. The note should document to whom a report was given, date/time, any interventional treatment undertaken, and the patient's response to the treatment.
- During the day-to-day interactions between the patient and nurses, the nurses are in an excellent position to assess the patient's mood and affect. Is the patient depressed? Is the patient optimistic about their recovery? Does the patient express fear? To what extent does the patient understand his/her medical condition? This information should certainly be documented into the nursing notes.
- The nursing notes should contain documentation of communications with all providers involved in the patient's care, the patient's

family, the substance of such conversations and communications, and accurate dates and time of the communication.

- Drugs administered to include the dose, frequency of administration, route of administration should be accurately documented. If the ordered medication was not administered, the reason for not administering the drug should be documented as well as any reason for altering the dose and/or frequency of administration. Any adverse reactions to medications should certainly be documented.
- If the patient leaves the floor for any reason, this too should be documented. For example, patient to X-ray date/time; patient to physical therapy date/time; patient back from X-ray, in room date/time.
- The nursing team should always be cognizant of the patient's safety. In other words, does the patient pose a risk for him/herself? What is the ability of the patient to ambulate or move from the bed to the bathroom? Does the patient require assistance to ambulate? Does the patient require a wheel chair or other special medical equipment? Is the patient a fall risk? Certainly, in the case of Mr. P, he would be a significant fall risk and certain precautions should be made. Should the bedside rails be raised? Is the patient such a danger to him/herself that restraints are necessary? Behaviors evidencing the need for restraints should be described and any information affecting the patient's safety should be thoroughly documented.
- In some instances, the patient may not speak or be able to read English, therefore an interpreter or translator may be required. The identity of any interpreter or translator should be documented.[1,2]

Medication administration record (Appendix 14)

The medication administration record (MAR) records the medications ordered by the physician and the dates and times the medication was administered. Upon examination of the MAR from Mr. P's chart we see that 0.9% NaCl infusion IV was ordered and the frequency was to be continuous. One can see that the medication was given 1/4/2015 at 17:51 at a rate of 75 mL/hr and a dose of 500 mL. We also see that Mr. P received Alprazolam 0.25 mg on 1/4/2015 at 17:00, 1/5/2015 at 09:00, 1/6/2015 at 09:30, and on 1/7/2015 at 10:10.

Laboratory and pathology reports (Appendix 15)

It is a common practice to obtain laboratory studies during a hospital admission. Physicians in a private practice setting also routinely obtain laboratory results. Common laboratory studies include blood tests of varying focus and urinalysis. In the case of Mr. P, a complete blood count (CBC) and a basic metabolic panel were ordered. The CBC measured white blood count, red blood count, hemoglobin, hematocrit, platelets, and other measurements. The basic metabolic panel measures blood levels of glucose, electrolytes, kidney function, liver function, carbon dioxide, potassium, sodium, calcium, blood urea nitrogen (BUN), and others.

Pathology reports provide the results of scientific study of certain tissues taken from a patient. Often pathology studies are conducted to examine abnormal tissue (lesions and tumors) to detect reasons for the abnormality or the presence of malignancies.[1,2] For example, a suspicious mole may require a biopsy (pathological study) to determine if it is melanoma.

Lab and pathology reports will contain name of the patient, the ordering physician, date and time of the order, the specimen collected (blood, urine, suspicious mole, etc.), the various components of the test, the values of the said components, the reference range (usually two values whereby above and below the range is considered normal), as well as any comments concerning unusual or abnormal results. Depending on what tests and studies are ordered by the treating physician, laboratory and pathology reports will differ from patient to patient.

Discharge summary (Appendix 16)

The discharge summary is an account of the chief events that occurred during a hospital stay.[1,2] Typically, the discharge summary is prepared by the attending physician or designee. The discharge summary contains the following information:

- Patient identification
- Admission date
- Discharge date
- Admitting physician
- Discharging physician
- Admission diagnosis (reason for hospitalization)
- Discharge diagnosis
- Hospital course (brief summary of the patient's course of treatment)
- Discharge examination
- Objective (vital signs upon discharge, lab results, etc.)
- Discharge condition
- Disposition (discharged home, skilled nursing facility, etc.)
- Patient instructions (home medications, follow-up, suture removal, activity as tolerated, etc.)

Incident reports (Appendix 17)

When an event occurs in the hospital that resulted, or could have resulted in patient injury, an incident report is prepared documenting the investigation of the event. Adverse events involve deviations from the standard of care and/or hospital policies and procedures. Incident reporting format will differ from institution to institution; however, they generally contain the same or similar information. Most incident reports will contain basic information concerning those involved, date, time and location of the incident, the nature of the event, patient outcomes, contributory factors, a narrative summary of the investigation, and action(s) taken as a result of the incident.[1,2]

Nature of event: Did the event involve malfunctioning equipment, medication error, wrong dose of medication, infection control issue, wrong site, wrong patient, etc.?

Patient outcomes: What happened to the patient? Death, injury, delay in treatment, near miss by chance, near miss by intervention, no adverse effect, etc.?

Contributory factors: Was a lack of knowledge and training a factor? Staffing issues, poor communication, poor documentation, etc.?

The narrative summary should include the results of interviews of all involved in the incident to include all caregivers, other staff, the patient, etc. The narrative should further describe the event and its attendant consequences.

Actions taken as a result of the event: What policy changes were made, personnel changes (reassignments, terminations, etc.), staffing issues addressed, additional training, etc.?

Incident reports may or may not be available via subpoena and may or may not be discoverable based on various state and federal laws. This matter should be vetted with the board's legal counsel. It should also be noted that incident reports are usually not contained in the patient's clinical record, therefore incident reports should be requested in addition to the clinical record.[2]

When reviewing an incident report, the investigator should determine the following:

- Who authored the report?
- Identities of personnel involved in the incident.
- Are names mentioned in the report that are not mentioned in the clinical chart?
- Does the report contradict events recorded in the clinical chart?[2]

Example: Some years ago, I was involved in an investigation involving a male teenage patient undergoing a procedure involving the sinuses and the nose. During the procedure, while under anesthesia, the patient's fingers were placed in a bowl of extremely hot water so as to make the patient urinate on himself. This abhorrent operating room (OR) prank left the patient with scarring and limited use of his fingers. The case resulted in the loss of the surgeon's hospital privileges, termination of employment of the other OR personnel, and a significant malpractice settlement, not to mention a complaint filed with the medical board. The incident report along with the clinical record in this case was crucial in helping to identify the other participants in the OR allowing for interviews to be conducted with these witnesses.

Autopsy report

Often in cases involving a death, an autopsy will be performed. Autopsy is defined as "the dissection of a dead body for the purpose of inquiring into the cause of death…a postmortem examination to determine the cause, seat, or nature of a disease."[6] In its simplest form, the autopsy seeks to determine the cause of death and the manner of death. What is the difference between the *cause* of death and the *manner* of death? The following is from an actual autopsy report reviewed by the author: Consider the unfortunate case of a man stepping out onto a busy interstate highway and being hit by several vehicles traveling at high rates of speed resulting in his death. Upon examination of the autopsy report, the medical examiner stated the cause of death was "traumatic injuries due to impact by motor vehicles (pedestrian struck by motor vehicles)." The manner of death is shown to be "suicide."

Cause of death speaks to the medical cause such as disease, injury, etc. Manner of death speaks to the classification or category of death such as homicide, suicide, accidental, natural, or undetermined. In the above case, evidence was discovered concerning the victim's long bout with depression and evidence that he had contemplated suicide previously. Therefore, the manner of death was ruled as suicide.

The Medical Examiner or forensic pathologist performing the autopsy will prepare a report detailing the examination and his/her findings and opinion as to the cause and manner of death. Autopsies may be performed at the hospital if the hospital is equipped to do so; however, victims of violent, unnatural, or unexplained death are typically autopsied by the local medical examiner's office or the state crime laboratory. A review of the autopsy report concerning the above case indicates the following information provided:

- Name of the agency or other entity conducting the autopsy
- Name of the patient/victim
- Evidence submitted (in this case the evidence is the decedent)
- Results and conclusions
  - Reason for examination
  - Examination time and place
  - Presentation of body and associated items (inventory of personal effects)
  - Evidence of medical intervention

    - External examination of the body
    - Internal examination of the body
    - Other procedures
    - Opinion
    - Cause of death
    - Manner of death
- Name and signature of medical examiner or forensic pathologist performing the autopsy
- Date of the autopsy

The author reviewed another autopsy report concerning a different case, that of a patient who died in the hospital of an apparent narcotic overdose. Additional information, not contained in the autopsy report of the suicide victim above, was observed. The autopsy report of the overdose victim included the same information and followed the same format as the suicide victim autopsy report, however, there were additional tests/examinations performed to include:

- Microscopic examination of major organs and tissues
- Toxicology analysis of blood, urine, and tissues
- Microbiologic analysis of blood or other bodily tissues

Altering and falsifying the medical record

It is held by most that the physician, the hospital, and all other healthcare providers and entities have a duty to maintain the integrity, accuracy, veracity, and reliability of patients' medical records. A patient's medical record may be relied upon by other healthcare practitioners who become involved in a patient's care.[7] Legislatures and courts have held that deliberate falsification of a medical record is considered gross malpractice endangering the life and health of the affected patient.[7] Most, if not all, state medical boards have adopted rules stating that falsification and/or tampering with medical records is considered unprofessional conduct and subject to licensure sanctions.

A brief discussion of the term *spoliation of evidence* is warranted. Spoliation is defined as:

> "The intentional destruction of evidence and when it is established, the factfinder may draw inference that evidence destroyed was unfavorable to the party responsible for its spoliation….The destruction or the *significant and meaningful alteration* of a document or instrument."[6] (emphasis added by author)

The following are considered acts of chart tampering or spoliation:

- Removing records from the chart
- Adding fraudulent records to the chart or adding information to an existing record at a later date
- Altering dates or facts and/or adding inaccurate or fictitious information into the chart
- Supplementing clinical notes at a later date but using a contemporaneous date
- Altering or supplementing another healthcare provider's notes
- Purposely omitting significant information that would tend to support clinical reasoning and actions
- Dating a record so as to appear as if it were written at an earlier time
- Destroying the record[1,2,7–9]

Detecting chart tampering

The following clues may suggest chart tampering:

- Crowded writing among existing entries
- Changes in slant and pressure
- Unnatural uniformity or other differences in handwriting, changes in the color of ink, use of margins, change of word spacing, change of writing style
- Erasures, obliterations, or omissions
- A photocopy of a page that has replaced the original
- Excessive number of late entries
- Differences between pages such as folds, stains, impressions, holes, and tears. Medical records are subject to a certain amount of abuse as they are handled by many caregivers and move from unit to unit. Charts often contain coffee and/or food stains, tears, and other signs of wear and tear. An immaculate sheet of paper among torn, soiled, and well-worn sheets may be suspect
- Use of new versions of forms not available at the time of the purported entry
- Entries that are out of chronological order[1,2,7–9]

Strategies to detect altered medical records

- Compare the medical records with the billing records. Look for discrepancies between the two. Is a note entered into the chart and no corresponding billing record?

- Compare medication administration records with the nursing notes. Are they consistent or are there discrepancies? Does the nursing note indicate one action and the medication administration record reflect another?
- Do documented observations of the nurse conflict with the physician's observations? Is an event or observation documented in one note and not the other?
- Compare staffing sheets and time cards. Was an entry made into the chart by an employee that was not at work?
- Compare the questioned document with other documents known to have been completed on the same day.[1,2,7–10]

Properly correcting the medical record

It must be made clear that legitimate documentation errors do occur at times. Policies and procedures should be in place to guide the physician, nurse, technician, etc. in the event a documentation error occurs and how to properly correct and document the error. Medical clinics and hospitals are busy places and healthcare personnel are subject to many interruptions, therefore errors and subsequent corrections are made.

With regard to handwritten records, if the error consists of incorrect information the mode of correction is to strike through the original erroneous entry with a single line. The erroneous entry should be able to still be read. The new corrected entry should be dated, timed, and signed by the person making the entry. Correction entries should never be back dated and the reader should be directed to the new corrected entry. Errors consisting of failure to include information that should have been included but inadvertently omitted should be noted as an addendum or late entry noting that the entry was inadvertently omitted at the time of the event.[9,10] Additions and corrections should be made in an open and honest approach to avoid an allegation of spoliation.[11]

With regard to electronic medical records (EMR), alterations are easier to identify. Most EMRs have date and time stamping (automatically records the date and time of the entry) and metadata (metadata will show deletions or changes made to the record), locks in all entries upon the author's sign off, and tracks all additions to the record.[12]

One can readily see that the medical record contains an abundance of valuable information. The chart contains information as to anyone who had access to the patient, their role, what they did, and when they did it. Depending on the nature of the investigation, the medical record identifies an array of potential witnesses. The medical investigator with little to no medical training should not fear the medical record. Even though there may be minimal understanding of the chart from a clinical perspective, the medical investigator should become very familiar with the organization of a medical chart and what information is available.

References

1. Brookshire, A. K. 2015. Allen & McCain, P. C. Interview by author. Atlanta, GA, September 23.
2. Darnell, S. A. 2015. Allen & McCain, P.C. Interview by author. Atlanta, GA, September 23.
3. Fishman, S. M. 2007. *Responsible Opioid Prescribing: A Physician's Guide*. Washington, DC: Waterford Life Sciences.
4. Federal Rules of Evidence, Rule 803(6), Exceptions to the Rule Against Hearsay, Records of a Regularly Conducted Activity. https://www.law.cornell.edu/rules/fre/rule_803
5. Steele, M. and Ellison, S. 2004. Trauma to the pelvis, hip, and femur. In *Emergency Medicine: A Comprehensive Study Guide*, 6th edition, Tintinalli, J., Kelen, G., and Stephan Stapczynski, J. (eds.), 1718–1722. New York: McGraw Hill, Inc.
6. Black, H. C. 1990. *Black's Law Dictionary*, 6th edition. St. Paul: West Publishing Company.
7. Quinn, C. 2005. *The Medical Record as a Forensic Resource*. Sudbury, MA: Jones and Bartlett Publishers.
8. Med League Support Services, Inc. 2015. Detecting Tampering with Medical Records. Accessed September 28, 2015. http://www.medleague.com/services/medical-record-analysis/detecting-tampering-with-medical-records/
9. Med League Support Services, Inc. 2015. Detecting Tampering with Medical Records—Subsections. Accessed September 28, 2015. http://www.medleague.com/services/medical-record-analysis/detecting-tampering-with-medical-records/subsections
10. Medical-Legal Topics. 2010. Pat Iyer's Dirty Dozen Tips for Detecting Altered Medical Records Part 3. Accessed September 28, 2015. http://www.medleague.com/blog/2010/07/05/pat-iyers-dirty-dozen-tips-for-detecting-altered-medical-records-part-3/
11. O'Farrell, J. 2010. Medical Records: Best Friend or Worst Enemy? Accessed September 28, 2015. http://www.princetoninsurance.com/downloads/Risk_Review_Downloads/Summer. 2010/08.2010_medical.records.pdf
12. Medicus Insurance Company. 2013. Making Changes to a Medical Record: Corrections vs. Alterations. Accessed September 28, 2015. http://www.medicusinsurance.com/june-email-2013-main

chapter seven

Evidence and evidence handling

This chapter will provide a discussion of typical types of evidence involved in medical practice investigations. Keep in mind that evidence common to medical investigations is the focus; however, nothing should be ruled out as potential evidence as the investigation develops. Prior to entering this discussion, a definition of evidence will prove useful. *Black's Law Dictionary*, 6th edition, defines evidence as *"testimony, writings, or material objects offered in proof of an alleged fact or proposition….that probative material, legally received, by which the tribunal may be lawfully persuaded of the truth or falsity of a fact in issue."*[1] In other words, evidence includes testimony, documents, and physical objects, legally obtained, that tend to prove a fact such that the court, hearing panel, medical board, etc. can be persuaded of that fact.

Purposes of evidence

The primary purpose of evidence is to prove a fact in issue. Other purposes of evidence include proof of the elements of the offense, impeachment of witnesses, and to reestablish the credibility of witnesses. The defense may offer evidence to establish a defense of the accused. Evidence may also be offered at the time of judgment which may include the accused's past offenses and prior conduct. The defense may also offer evidence of the accused's character and good reputation.[2]

Types of evidence

Evidence can be categorized in several ways, three of which are:

- *Physical evidence* (sometimes referred to as *real* evidence): Physical tangible objects such as syringes, pills, etc.[3,4]
- *Documentary evidence*: Documents, writings, photographs, print material, medical records, prescriptions, etc.[2,3,6]
- *Testimonial evidence*: Witness statements, victim statements, etc.[5,6]

Evidence may be further characterized as:

- *Direct evidence*: Evidence that proves the fact in dispute without the support of any other evidence, such as eyewitness evidence, evidence based on firsthand knowledge.[3,5–7]

- *Circumstantial evidence/indirect evidence*: Evidence that does not directly prove a fact in issue; evidence whereby inferences are drawn; evidence that implicates or logically connects an offender with the offense.[1,3,5–7]
- *Demonstrative evidence:* (sometimes referred to as *illustrative* evidence): Evidence in the form of certain tangible items used to demonstrate or illustrate facts. May include maps, charts, models, x-rays, CT scans, MRI images, photographs, etc.[7]
- *Opinion evidence*: Commonly referred to as expert testimony, is evidence provided by a witness that is qualified by the court, or other trier of fact (administrative law judge, etc.) as an expert; someone with special knowledge or skills not ordinarily possessed by others.[7] In the criminal arena, an expert witness may be a scientist or chemist from the crime lab testifying regarding blood/alcohol analysis or DNA analysis. In the administrative arena involving a medical practice issue, an expert witness may be a physician who has expertise in a specific surgical procedure or area of medical practice based on their training and experience. The medical expert witness will review all pertinent records, images, and other applicable information in order to render an opinion on the standard of care standard of care (SOC).
- *Competent evidence*: Evidence that is adequately sufficient, reliable, and relevant to the case and presented by a qualified, competent, and credible witness; evidence that has been properly collected, identified, and properly secured.[2,5]

Rules of evidence

The admissibility of evidence is governed by a set of rules, commonly referred to as *rules of evidence*. Said rules are found at the federal and state court levels. The rules provide a foundation by which to qualify evidence to ensure the evidence is credible, dependable, material (evidence having a relationship to the case at hand), and dependable before the evidence is admitted into the record.[2] A complete understanding of the rules of evidence perhaps should be left to the prosecuting attorney as the rules are extensive and complex, however, there are two very important rules concerning evidence that the investigator should be very familiar; the exclusionary rule and the rule against hearsay.

Exclusionary rule

The *exclusionary rule* maintains that evidence obtained illegally, in violation of the 4th Amendment to the U.S. Constitution, is inadmissible and may not be used as evidence against the accused.[3–5,8] It is important to note that over the years, the U.S. Supreme Court has carved out many exceptions to the exclusionary rule and such may warrant further study. Other bases that may exclude evidence from admission are relevancy, materiality, and competency.[9]

Relevancy is concerned with whether there is a connection between the evidence and the fact to be proven. *Materiality* is concerned with whether the evidence is sufficiently important to influence the outcome of the issue under consideration. *Competency* is concerned with the quality and kind of evidence being offered. Competent evidence is admissible for the purpose of proving a relevant fact.[9]

Hearsay rule

The rule against hearsay, commonly referred to as the *hearsay rule*, is found in the Federal Rules of Evidence 802 and states:

"Hearsay is not admissible unless any of the following provides otherwise:

- A federal statute;
- These rules; or
- Other rules prescribed by the Supreme Court."

Hearsay is defined as "testimony given by a witness who relates, not what he knows personally, but what others have told him, or what he has heard said by others."[1] Hearsay evidence does not rely on the credibility of the witness but relies on the competency and credibility of those who made the statement(s). Given the obvious weakness of hearsay evidence, it is usually inadmissible unless it meets one or more of several exceptions set out in the rules.[1]

Given the fact that medical investigations, by their nature, tend to rely heavily on documentary evidence, further discussion of such is warranted. *Black's Law Dictionary Free Online Legal Dictionary*, 2nd edition defines documentary evidence as "such evidence as is furnished by written instruments, inscriptions, documents of all kinds, and also any inanimate objects admissible for the purpose, as distinguished from 'oral' evidence, or that delivered by human beings via voce."[10] One should be careful, however, not to confuse *documentary* evidence with *physical* evidence.

Physical evidence is used to prove a fact that is based on the physical characteristics of the evidence.[11] Documentary evidence is used to prove a fact that is included in the information contained in the document.[11] For example: A physician is charged with unprofessional conduct for allegedly failing to maintain a medical record on a patient as required by statute or rule. He is also accused of practicing medicine below the SOC on the same patient by failing to timely diagnose prostate cancer. For over a year, the patient has made multiple visits to the physician's office complaining of frequent urination, painful/burning urination, some erectile dysfunction, and blood in the urine. During the investigation, a subpoena is issued to the physician calling for a copy of the patient's medical record. The medical record is produced. In this instance, the mere existence of the medical record is what is important in that it refutes the first allegation (failure to maintain a medical record). However, when the contents of the record (what is written in the record) is reviewed, it is revealed that the physician failed to obtain PSA tests on this patient at any time to rule out prostate issues and the record contained no note referring the patient to a urologist. It is the content, or what is written (in this case what is not documented) that is important. Evidence is *documentary* when its *contents* are the important part and *physical* when its *existence* is what is important.[11]

Authentication of documentary evidence

Another important aspect relating to documentary evidence is that it is required to be properly authenticated.[12] Federal Rules of Evidence rule 803 pertains to exceptions to the rule against hearsay. Rule 803(6) cites specific records exempted from the hearsay rule when meeting certain criteria. Records of a regularly conducted activity are excepted as long as they meet the following criteria:

- If the record was made at or near the time by—or from information transmitted by—someone with knowledge;
- If the record was kept in the course of a regularly conducted activity of a business, organization, occupation, or calling, whether or not for profit;
- If making the record was a regular practice of that activity;
- If all of these conditions are shown by the testimony of the custodian or another qualified witness, or by a certification that complies with Rule 902(11), or with a statute permitting certification.[13]

Documentary evidence in the medical investigation will likely consist of *certified copies* (properly authenticated) of original document(s) as opposed to the original document itself. If an original document is obtained, it should be treated as evidence, that is, properly collected, properly handled, properly documented, and properly secured. It should also be stressed that certified copies of documents should not be altered in any way. Alterations to the record may be considered acts of spoliation which was discussed in Chapter 6. If the investigator needs a working copy of the document, a photocopy should be made and the original certified copy secured.

One is strongly encouraged to become familiar with the rules of evidence in your state. The attorney representing your medical board will be an excellent resource in this area.

As stated earlier, medical practice investigations by and large are concerned with documentary evidence and testimonial evidence. There are cases, however, that may involve the need to obtain physical and demonstrative evidence such as pills, pill bottles, original prescriptions, imaging (X-rays, MRI, CT scan, etc.), medical instruments, audio/video recordings, and to name a few.

Obtaining evidence

Physical, documentary, and demonstrative evidence may be obtained in a variety of ways:

- Voluntarily relinquished to the investigator
- Subpoena (or other statutory authority granted to the board compelling release of evidence)
- Search Warrant

Voluntary relinquishment

While not often the most successful means of obtaining evidence, voluntary relinquishment of certain evidentiary items may be obtained from victims, patients, or patient/victim family members. Such items may include medications, prescriptions, medical records in the patients' possession, receipts for service, photographs, audio recordings, and text messages between the patient and physician. With regard to voluntarily relinquished documents, a copy may be made and provided to the donor, or a copy made for the investigator and the original returned to the donor. In this scenario, it would be advisable for the investigator to make the copies him/herself so that he/she can testify to the authenticity of the copies. If the originals are given to another staff person to copy, the integrity of the evidence and the authenticity of the copies may be challenged in court or in a hearing.

Subpoena

Obtaining evidence via administrative subpoena is perhaps the most efficient and effective method when conducting administrative investigations. A survey of 65 medical boards in the United States and District of Columbia revealed that 59 boards (90%) have some form of statutory subpoena authority. The survey failed to confirm subpoena authority in six states and an email sent requesting confirmation of such to those six state boards was met with no response. It is possible that these six boards do possess some form of subpoena authority; therefore, the percentage may be higher.

Subpoenas should not be "over-broad," or lacking specificity. This means that the subpoena must be written so as to specify the exact material to be produced. For example, a subpoena issued to a physician for *all patient records* would be considered over-broad. Such may imply a "fishing expedition" being conducted. Subpoenas should be specific citing the patient's name, date of birth (if available), and other identifying information such as dates of services were rendered, medical record number (if applicable and known). With regard to investigations of excessive prescribing, several patients may be identified as problematic from the pharmacy data. The subpoena should contain the same specific identifying information for each patient's record sought.

It is important to note that administrative subpoena authority may not extend to unlicensed individuals such as complementary and alternative medical practitioners (discussed in Chapter 14). Knowledge of the specific statutory authority granted and the requirements for a valid subpoena in the specific state statutes will be necessary.

Another important aspect concerning administrative subpoenas involves criminal proceedings. Specifically, the issue concerns utilizing evidence obtained via an administrative subpoena against a defendant in a criminal proceeding. Again, statutes and case law vary among the states; therefore, this issue should be thoroughly vetted with the board's legal counsel and the criminal prosecutor. A specific case in Georgia, King v. The State, illustrates this issue. Figure 7.1 discusses the specifics of King v. State as it pertains to medical record evidence.

In some states, medical board investigators are considered sworn law enforcement officers and as such have the powers of arrest and search and seizure. The *King v. State* issue often arises when nonsworn medical investigators conduct an investigation jointly with law enforcement agencies. If evidence is obtained by the medical board agent via administrative subpoena, then turned over to law enforcement authorities to be used as evidence in a criminal proceeding, said evidence is open to defense challenges and may be inadmissible.

If the law enforcement agency utilizes a search warrant to seize original evidence, the original evidence may not be made available to the medical board investigator. A possible remedy to this dilemma is for the medical investigator to accompany the law enforcement officer on the search warrant execution and serve to the practitioner a subpoena for the same evidence being seized. After the warrant execution is complete, the medical investigator may obtain copies of the original seized evidence from the participating law enforcement agency. It should be noted that this process will rely heavily on sound and positive professional relationships with law enforcement.

272 Ga. 788

Supreme Court of Georgia.

KING v. The STATE.
No. S99A1490.
Oct. 2, 2000.

Defendant was convicted in the Superior Court, Barrow County, of driving under the influence of alcohol to the extent that it was less safe for her to drive. Defendant appealed. The Supreme Court held that: (1) defendant's medical records were protected by fundamental constitutional right of privacy, and (2) prosecution's use of ex parte subpoena to obtain defendant's medical records violated defendant's constitutional right to privacy.......Defendant's medical records were within the ambit of protection provided by fundamental constitutional right of privacy; medical information, as reflected in the records maintained by medical providers, was a matter which a reasonable person would consider to be private, even if medical provider was the technical "owner" of actual records. Const. Art. 1, § 1, Par. 1.......Prosecution's use of ex parte subpoena to obtain defendant's medical records violated defendant's constitutional right to privacy, requiring that subpoena seeking results of blood-alcohol test that hospital administered to defendant be quashed, where defendant did not have notice and opportunity to object to state's subpoena of medical records in which she had not waived her right of privacy. Const. Art. 1, § 1, Par. 1; O.C.G.A. § 24–9–40(a)........ Medical records, protected by the constitutional right of privacy, cannot be disclosed without patient's consent unless their prohibition is required by law effectuating a compelling state interest and which is narrowly tailored to promote only that interest. Const. Art. 1, § 1, Par. 1........**The state is not entitled to exercise indiscriminate subpoena power as an investigative substitute for procedural devices otherwise available to it in the criminal context, such as a search warrant.**

Reversed.

Figure 7.1 *King v. The State.* (From King, v. The State of Georgia, 272 Ga. 788, Supreme Court of Georgia, No. S99A1490, October 2, 2000. http://biotech.law.lsu.edu/cases/privacy/king_v_state.htm)

Search warrant

When conducting criminal investigations, a search warrant will be necessary to obtain required evidence. As mentioned earlier, medical board investigators in some states are granted law enforcement powers and as such are authorized to obtain and execute search warrants. In situations whereby the medical board investigator is not vested with law enforcement authority, the medical investigator may seek to partner with local or state law enforcement if criminal violations are suspected.

Chain of custody

Maintaining the *chain of custody* is extremely important when handling evidence. Chain of custody refers to the chronological documentation or paper trail, showing the seizure or otherwise obtaining, custody, control, transfer, analysis, and disposition of evidence. All evidence must be accounted for in terms of where it has been, who has handled it, for what purpose, and change of possession.

When obtaining evidence, the investigator should complete an "evidence receipt/chain of custody" form (Appendix 18). This form provides for a complete detailed description of the evidence, the date and time the evidence was obtained, date and time of all transfers of the evidence from one person to another, and the purpose of the transfer. The item of evidence should be secured in a paper or plastic bag along with the original evidence receipt form. A copy of the evidence receipt form should be placed in the investigative file and another copy placed in the evidence log book which is typically maintained in the secure evidence storage room. In the best case scenario, the evidence, once properly packaged, should be secured in a locked area used for evidence storage only and accessed by a designated evidence custodian or an alternate evidence custodian. Do not store evidence in an area accessible by other staff as this will place the integrity of the evidence in question and may open up challenges to its authenticity and possible alteration. It is also advisable not to carry evidence in one's vehicle nor to keep in the investigator's house. This too can open up challenges to the evidence's integrity.

An evidence receipt or chain of custody form enables the investigator to properly and accurately document the above. An accurate chain of custody is essential to protect and maintain the integrity of the evidence otherwise the evidence may be successfully challenged by the defense and barred from admission in a hearing or other legal proceeding.

Another important aspect of evidence and the chain of custody concerns the investigator's appearance in court or a hearing. When called to testify and at the time the board attorney or prosecutor intends to tender the evidentiary items into the record, the investigator will be required to satisfy certain legal requirements. The investigator must be able to:

- Identify the evidence
- Describe where it was found and/or how it was obtained
- Establish integrity of the chain of custody
- Describe and explain any changes in the evidence that may have occurred since it was obtained.[7]

Evidence could be considered the linchpin of the investigation. If the evidence is improperly obtained or haphazardly handled without proper chain of custody documentation, an otherwise strong investigative effort will be for naught.

References

1. Black, H. C. 1990. *Black's Law Dictionary*, 6th edition. St. Paul: West Publishing Company.
2. Lee, G. D. 2007. *Practical Criminal Evidence*. Upper Saddle River, NJ: Pearson/Prentice Hall.
3. Gilbert, J. N. 2007. *Criminal Investigation*, 7th edition. Upper Saddle River, NJ: Pearson/Prentice Hall.
4. Becker, R. F. 2000. *Criminal Investigation*. Gaithersburg, MD: Aspen Publishers.
5. Bennett, W. W. and K. M. Hess. 2007. *Criminal Investigation*, 8th edition. Belmont, CA: Thompson Higher Education.

6. Palmiotto, M. J. 1998. *Criminal Investigation,* 2nd edition. Bethesda, MD: Austin & Winfield Publishers.
7. Swanson, C., N. Chamelin, L. Territo, and R. Taylor. 2006. *Criminal Investigation,* 9th edition. New York: McGraw-Hill Higher Education.
8. Law Dictionary. *Black's Law Dictionary Free Online Legal Dictionary,* 2nd edition. (accessed March 2, 2014). www.thelawdictionary.org
9. Osterburg, J. W. and R. H. Ward. 1997. *Criminal Investigation,* 2nd edition. Cincinnati, OH: Anderson Publishing.
10. Law Dictionary. *Black's Law Dictionary Free Online Legal Dictionary,* 2nd edition. (accessed September 22, 2015). www.thelawdictionary.org
11. Rottenstein Law Group, LLP. 2011. What Is Documentary Evidence? (accessed April 19, 2014). http://www.rotlaw.com/legal-library/what-is-documentary-evidence/
12. Jackson, K. Documentary Evidence. Paper presented at the National Business Institute Seminar, Birmingham, Alabama, July 30, 2009.
13. Federal Rules of Evidence, Rule 803(6), Exceptions to the Rule Against Hearsay, Records of a Regularly Conducted Activity. https://www.law.cornell.edu/rules/fre/rule_803
14. King, v. The State of Georgia, 272 Ga. 788, Supreme Court of Georgia, No. S99A1490, October 2, 2000. http://biotech.law.lsu.edu/cases/privacy/king_v_state.htm

chapter eight

Standard of care investigations

The standard of care... what is it? Medical boards in all states have a statute or rule providing for disciplinary action against a physician for practicing medicine below the standard of care.

Definition

The standard of care (SOC) is often viewed as an idea referring to a generally accepted or agreed upon, community way of doing things as it pertains to treating a patient for a specific malady at a specific place in time.[1] The standard of care changes over time. With the advent of technological advances and advances in research and knowledge, the SOC in 2015 is vastly different from what it was in the early twentieth century.

Definitions of the SOC will differ from state to state; however, similarities will be noticed. The medical practice act of three states from different regions of the country was examined and they revealed similarities and differences as they define the SOC. The state of Florida defines the SOC as "the prevailing professional SOC for a given healthcare provider shall be that level of care, skill, and treatment, which, in light of all relevant surrounding circumstances, is recognized as acceptable and appropriate by reasonably prudent similar healthcare providers."[2] Oregon's statute addresses a "duty of care" and it reads "A physician licensed to practice medicine...by the Oregon Medical Board has the duty to use that degree of care, skill and diligence that is used by ordinarily careful physicians in the same or similar circumstances in the community of the physician or a similar community."[3] The Ohio medical practice act contains language as it pertains to unprofessional conduct; "a departure from, or the failure to conform to minimal standards of care of similar practitioners under the same or similar circumstances, whether or not actual injury to a patient is established..."[4]

Closer scrutiny of these three definitions reveals a consistency with regard to the use of the words "care," "skill," "same," "similar," and "circumstances." Physicians must use a degree or level of care and skill as other physicians in the same or similar circumstances or community. It is important to note that the SOC may vary from locale to locale. In other words, the SOC in Atlanta, GA may be much different than the SOC in Kingsland, GA (an extremely small remote southeast Georgia town). The physician in rural Georgia would not be in a similar circumstance as a physician in Atlanta given the high level of technology, state-of-the-art medical facilities, and research institutions located in Atlanta.

A very early court ruling addressing the SOC came from the Illinois Supreme Court in 1860. The plaintiff was patient Richie who alleged that the defendant physician Dr. West was negligent when applying a plaster cast. The court ruled in favor of the plaintiff (patient) and stated "When a person assumes the profession of physician and surgeon, he must be… held to employ a reasonable amount of skill and care."[5] Anecdotally, it is interesting to note that the defendant's legal counsel was Abraham Lincoln.

When discussing the concept of the SOC (or substandard care) it is often equated to medical malpractice, however, this is not always the case. Medical malpractice typically refers to claims for damages and civil suits alleging negligence resulting in some form of harm or injury. However, not all cases involving substandard care result in medical malpractice claims or lawsuits. A physician may practice below the SOC with regard to aberrant prescribing of drugs, failure to perform an appropriate physical examination, failure to timely inform a patient of diagnostic test results, etc. While medical malpractice suits must demonstrate deviance from the SOC to succeed, many incidences of substandard care, fortunately, do not result in a harm or injury, resulting in no claim or lawsuit. A brief discussion of medical malpractice is warranted in that matters of substandard care and legal claims of medical malpractice often go "hand in hand."

Medical malpractice

Medical malpractice is defined as professional negligence by a physician or other healthcare practitioner that causes physical or emotional harm to a patient. That negligence can come in the form of an act or an omission of an act. A claim or suit of medical malpractice must prove four essential elements:

1. Duty—A duty must have been owed to the patient by a physician charged with the patient's care (established by creation of the physician/patient relationship).
2. Breach of Duty—The physician who had the duty of care must have failed in his/her duty by not exercising the degree of care or skill that another physician in the same/similar circumstances would have used (often established via expert testimony).
3. Damage—The patient must have suffered emotional or physical injury while in the care of the physician.
4. Cause—There must be proof that the breach of duty by the physician caused the patient's injury.[6]

Physician/patient relationship

Often the physician/patient relationship will be based on one of three models, the authoritative model, the contractual model, or the fiduciary model.[7]

1. Authoritative Model—This model is perhaps the most traditional. It is based on the premise that the physician is in charge and the patient blindly follows the physician's orders and recommendations.
2. Contractual Model—In this model, the physician and patient are simply two individuals legally contracting for services and payment for said services.
3. Fiduciary Model—This model is often referred to as the friendship model. The physician/patient relationship consists of mutual trust, mutual dependence, and mutual respect.[7]

Common SOC issues

Practice below the SOC can encompass many, many acts or omissions, however, several of the more common issues are discussed.

Failure to obtain consultation and referral

In this day and age of specialization, medical consultations are often considered the norm. When a physician is confronted with a situation with which they are unfamiliar or insufficiently trained, or if they surmise that their treatment plan is not working, a consultation with a specialist or a referral would be in order.[7] Consultations and referrals should be timely and to the appropriate specialist. A family practice physician treating a high risk pregnancy patient should perhaps consider a consult with or referral to an OB/GYN. If an internist sees elevated PSA values on his male patient's lab work, a referral to a urologist would be in order. Failure to do so may be considered substandard practice. A consultation with the patient's prior treating physician may be warranted to better understand the case and model an appropriate course of treatment.[7]

Physician/patient communication failure

Physicians are busy people; however, being busy should not interfere with their obligation to listen to their patients. During hasty clinic visits, medical histories can be inadequate and physical examination is cursory at best. Patient complaints that are ignored or rejected could result in a course of treatment that is not adequate to treat the problem or lead to missed diagnoses of more serious problems.[7]

Failure to diagnose/misdiagnosis

A diagnosis is a process whereby a physician, by examination and observation, distinguishes between a variety of clinical possibilities; differentiating two or more diseased states.[7] Misdiagnosis typically manifests in one of three ways:

1. Failure to render any diagnosis whatsoever; failure to recognize that a particular malady or condition exists.
2. Making an incorrect diagnosis; diagnosing a condition that the patient does not have or a condition different than what the patient actually has.
3. Rendering a diagnosis of disease or other malady when the patient has no disease.[7]

Diagnostic problems often result from an inferior medical history taken from the patient, inadequate physical examination, and inadequate or incorrect diagnostic studies (blood work, imaging, etc.).[7]

Treatment errors

Error in treatment covers a broad spectrum ranging from prescribing the wrong medication(s), prescribing an insufficient dose or a too strong dose, surgical errors such as wrong site surgery, hemorrhage during surgery, problems involving anesthesia, improper monitoring of patient during administration of anesthesia, failure to perform a timely Cesarean section, and to name but a few.[7]

Prescribing of drugs

Physicians receive little training in pharmacology. Substandard care with regard to prescribing may involve the prescribing of a drug causing an adverse reaction to other drugs being taken, allergic reactions to certain drugs, excessive prescribing of controlled substances, and potential adverse interactions with over-the-counter drugs.[7]

Investigation

The SOC cases typically originate via a complaint from a patient, family member of a patient, another healthcare provider, an attorney on behalf of a patient, or a malpractice suit settlement or judgment. The SOC complaints allege that the physician breached the SOC by performing certain acts, failing to perform certain acts, or performing certain acts improperly. Failure to perform certain diagnostic studies leading to a failure to timely diagnose a disease or other malady; performing a procedure improperly causing injury; prescribing the wrong medication to treat an illness; and performing a procedure on the wrong site are just a few examples. The complaint should be thoroughly reviewed as described in Chapter 4 and once the investigator has an overall impression as to the nature of the complaint and who is, or should be involved, the investigation can commence.

Interview of complainant

The first step is to interview the complainant. Allow the complainant to tell their story uninterrupted while the investigator takes notes. When the complainant finishes telling their story, go back and ask pertinent questions to close any gaps and to obtain specific details using the journalistic technique. Specific details are essential as to dates, times, locations of treatment, what happened, witnesses present, what was said, what was heard, to whom and by whom. If the patient sought treatment from a subsequent treating physician, it will be important to determine from whom, when the treatment was provided, and obtain a copy of the patient's chart from this practitioner. If the complainant is the patient, it is a good idea to go ahead and obtain signed medical record releases for each location where treatment was obtained in case they are needed, especially in psychiatric or substance abuse cases. If possible, obtain a written statement from the complainant and patient so as to lock in their account of what happened.

Interview of witnesses

After the complainant and patient have been interviewed, all witnesses should then be interviewed. Again, planning is essential. The same basic interview process will suffice. Allow the witness to tell their story, then go back and ask specific questions to close any gaps. Again, the journalistic technique is very effective. After the witness has been thoroughly interviewed, obtain a written statement if possible.

Obtaining records

Thorough interviews with the patient/complainant, and all relevant witnesses should assist in identifying the necessary records needed for the investigation. Request documents (subpoenas, demand letters, orders to produce, etc.) should then be drafted and approved by one authorized to do so at the agency. The request documents should then be served to the corresponding entities, that is, the physician's office, hospital(s), subsequent treating physicians, nursing home, etc.

Reviewing the records

Depending on the nature of the complaint, a cursory review of the records may be in order. Ultimately a medical professional affiliated with the agency will be required to review them in order to render an opinion as to the SOC. Based on this opinion, the board may wish to proceed with an outside independent peer review (see below). A review of the records as described in Chapter 6 will assist the investigator in establishing the legitimacy of the complaint. For example, if the patient states the injury was caused by an improperly administered steroid injection in the left knee on a certain date and the record reflects that the patient was not seen on that date and there is no documentation of a steroid injection whatsoever, the validity of the complaint may be questioned. A re-interview of the patient would be in order in a case such as this.

Interview of the respondent

Standard of care cases examine just that…the standard of care. An allegation has been made that the physician breached the SOC in the treatment of a particular illness or condition. Did the physician fail to properly diagnose the condition, did the physician improperly perform a particular surgical procedure, did the physician prescribe inappropriate medications, etc.? It should be noted that the investigator is not charged with rendering a medical opinion. The investigator's duty is to gather all of the facts to enable a medical expert to render an opinion. In these types of cases, the investigator should have the physician explain, in writing, his/her approach to the particular patient, diagnostic studies conducted, consults obtained, and his/her rationale in treating the condition or performing the particular procedure. Basically, a detailed discussion of the patient's complete course of treatment is required for this type of case.

Peer review

As stated, the standard of care is often hard to identify or precisely define. Medical boards often rely on experts to render opinions as to specific cases in which the standard of care has come into question. This is known as *peer review*. Peer review is a process whereby a physician of the same specialty, who is not familiar with the subject physician, is contracted by the board to review all of the pertinent patient records related to the instant case. Based on this review, the peer reviewer is asked to render an opinion as to whether or not the subject physician practiced below the standard care.

The peer review report should be clear and detailed as to the commissions and omissions by the subject physician resulting in the breached

SOC. The process of peer review is often used in cases involving questions of quality of care, prescribing of drugs, and malpractice judgments and settlements. See Appendix 19 for a sample peer review report.

References

1. Cooper, D. C. 2007. Investigating standard of care cases. Presentation given at *Administrators in Medicine Investigator Training Conference*, Orlando, Florida, June 2007.
2. Laws of Florida, Title 45, 766.102(1).
3. Oregon Revised Statutes 677.095.
4. Ohio Revised Code 4731.22(6).
5. *Richie v. West*, 23 Ill. 329 (1860).
6. G. Eric Nielson & Associates. 2015. What Are the Four Elements That Constitute Medical Malpractice? Accessed September 9, 2015. http://ericnielson.com/four-elements-medical-malpractice.html
7. Blackman, N. S. and C. P. Bailey. 1990. *Liability in Medical Practice: A Reference for Physicians*. New York, NY: Harwood Academic Publishers.

chapter nine

Controlled substance prescribing investigations

Controlled substances are specific drugs identified by government as having the potential for abuse, dependence, and addiction. Controlled substances are identified and the laws governing the possession, prescribing, dispensing, and administering of controlled substances are codified in both federal and state laws.

Definitions

The federal controlled substances act, as well as most state codes, identifies five groups (referred to as *schedules*), of controlled substances:

- Schedule I
  - The drug or other substance has a high potential for abuse.
  - The drug or other substance has no currently accepted medical use in treatment in the United States.
  - There is a lack of accepted safety for use of the drug or other substance under medical supervision.[1]
- Schedule II
  - The drug or other substance has a high potential for abuse.
  - The drug or other substance has a currently accepted medical use in treatment in the United States or a currently accepted medical use with severe restrictions.
  - Abuse of the drug or other substances may lead to severe psychological or physical dependence.[1]
- Schedule III
  - The drug or other substance has a potential for abuse less than the drugs or other substances in schedules I and II.
  - The drug or other substance has a currently accepted medical use in treatment in the United States.
  - Abuse of the drug or other substance may lead to moderate or low physical dependence or high psychological dependence.[1]
- Schedule IV
  - The drug or other substance has a low potential for abuse relative to the drugs or other substances in schedule III.

    - The drug or other substance has a currently accepted medical use in treatment in the United States.
    - Abuse of the drug or other substance may lead to limited physical dependence or psychological dependence relative to the drugs or other substances in schedule III.[1]
- Schedule V
    - The drug or other substance has a low potential for abuse relative to the drugs or other substances in schedule IV.
    - The drug or other substance has a currently accepted medical use in treatment in the United States.
    - Abuse of the drug or substance may lead to limited physical dependence or psychological dependence relative to the drugs or substances in schedule IV.[1]

Controlled substances can also be classified as to their legitimate medical use. There are three primary categories; Opioids/Narcotics, Stimulants, and Central Nervous System Depressants.

Opioids/narcotics

Opioids are used primarily to treat pain. They diminish pain signal intensity reaching the brain and affect certain brain areas controlling emotion, thus diminishing the effects of a painful stimulus.[2] Medications within this group include hydrocodone, oxycodone, morphine, codeine, and related drugs.[2] Opioids are found in all schedules.

Effects on the brain and body

Opioids affect the brain and body by attaching to specific proteins called opioid receptors, which are found in the brain, spinal cord, gastrointestinal tract, and other organs in the body. When these drugs attach to their receptors, they reduce the perception of pain. Drowsiness, mental confusion, nausea, constipation, and, depending upon the amount of drug taken, depressed respiration are other effects of opioid use.[2]

Opioid use can also cause a euphoric effect in that these drugs affect the "reward" regions in the brain. Those who abuse opioids may seek to heighten their experience by taking the drug in ways other than those prescribed. For example, oxycodone is a tablet meant to be taken orally and relieves pain via a slow and steady release of the opioid. Opioid abusers may crush the tablet then snort or inject it to heighten the euphoric effect further increasing their risk of overdose.[2]

Potential consequences of opioid use and abuse

Taken as prescribed, opioids can be used to manage pain safely and effectively. When abused, even a single large dose can cause severe respiratory depression and death. Properly managed, short-term medical use of opioid analgesics rarely cause addiction which is characterized by compulsive drug seeking behavior and use despite serious adverse consequences. Regular (e.g., several times a day, for several weeks or more) or longer term use or abuse of opioids can lead to physical dependence and, in some cases, addiction. Physical dependence is a *normal* adaptation to chronic use of a drug and is not the same as addiction. In either case, withdrawal symptoms may occur if drug use is suddenly reduced or stopped. These symptoms can include restlessness, muscle and bone pain, insomnia, diarrhea, vomiting, cold flashes with goose bumps ("cold turkey"), and involuntary leg movements.[2]

Stimulants

Stimulants increase alertness, attention, and energy, as well as elevate blood pressure, heart rate, and respiration. Stimulants are prescribed to treat only a few health conditions, including attention deficit hyperactivity disorder (ADHD), narcolepsy, and occasionally depression in patients who have not responded to other treatments.[2] Some lower scheduled stimulants are prescribed for relatively short-term treatment for obesity (weight loss).

Effects on the brain and body

Stimulants, such as amphetamine, dextroamphetamine, and methylphenidate, act in the brain similar to a group of key brain neurotransmitters called monoamines, which include norepinephrine and dopamine. Stimulants enhance the effects of these chemicals in the brain and the resulting increase in dopamine can bring about a feeling of euphoria when taken nonmedically. Stimulants also increase blood pressure and heart rate, constrict blood vessels, increase blood glucose, and open up breathing passages.[2]

Dramatic increases in the prescribing of stimulants over the past two decades have led to greater availability and increased risk for diversion and abuse. For patients taking these medications to treat properly diagnosed conditions, they can greatly enhance a person's quality of life. Stimulants are perceived by many to be generally safe and effective, however, prescription stimulants are increasingly being abused to "treat" nonmedical conditions or situations. Reports suggest that nonmedical use of stimulants is occurring among some academic professionals, athletes, performers, older people, and both high school and college students. Such nonmedical cognitive enhancement poses potential health risks, including addiction, cardiovascular events, and psychosis.[2]

Potential consequences of stimulant use and abuse

As with other drugs of abuse, it is possible for individuals to become dependent upon or addicted to stimulants. Withdrawal symptoms associated with discontinuing stimulant use include fatigue, depression, and disturbance of sleep patterns. Repeated abuse of some stimulants (sometimes within a short period) can lead to feelings of hostility or paranoia, even psychosis. Further, taking high doses of a stimulant may result in dangerously high body temperature and an irregular heartbeat. There is also the potential for cardiovascular failure or seizures.[2] Like opioids, stimulants are found in all schedules.

Central nervous system (CNS) depressants

CNS depressants are often referred to as sedatives and tranquilizers. These substances can slow brain activity and make them useful for treating anxiety and sleep disorders.[2] Medications commonly prescribed for these purposes are the following:

- *Benzodiazepines*, such as diazepam and alprazolam, are sometimes prescribed to treat anxiety, acute stress reactions, and panic attacks. The more sedating benzodiazepines, such as triazolam and estazolam, are prescribed for short-term treatment of sleep disorders. Benzodiazepines should not be prescribed for long-term use because of the risk for developing tolerance, dependence, or addiction.[2]
- *Non-benzodiazepine sleep medications*, such as zolpidem, eszopiclone, and zalepon, have a different chemical structure, but act on some of the same brain receptors as benzodiazepines. They are thought to have fewer side effects and less risk of dependence than benzodiazepines.[2]
- *Barbiturates*, such as mephobarbital, phenobarbital, and pentobarbital sodium, are used less frequently to reduce anxiety or to help with sleep disorders because of their higher risk of overdose compared to benzodiazepines. Many barbiturates are classified in schedule II whereas most benzodiazepines are classified in schedules III, IV, and V. However, barbiturates are still used in surgical procedures and for seizure disorders.[2]

Effects on the brain and body

Most CNS depressants act on the brain by affecting the neurotransmitter gammaaminobutyric acid (GABA). Neurotransmitters are brain chemicals that enable communication between brain cells. Each class of CNS depressants work in unique ways, however, their ability to increase GABA inhibits brain activity, producing a drowsy or calming effect which can be beneficial to those suffering from anxiety or sleep disorders.[2]

Potential consequences of CNS depressant use and abuse

CNS depressants have the potential for abuse and should be used only as prescribed. The use of nonbenzodiazepine sleep aids is less well studied, but certain indicators have raised concern about their abuse potential as well. During the first few days of taking a prescribed CNS depressant, one may feel sleepy and uncoordinated. As the body becomes accustomed to the effects of the drug and tolerance develops, these side effects will likely begin to disappear. As one uses these drugs long-term, larger doses may be required to achieve the same therapeutic effects. Continued use may lead to physical dependence and withdrawal symptoms when use is abruptly reduced or stopped. All CNS depressants work by slowing brain activity. When an individual stops taking them there can be a rebound effect, resulting in seizures or other harmful consequences.[2]

Tolerance versus dependence versus addiction

In the proceeding discussion of opiates, stimulants, and CNS depressants, the terms tolerance, dependence, and addiction were mentioned. These terms are often used synonymously or interchangeably. Such interchangeable use of these terms is inaccurate and can be misleading, therefore, it is necessary to define and differentiate the three.

Tolerance

Tolerance is defined as a state of progressively decreased response to a drug resulting in a larger dose needed to achieve the effect originally obtained by a smaller dose. In other words, it takes a higher dose of the drug to achieve the same level of response achieved initially. It is essentially the body's ability to adapt to the presence of the drug.[3,4]

Dependence

Dependence refers to a state where the individual is dependent upon the drug for normal physiological functioning.[5] Dependence develops when the neurons in the brain adapt to repeated exposure to the drug and only function normally when the drug is present.[4] Cessation of the drug will likely result in withdrawal symptoms that can be severe, even life threatening. The body has become so dependent on the drug that withdrawal now interferes with "normal" physiological processes.[3,4]

Dependence is characterized two ways; *physical dependence* and *psychological dependence.*

Physical dependence

Physical dependence occurs when the body has adjusted to the presence of a drug, resulting in withdrawal symptoms when its use stops. One physically dependent on a drug requires that drug in order to function normally. The state of physical dependence is revealed by the manifestation of withdrawal symptoms after the drug is withheld. Symptoms of withdrawal can be terminated by re-administering the drug.[3]

Symptoms of withdrawal tend to be the opposite of the effects of the drug. If the effect of the drug is sedation, the withdrawal effect will likely be hyperexcitability. If the effect was stimulation, the withdrawal effect will likely be a form of depression.[3]

Psychological dependence

Psychological dependence is characterized by emotional and mental preoccupation with the drug's effects and by a persistent craving for it. The symptoms are not physical symptoms and craving seems to be the most common withdrawal symptom. Psychological dependence is usually manifested by compulsive drug-taking, but the frequency and pattern of use can differ considerably from one individual to another.[3]

Addiction

The World Health Organization (WHO) defines *addiction* as:

> A behavioral pattern of drug use, characterized by overwhelming involvement with the use of a drug (compulsive use), the securing of the supply, and a high tendency to relapse after withdrawal. Addiction is viewed as an extreme on a continuum of drug use patterns. It refers, in a quantitative rather an a qualitative sense, to the degree to which drug use pervades the total life activity of the user, and to the range of circumstances in which drug use controls his/her behavior [sic].

Addiction is a behavioral syndrome where the acquisition and use of a drug dominates the person's motivation and where normal constraints on behavior are ineffective. Inherent in this definition is the overwhelmingly powerful motivation to obtain and self-administer the drug.[5]

Regulation

Federal regulations, and state codes have specific requirements as they pertain to the proper prescribing of a controlled substance. Title 21 of the US Code of Federal Regulations, Part 1306.04(a) provides for the following:

21 CFR § 1306.04 Purpose of issue of prescription

a. A prescription for a controlled substance to be effective must be issued for *a legitimate medical purpose by an individual practitioner acting in the usual course of his professional practice*. The responsibility for the proper prescribing and dispensing of controlled substances is upon the prescribing practitioner, but a corresponding responsibility rests with the pharmacist who fills the prescription. An order purporting to be a prescription issued not in the usual course of professional treatment or in legitimate and authorized research is not a prescription within the meaning and intent of Section 309 of the Act (21 U.S.C. 829) and the person knowingly filling such a purported prescription, as well as the person issuing it, shall be subject to the penalties provided for violations of the provisions of law relating to controlled substances.[6]

Title 21 of the US Code of Federal Regulations, Part 1306.05(a) sets out the required manner of issuance of prescriptions and it reads as follows:

21 CFR § 1306.05 Manner of issuance of prescriptions

a. All prescriptions for controlled substances shall be dated as of, and signed on, the day when issued and shall bear the full name and address of the patient, the drug name, strength, dosage form, quantity prescribed, directions for use, and the name, address, and registration number of the practitioner.[7]

Figure 9.1 shows a sample prescription with the above-mentioned components labeled.

When we examine Figure 9.1, we can readily see how the information contained on the prescription matches with the requirements set forth in 21 CFR 1306.05(a).

Item #1 is the patient's identifying information, item #2 is the date the prescription was issued, item #3 is the name of the drug being prescribed, item #4 is the dosage, items #5, 6, and 7 constitute the directions for taking the drug. In this example, Sig is an abbreviation of the Latin word *signetur* which means "let it be labeled." The directions go on to say "i or ii" (1 or 2 tablets) "po" (by mouth), "qid" (4 times per day), "prn" (as needed). Item #8 is the quantity of tablets to be dispensed, #9 indicates the number of times the prescription may be refilled, #10 is the DEA registration number of the prescribing practitioner, and #11 is the prescribing practitioner's signature.

If a prescription is issued in violation of this regulation, it is then not considered a prescription resulting in the unlawful prescribing,

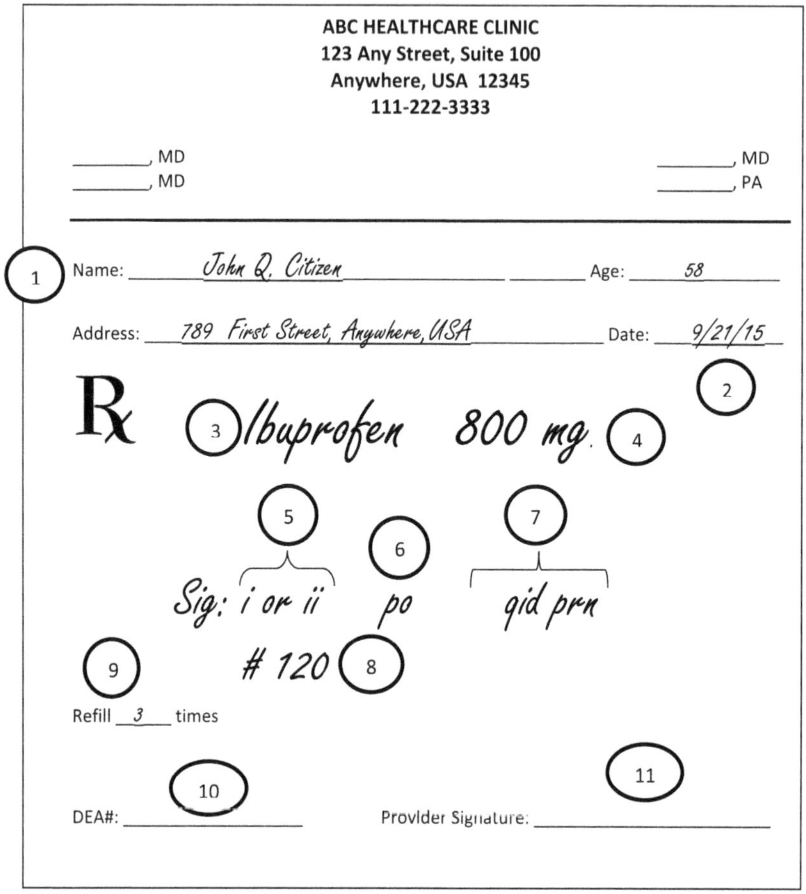

Figure 9.1 Sample prescription. (From prescription format taken from actual prescription issued to the author.)

dispensing, and possession of the controlled substance. The physician is required by law to prescribe controlled substances for legitimate medical purposes while acting in the usual course of his/her professional practice.

The following is a quote from the decision of the US Circuit Court of Appeals, 5th Circuit, affirming the criminal conviction of Henry M. Collier, MD in 1973:

> A licensed practitioner is not immune from the law solely due to his status....but rather, because he is expected to prescribe or dispense drugs within the bounds of his professional practice of medicine. A physician is restricted to dispensing or prescribing

> drugs in the bona fide treatment of a patient's disease...However, under the guise of treatment a physician cannot sell drugs nor distribute drugs intended to cater to the cravings of an addict... Congress did not intend for doctors to become pushers.[8]

Scope of the problem

Prescription drug abuse has become a national epidemic. It is believed that prescription drug overdose deaths account for more than all other drug-related deaths combined. According to research published by the U.S. Department of Justice, National Drug Intelligence Center, approximately seven million people aged 12 or older were current nonmedical users of prescription controlled drugs in 2009, a 12% increase from 2008. Adolescents showed a significantly higher rate of nonmedical use of opioids than the overall population. Current nonmedical use of opioids increased from 2.3% of 12- to 17-year olds in 2008 to 2.7% in 2009 according to the National Survey on Drug Use and Health (NSDUH).[9]

In 2007 11,528 people died in the United States from unintentional opioid overdoses up from 11,001 in 2006.[9] Statistics from the Centers for Disease Control and Prevention (CDC) indicate the number of opioid-related deaths has increased steadily over the past decade.[9] It is believed that deaths from prescription opioid overdoses exceed deaths from all other illegal drugs combined.[10] Figure 9.2 shows death data whereby opioid caused deaths surpass deaths from illicit drugs.

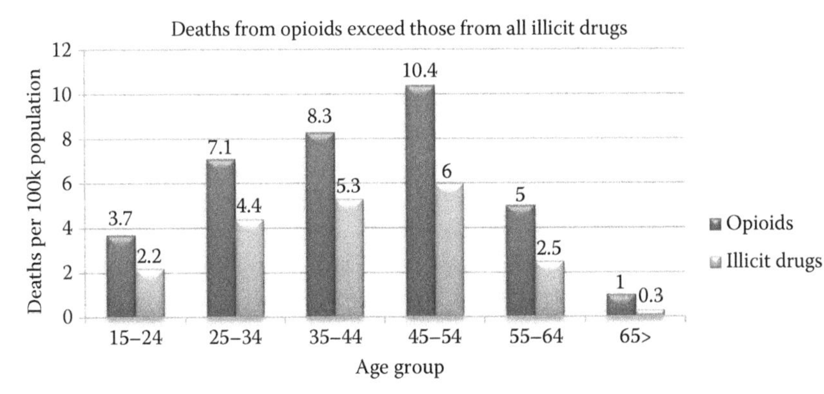

Figure 9.2 Opioid deaths surpass those from illicit drugs. (From Centers for Disease Control and Prevention, 2011. *Morbidity and Mortality Weekly Report*, 60(43): 1489.)

The estimated number of Emergency Department visits involving nonmedical use of prescription opioids increased approximately 30% between 2008 and 2009.[9]

On a positive note, those abusing prescription drugs decreased from 6.8 million users in 2012 to 6.5 million users in 2013. Rates of prescription drug abuse among adolescents (ages 12–17) decreased from 2.8% to 2.2% maintaining a gradual decline from a rate of 4% in 2002.[11]

The problem of prescription drug abuse on the state level is evidenced by the startling statistics from the Georgia Bureau of Investigation, Division of Forensic Sciences (GBI). The GBI began collecting this data in 2008. The data reveal the following:

- 2008—638 autopsies performed attributed to drug overdose; of those, 543 were prescription drug related or 85%
- 2009—670 autopsies performed attributed to drug overdose; of those, 584 were prescription drug related or 87%
- 2010—729 autopsies performed attributed to drug overdose; of those, 628 were prescription drug related or 86%
- 2011—664 autopsies performed attributed to drug overdose; of those, 582 were prescription drug related or 88%
- 2012—686 autopsies performed attributed to drug overdose; of those, 592 were prescription drug related or 86%
- 2013—630 autopsies preformed attributed to drug overdose; of those, 524 were prescription drug related or 83%[12]

As one can see the trend of prescription, drug abuse has remained at a high steady rate over the six-year period. Figure 9.3 shows a six-year period comparison of deaths attributed to prescription drug use versus nonprescription drug use.

Further examination of the 2013 GBI data reveals that on average there were over two different drugs found for each death. Alprazolam appeared in 211 cases, oxycodone in 164, methadone in 118, hydrocodone in 125, morphine in 62, citalopram in 45 cases, and fentanyl in 47 cases. The toxicology studies revealed 83 different drugs found in the 630 deaths and 1693 instances of the 83 drugs. An astonishing 46% of all drugs found in the 630 deaths were comprised of the aforementioned seven drugs. About 72% of the 630 deaths were those whose ages were between 25 and 54 years of age. About 87% of the cases were attributed to accidental overdose.[12]

Even though controlled substances require a prescription from a physician or other authorized healthcare provider prior to dispensing, many are stolen and diverted at the manufacturer, distributor, wholesale, and retail levels, however, unscrupulous prescribers do

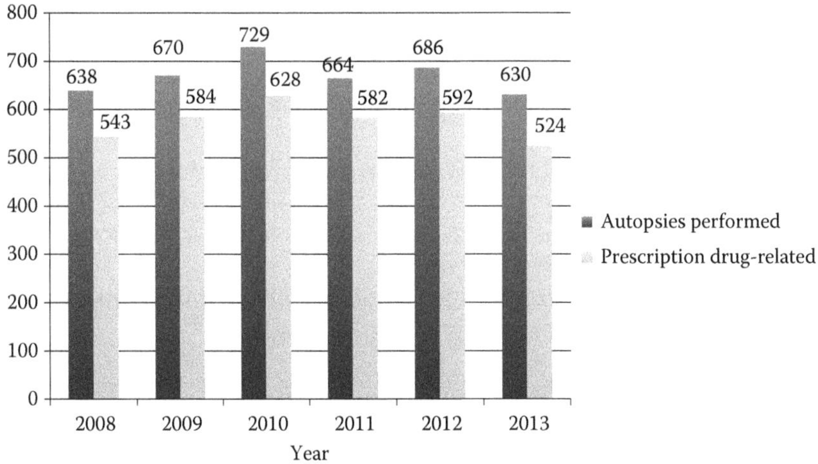

Figure 9.3 Georgia Bureau of Investigation statistics for six year period comparing deaths attributed to prescription drug use versus nonprescription drug use. (From Georgia Bureau of Investigation, Division of Forensic Sciences Reports (2008–2013).)

contribute to the problem. Cases of alleged violations of prescribing controlled substances can involve rather simple cases of poor judgment and relatively few prescriptions to cases of extreme prescribing abuse giving rise to licensure sanctions and potential criminal violations, and the investigation of said cases can range from rather simple straightforward investigations to lengthy, complex, and time-consuming investigations.

Research suggests several reasons why physicians have problems related to their prescribing patterns. The research indicates that the problem prescriber will fall into one of four categories:

- Deficient
  - Too busy to maintain continuing education in the area of prescribing
  - Unaware of the laws and rules governing the prescribing of controlled substances
  - Prescribing drugs that were once thought nonaddictive but have been proven otherwise
  - Prescribing for friends or family[13]
- Duped
  - Gullible, too trusting
  - "Buys" the sad story of the patient[13]

- Deliberate
  - Physician becomes a mercenary
  - Practice becomes a "pill mill" full of drug seekers
  - Sells his prescriptions, splits the money with drug dealers who sell the drugs
  - Exchanges prescriptions for sex, illicit drugs, etc.[13]
- Drug Dependent
  - Physician begins taking samples of controlled substances
  - Progresses to diverting drugs
  - Phones in prescriptions for family members or fictitious patients
  - Becomes more brazen as addiction progresses[13]

Prescription drug monitoring programs

A prescription drug monitoring program (PDMP) is a statewide electronic database that collects designated data on controlled substances dispensed in the particular state.[14] The data are collected from pharmacies and other dispensaries when a controlled substance is filled. The law in some states provide for the collection of data on all schedules of controlled substances while other states are permitted to collect data on specified schedules, usually schedules II and III. The PDMP is managed by a specified statewide regulatory, administrative, or law enforcement agency, not the Drug Enforcement Administration. The managing agency distributes data from the database to individuals who are authorized under state law to receive the information for purposes of their profession.[14]

The National Alliance for Model State Drug Laws (NAMSDL) identifies the benefits of a PDMP as a tool used by states to address prescription drug abuse, addiction, and diversion. It may serve several purposes such as:

1. Support access to legitimate medical use of controlled substances.
2. Identify and deter or prevent drug abuse and diversion.
3. Facilitate and encourage the identification, intervention with, and treatment of persons addicted to prescription drugs.
4. Inform public health initiatives through outlining of use and abuse trends.
5. Educate individuals about PDMPs and the use, abuse, and diversion of and addiction to prescription drugs.[15]

According to the NAMSDL, 48 states have an operational PDMP. The state of New Hampshire and the District of Columbia has enacted legislation establishing a PDMP, however, the program is not yet operational. The state of Missouri has legislation pending.[15] A list of the state PDMPs and contact information is located in Appendix 20.[16]

Investigation

Complaints of inappropriate prescribing will likely generate from family members of patients, law enforcement, or pharmacists. Pharmacists, by the nature of their job, are in an excellent position to know what drugs physicians are prescribing, quantities, dosages, and over what period of time. Local law enforcement may be experiencing problems in their community with a local clinic known for ease of obtaining controlled substances attracting large crowds of unruly patrons or having made several DUI arrests finding a certain physician's prescription on the pill bottles rolling around in the floor of the vehicle. Family members may complain of a loved one who is routinely impaired and suffering from addiction.

There are two basic approaches to a prescribing investigation. One approach is a covert "undercover" investigation and the other approach is an overt approach commonly referred to as a "paper case." The goal of the investigation should be considered when deciding on what approach to take. Investigations of alleged criminal violations with regard to the prescribing of controlled substances often begin with a covert approach and then supplemented by an overt approach. Strictly administrative investigations often take an overt approach eliminating a potentially costly undercover operation.

Covert approach

The undercover investigation involves an informant or an investigator posing as a patient and making multiple visits to the physician's office in an effort to obtain prescriptions for controlled substances. If this type of approach is deemed most appropriate, it is advisable to contact local law enforcement to determine if they are investigating the physician. They may already be in the process of conducting undercover operations and may have a wealth of intelligence to share. Undercover operations are typically used when conducting criminal investigations, however, this approach may prove useful in an administrative or licensing investigation as well. In that state medical boards are concerned with the SOC as opposed to criminal prosecutions, this approach is not commonly used. However, a brief series of undercover visits to the clinic may produce useful intelligence, that is, to what extent is the undercover operative given a physical examination, what, if any, diagnostic tests are administered, how easy is it for the operative to obtain a prescription? Undercover investigations can be extremely costly and time consuming and investigative resources should be considered. Does the board have the necessary personnel to conduct the undercover operation, does the board have the cash funds to finance the investigation (pay for office visits, investigator overtime, etc.), and does the board have the necessary electronic surveillance equipment needed to properly record and monitor the undercover visits? This type of sophisticated electronic equipment is extremely costly and likely not included in the medical board's investigative resources. Even though undercover investigations have some drawbacks, it should not be totally dismissed outright. It may be an appropriate method of collecting intelligence, identifying witnesses, and obtaining evidence of inappropriate and possibly illegal prescribing; however, it will depend on the information and intelligence developed early on in the investigation.

Statutes dealing with the prescribing of controlled substances require the prescription be for a legitimate medical purpose. If the goal of the investigation is to determine if the physician is prescribing controlled substances for nonlegitimate medical purposes, it is important for the operative to not provide the physician a legitimate medical problem which would justify the prescription. A sound undercover scenario should be developed to maximize the attainment of the operation's goals and to minimize legal challenges such as entrapment.

Overt approach

This approach is more commonly used in the development of what is often termed a "paper case" or documentary investigation. Documentary investigations involve the collection of prescribing data, patient records, and any other documents necessary for the medical board or other medical expert to render an opinion as to the legitimacy of the prescribing as it relates to the SOC.

Interview of complainant and witnesses

The first step in the investigation should be to interview the complainant. During this interview, the investigator can determine the scope of the case. Does this case involve numerous patients or just a few? The complainant may be able to identify specific patients and which pharmacies they are using especially if they are a family member of the patient(s). They may be able to identify other witnesses that will require interviewing.

What drugs are being prescribed and at what dosages and quantities? To what extent should a survey of pharmacies be conducted? Is a survey of local pharmacies in order or will this case require a widespread survey of multiple pharmacies? Pharmacists are in an excellent position to observe a physician's prescribing patterns. Are the patients known to them or are they from out of town or out of state? Does the physician typically prescribe the same drugs to each patient? This has become more of an issue with the advent of rogue pain clinics. Investigations of these clinics reveal that mostly every patient receives a prescription, commonly called a "cocktail," for the same drugs; oxycodone 30 mg. #280, oxycodone 15 mg. #240, alprazolam 2 mg. #120, and carisoprodol 350 mg. #90. Pharmacists have access to a wealth of information and pharmacy data will be the foundation on which the case is made.

Collecting pharmacy data

After interviewing the complainant and other witnesses, the investigator should have a better idea as to the scope of the case. The next step is to conduct pharmacy surveys. Pharmacy surveys involve the collection of prescribing data from the pharmacies identified by the complainant. If no specific pharmacies were identified, a broader survey will be necessary. Pharmacy information is considered protected health information and will require a subpoena, order to produce, or other legally compelling document to authorize the pharmacy to release the information. Most of the large corporate pharmacy chains will have a legal department that handles such requests and the request document may be served to them via certified mail. Small privately owned pharmacies can be served by certified mail or in person if necessary.

If the complainant was able to identify specific patients to whom the physician is prescribing, the request document should contain these names and identifying information if available, such as date of birth, etc. For a broader pharmacy survey, request documents should be sent to all of the major corporate pharmacies and to local privately owned pharmacies in the physician's community. The request document should include the physician's name, his/her DEA registration number, and the time period for the survey to cover. A standard time frame is one year. This will provide a good look at the physician's prescribing patterns. The request should state precisely what is requested, for example, "a certified computer generated printout of all controlled substance prescriptions issued by John Doe, MD, DEA# JD1234567, for the period of 1/1/2013 to present," or "a certified computer generated printout of all controlled substance prescriptions issued by John Doe, MD, DEA# JD1234567 to the following patients for the period of 1/1/2013 to present: Jane Smith date of birth 2/3/1973, Mary Jones date of birth 3/4/1979, and James Jones date of birth 9/11/1983." Another source of prescribing data that will likely be more efficient is the state PDMP discussed earlier in the chapter provided the medical board is authorized access to the data.

Organizing the pharmacy data

When the pharmacy data begins to come in, the investigator will quickly realize that the amount of data can be overwhelming, unless the investigation is targeting only a few selected patients. Pharmacy data output may be organized differently from pharmacy to pharmacy. Most printouts will include the patients' names, dates of birth, drug prescribed, dosage, quantity, number of authorized refills, directions for taking the drug, prescription number, date the prescription was written or ordered by the physician, and the date the prescription was filled (Appendix 21). Some printouts may be organized in alphabetical order by patient last name, some in chronological date order by the date filled, and some may be organized in alphabetical order by drug name. If the data can be requested from the pharmacy sorted in alphabetical order by patient last name and then secondarily sorted in chronological date order, it will save considerable time when reviewing the data.

Some pharmacies will provide data on a compact disk. This is highly recommended in that it may be able to be converted to a computerized spreadsheet and can then be sorted in a variety of ways. The goal when organizing prescription data is to be able to readily identify the patients who are being prescribed controlled substances more questionably than other patients.

Reviewing the pharmacy data

The review of the pharmacy data should include an analysis of the physician's prescribing patterns to include the drugs consistently prescribed (narcotics, stimulants, benzodiazepines, etc.), unusual or high doses, unusual or contraindicated combinations of drugs, ongoing refills with no documented office visits, frequency of the prescribing (monthly, every 90 days, etc.), quantity of pills, patients whose name continues to repeat in the data, and over what time period the patient has been on the drugs.

Using the aforementioned rogue pain clinic example, the pharmacy data revealed that the physician was prescribing the same drugs, the same quantities, and the same dosages to almost every patient. The data also showed that many of the patients were on this drug regimen for many months, even years. That is not to say that someone suffering from legitimate chronic pain should not be provided medication after legitimate diagnostic testing and physical examination supports such. However, when the clinic is seeing 50–60 patients per day, 5 days per week, and everyone gets the same cocktail of drugs, red flags should be going up.

Another important piece of information not to overlook is the patient's address. Most pharmacies provide this information in their printouts. Are the patients local or are they coming from out of town or out of state? While it is not a violation of the law to treat a patient from out of state, it is interesting however, when over 75% of the clinic's patient base is from another state. Why are dozens of patients coming to Atlanta, GA from Kentucky, West Virginia, Ohio, Kansas, Oklahoma, Texas, etc. to be treated for low back pain? Just a thought.

It should also be noted that patients may fill their prescriptions at different pharmacies; therefore the investigator may find the same patient names showing up in data from different pharmacies. The patient may use different pharmacies in an effort to minimize their being identified as a "doctor shopper" and in some cases the physician will direct the patient to go to different pharmacies to avoid detection.

The actual original prescription will not be needed right away, or may not be needed at all. Some cases may be resolved without proceeding to a hearing in which case the computer data will suffice. If a case is contested and proceeds to a hearing, the original prescriptions may be needed as evidence. If so, the investigator will then need to prepare request documents for the specific prescriptions needed and properly serve the pharmacy. Obtaining original documents for a medical board hearing may trigger certain legal obstacles. In such a case, it may be necessary to have the board's legal representative get involved.

Obtaining patient records

Once the pharmacy data has been organized and specific patients identified as to questionable or inappropriate prescribing based on the above analysis, request documents should be prepared so as to obtain certified copies of the patient records from the physician. Keep in mind that at some point, a medical expert may be asked to review the charts so it will be important to obtain a number of charts that will be manageable.

The pharmacy data may indicate dozens of questionable patients, so careful selection of charts is important. It is recommended that 15–20 charts representing the most egregious cases be selected based on the pharmacy data. Fifty to one hundred charts would be unwieldy and will increase the cost of the expert review.

As stated earlier, the medical record will be a crucial piece of evidence and should be treated as such. The request document should contain the patient's name, date of birth, and any other identifying information, and then properly served to the physician.

Reviewing the patient records

When the medical records are received, a thorough review is necessary. Remember to keep the certified copies in a secure location and make a working copy for note-taking and highlighting. The review should follow the guidelines set out in Chapter 6. The records should be reviewed as to the patient's medical history, current medical condition, diagnostic studies, consults, diagnosis, and the type and number of controlled substances prescribed. Charts devoid of this basic information will tend to lend support to a charge of substandard practice. For example, consider a female patient who is 5′10″ tall and weighs 110 pounds. She has been receiving prescriptions for controlled diet medications for two years with no gain or loss of weight. Query: Did this patient need the weight loss medication in the first place? In cases of controlled diet medication prescribing, it is also interesting to note contraindications for the drug, for example, a patient presenting with obvious hypertension, BP of 160/110, and prescribed a stimulant. Much of the research on controlled weight loss drugs indicate effectiveness for approximately 6 months of therapy. A patient chart indicating an initial height and weight of 5′10″ and 250 lbs. and drug therapy for 2 years with an ending weight of 275 lbs. should be questioned.

Another example may concern a patient being treated for chronic pain whose chart indicates that he suffered a back injury in a car accident several years ago and is receiving oxycodone for pain on a routine and frequent basis. If the chart contains no documentation of diagnostic studies or consults, or prior treatment records from a prior treating physician to support the diagnosis, the physician may encounter difficulty supporting his/her long-term prescribing of narcotics.

As the charts are being reviewed, it is advisable to enter review notes on a separate sheet. This will allow for ease in organization of the information gleaned from the chart and will also provide for consolidation and ease of reference when interviewing the physician and preparing the eventual report of investigation (Appendix 22).

Interviewing the physician

After the patient charts have been thoroughly reviewed along with the pharmacy data, the physician should be interviewed. The physician should be afforded his/her right to explain his/her treatment and justification for his/her prescribing. The physician should be told of the medical board's concerns and asked to address the treatment of each patient whose records were obtained.

The physician should be asked to provide a written narrative discussing each individual patient's course of treatment, diagnosis, how arrived at the stated diagnosis, his/her rationale for the specific drug treatment regimen, and explanations for any lack of thorough documentation such as medical history, physical exam, diagnostic studies, consults, prior treatment records, explanation of the risks of the treatment regimen, etc. The physician's narrative along with the pharmacy data and patient charts should then be reviewed by a physician on the board or by a physician consultant preferably in the same specialty field as the subject of the investigation (peer review). At this point, an opinion as to whether the SOC was met or breached can be rendered.

Internet prescribing

Advancements in technology have enhanced our lives beyond description. Unfortunately, some of these advancements are used for other not so altruistic endeavors. One of these is the prescribing of drugs via the internet. Positively speaking, the internet provides several advantages as it pertains to the practice of medicine. It provides opportunities to improve the delivery and access to health care.[17] The internet provides a massive amount of information on virtually all medical issues within seconds. It also allows for far more timely consultations with other healthcare providers. Coming with these advantages, however, are concerns regarding patient safety and these concerns have brought about complex regulatory challenges, one of them being internet prescribing.[17]

There are several hundred websites, or "internet pharmacies," offering prescription drugs; however, very few of them are considered legitimate. An excellent source to use to verify the legitimacy of an online pharmacy is to check the Verified Internet Pharmacy Practice Sites (VIPPS) located on the National Association of Boards of Pharmacy website, www.nabp.net. Often, the way these pharmacies operate is to provide an on-line questionnaire for the "patient" to complete. This questionnaire consists of very basic cursory medical history questions. The questionnaire is then sent by the online pharmacy to a physician who is under contract with the online pharmacy and unknown to the patient. The physician approves the prescription and the prescription is then filled and shipped to the patient. There is no face-to-face meeting with a physician or even a telephonic discussion with a physician.

There are several risks when dealing with an online pharmacy and these should be very thoughtfully considered by potential patients. Risks include:

- Illegal or unethical pharmacies sending outdated, substituted, or counterfeit medications.[18,19]
- The online pharmacy may not be located in the country that is claimed. For example, one study of drug shipments claiming to be from Canada revealed many actually originated in several different countries and were often bogus medications.[20]
- Minors or children ordering controlled substances without adult supervision.[20]
- Other concerns include potential lack of confidentiality, improper packaging, and inability to check for drug interactions.[21]

Following are three red flags indicative of a potentially illegal internet pharmacy:

- No Prescription Required
  Obtaining a prescription takes time, effort, and money. Many outlaw pharmacies willingly sell medications without a physician's prescription. The pharmacy is preying on the customer that does not want the "inconvenience" of having to make a doctor's visit for a prescription.[21]
- Location Unknown
  Pharmacies are regulated by state and federal agencies and internet pharmacies that fail to disclose their location make it virtually impossible to know if they are regulated at all, and if regulated, by what agency. Drugs are required to be properly stored and labeled with lot numbers and expiration dates. Without appropriate regulation, this could pose additional safety issues.[21]
- Lowest Prices
  When the internet pharmacy advertises the "lowest prices," one should question how they provide the lowest prices. The first question I would ask is what safety precautions are they not implementing in order to save money.[21]

The following statutes and notices provide some guidance on the issue of internet prescribing:

In April 2001, the DEA issued a notice concerning internet prescribing. It states in part:

> ….Completing a questionnaire that is then reviewed by a doctor hired by the internet pharmacy could not be considered the basis of a doctor/patient relationship….It is illegal to receive a prescription for a controlled substance without the establishment of a legitimate doctor/patient relationship, and it is unlikely for such a relationship to be formed through internet correspondence alone….[22]

The Food, Drug, and Cosmetic Act prohibits the manufacture and distribution of misbranded or adulterated drugs.[23] The Controlled Substances Act prohibits the dispensing of a controlled substance without a valid prescription and 21 CFR 1306.04 defines a valid prescription: "a prescription for a controlled substance to be effective must be issued for a legitimate medical purpose by an individual practitioner acting in the usual course of his professional practice."[6] The Controlled Substances Act goes on to state that the distribution of a controlled substance without a valid prescription can result in a violation of 21 USC §841(a), a criminal violation.[24] The investigation should attempt to show that the drugs were dispensed for a non-legitimate medical purpose and that the physician was not acting in the usual course of his/her professional practice.[24] In other words, the investigation will likely have to demonstrate what the usual and ordinary course of professional practice is, and that the conduct of the physician fell outside the usual and ordinary course of professional practice. It is not enough to prove that internet prescribing was merely occurring.[25]

A criminal prosecution has a higher burden of proof as opposed to an administrative licensure proceeding. Criminal prosecutions must prove the case "beyond a reasonable doubt," whereas most administrative proceedings must "show a preponderance of the evidence." As examined above, the success or failure of a case may hinge on the ability to show that the conduct fell outside the usual course of professional practice. This may be more critical for criminal prosecutions, however, it should be no less important for administrative proceedings.

What is "the usual course of professional practice"? Suffice it to say that there is no consensus. The law tends to utilize normative standards, that is, "A pattern or trait taken to be typical in the behavior of a social group, a widespread or usual practice, procedure, or custom."[25] Such standards will require that the "standard" be proven for each case in that the "standard" differs from region to region, state to state, and community to community.[25] Examination of the positions of several government agencies, regulatory, and medical organizations may provide some insight as to what the "usual course" is, or perhaps, should be.

DEA Guidance 66 FR 211810-01, April 27, 2001, referred to earlier, states as follows:

> Where a doctor/patient relationship exists, you may use the Internet to receive requests for treatment to include prescriptions. Under federal and state law, for a doctor to be acting in the usual course of professional practice, there must be a bona-fide doctor/patient relationship.[22,25]

The Federation of State Medical Boards (FSMB) developed model guidelines for consideration of adoption by state medical boards concerning internet prescribing. Section three of the model guidelines addresses the doctor/patient relationship. It states:

> Although the Board recognizes that it may be difficult in some circumstances, particularly in an online setting, to define precisely the beginning of the physician-patient relationship, it tends to begin

> when an individual seeks assistance from a physician with a health-related matter for which the physician may provide assistance. However, the relationship is clearly established when the physician agrees to undertake diagnosis or other treatment of the patient and the patient agrees, whether or not there has been a personal encounter between the physician (or other supervised health care practitioner) and the patient.[25,26]

The American Medical Association (AMA) takes the following position:

> Physicians who prescribe medications via the Internet shall establish, or have established, a valid patient–physician relationship, including, but not limited to the following components:
>
> The physician shall obtain a reliable medical history and perform a physical examination, adequate to establish the diagnoses for which the drug is being prescribed…Exceptions to the above criteria exist in the following specific instances: treatment provided in consultation with another physician who has an ongoing professional relationship with the patient… and on-call or cross-coverage situations.[25,27]

The various states, however, do not reflect the above-purported consensus. A total of 29 states (58%) have medical board policies addressing online prescribing. Most states deem it "unprofessional conduct," however, none declares that it is outside the usual course of professional practice or constitutes an invalid prescription.[25] A total of 15 states (30%) have statutes addressing online prescribing, however, some merely address cross-border licensing and most deem it as "unprofessional."[25] The article cited in reference 15 contains detailed discussion of numerous state level cases demonstrating the lack of consensus as to the usual course of professional practice and what constitutes a valid doctor–patient relationship.[15] The reader is encouraged to study this excellent article.

In summary, as it pertains to the position of the DEA regarding the usual course of professional practice, neither the medical community, the legal community, Congress, other government agencies, nor individual states share a consensus. While some consider online prescribing unprofessional, the overwhelming majority do not treat it as outside the usual course to the extent that results in an invalid prescription.[25]

Be prepared to prove "outside usual course." Use computers to show how long the doctor spent on each review and to show how many prescriptions the doctor denied. Consider other statutes such as labeling laws, fraud, false statements on the websites about legality, false statements on the websites about business model, use of "licensed doctors," sales to minors, and HIPAA violations. The defense will likely take the position that "we're just practicing medicine." Anything that challenges this claim will help make the case.[25]

References

1. Food, Drug, and Cosmetic Act (Controlled Substances), 21 USC 13(1), Part B, §812(b).
2. National Institutes of Health, National Institute on Drug Abuse. 2011. Accessed May 25, 2013. http://www.drugabuse.gov/drugs-abuse/prescription-drugs-cold-medicines
3. Kupferschmidt, G. 2004. Consulting Services Ltd., ForCon—Forensic Consulting. Pharmacology of Drugs. Accessed May 25, 2013. http://www.forcon.ca/learning/pharmacology.html
4. National Institutes of Health, National Institute on Drug Abuse. 2007. Accessed May 25, 2013. http://www.drugabuse.gov/publications/teaching-packets/neurobiology-drug-addiction/section-iii-action-heroin-morphine/6-definition-tolerance
5. Addiction Science Network, Addiction Science Forum. 2009. Why Distinguishing Between Drug Dependence and Drug Addiction Is Important. Accessed June 5, 2013. http://addictionscience.net/b2evolution/?blog=1&paged=4
6. Code of Federal Regulations, 21 CFR 1306.04.
7. Code of Federal Regulations, 21 CFR 1306.05.
8. US v. Collier, 1973. 478 F.2d 268. Accessed July 26, 2013. http://law.justia.com/cases/federal/appellate-courts/F2/478/268/373123/
9. US Department of Justice, National Drug Intelligence Center. 2011. National Drug Threat Assessment, Controlled Prescription Drugs. Accessed June 15, 2014. http://www.justice.gov/archive/ndic/pubs44/44849/44849p.pdf
10. Centers for Disease Control and Prevention, Morbidity and Mortality Weekly Report. 2011. Vital Signs: Overdoses of Prescription Opioid Pain Relievers—United States, 1999—2008. Accessed June 17, 2014. http://www.cdc.gov/mmwr/preview/mmwrhtml/mm6043a4.htm?s_cid=mm6043a4_w
11. Substance Abuse and Mental Health Services Administration, Center for Behavioral Health Statistics and Quality. 2014. The NSDUH Report: Substance Use and Mental Health Estimates from the 2013 National Survey on Drug Use and Health: Overview of Findings. 2014. Accessed September 12, 2014. http://store.samhsa.gov/shin/content/NSDUH14-0904/NSDUH14-0904.pdf
12. Georgia Bureau of Investigation. 2013. Deaths Related to Drug Overdoses Decrease Overall While Deaths Related to Illicit Drugs Increase in 2013. Accessed June 4, 2014. http://gbi.georgia.gov/press-releases/2014-07-31/deaths-related-drug-overdoses-decrease-overall-while-deaths-related

13. Vanderberry, R. 1995. Inappropriate prescribing. *Contribution to Problem Physicians—A National Perspective: A Report to the Georgia Composite Medical Board*; G. Douglas Talbott, and L.R. Crosby editors. http://www.talbottcampus.com/pdf/Perspective.pdf
14. US Drug Enforcement Administration. 2011. State Prescription Drug Monitoring Programs. Accessed May 23, 2014. http://www.deadiversion.usdoj.gov/faq/rx_monitor.htm
15. National Alliance for Model State Drug Laws. 2014. Status of State Prescription Drug Monitoring Programs. Accessed May 23, 2014. http://www.namsdl.org/prescription-monitoring-programs.cfm
16. National Association of State Controlled Substance Authorities. Membership List. Accessed March 25, 2015. www.nascsa.org/statecontacts.htm
17. Rawson, J. 2007. Regulation of internet prescribing. *Presentation Given at Administrators In Medicine Investigator Training Conference*, Orlando, Florida, June.
18. Davidson, M. 2011. *Pharmaceutical Anti-Counterfeiting: Combating the Real Danger from Fake Drugs*. Hoboken, NJ: Wiley.
19. U.S. Food and Drug Administration. 2007. FDA Alerts Consumers to Unsafe, Misrepresented Drugs Purchased Over the Internet. Accessed July 26, 2014. http://www.fda.gov/NewsEvents/Newsroom/PressAnnouncements/2007/ucm108846.htm
20. U.S. Food and Drug Administration. 2005. FDA Operation Reveals Many Drugs Promoted as "Canadian" Products Really Originate From Other Countries. Accessed July 26, 2014. http://www.fda.gov/NewsEvents/Newsroom/PressAnnouncements/2005/ucm108534.htm
21. Griffin, R. M., Beyond the Pharmacy, Online and Mail-Order Prescription Drugs. Accessed April 10, 2013. http://www.webmd.com/healthy-aging/features/beyond-the-pharmacy-online-and-mail-order-prescription-drugs
22. DEA Notice, Federal Register, April 27, 2001, Volume 66, No. 92.
23. Food, Drug, and Cosmetic Act, 21 USC §331(a), §353(b).
24. Food, Drug, and Cosmetic Act (Controlled Substances), 21 USC §841(a).
25. Gluck, B. 2008. Case Strategy: How to Investigate an Internet Pharmacy. Accessed April 11, 2013. Used with permission. https://www.nabp.net/events/assets/CaseStrategy.pdf
26. Federation of State Medical Boards of the United States, Inc. 2002. Model Guidelines for the Appropriate Use of the Internet in Medical Practice. Accessed May 5, 2013. Used with permission. http://www.fsmb.org/policy/publications-media/
27. American Medical Association. Guidance for Physicians on Internet Prescribing. Accessed April 24, 2013. http://www.ama-assn.org/resources/doc/PolicyFinder/policyfiles/HnE/H-120.949.htm

chapter ten

Professional sexual misconduct investigations

Professional sexual misconduct occurs when a physician (or other healthcare provider) engages in certain behaviors with a patient that could be considered inappropriate from an intimate or sexual perspective. It is widely held that professional sexual misconduct adversely affects the public welfare and harms patients individually and collectively as well as physically and mentally.[1] Sexual misconduct may be viewed as originating from some form of impairment, that is, addictive disorder, mental disorder, sexual disorder, etc., however, this should not assuage the medical board's mandate to protect the public.[1]

Definition

The Federation of State Medical Boards (FSMB) defines physician sexual misconduct as "behavior that exploits the physician/patient relationship in a sexual way." The FSMB asserts that physician sexual misconduct is neither diagnostic nor therapeutic. The behavior may be verbal, physical, and may include feelings or gestures that are sexual or that could reasonably be construed by the patient as sexual.[1]

What leads to professional sexual misconduct? Many researchers describe a breakdown of *boundaries* that leads to inappropriate behavior with patients. So, what are boundaries as used in this context? A boundary can be considered "the containing edge of appropriate behavior."[2,3] Establishing clear boundaries is intended to create a safe and predictable place where treatment and healing can occur.[2]

Boundaries

Boundaries in the doctor/patient relationship are considered parameters that describe the limits of a fiduciary relationship, implying professional distance and respect.[3]

Boundaries can also be viewed as a frame around the doctor/patient relationship that defines the characteristics of the relationship.[2,3] The physician must work within these boundaries or within this framework so as to preserve the therapeutic relationship so that proper treatment, unclouded judgment, and optimum therapeutic results can occur.[2,3] When the frame is altered, the physician's role and function then becomes altered not only in practice, but also in the mind of the patient, resulting in a shift in the doctor/patient relationship.[2]

Research into this phenomenon reveals that sexual misconduct is often preceded by a progressive series of nonsexual boundary violations.[4] Examples of such nonsexual boundary issues include dual relationships, business relationships, gifts, free services, use of certain language, certain types of physical contact, time and duration of appointments, location of appointments, and misuse of the physical examination.[4] It should also be noted that there exists a power *differential* within the physician/patient relationship. The displacement of feelings by the patient (transference) placed on the relationship places the patient in a vulnerable position and the physician in a "powerful" position. The power derived by the physician may be due to greater knowledge and skills, higher socioeconomic and educational status, or from an inherent social or charismatic power. The combination of transference and the power differential makes mutual consent highly unlikely.[4]

The AMA issued a 1991 statement titled: Sexual contact or romantic relationships concurrent with the physician/patient relationship may be unethical. The AMA statement proposes certain ethics standards and addresses a wide range of situations encountered in medical practice to include:

- Predatory physicians with serious personality disorders
- Using sex for therapeutic purposes
- Abusing the physical examination
- Soliciting a date with a patient
- Longstanding physician/patient relationship evolving into intense infatuation
- Rural physician dating a patient because anyone who may be a potential romantic partner is also a patient
- Patients who are raped or fondled whether under anesthesia or not
- Sexual harassment to include erotic or suggestive comments to the patient[4]

Why is physician/patient sex considered unethical? Researchers and various medical organizations assert that it is a breach of the trust that is fundamental in a fiduciary relationship. It calls into question the physician's capacity for objective professional judgment, and exploits the psychological state of the patient resulting in an overall negative effect on the physical and psychological wellbeing of the patient.[4]

As stated earlier, professional sexual misconduct usually begins with a series of nonsexual boundary violations. Five types of boundary violations will be discussed in the order of their progressive seriousness.

Boundary blurring

Boundary blurring occurs when the physician steps outside of his/her role as a clinician and functions in some other capacity. An example of this would be the physician loaning the patients a few dollars to pay for their parking, allowing the patient to use the physician's cell phone, etc. Such boundary blurring may not exploit or harm the patient, however, it is extremely important that the physician considers that when the boundary is blurred, the frame of treatment has been altered and the possible consequences should be appreciated.[2]

Dual relationships

This situation occurs when the physician becomes confused about his/her role in the physician/patient relationship. Dual relationships involve the physician playing two or more roles in relation to the patient simultaneously. An example could include engaging in nonclinical business transactions with patients, loaning or borrowing money, etc.[2]

Sexual impropriety

Sexual improprieties are considered sexually provocative, demeaning, or explicit comments about a patient's body or clothing. Such improprieties may comprise behavior, gestures, or expressions that are seductive, sexually suggestive, disrobing or draping practices that reflect a lack of respect for the patient's privacy, and deliberately watching a patient disrobe, etc.[2,4] Other behaviors that may be considered sexual improprieties are the physician initiating conversation regarding his/her (the physician's) sexual problems, preferences or fantasies, criticizing the patient's sexual orientation and/or potential sexual performance, discussing sexual likes/dislikes when not clinically indicated, and using the physician/patient relationship to solicit a date.[1]

Boundary transgressions

Boundary transgressions are behaviors that are considered exploitive of the doctor/patient relationship. Boundary transgressions refer to the physician touching the patient in an explicit or circuitous manner. Examples of such behaviors include kissing, fondling of the patient's body parts, frotteurism, etc.[2,4]

Sexual violations

Sexual violations are considered to be the most damaging of boundary incursions (even if patient initiated). Sexual violations involve explicit sexual contact to include, sexual intercourse, oral and/or anal sex, or mutual masturbation.[2,4]

How common is the issue of professional sexual misconduct? A review of the literature indicates that this problem is becoming more prevalent. A 1986 national survey of psychiatrists in the United States (1057 males and 257 females) revealed that 7.1% of male respondents and 3.1% of female respondents acknowledged sexual contact with their patients. About 88% of the sexual contacts involved male psychiatrists and female patients.[5]

Another survey conducted in 1992 involved 10,000 family practitioners, internists, obstetrician-gynecologists, and surgeons. About 1891 responded to the survey (19%). Of the 1891 respondents, 9% acknowledged sexual contact with one or more patients, or 170 physicians having had sexual contact with one or more patients.[6] Lamont and Woodward[7] conducted a survey of all members of the Society of Obstetricians and Gynecologists of Canada (792 members). About 618 responded to the survey (78%). The survey revealed that 10% of respondents indicated that they knew of another OB/GYN who at some time had been sexually involved with a patient. About 3% of the male respondents (23 physicians) and 1% of the female respondents (approx. 8 physicians) reported sexual involvement with a patient. Of note, 37% of the female OB/GYNs reported awareness of a colleague's sexual involvement with a patient as opposed to 19% of male OB/GYNs.[7]

The next research effort, conducted in 1996, consisted of a nationwide, random sample of 1600 physicians to include internists, family practice physicians, OB/GYNs, and ophthalmologists. The response rate was 52% (787). About 4.5% (approx. 35 physicians) reported having dated a patient and 3.4% (approx. 26 physicians) reported having had sexual contact with a patient to include genital–genital, oral–genital, or anal–genital. The survey further revealed that physicians aged 50 and older and physicians who were unmarried were significantly more likely to have dated patients.[8]

In an effort to determine the frequency and severity of discipline against physicians committing sex-related offenses, Dehlendorf and Wolfe[9] examined sex-related disciplinary orders issued by state medical boards and federal agencies. A total of 761 physicians were disciplined for sex-related offenses from 1981 through 1996. The study's findings reveal that the number of physicians disciplined per year increased from 42 in 1989 to 147 in 1996 and the proportion of all disciplinary orders that were sex-related increased from 2.1% in 1989 to 4.4% in 1996. It was also revealed that discipline for sex-related offenses tended to be significantly more severe than for nonsex-related offenses, with 71.9% involving revocation, surrender, or suspension of the medical license. Of the 761 physicians disciplined, 567 (75%) involved patients and the offenses included sexual intercourse, rape, sexual molestation, and sexual favors in exchange for drugs.[9]

It should also be noted that charges of sexual abuse by healthcare professionals, primarily psychiatrists and other psychotherapists, have resulted in one of the fastest growing categories of malpractice insurance claims. Jury verdicts can also be extremely high, one of the largest being $4.6 million. Another case concerned a schizophrenic teenager who sued her psychiatrist and was awarded $650,000.00 by a Virginia jury after the defendant psychiatrist admitted to approximately 60 sexually related incidents.[10]

Investigation

The investigation of professional sexual misconduct should receive the highest priority given the potential for significant harm to patients. Consideration should also be given to the fact that the allegations may be false or significantly exaggerated. Therefore, investigations of this type should be conducted as discretely as possible to avoid unwarranted embarrassment and stigma to the physician as well as the patient.

Complaints of professional sexual misconduct may originate from a variety of sources. Common complaint sources are the patient/victim themselves, family members of the patient, other healthcare providers to whom the patient has confided (therapist, etc.), and local law enforcement. The complaint may range from behaviors discussed earlier such as acts of boundary blurring, dual relationships, acts of sexual impropriety, boundary transgressions, and/or sexual violations.

Interview of complainant

The first phase of the investigation should be to interview the complainant. If the complaint originates from a law enforcement agency, the investigator should obtain a complete copy of the agency's report to include statements made by the victim, all witnesses, and evidentiary reports, for example, lab reports, reports of physical examination, polygraph reports, copies of any audio or video recordings of all interviews, etc. It will also be helpful to meet with the investigating officer in an effort to determine their assessment of the victim's credibility as well as the credibility of the witnesses.

If the complaint originates from another healthcare provider, the investigator should meet with and interview this individual as to the circumstances surrounding the victim's disclosure of sexual misconduct. If this provider is contacting the board to report a sexual boundary matter, it is likely that the patient has granted permission for the provider to do so. When meeting with this provider, determine if the patient/victim is willing to speak to the investigator about the incident. The patient/victim may be more comfortable being interviewed by the investigator in the presence of the provider. In the interest of HIPAA and patient confidentiality, the provider will require a release from the patient to share the patient's record with the investigator, however, the issuance of a subpoena to the provider should occur. A written statement from this provider as to the specifics of their conversation with the victim and what the victim specifically stated will be very important. The treatment records from this provider should contain notes made by the provider as to the victim's statements.

Interview of victim/patient

In most cases the complainant will be the patient/victim. It is important to note from the outset that good listening skills are essential when interviewing the witnesses, especially the victim/patient (Chapter 5). The victim/patient will likely provide a great deal of information and it will be important for the investigator to be able to sift through the extraneous details.[11] Of course, each case is unique and should be treated as such. The victim is likely going to be emotional, angry, and possibly traumatized to some extent. The extent of these emotions will be affected by the lapse of time since the incident. It is also important to try to be sensitive to the victim's feelings, however, it is imperative that the investigator maintain control over the interview. The victim may desire a support person be present and this is acceptable as long as the support person does not interfere with the interview. Allowing the husband or boyfriend to be present is typically not recommended.[11]

Preparing for the interview is critical. Based on the information provided in the complaint, the investigator should prepare a set of questions on basic topics, then progress to more specific questions as to the physician's specific behaviors. What specific elements of the violation must be proved? This knowledge, along with a thorough review of the allegations in the complaint, will allow the investigator to tailor their questions so as to maximize the amount and quality of information gained. The interview should be conducted as soon as possible so as to avoid the loss of essential details and facts.[12]

Allow the victims to tell their story with as minimal interruption as possible. Notes should be taken so that gaps in the story can be probed and inconsistencies reconciled. The following questions provide for a basic foundation for the interview, a starting point; however, this is not to be considered all-inclusive as each case in unique and may require additional information and probing:

- Date, time of incident
- Identity of witnesses

- What was the purpose of the patient's visit to the physician?
  - Example: patient presents for treatment of a sore throat and physician demands that a breast or vaginal exam be performed.
- Was a chaperone present in the exam room?
- Was the chaperone in and out of the room or did the physician tell her to leave the room at any time?
- Specific details as to what was done; describe the assault.
- Specific details as to what was spoken; by whom to whom.
- Obtain necessary releases for records if necessary.
- When was the first appointment?
- Did the office have the patient complete a physical history form?
- Was consent for treatment form signed?
- How was the billing or payment for treatment arranged?
- What time of day was the first appointment?
- Were staff members present in the office?
- Did a staff member do a pre-exam for vital signs?
- Was the patient asked to change into a gown?
- Was a gown provided?
- Was the patient instructed on what clothing items to remove?
- Was the patient given privacy in order to change into the gown?
- Was there an initial physical exam by the doctor?
- Did the doctor wear gloves during the exam?
- Was a treatment plan discussed and decided upon?
- Were prescriptions written or samples provided?
- Were follow-up appointments discussed and arranged?
- How was the appointment completed?

Determine from the victim the names and contact information for all potential witnesses as well as the relationship of the witnesses to the case, for example, friend or family of the patient, staff employed at the facility, etc. Are there any subsequent treatment providers (physicians, counselors, etc.) that should be interviewed?

The investigator should also query the victim as to their knowledge and description of the scene and any information they can relate which would specifically identify the physician, for example, specific physical markings that could only be known by the victim, clothing, if the incident occurred away from the physician's office a description of that location as to furniture and other specific identifying items will be useful. If the incident occurred at a hotel, the investigator should seek to obtain hotel receipts and reservation information.

Emails and text messages may be saved on the victim's computer or cell phone. These too, should be obtained. Note that some cases of sexual misconduct may involve multiple patients/victims. Each victim should be interviewed separately at a location in which they are comfortable; their home with another person present, or at a neutral site.[11] Efforts should be made to obtain a written statement from each victim.

Assessing the victim/patient's credibility

During the interview with the victim/patient, it is important to attempt to assess their credibility. As discussed earlier, credibility has to do with believability. Is the story believable? Does the victim have a motive? If so, what is their motive? Is there some underlying issue between the victim and physician that may lead the victim to attempt to carry out some nefarious scheme? To assess the victim/patient's credibility, examine the internal consistency of their story after they have an opportunity to tell the complete story. Are there any inconsistencies? What are they? Can they be resolved? Discontinuities can be the sign of a lack of accuracy or even dishonesty. Be careful not to "lead the witness." Is there a common recurring theme or pattern of the physician's behavior across different victims? Is their story believable at face value or outlandish?[1] The information obtained in this interview and the investigator's assessment of the victim's credibility will impact the investigator's pre-interview planning and approach when interviewing the physician.

Interview of witnesses

After a thorough interview of the victim/patient, all witnesses should be interviewed. They should be interviewed as soon as possible to avoid loss of critical details and should be interviewed separately to avoid collaborative details being shared.[12] A basic interview protocol as previously discussed will suffice. Allow the witness to describe what they saw, heard, etc. while the investigator takes notes. The investigator can then revisit the portions of the witness' account to close any gaps and reconcile any discrepancies. Written statements from each witness should be obtained.

Documentary evidence

Once the victim/patient and all witnesses have been interviewed, necessary documents pertinent to the case should be obtained. Such documents will include, but not necessarily be limited to:

- Treatment records from the respondent (accused physician)
- Treatment records from subsequent treating physicians, counselors, therapists, etc.
- Records from law enforcement agencies as necessary

- Hotel/motel receipts if applicable
- Cards, letters, text messages, and email messages if applicable
- If the physician is employed by a clinic or hospital, the personnel file of the physician should also be obtained. This record may reveal prior in-house investigations on similar behaviors.

Interview of the respondent/physician

After thorough interviews of all victims/patients, all witnesses, and the collection of all pertinent documentation/evidence, the physician should be interviewed. Allegations of sexual misconduct are serious and can have enormous implications for the physician's career and reputation. That is not to say that the physician should be feared or that a proven case of sexual misconduct should not be aggressively pursued. As stated earlier, the investigator's duty is to gather facts in an unbiased and professional manner, treating both victim and physician with courtesy, respect, and imperturbability.

Once again, planning and preparation for the interview is essential. This is not the time to just "wing it," nor is there ever a time to "wing it." With all of the acquired information, the investigator is now able to develop a list of appropriate and competent questions. The physician will likely be at somewhat of a disadvantage because he/she does not know what the investigator knows.[11] Depending on the severity of the allegations, the physician may react in varying ways to include:

- Disbelief—who me?
- Anger—How dare she make such ridiculous assertions?
- Quiet—Often the physician that quietly denies the allegations and "just cannot believe this is happening" is ripe for thorough probing.[11]

When interviewing the physician, the investigator should set the tone and maintain control of the interview. The tone of the interview should be cordial rather than confrontational.[11] Allow the physician to tell his/her version of the event. After the physician has provided his version, the investigator should probe to fill in gaps or resolve inconsistencies. During this account, the physician may provide the identities of witnesses to support his version such as nurses, chaperone, and others who may have interacted with the patient. These witnesses must be interviewed.

Assessing the physician's credibility

Just as with the victim and witnesses, it is important for the investigator to make some assessment of the physician's credibility. In order to do so, we must examine the consistency of the doctor's story. Are there any inconsistencies?[1] If so, when do they occur and what are they? Can they be reconciled? Inconsistencies can be the sign of a lack of accuracy or perhaps dishonesty. The physician should be asked to reconcile the inconsistencies. If he/she is unable to do so, it is likely that they are not being fully truthful. Does the physician degrade, blame, or demean the victim/patient? If so, this can sometimes be indicative of a personality disorder.[1]

The investigator should ask him/herself, "how well does the doctor's story line up with the complainant's story?" How do the two versions differ? Can these differences be reconciled? If not, it could mean that the physician is either purposefully lying or reluctant to disclose the truth. It is possible that certain incidents did not occur or the victim/patient may be exaggerating or lying.[1] It is extremely important to thoroughly follow up on any alibi or other information provided by the physician. A thorough review of the patient's medical records from the physician is also necessary to look for inconsistencies.[1] If any inconsistencies are found, the physician may need to be re-interviewed.

Potential outcomes

When the investigation is complete, the medical board will consider several factors based on the investigative findings. Several factors considered by the board are:

- Patient harm
- Severity of impropriety
- Culpability of the respondent
- Psychotherapeutic relationship
- Age of patient (minor, etc.)
- Number of times behavior occurred
- Period of time relationship existed
- Inappropriate termination of physician/patient relationship
- Context within which impropriety occurred
- Opportunity (type of practice)
- Vulnerability of the patient
- Number of patients involved
- Prior history of similar conduct

Another option available to most medical boards is to order the physician to undergo a comprehensive mental and physical evaluation. A board's authority to exercise this option will be found in the board's laws as it is a statutorily granted authority. There are several facilities throughout the United States that specialize in the treatment of sexual deviance and some that focus on the treatment of healthcare professionals.

The results of this type of evaluation will also be considered by the board as it determines the appropriate course of action.

References

1. Federation of State Medical Boards of the United States, Inc. 2006. Addressing Sexual Boundaries: Guidelines for State Medical Boards. Accessed August 3, 2014. http://www.fsmb.org/Media/Default/PDF/FSMB/Advocacy/GRPOL_Sexual%20Boundaries.pdf
2. Stacy, S. 2003. The Misuse of Power: Professional Sexual Misconduct. Accessed September 22, 2013. http://www.fclb.org/Portals/7/Home/MisuseofPower.pdf
3. Gutheil, T. and G. Gabbard. 1993. The concept of boundaries in clinical practice: Theoretical and risk-management dimensions. *American Journal of Psychiatry*, 150: 188–196.
4. Gabbard, G. and C. Nadelson. 1995. Professional boundaries in the physician-patient relationship. *Journal of the American Medical Association*, 273(18): 1445–1449.
5. Gartrell, N., J. Herman, S. Olarte, M. Feldstein, and R. Localio. 1986. Psychiatrist-patient sexual contact: Results of a national survey. I: Prevalence. *American Journal of Psychiatry*, 143(9): 1126–1131.
6. Gartrell, N., N. Milliken, W. Goodson III, S. Thiemann, and B. Lo. 1992. Physician-patient sexual contact: Prevalence and problems. *Western Journal of Medicine*, 157(2): 139–143.
7. Lamont, J. and C. Woodward. 1994. Patient-physician sexual involvement: A Canadian survey of obstetrician-gynecologists. *Canadian Medical Association*, 150(9): 1433.
8. Bayer, T., J. Coverdale, and E. Chiang. 1996. A national survey of physicians' behaviors regarding sexual contact with patients. *Southern Medical Journal*, 89(10): 977–982.
9. Dehlendorf, C. and S. Wolfe. 1998. Physicians disciplined for sex-related offenses. *Journal of the American Medical Association*, 279(23): 1883–1888.
10. Schwartz, H. A. 2007. Sexual Abuse of Patients by Health Care Professionals. Accessed April 17, 2013. http://www.stanford.edu/group/psylawseminar/Sex.htm
11. Schrock, K. 2007. Complaints of sexual misconduct. Presentation given at *Administrators in Medicine Investigator Training Conference*, Orlando, FL, June 2007.
12. Arizona State Board of Nursing. 1997. Guidelines for Sexual Misconduct and Boundary Violation Cases. Accessed April 22, 2013. https://www.azbn.gov/documents/Substantive%20Policies/Guidelines%20for%20Sexual%20Misconduct%20&%20Bondary%20Violation%20Cases.pdf

chapter eleven

Mental and physical impairment investigations

As stated throughout this text, state medical boards are charged with the protection of the public. Perhaps one of the most important, if not the most important, problem state medical boards face is the impaired physician. Organized medicine should be accountable to the public in assuring competent care to patients by competent physicians.[1] This accountability is strained when a physician becomes unable to practice with reasonable skill due to an impaired condition.[1] The term "impairment" is often equated or synonymous with "illness."[2] According to the literature, a distinction between these two terms is critical when it comes to dealing with an impaired physician in terms of public protection and in terms of what is best for the physician by way of treatment. This will be discussed in detail later in the chapter.

Definitions

First, some definitions are in order so as to gain better insight into this area. *Webster's II New College Dictionary* defines the word "impair" as "to worsen; to *decrease* in strength, value, amount, or *quality*."[3] In terms of physician impairment, it is the *decreased quality* of medical care rendered that becomes the concern of the medical board. The American Medical Association (AMA) defines physician impairment as "the inability to practice medicine with reasonable skill and safety due to (1) mental illness, (2) physical illnesses, including but not limited to deterioration through the aging process, or loss of motor skill, or (3) excessive use or abuse of drugs, including alcohol."[2] A physician whose skills and judgment are impaired may pose a significant threat to patient safety.

Illness versus impairment

The AMA definition of impairment has been adopted by most medical boards and this language often appears in most state Medical Practice Acts.[2] Often impairment is equated with illness which is not an accurate assumption. A clear understanding of these terms and distinction between the two is necessary.

Illness is the existence of a disease. Impairment is a functional classification and implies the inability of the person affected by disease to perform specific activities. Illness and impairment exist on a continuum with illness typically predating impairment. Physicians who become ill are often able to function effectively during the earlier stages of their illness. If illness progresses to cause impairment, treatment often results in remission of the illness and restoration of function.[2] Substance abuse or addiction is an illness. The illness, if not timely treated, will likely result in the impairment of skills and judgment. Parkinson disease is an illness. As Parkinson's advances, motor skills thus become impaired. Many impairment causing maladies, if treated timely, may avoid or diminish actual impairment.

There are several obstacles to an ill physician seeking care to include denial, aversion to the patient role, stigma, and fear of disciplinary action by the medical board. Overt impairment will likely manifest in the workplace if ill physicians remain without treatment.[2] Manifestation of impairment in the workplace may then come to the attention of the medical board. Common maladies that may bring about a state of impairment include substance abuse/addiction, psychiatric disorders, and physical disabilities. Another potential cause of impairment is the aging process.

It is estimated that approximately 15% of physicians will be impaired at some point in their career.[4] Physicians typically possess a strong drive for achievement, conscientiousness, and the ability to deny personal problems. While these attributes are beneficial for success in medicine, they may predispose to impairment, especially drug use, mental illness, and depression.[4] One study examined several different causes of physician impairment to include depression, alcohol and drug dependence, physical illness, and diminished skill competency. The findings concluded that "when all conditions are considered, at least one-third of all physicians will experience, at some point in their career, a period during which they have a condition that impairs their ability to practice medicine safely."[4]

Thomas Wallace, MD, JD, MBA, a Joint Commission Resources consultant, identifies several signs of impairment in terms of physical appearance, behavior in the hospital, and behavior in the community.

- Physical Appearance
    - Personality or behavior changes
    - Deterioration of hygiene or appearance
    - Frequent or unusual accidents
    - Multiple prescriptions
    - Frequent or unexplained absences
    - Complaints of excessive work load

- Inaccessible ("locked door syndrome")
- Excessive ordering of drugs or excessive personal drug use
- Complaints by patients or staff[5]
- In the Hospital
  - Frequent trips to the restroom
  - Frequently late, absent, or ill
  - Desire to work alone or refusing work relief
  - Lack of or inappropriate responses to pages or calls
  - Decreasing quality of performance or patient care[5]
- In the Community
  - Unreliability or neglect of commitments
  - Isolation or withdrawal
  - Unpredictable behavior
  - Embarrassing behavior at social functions
  - Arrest(s) for driving under influence (DUI) or other legal problems[5]

Substance abuse/addiction

Definitions

Substance

- Mind and mood altering substances defined in law as controlled substances;
- Alcohol or other legal or illegal substances that are mood altering and can potentially impact the ability to practice[6]

Substance use disorder (according to DSM-IV)

- Substance Abuse: "a maladaptive pattern of substance use manifested by recurrent and significant adverse consequences related to the repeated use of substances..."
- Substance Dependence: "a cluster of cognitive behaviors and psychological symptoms indicating that the individual continues use of the substance despite significant substance related problems..."[6,7]

Addictive illness

- The American Society of Addiction Medicine (ASAM) defines addictive illness as "a biochemical, psychosocial, genetically influenced primary illness hallmarked by loss of control or continued use of mind and/or mood altering substances regardless of negative consequences frequently accompanied by a powerful denial of the existence and effects of the illness."[6]

Studies indicate that the lifetime prevalence of any substance abuse or dependence disorder is estimated at 26.6% for the general U.S. population and the lifetime incidence of alcohol dependence is 14.1%, and of drug dependence is 7.5%. It is believed that physicians have a greater lifetime probability of developing substance-related disorders than the general population partly due to easy access to drugs. Substance dependence is characterized by a continuous or periodic loss of control over drinking or drug use, preoccupation with the drug or alcohol, use of alcohol or other drugs despite adverse consequences, and distortions in thinking, primarily denial.[8]

Other studies estimate that 10–15% of all healthcare professionals will misuse drugs or alcohol at some time during their career and healthcare professionals tend to have higher rates of abuse with benzodiazepines and opiates.[9,10] Research also suggests that attending physicians and resident physicians tend to use drugs of abuse for performance enhancement and to self-treat pain, anxiety, or depression.[9] This is concerning in that physicians have a high rate of self-treatment with controlled substances which could lead to abuse or dependence.[10] Substance abuse is the most common form of impairment that results in discipline from a state medical board.[9] Alcohol tends to be the most abused followed by opiates and physicians are estimated to use opiates and benzodiazepines at a rate five times higher than the general public.[10,11] Prescription drugs most commonly used by physicians in order of descending prevalence were minor opiates (codeine, propoxyphene, etc.), benzodiazepines, amphetamines, barbiturates, major opiates (oxycodone, fentanyl, etc.), and steroids.[10,12] Predisposing factors in physician substance abuse include:

- Obsessive-compulsive personality
- Family history of substance use disorders or mental illness
- Childhood family problems
- Personal mental illness
- Sensation seeking behavior
- Denial of personal and social problems
- Perfectionism
- Idealism[11]

Psychiatric disorders

This section will examine other psychiatric disorders as they relate to the impaired physician. Studies estimate that 4–10% of physicians come to the attention of medical boards due to problems related to nonsubstance-related major psychiatric disorders. The most common psychiatric disorders suffered by physicians include the mood disorders (depression and bipolar disorder), anxiety disorders, and cognitive disorders. Some personality disorders may manifest as behavioral disruption and antisocial, unscrupulous, or unethical behavior.[13]

An important tool used by physicians and other healthcare professionals in the diagnosis of psychiatric disorders is the *Diagnostic and Statistical Manual of Mental Disorders, 4th edition* which is commonly referred to as the DSM-IV. A basic understanding of the DSM-IV classifications and its multiaxial system will be of great value to the investigator when evaluating treatment records obtained during an investigation. The DSM-IV consists of three major components: diagnostic classification, diagnostic criteria sets, and descriptive text.[14]

The diagnostic classification is the list of the mental disorders that are officially part of the DSM system. Making a DSM diagnosis consists of selecting those disorders from the classification that best reflect the signs and symptoms that are exhibited by the individual being evaluated.[14] For each disorder there is a set of diagnostic criteria that indicate what symptoms must be present (and for how long) as well as symptoms, disorders, and conditions that must not be present in order to qualify for a particular diagnosis. The third component of the DSM is the descriptive text that accompanies each disorder and methodically describes each disorder under various headings.[14]

The DSM-IV organizes each psychiatric diagnosis in five dimensions, or axes, relating to different aspects of disorder or disability:

- Axis I: All diagnostic categories except mental retardation and personality disorder
- Axis II: Personality disorders and mental retardation
- Axis III: General medical condition; acute medical conditions and physical disorders
- Axis IV: Psychosocial and environmental factors contributing to the disorder (family dysfunction, legal issues, financial problems, etc.)
- Axis V: Global Assessment of Functioning[7]

Common Axis I disorders include, but not limited to, depression, anxiety disorders, bipolar disorder, attention deficit hyperactivity disorder (ADHD), autism, and eating disorders. Common Axis II disorders include personality disorders: paranoid personality disorder, schizoid personality disorder, borderline personality disorder, narcissistic personality disorder, obsessive-compulsive personality disorder, and intellectual disabilities. Axis III disorders include brain injuries and other medical/physical disorders which may aggravate existing diseases or present symptoms similar to other disorders.[7]

Axis V is the global assessment of functioning or GAF. The GAF is a numeric scale ranging from 1 to 100. Mental health practitioners and physicians use this scale to subjectively rate the social, occupational, and psychological functioning of adults. For example, a GAF score of 1–10 would indicate a consistent risk of injuring oneself or others or a serious suicide attempt indicating a calculated effort to bring about death. A GAF score of 90–100 indicates an exceptionally high level of functioning. A GAF score of 51–60 indicates "some mild symptoms (depressed mood, mild insomnia) or some difficulty in social, occupational, or school functioning, but generally functioning pretty well and has some meaningful interpersonal relationships."[7]

An Axis I or Axis II diagnosis does not necessarily lead to, or equate with impairment. A physician's depression, eating disorder, and obsessive-compulsive disorder may not have progressed to the point that it affects their medical judgment, competence, or safety.[15] Many disorders respond well to treatment and many physicians with a diagnosis practice at very high levels. Untreated or inadequately treated disorders are more likely to cause impairment.[13] Examples of physicians who may not be able to practice safely include:

- Active bipolar disorder in a manic phase who is showing poor judgment and insight and is refusing treatment
- Panic disorder resistant to medications, phobic to the point that work duties and patient care duties are avoided and neglected
- Exhibiting marked irreversible memory impairment from early dementia
- Psychotic as a sign of incipient schizophrenia, not responding to medication[13]

Examples of physicians with a diagnosis who may not pose a safety threat to patients include:

- Bipolar disorder in a somewhat depressed state, compliant with treatment, maintaining appropriate therapeutic lithium levels, showing good insight and judgment
- Panic disorder responding well to treatment and avoiding certain situations that do not interfere with work[13]

Research indicates that risk factors for depression in the physician are similar to those in the general public, however, physicians do have certain biologic, psychologic, and social risk factors making them vulnerable to mood disturbances. Due to the erratic schedules of physicians they often do not get enough sleep, exhibit poor/irregular eating habits, and lack of exercise contributing to biologic risk factors. Other biologic risk factors include a family history of mental illness and physical illness. Psychologic factors may include the need for control and perfection, a need for approval, a distinct sense of responsibility, and self-doubt. Social risk factors include managing difficult patients, outside scrutiny, certain occupational endangerments such as contracting an illness, the stress of dealing with managed care organizations, and the like.[12]

Stress and burnout are another set of potential problems that may lead to impairment. Physicians are presented with a host of stressors from medical school, through residency, and into their daily practice. When these stressors cause a feeling of being overwhelmed, burnout can occur. Signs of burnout may include signs of weariness, worrisome, inability to sleep, lack of concentration, and perhaps an increase in the use of mood-altering substances.[16] Physicians experiencing burnout are more likely to make mistakes than less stressed physicians.[17] Burnout may reveal itself by exhibiting increases in physical problems and illness, relationship problems, and the taking on of unhealthy habits such as overeating, smoking, drinking, tardiness, and to name a few.[12]

Depressive disorders and substance dependence are common disorders among physicians who commit suicide.[12] The President's Commission on Mental Health (1978) estimates that 100–300 physicians commit suicide each year and is reported to be the second largest cause of death among medical students.[18] Studies reveal that the suicide risk in male physicians ranged from 1.1 to 3.4 times higher than the general public.[12] The suicide risk in female physicians was 2.5–5.7 times higher than the general population and the actual suicide rate ratio of female physicians is substantially higher than that of male physicians.[12]

A physician at high risk for suicide usually does not lean toward one gender or the other. The high risk physician typically falls within an age range of 45 and over for females and 50 and over for males and they are usually Caucasian. They are often divorced or separated or otherwise experiencing marital dysfunction. The high risk physician is likely a substance user, "workaholic," and takes excessive risks. They will exhibit psychiatric symptoms (depression, anxiety) and physical symptoms (chronic pain, etc.). They will likely have experienced significant changes in their professional status or a threat to that status, financial problems, and recent losses.[12]

Disruptive behavior

Disruptive behavior can be described as a chronic pattern of contentious, threatening, intractable, litigious behavior that significantly deviates from the cultural norm.[19] Such behavior creates a work environment that interferes with the efficient functioning of the healthcare team impacting patient safety and the delivery of quality care.[19,20] The word "chronic" is used to describe a habitual pattern of behavior as opposed to the occasional outburst from a stressed and overworked physician. The distinguishing characteristic of this physician is chronic malcontent and frequent ebullitions of anger resulting in inappropriate outbursts towards nurses, technicians, and patients.[19]

Inappropriate behaviors

- Intimidation
- Abusive language
- Demeaning other staff
- Blaming or shaming others for adverse outcomes
- Threats of violence, retribution, or litigation
- Throwing instruments or charts[19,20]

Inappropriate words or actions

- Sexual comments, jokes, innuendo
- Flirtation, sexual harassment
- Seductive, aggressive, or assaultive behavior
- Racial, ethnic or socioeconomic bias, or slurs
- Lack of regard for personal comfort and dignity of others[19]

Inappropriate responses to patient needs or staff requests

- Uncooperative, defiant, rigid, inflexible
- Avoidant, unreliable
- Late or unsuitable replies to pages and calls
- Unprofessional demeanor or conduct
- Arrogant, disrespectful
- Inadequate communication in quantity, quality, and promptness
- Recurrent conflict with others, particularly with authority figures, irrational, oppositional[19]

Much of the research suggests that disruptive behavior leads to medical errors, contributes to poor patient satisfaction and to preventable adverse outcomes.[21] Patient safety and the delivery of quality medical care is dependent on teamwork, communication, and collaboration.[21] In the Joint Commission's root cause analysis of sentinel events, it is reported that almost 70% of sentinel events can be traced to a problem with effective communication.[22] Often members of the healthcare team will avoid the disruptive physician, hesitate to ask for clarification of orders, and hesitate to collaborate in patient care thus leading to a higher risk for medical errors and diminished patient safety. When patients witness disruptive behavior, their confidence in the physician and the institution is undermined and the patient will often opt out of participating or partnering in their own care. Such behavior threatens patient safety and engenders a destructive effect on morale in the workplace.[20]

Studies suggest that disruptive behavior derives from two factors: individual factors and systemic factors.[21] The inherent stress of medical practice, high stakes and high emotion situations, and fatigue may contribute to unprofessional behavior. Characteristics such as self-centeredness, immaturity, or defensiveness may cause one to be more prone to disruptive behavior as well as a lack of interpersonal, coping, and conflict management skills.[21]

Systemic factors evolve from the healthcare cultural environment wherein there exists heightened pressure to increase productivity, contain costs, embedded hierarchies, and fear or stress from lawsuits. The lack of or diminished autonomy and empowerment, continual flux in shifts and work hours creates a challenge for effective interpersonal communication and the development of trust among team members.[21] Other studies suggest that physician behaviors may be molded in medical school in that physicians learn to think on their own and take responsibility for their actions.[23] This type of self-preservation promotes autonomy, independence and an autocratic, domineering behavior pattern; behavior contrary to team building and collaboration.[23]

Often disruptive physicians go unreported primarily due to a fear of retaliation, the stigma of being a "whistleblower," and the general reluctance to confront an intimidator.[21] Other reported reasons for not reporting the behavior include assertions that "nothing ever changes," a lack of confidentiality, lack of administrative support, and the physician's lack of awareness or unwillingness to change.[23] Disruptive physicians rarely seek help as they characteristically lack insight into the nature of their problematic behavior.[19] When this type of behavior crosses the threshold from the rare outburst caused by fatigue or frustration to a chronic habitual pattern of abusive behavior, intervention may be necessary, either by the institution, the medical board, or both.

A review of the literature indicates that disruptive physician behavior is quite prevalent. A west coast study of disruptive behavior in obstetric labor and delivery units revealed that disruptive behavior was occurring on 60.7% of the participating units and crossed multiple professions. The study further indicated that such behavior contributed to a nursing shortage in the units, near misses, and adverse occurrences.[24]

Additional studies examined the effect of disruptive behavior on the nursing shortage. The studies suggest that daily interactions between nurses and physicians strongly influence nurses' morale. One study found a direct link between disruptive physician behavior and nurse satisfaction and retention.[25] A 2002 survey examining physician/nurse relationships discovered a very high prevalence of physician disruptive behavior negatively affecting nurse retention. Over 90% of the survey participants reported witnessing disruptive behavior and at least one-third reported knowing at least one nurse leaving the institution due to disruptive physician behavior. The survey indicated that the most frequent types of disruptive behaviors were disrespect, berating colleagues, abusive language, and condescending behaviors. The most common circumstances involved placing calls to physicians to clarify orders for treatment. This study found that disruptive outbursts occurred most frequently in operating rooms, surgical units, intensive care units, emergency departments, and obstetric units. The specialties exhibiting the most disruptive behavior were general surgery (ranked #1), then cardiology, cardiovascular surgery, neurology, neurosurgery, orthopedics, obstetrics, and anesthesia. The survey asked how important a factor disruptive behavior is for nurse satisfaction and morale. The participants were asked to assign a score between 1 and 10 with 10 being extremely important. The score was 8.01 indicating extremely high importance.[23]

A follow-up study to the 2002 study previously discussed found that most respondents perceived disruptive behavior as having negative or worsening effects on stress, frustration, concentration, communication, collaboration, information transfer, and workplace relationships.[26] The study further revealed disquieting perceptions of negative or worsening effects on adverse events, medical errors, patient safety, patient mortality, and quality of care.[26]

Another research effort examined disruptive physician behavior in the perioperative arena. This study found that disruptive behaviors were very prevalent in the perioperative setting with the most prevalent offenders being attending surgeons. This study, like others, found that such behavior increased stress and frustration leading to impaired concentration and the thwarting of the flow of communication, events perceived to increase medical errors, adverse events, and diminish patient safety and quality of care.[27]

The final study reviewed is a 2008 survey of respondents in 102 hospitals on the west coast. The respondents participating included 2846 nurses, 955 physicians, 40 administrators, and 700 "other." The "other" respondents consisted of pharmacists, respiratory therapists, physical therapists, and other ancillary healthcare workers. The survey revealed that 77% of the respondents had witnessed disruptive behavior in their hospital. Eighty-eight percent of the nurses reported witnessing disruptive behavior and 51% of the physicians reported the same. Sixty-seven percent felt that there was a linkage between disruptive behavior and adverse events, 71% medical errors, and 27% to patient mortality. Of interest, and worth noting, are several respondent comments from this survey:

- "Most nurses are afraid to call Dr. XX when they need to, and frequently won't call. Their patients' medical safety is always in jeopardy because of this."

- "Disruptive behavior results in medication errors, slow response times, and treatment errors."
- "Disruptive behavior caused increased stress and lack of concentration, which caused a nurse to make a mistake."
- "Poor communication postop because of a disruptive reputation, resulted in delayed treatment, aspiration, and the patient's death."[28]

Anecdotally, while researching this chapter, an Indiana Supreme Court case was found dealing with this very issue. The case is Daniel Raess, MD v. Joseph Doescher. Doescher is a perfusionist at his employing hospital in Indiana. Raess is a cardiac surgeon. Doescher sued Raess for assault and was awarded monetary damages. Raess appealed to the Indiana Court of Appeals who reversed the trial court decision. The facts of the case are as follows taken from the record of the Indiana Court of Appeals:

> On October 25, 2001, Doescher, who was acting as a perfusionist in an open-heart surgery being performed by Dr. Beth Ashworth ("Ashworth") at St. Francis Hospital ("the Hospital") in Beech Grove, Indiana, left during the surgery to attend to personal business. As a perfusionist, Doescher operated the "heart/lung" machine that kept the patient alive during the surgery. Prior to the beginning of the procedure, Doescher had arranged for Jennifer Lee, another perfusionist, to fill in for him after his departure. Although it was customary for a perfusionist to give notice of an absence to the physician conducting a surgical procedure, hospital policy did not require such notice. Doescher did not give notice to Ashworth or to any other doctor. The combination of Doescher's absence, Lee's commitment as Doescher's replacement, and the involvement of the third perfusionist, Joe Borondy ("Borondy"), in a scheduled surgery left the hospital with no available perfusionists for a short amount of time. Accordingly, Raess, who is a heart surgeon, was not immediately able to conduct an emergency heart surgery. Raess became angry and yelled at both Lee and Borondy. The following day Borondy told Doescher about Raess' outburst. Doescher testified that he then resigned his Chief Perfusionist position as a form of "protest." However, Doescher

continued working as a staff perfusionist at the hospital. On November 2, 2001, Doescher acted as a perfusionist in a heart surgery performed by Raess. Afterwards, Raess approached Doescher to talk about "coverage issues" such as the one caused by Doescher's previous absence. Doescher informed Raess that he was no longer Chief Perfusionist and that coverage issues were not his concern. The two men separated without further discussion. Later in the day, Doescher and Raess were together in the "pump room" located between the operating rooms in the Hospital's open-heart surgery area. An argument ensued and Raess became angry, causing his body to stiffen, his face to turn red, and his jugular vein to extend. Raess walked toward Doescher and exited out the door close to Doescher. At trial, Doescher testified that Raess walked toward him in a manner that caused Doescher to think that Raess was going to "smack the s*** out of me." Transcript at 484. Doescher also testified that although Raess' balled fists were at his side, Raess' demeanor and purposeful walk caused Doescher to back up against the wall and raise his hands in defense. Doescher then declared an end to the conversation, and Raess walked out after yelling, "You're over. You're history. You're finished." Doescher further testified that he felt assaulted because of "the advancement, the look in [Raess'] eye, [and] his body positioning." Transcript at 492. After the November 2, 2001 incident, Doescher testified that he became depressed and anxious, exhibited heightened anxiety, developed sleep problems, and experienced loss of appetite. Doescher further testified that he lost his confidence and did not return to his position as a staff perfusionist. Doescher presented medical experts who testified as to Doescher's mental and physical health. On June 26, 2002, Doescher filed a complaint against Raess for assault, intentional infliction of emotional distress, and intentional interference with his employment relationship. The trial court entered summary judgment in Raess' favor on the intentional interference with an employment relationship claim, and the suit went to trial on the remaining issues. Prior to the jury trial,

> Raess filed a motion in limine seeking to preclude any witness, including any expert witness, from giving testimony depicting Raess as a "workplace bully." Raess also filed a motion to exclude the testimony of Doescher's "workplace bully" expert, Gary Namie ("Namie"). The trial court ruled that Namie could testify that Raess was a workplace bully as to Doescher, but not "against the world." Transcript at 165. Over Raess' objection, Namie testified that the November 2, 2001 altercation was an "episode of workplace bullying" and that Raess is "a workplace abuser … a person who subjected [Doescher] to an abusive work environment." Transcript at 409; 413–14. The jury found for Raess on the intentional infliction of emotional distress claim and for Doescher on the assault claim. It awarded damages of $325,000.[29]

The case was transferred from the Court of Appeals to the Indiana Supreme Court. Following is an excerpt from the Indiana Supreme Court ruling:

> "This is an appeal by defendant Daniel Raess, M.D., a cardiovascular surgeon, challenging a $325,000 jury verdict and judgment on a claim for assault brought by plaintiff Joseph Doescher, a hospital operating room perfusionist (the person who operates the heart/lung machine during open heart surgeries). The Court of Appeals reversed and remanded for a new trial. *Raess v. Doescher,* 858 N.E.2d 119 (Ind. Ct.App.2006), *aff'd on reh'g.,* 861 N.E.2d 1216 (Ind. Ct.App.2007). We granted transfer and now *affirm* the judgment of the trial court."[29]

Physical and medical disability and the aging physician

Physicians, like everyone else, are susceptible to illness and medical conditions as well as advancing age. When a physician's medical condition negatively affects his/her ability to practice medicine with reasonable skill and safety, the public welfare must be considered.[30] It should be noted, however, that a physician with a physical disability may not necessarily be impaired and many physicians have practiced safely well into their advanced years.[31]

Physical disabilities may occur at any point in a physician's life and the type of disability may range from a spinal cord injury to age-related disabilities such as Parkinson disease to hearing and vision loss. Physicians with disabilities face unique challenges in medicine where cognitive and physical demands are high.[12]

The AMA Physician Masterfile data indicates an increase in the aging physician population. The data revealed that in 1985, the number of active physicians in practice was 476,683 with 9.4% age 65 or older. In 2005, there were 672,531 active physicians in practice with 11.7% age 65 or older. The 2011 data shows 697,340 active physicians with 15.1% age 65 or older. The 2005 data further revealed the mean age of the 672,531 active physicians was 50 years old and the mean age of the 697,340 active physicians in 2011 was 52 years old.[32]

A 1987 study examined this issue by collecting data on physicians and medical students who had communicated with the American Society of Handicapped Physicians between 1982 and 1984. A total of 155 physicians were included in the study and the majority worked full time and represented 20 different areas of medicine. Two-thirds of the group were in internal medicine, family medicine, rehabilitation medicine, psychiatry, and pediatrics. The majority had neurologic disabilities followed by musculoskeletal, visual, auditory, and medical-surgical etiologies. The study identified seven specific disorders that accounted for half of all disabilities including spinal cord injury, multiple sclerosis, stroke, arthritis/connective tissue disease, postpolio weakness, lower limb amputation, and diabetic retinopathy. The study further indicated that the participating physicians were capable of safely practicing in many professional specialties despite certain medical conditions and physical disabilities.[33]

A Canadian study from 2001 to 2010 revealed some interesting findings. The study of 1618 Quebec physicians involved an on-site visit by the researchers for the purpose of reviewing the subjects' practices to include reviews of documentation, prescribing habits, billing practices, and clinical outcomes. The physicians were contacted two to three months in advance of the visit to inform them of the impending visit. After the on-site review, each physician was placed in one of five categories:

Level 0: No action required, satisfactory
Level 1: Recommendations for improvement
Level 2: Recommendations given and control visit follow-up
Level 3: Refresher course or retraining or limitation of practice
Level 4: Cancellation of licensure (surrender or revocation)[32]

The study revealed that physicians over the age of 70 had a three times higher rate of licensure cancellation (31%) compared to the group less than 70 years old (10%). Physicians aged 65–69 had almost double the rate of Level 3 recommendations than for the age group less than 65. The study also noted that physicians in the over 70 group had less favorable clinical outcomes even with remediation.[32]

Physician health programs

Physician Health Programs (PHP), sometimes referred to as Professional Health Programs, are organizations established for the purpose of promoting early detection, assessment, evaluation, and referral to abstinence-oriented treatment for 60–90 days. Often this treatment is in a residential treatment facility.[34] PHPs typically do not provide treatment, however, they usually provide initial triage, referral into treatment, post-treatment monitoring, and long-term care for addictive disorders.[35] In many situations, entering treatment under the auspices of a PHP will avoid involvement by the medical board.

Forty-seven states and Washington, DC have some form of a PHP (Appendix 23). An excellent resource for PHPs nationwide is the Federation of State Physician Health Programs (FSPHP), (Contact information found in Appendix 31). Most treatment programs provide specialized and individualized treatment plans tailored for the individual health professional as well as tailor a specific aftercare monitoring program for each patient.[36]

The AMA issued a statement on physician health programs in February 2008 supporting state physician health programs in that "they are essential to ensure the safety and protection of patients."[37] In 2011, the AMA issued a report stating their desire to work closely with the FSPHP to educate their members about the availability of state PHPs and work with FSPHP to establish guidelines for the establishment, design, and limitations of PHPs, and to collaborate on legislation positively affecting PHPs.[38]

A 2009 study examined the way physicians are treated as opposed to the general population with regard to substance abuse disorders. The study consisted of a survey of the then 49 existing PHPs in an effort to characterize their treatment, support, and monitoring programs. It was found that physicians receive care that is qualitatively different from and reputedly more effective than what is offered to the general public. Aftercare monitoring consisted of a period of typically five years. (The five year monitoring period is also endorsed by the FSPHP.[39]) The study further concluded that only 22% of physicians tested positive at any time during the five years and 71% remained licensed and employed at the five-year mark.[34]

A study conducted a year earlier in 2008 examined the effectiveness of state physician health programs. This research effort consisted of a five-year longitudinal study of 904 physicians admitted to one of 16 PHP programs from September 1995 to September 2001. The study revealed the following:

- 19% failed the program and did not complete treatment.
- 81% completed treatment and had a 19% occurrence (over five years) of alcohol/drug misuse.
- At the five-year follow-up, 79% were licensed and working, 11% had their licenses revoked, 3.5% had retired, 3.7% had died.[40]

The consensus is that PHPs play a very important role in the care of physicians who suffer from various impairments due to alcohol or substance abuse. Studies have shown that approximately 75% of physicians treated for substance abuse and followed by their PHP had favorable outcomes over five years.[40] PHPs in many states share a dual role of helping physicians attain sobriety and personal recovery as well as providing assurance to colleagues, hospitals, insurers, licensing boards, and the general public that these physicians can practice safely.[40]

One is urged to make contact with the PHP in your state to learn of their policies, programs, and procedures. Having strong points of contact with your PHP will be very helpful when conducting investigations of this sort.

Investigation

Prior to discussing the various investigative protocols, it is important to discuss an extremely important resource available to most state medical boards. About 60 of 65 (92%) medical or osteopathic boards in the United States and the District of Columbia have statutory authority to order a physician to undergo a mental/physical evaluation based on *reasonable grounds*. The burden of establishing reasonable grounds rests with the board. Reasonable grounds may take on different meanings in different states. The burden of establishing reasonable grounds may be more stringent in some states and less so in others. It would be advisable to discuss this issue with the attorneys representing your medical board to gain an understanding of what is required to establish reasonable grounds for this type of investigation. Some examples of behaviors that may establish reasonable grounds include, but are not limited to, the following:

- Prescribing controlled substances in the physician's own name for self-use
- Prescribing controlled substances in fictitious names, family members' names, etc.
- Receiving prescriptions for controlled substances from a colleague
- Other forms of drug diversion, theft, use of samples, etc.

- Two or more DUI arrests in a relatively short period of time
- Results of a hospital internal investigation leading to the suspension of privileges
- Physical indicators observed by the investigator
- Thorough interviews with the physician's employees and colleagues

Investigations of alleged impairment may originate from a variety of sources. The physician may self-report his/her impairment and entry into treatment to the board. A concerned patient, colleague, or office staff may report allegations of atypical behavior exhibited by the physician. Family members of the physician may also come forward expressing concern for their loved one seeking a form of intervention by the board. Hospital adverse actions are another way these investigations can be initiated.

Self report

The physician who self-reports their impairment makes for a relatively straight forward investigation. Conduct a face-to-face interview with the physician making note of his/her mannerisms, speech, gait, etc. Make note of any behaviors that may indicate impairment. Request that he/she describe the nature of their illness and if substance abuse, indicate the substances used such as alcohol, narcotics, amphetamines, etc. How are these substances obtained? Were there instances of diversion, theft, fraud, etc.? Have the physician describe their methods for obtaining the substances. If drug diversion was involved, it will be necessary to obtain pharmacy records and applicable patient records. Often an impaired physician suffering from substance abuse will prescribe the drug of choice in fictitious names, friends' names, or patients' names. Determine these names and issue a subpoena for these specific patients' medical records. Upon examination of the charts one will likely find that no entries were made into these records and in some cases there exists no record whatsoever. Such information or lack thereof will provide the necessary "reasonable grounds" for the board to issue an order for a mental/physical evaluation if necessary. The self-reporting physician is likely to have already been evaluated and referred for treatment. If this is the case, request the physician to provide a release of the evaluation records and records of any treatment.

Determine if the physician has been experiencing problems at his practice or at the hospital and detail the nature of such problems: tardiness, missing work, coming to work smelling of alcohol, and erratic behaviors. Interviews with office staff and colleagues may be warranted to corroborate this information. Was there a sentinel event that prompted the physician to self-report? If a patient was harmed as a result of the physician's impairment, further investigation is certainly warranted to include an interview with the patient and obtaining a copy of the specific patient's medical records at a minimum.

Other areas to explore would include whether the physician used their substance of choice prior to arriving to work, while on call, or during the work day. Complete details of these instances will be necessary to establish reasonable grounds for an ordered evaluation. Is the physician currently in treatment or does he/she plan to enter treatment? If so, determine the identity of the facility and anticipated dates for treatment. Does he/she plan to make contact with and enter the Physicians Health Program (PHP)? If possible, a HIPAA release should be obtained so as to access these records if/when necessary.

Report from family, co-worker, pharmacist, et al.

Allegations of impairment may originate from others closely associated with the physician to include family members, coworkers, colleagues, and pharmacists, among others. The first step is to interview the party or parties bringing the allegations. This interview should explore the substances being used, how they are being obtained, and pharmacies being used to cash fraudulent prescriptions. The interview should also explore behavioral changes such as unusual mood swings, increased anger outbursts, easy loss of temper, lethargy, loss of interest in activities once enjoyed, and to name a few. Is the physician experiencing problems at work as mentioned earlier? Details of such should be thoroughly explored.

The initial complainant may be able to provide other witnesses to further corroborate the allegations. Interviews with these witnesses should be conducted and developed leads thoroughly explored. If the workplace has documentation of having counseled the physician about certain problems, incident reports, Drug Enforcement Administration (DEA) drug order forms indicating drugs ordered by the physician, or documentation of an in-house investigation, copies of such should be obtained.

Another form of drug diversion carried out within the hospital setting involves the physician taking medication ordered for a patient(s). There are several things to look for in a case involving theft from an institution or patient. Interview the complainant and any other witnesses identified. Always talk to the institutional pharmacist. If individual patients are involved, an interview with them may be warranted. The patients may be able to confirm that they did not get a dose or injection of a specific drug at a specific time. The patient's family may have been present and can also corroborate the information. If specific patients are identified, obtain a copy of their hospital chart and examine the attending physicians' medication orders to determine if the patient was actually ordered the drug in question. Then check the medication administration record in the patient chart to ascertain if the drug was documented as being administered: date, time, etc. The secure area where controlled substances are stored should have some form of documentation indicating who signed for the drug when a drug is taken for patient administration.

Often these documents are referred to as medication sign-out sheets; however, such documentation is widely kept electronically today. Compare the physician's orders, sign-out sheets, and the medication administration record, and note any discrepancies. It is also advisable to examine the nurses notes contained in the patient chart in that a note should be entered by the nurse administering the medication. Discrepancies in this area can be extremely strong when establishing reasonable grounds. It is important that all witnesses identified be thoroughly interviewed, and all leads developed prior to interviewing the subject physician.

Physician interview

In many cases, it is suggested that an unannounced visit to meet with the physician be considered. If an appointment is made to meet with the physician, an opportunity for the physician to "clean up" is provided. Some physicians will refuse to meet with an investigator without an appointment being made and many will retain legal counsel prior to meeting with an investigator. If such should occur, then an appointment will have to be made.

The interview is intended to glean additional information and allow the physician to tell his/her side of the story. Remember, the role of the investigator is to gather facts, not convict. After introductions are made and the purpose of the interview is disclosed, the investigator should present the information garnered in the investigation. If the physician requests to see the questioned documents, such can be done to allow him/her to respond. Do not provide any documents from your investigation to the physician for him/her to keep. It may be appropriate for him/her to look at certain documents but they should be returned to you. Said documents may include alleged questionable prescriptions, excerpts from altered medical records, certain hospital records, etc. Do not provide copies of documents or other evidence obtained during the investigation.

Allow the physician to respond and provide his/her explanation. Take notes during this time. After the physician is finished with their explanation, continue to probe any gaps or discrepancies. Take note of the physicians' nonverbal responses (body language). Is he/she exhibiting an unusually higher rate of speech, acting fidgety, showing signs of anxiousness, becoming nonchalant, disengaging, etc.? These could be signs of untruthfulness or perhaps fear when becoming disengaged. It is important to know that persons suffering from substance abuse disorders and addiction have likely been hiding such from their families and peers for a long time. As such they have become exceedingly able to effectively conceal their illness via their prevarications. At the conclusion of the interview, request from the physician a written statement or written response addressing the issue at hand.

Report of adverse action by hospital or practice

Often allegations of impairment originate by virtue of an adverse action taken by a hospital or practice group. Certain adverse actions are required to be reported to the National Practitioner Data Bank (NPDB) as well as to state medical boards. What action was taken by the hospital; suspension of privileges, leave of absence, etc.? The investigation generally starts with the person from the hospital reporting the adverse action. An interview with this individual will likely lead to others involved such as the CEO of the hospital, Chairman of the Medical Executive Committee, and others. Determine to what extent the hospital conducted its own internal investigation. Much of the investigator's leg work may have already been accomplished. It will be necessary to obtain a copy of the hospital's investigative file if at all possible. The hospital's investigative file will identify other witnesses and documentary evidence such as urine drug screens, etc. It may be necessary to conduct follow-up interviews with other identified witnesses to corroborate their statements.

Upon completion of the investigation, an interview with the physician is necessary. As covered previously, allow the physician to relate their version of the events. He/she is likely to have already been confronted by hospital officials, so the board's investigation should come as no surprise. The physician may have already prepared a written statement for the hospital and a copy of such should be obtained. If such a statement exists, it may not address all of the issues developed from your investigation. If that is the case, a written statement from the physician should be sought covering the issues from your investigation.

References

1. American Medical Association Council on Mental Health. 1973. The sick physician: Impairment by psychiatric disorders, including alcoholism and drug dependence. *Journal of the American Medical Association*, 223: 684–687.
2. Federation of State Physician Health Programs, Inc. 2008. Public policy statement: Physician illness vs. impairment. Accessed July 27, 2013. http://www.fsphp.org/Illness_vs_Impairment.pdf
3. *Webster's II New College Dictionary*. 2001. Boston: Houghton Mifflin Company, p. 553.
4. Boisaubin, E. and R. Levine. 2001. Identifying and assisting the impaired physician. *American Journal of the Medical Sciences*, 322(1): 31–36.
5. Joint Commission Resources. 2006. Identifying impaired physicians: How to address problem physicians quickly. *Patient Safety*, 6: 1–13.

6. Federation of State Medical Boards, Inc. 2011. Policy on Physician Impairment. Accessed July 27, 2013. http://www.fsmb.org/Media/Default/PDF/FSMB/Advocacy/grpol_policy-on-physician-impairment.pdf
7. American Psychiatric Association. 1994. *Diagnostic and Statistical Manual of Mental Disorders, 4th edition.* Arlington, VA: American Psychiatric Association.
8. Earley, P. 1995. Substance abuse related disorders. *Contribution to Problem Physicians: A National Perspective; A Report to the Georgia Composite State Board of Medical Examiners.* http://www.talbottcampus.com/pdf/Perspective.pdf
9. Baldisseri, M. 2002. Impaired healthcare professional. *Critical Care Medicine,* 35(2): 106–116.
10. Hughes, P., N. Brandenburg, D. Baldwin, C. Storr, K. Williams, J. Anthony, and D. Sheehan. 1992. Prevalence of substance abuse among US physicians. *Journal of the American Medical Association,* 267(17): 2333–2339.
11. Bright, R. and L. Krahn. 2010. Impaired physicians: How to recognize, when to report, and where to refer. *Current Psychiatry,* 9(6): 11–20.
12. Izenour, S. 2008. The impaired physician. Contribution to hospital physician: Psychiatry board review manual. *Psychiatry,* 11(4): 2–11.
13. Howell, E. 1995. Psychiatric disorders. *Contribution to Problem Physicians: A National Perspective; A Report to the Georgia Composite State Board of Medical Examiners.* http://www.talbottcampus.com/pdf/Perspective.pdf
14. American Psychiatric Association. 2012. DSM. Accessed August 15, 2013. http://www.psych.org
15. Myers, M. 1997. Treatment of the mentally Ill physician; position paper of the Canadian psychiatric association. *The Canadian Journal of Psychiatry,* 42(6).
16. Gunderson, L. 2001. Physician burnout. *Annals of Internal Medicine,* 135: 145–148.
17. Crane, M. 1998. Why burned-out doctors get sued more often. *Journal of Medical Economics,* 198(75): 210–212, 215–218.
18. Collins, J. 1982. The impaired physician. *Journal of the National Medical Association,* 74(3): 221–223.
19. Dodd, D. 1995. Disruptive behavior. In: G. Douglas Talbott, Linda R. Crosby (eds), *Contribution to Problem Physicians: A National Perspective; A Report to the Georgia Composite State Board of Medical Examiners,* 1995. http://www.talbottcampus.com/pdf/Perspective.pdf
20. Leape, L. and J. Fromson. 2006. Problem doctors: Is there a system-level solution? *Annals of Internal Medicine,* 144(2): 107–115.
21. The Joint Commission; Sentinel Event Alert. 2008. Behaviors That Undermine a Culture of Safety. Accessed August 15, 2013. http://www.jointcommission.org/SentinelEventAlert/sea_40.htm
22. The Joint Commission. 2008. Sentinel Event Root Cause and Trend Data. Accessed May 20, 2013. http://www.jointcommissionreport.org/performanceresults/sentinel.aspx
23. Rosenstein, A., H. Russell, and R. Lauve. 2002. Disruptive Physician Behavior Contributes to Nursing Shortage. *Physician Executive Journal,* 28: 8–11.
24. Veltman, L. 2007. Disruptive behavior in obstetrics: A hidden threat to patient safety. *American Journal of Obstetrics and Gynecology,* 196(6): 587.e1–587.e5.
25. Rosenstein, A. 2002. Nurse-physician relationships: Impact on nurse satisfaction and retention. *American Journal of Nursing,* 102(6): 26–34.

26. Rosenstein, A. and M. O'Daniel 2005. Disruptive behavior and clinical outcomes: Perceptions of nurses and physicians: Nurses, physicians, and administrators say that clinicians' disruptive behavior has negative effects on clinical outcomes. *American Journal of Nursing*, 105(1): 54–64.
27. Rosenstein, A. and M. O'Daniel. 2006. Impact and implications of disruptive behavior in the perioperative Arena. *Journal of the American College of Surgeons*, 203(1): 96–105.
28. Rosenstein, A. and M. O'Daniel. 2008. A survey of the impact of disruptive behaviors and communication defects on patient safety. *Joint Commission Journal on Quality and Patient Safety*, 34(8): 464–471.
29. Raess v. Doescher. 2008. 858 N.E.2d 119 (Ind.Ct.App.2006); Raess v. Doescher, 861 N.E.2d 1216 (Ind.Ct.App.2007); Raess v. Doescher; Indiana Supreme Court; 883 N.E.2d 790.
30. Pomm, R. 1995. Physically or medically disabled. *Contribution to Problem Physicians: A National Perspective; A Report to the Georgia Composite State Board of Medical Examiners*. http://www.talbottcampus.com/pdf/Perspective.pdf
31. Hobbs, T. 1995. Age related issues. *Contribution to from Problem Physicians: A National Perspective; A Report to the Georgia Composite State Board of Medical Examiners*. http://www.talbottcampus.com/pdf/Perspective.pdf
32. Moutier, C., D. Bazzo, and W. Norcross. 2013. Approaching the issue of the aging physician. *Journal of Medical Regulation*, 99(1): 10–18.
33. Wainapel, S. 1987. The physically disabled physician. *Journal of the American Medical Association*, 257(21): 2935–2938.
34. DuPont, R., T. A. McLellan, G. Carr, M. Gendel, and G. Skipper. 2009. How are addicted physicians treated? A national survey of physician health programs. *Journal of Substance Abuse Treatment*, 37(1): 1–7.
35. Georgia Professionals Health Program, Atlanta, GA. 2012. The Georgia PHP. Accessed July 25, 2013. www.gaphp.org.
36. Elements Behavioral Health-Physician Health Program, Long Beach, CA. 2013. FAQs About Physician Health Programs. Accessed July 25, 2013. www.elementsbehavioralhealth.com
37. Patchin, R. 2006. AMA Statement on Physician Health Programs. http://fsphp.org/AMA_statement.pdf
38. American Medical Association Official Observer Report. 2011. Educating Physicians About Physician Health Programs. Accessed July 30, 2013. http://www.fsphp.org/FSPHP%20Newsletter%202012%20FInal.pdf
39. Federation of State Physician Health Programs. 2000. Public Policy Statement Regarding Recommendations for Length of Monitoring of Physicians with Substance Abuse Disorders. Accessed August 1, 2013. http://www.fsphp.org/Monitoring.pdf
40. McLellan, A. T., G. S. Skipper, and R. L. DuPont. 2008. Five year outcomes in a cohort study of physicians treated for substance use disorders in the United States. *British Medical Journal* 337: a2038.

chapter twelve

Investigating healthcare fraud

Healthcare fraud is an enormous problem in the Unites States costing billions of wasted dollars as well as placing the health and safety of patients at risk. As medical board investigators, we should seek to participate and assist other primary investigative agencies in stemming this problem. Healthcare fraud is rampant among both public and private healthcare benefit programs with Medicare and Medicaid perhaps being the most visible in that these programs are publicly funded.

Scope of the problem

The Centers for Medicare and Medicaid Services (CMS) projects that total healthcare expenditures could reach over \$4.1 trillion dollars by the year 2016 and to \$4.3 trillion by 2017, comprising almost 20% of the Gross Domestic Product (GDP) of the United States.[1,2] Estimates of fraudulent billings to healthcare benefit programs, both public and private, constitute between 3% and 10% of healthcare expenditures.[1–3] Recent CMS estimates indicate that current healthcare expenditures are at \$2.4 trillion dollars and as mentioned above, are expected to increase to \$4.3 trillion by 2017.[1,2] If estimated fraud is between 3% and 10%, doing the math will reveal how lucrative and tempting healthcare fraud can be.

Current expenditure estimates at \$2.4 trillion at 3% fraud amounts to \$72 billion dollars lost to fraud; at 10% the amount lost to fraud is \$240 billion. If we examine the 2017 projection of \$4.3 trillion total expenditures, at 3% fraudulent dollars equal \$123 billion and at 10% equal \$410 billion.

Aside from the economic impact of healthcare fraud, it is necessary to examine the human impact. Victims of healthcare fraud are those who are exploited and used for profit by unscrupulous providers. As a result of certain fraud schemes, these victims are subjected to unnecessary surgeries, procedures, and treatments placing their safety and health at risk. The commission of healthcare fraud also involves the falsification of a patient's medical record in order to cover up the fraud. Inaccurate falsified medical records can be devastating for a patient seeking medical care from various providers and facilities. Fraudulent records can lead to inaccurate diagnoses, inappropriate treatments, and improper healthcare decisions by other providers as well as the patient.[4]

As has been discussed earlier in this text, the concept of trust between patient and physician is crucial to enhance the healing process. Healthcare fraudsters violate the confidence placed in them by taking advantage of the patient subjecting them to unnecessary procedures, and using the patient's personal information to continue filing false claims to the patient's insurers. When devising fraud schemes, healthcare fraudsters enjoy the advantage of having access to an immense range of options with which to devise simple to very complex fraud schemes to include:

- The entire population of patients;
- The entire range of potential medical conditions and treatments on which to base false claims;
- The ability to spread false claims among many health benefit programs simultaneously increasing proceeds and minimizing their chances of detection.[4]

Definitions

Prior to discussing the various statutes addressing healthcare fraud, prevalent fraud schemes, and investigative techniques certain definitions are in order. First a general definition of fraud will be examined followed by a more specific definition as it pertains to healthcare fraud.

General definition of fraud

Black's Law Dictionary defines fraud as:

> An *intentional* perversion of truth for the purpose of *inducing another* in reliance upon it to *part with some valuable thing* belonging to him or surrender a legal right. A *false presentation of a matter of fact*, whether by words or by conduct, by false or misleading allegations, or by concealment of that which should have been disclosed, *which deceives* and is intended to deceive another so he shall act upon it to his legal injury. Anything calculated to deceive.....or by suppression of truth.....[5]
>
> (Emphasis added by author)

Certain terms in the above definition have been highlighted to bring attention to certain elements of the crime of fraud. The same or similar terms will be found in the various statutes to be examined later in this chapter. Fraud is intentional, induces another (in our present context "another" would be the health benefit program/insurance company) to part with some valuable thing (money). Healthcare fraud is committed by a false presentation of a material fact (insurance claim form containing false information).

Definition of healthcare fraud

Cornell Law defines healthcare fraud as:

> A type of white collar crime that involves the filing of dishonest healthcare claims in order to turn a profit."[6]

The National Healthcare Anti-Fraud Association defines it as:

> ….an intentional deception or misrepresentation that the individual or entity makes knowing that the misrepresentation could result in some unauthorized benefit to the individual, or the entity or to some other party.[4]

Healthcare fraud relies heavily on one or both of two key components which are *misrepresentation* of material facts and *concealment* of material facts. The basic elements of a case of fraudulent misrepresentation include:

- A material false statement
- Knowledge of its falsity
- Reliance on the false statement by the victim
- Damages suffered by the victim[1]

Material fact is defined by *West's Encyclopedia of American Law* as:

> ….an occurrence, event, or information that is sufficiently significant to influence an individual into acting in a certain way, such as entering into a contract. In formal court procedures, a material fact is anything needed to prove one party's case, or tending to establish a point that is crucial to a person's position.[7]

Federal statutes relating to healthcare fraud

There are several federal statutes that relate to healthcare fraud. It should be noted that every state has statutes that deal with healthcare fraud as well. Healthcare fraud is almost always criminalized; however, the specific nature or degree of the criminal acts may vary from state to state.[4] A review of the 65 medical practice acts in the United States revealed that each state has certain language that prohibits the making of dishonest, fraudulent statements in the practice of medicine. Therefore, a healthcare fraudster may not only violate the criminal law but the administrative/regulatory law as well.

18 United States Code (USC) §24—Definitions Related to Federal Healthcare Offense[1]

1. As used in this title, the term "Federal health care offense" means a violation of, or a criminal conspiracy to violate—
   a. Section 669, 1035, 1347, or 1518 of this title or Section 1128B of the Social Security Act (42 U.S.C. 1320a–7b); or
   b. Section 287, 371, 664, 666, 1001, 1027, 1341, 1343, 1349, or 1954 of this title Section 301 of the Federal Food, Drug, and Cosmetic Act (21 U.S.C. 331), or Section 501 of the Employee Retirement Income Security Act of 1974 (29 U.S.C. 1131), or Section 411, 518, or 511 of the Employee Retirement Income Security Act of 1974,[1] if the violation or conspiracy relates to a healthcare benefit program.
2. As used in this title, the term "healthcare benefit program" means any public or private plan or contract, affecting commerce, under which any medical benefit, item, or service is provided to any individual, and includes any individual or entity who is providing a medical benefit, item, or service for which payment may be made under the plan or contract.

31 USC §3729—False Claims Act[1]

1. Liability for Certain Acts—
   a. In general—Subject to paragraph (2), any person who—
      i. Knowingly presents, or causes to be presented, a false or fraudulent claim for payment or approval;
      ii. Knowingly makes, uses, or causes to be made or used, a false record or statement material to a false or fraudulent claim.....
2. Definitions—For purposes of this section—
   a. The terms "knowing" and "knowingly"—
      i. Mean that a person, with respect to information—
         A. Has actual knowledge of the information;
         B. Acts in deliberate ignorance of the truth or falsity of the information; or
         C. Acts in reckless disregard of the truth or falsity of the information; and
      ii. Require no proof of specific intent to defraud;

b. The term "claim"—
   i. Means any request or demand, whether under a contract or otherwise, for money or property and whether or not the United States has title to the money or property, that—
      A. Is presented to an officer, employee, or agent of the United States.....

The False Claims Act is lengthy and involves other forms of fraud not involving health care per se. The pertinent portions are listed above.

18 USC §1347—Healthcare Fraud[1]

1. Whoever knowingly and willfully executes, or attempts to execute, a scheme or artifice—
   a. To defraud any healthcare benefit program; or
   b. To obtain, by means of false or fraudulent pretenses, representations, or promises, any of the money or property owned by, or under the custody or control of, any healthcare benefit program, in connection with the delivery of or payment for healthcare benefits, items, or services, shall be fined under this title or imprisoned not more than 10 years, or both. If the violation results in serious bodily injury (as defined in Section 1365 of this title), such person shall be fined under this title or imprisoned not more than 20 years, or both; and if the violation results in death, such person shall be fined under this title, or imprisoned for any term of years or for life, or both.
      i. With respect to violations of this section, a person need not have actual knowledge of this section or specific intent to commit a violation of this section.

18 USC §1035—False Statement Relating to Healthcare Matters[1]

1. Whoever, in any matter involving a healthcare benefit program, knowingly and willfully—
   a. Falsifies, conceals, or covers up by any trick, scheme, or device a material fact; or
   b. Makes any materially false, fictitious, or fraudulent statements or representations, or makes or uses any materially false writing or document knowing the same to contain any materially false, fictitious, or fraudulent statement or entry, in connection with the delivery of or payment for healthcare benefits, items, or services, shall be fined under this title or imprisoned not more than 5 years, or both.
2. As used in this section, the term "healthcare benefit program" has the meaning given such term in Section 24 (b) of this title.

18 USC §287—False, Fictitious or Fraudulent Claims[1]

Whoever makes or presents to any person or officer in the civil, military, or naval service of the United States, or to any department or agency thereof, any claim upon or against the United States, or any department or agency thereof, knowing such claim to be false, fictitious, or fraudulent, shall be imprisoned not more than 5 years and shall be subject to a fine in the amount provided in this title.

18 USC §1001—Statements or Entries Generally[1]

1. Except as otherwise provided in this section, whoever, in any matter within the jurisdiction of the executive, legislative, or judicial branch of the Government of the United States, knowingly and willfully—
   a. Falsifies, conceals, or covers up by any trick, scheme, or device a material fact;
   b. Makes any materially false, fictitious, or fraudulent statement or representation; or
   c. Makes or uses any false writing or document knowing the same to contain any materially false, fictitious, or fraudulent statement or entry, shall be fined under this title, imprisoned not more than 5 years or, if the offense involves international or domestic terrorism (as defined in Section 2331), imprisoned not more than 8 years, or both. If the matter relates to an offense under Chapter 109A, 109B, 110, or 117, or Section 1591, then the term of imprisonment imposed under this section shall be not more than 8 years.

18 USC §1031—Major Fraud Against the US[1]

1. Whoever knowingly executes, or attempts to execute, any scheme or artifice with the intent—
   a. To defraud the United States; or
   b. To obtain money or property by means of false or fraudulent pretenses, representations, or promises, in any grant, contract, subcontract, subsidy, loan, guarantee, insurance, or other form of Federal assistance, including through the Troubled Asset Relief Program, an economic stimulus, recovery or rescue plan provided by the Government, or the Government's purchase of any troubled asset as defined in the Emergency Economic Stabilization Act of 2008, or in any procurement of property or services as a prime contractor with the United States or as a subcontractor or supplier on a contract in which there is a prime contract with the United States, if the value of such grant, contract, subcontract, subsidy, loan, guarantee, insurance, or other form of Federal assistance, or any constituent part thereof, is $1,000,000 or more shall, subject to the applicability of subsection (c) of this

section, be fined not more than $1,000,000, or imprisoned not more than 10 years, or both.

42 USC §1320A-7b—Criminal Penalties for Acts Involving Federal Healthcare[1]

1. Making or causing to be made false statements or representations Whoever—
   a. Knowingly and willfully makes or causes to be made any false statement or representation of a material fact in any application for any benefit or payment under a Federal healthcare program (as defined in subsection (f) of this section),
   b. At any time knowingly and willfully makes or causes to be made any false statement or representation of a material fact for use in determining rights to such benefit or payment,
   c. Having knowledge of the occurrence of any event affecting
      i. His initial or continued right to any such benefit or payment, or
      ii. The initial or continued right to any such benefit or payment of any other individual in whose behalf he has applied for or is receiving such benefit or payment, conceals or fails to disclose such event with an intent fraudulently to secure such benefit or payment either in a greater amount or quantity than is due or when no such benefit or payment is authorized,
   d. Having made application to receive any such benefit or payment for the use and benefit of another and having received it, knowingly and willfully converts such benefit or payment or any part thereof to a use other than for the use and benefit of such other person,
   e. Presents or causes to be presented a claim for a physician's service for which payment may be made under a Federal healthcare program and knows that the individual who furnished the service was not licensed as a physician, or
   f. For a fee knowingly and willfully counsels or assists an individual to dispose of assets (including by any transfer in trust) in order for the individual to become eligible for medical assistance under a State plan under subchapter XIX of this chapter, if disposing of the assets results in the imposition of a period of ineligibility for such assistance under Section 1396p (c) of this title, shall
      i. In the case of such a statement, representation, concealment, failure, or conversion by any person in connection with the furnishing (by that person) of items or services for which payment is or may be made under the program, be guilty of a felony and upon conviction thereof fined not more than $25,000 or imprisoned for not more than 5 years or both....

This statute is also very lengthy and only certain parts of the statute are presented here. The statute should be thoroughly reviewed for other applicable violations and penalties.

Health Insurance Portability and Accountability Act of 1996

The Health Insurance Portability and Accountability Act (HIPAA) is perhaps one of the most comprehensive pieces of legislation that deals with healthcare fraud. HIPAA expanded the scope of healthcare fraud prevention in several ways. HIPAA authorized the first stable source of funding to combat healthcare fraud. HIPAA also extended the scope of the Anti-Kickback Statute to cover all federal healthcare programs and was the first legislation to regulate private health care and increased the government's power to prosecute healthcare fraud.[8] HIPAA makes it illegal for anyone to knowingly and willfully:

- Defraud any healthcare benefit program or to obtain by means of false representations any money or property of a healthcare benefit program;
- Make false or fictitious statements in any matter involving a healthcare benefit program;
- Embezzle, convert, or steal any funds, property, or assets of a healthcare benefit program; or
- Obstruct, delay, prevent, or mislead the investigation of federal healthcare offenses.[8]

Types of fraud schemes

Healthcare fraud schemes range from rather simple schemes to elaborate and complex with multiple providers and entities involved. A rather simple scheme may involve a provider sporadically billing for services that were never rendered. Complex schemes may involve the fraudulent billing of numerous insurance companies and involve multiple providers and entities conspiring to defraud. Physicians, other healthcare practitioners, mid-level practitioners, nursing homes, hospitals, insurance company employees, and others may all be involved in a scheme of widespread fraudulent activity. Such a complex enterprise may also involve several different schemes affecting many patients.

Several schemes have emerged as being the most common or prevalent.

- Billing for services not rendered
- Up-coding of services
- Up-coding of medical equipment and devices

- Substitute providers
- Unnecessary tests and/or services
- Unnecessary surgeries and procedures
- Unbundling
- Billing noncovered procedures as medically necessary
- Kickbacks[2,3,4,9]

Billing for services not rendered

This scheme involves the provider filing a claim to the insurer for payment of services that were not provided. For example, the provider files a claim for an office visit that never occurred or files a claim for tests or procedures that were not performed.[2,4,9]

An interesting anecdote illustrating this scheme is provided by Charles Piper in his article "10 Popular Health Care Provider Fraud Schemes." Alzheimer patients were sitting unsupervised in a small room inside a medical care facility watching a movie which had been played for them on many prior occasions. Each time the patients sat in front of the television watching it, the clinic submitted insurance claims for providing group therapy.[9]

Up-coding of services

Up-coding is a scheme whereby the provider files a claim using a procedure code for a higher cost service than the service that was actually provided. Examples of up-coding include:

- A routine follow-up office visit claimed as an initial comprehensive office visit
- Group therapy billed as individual therapy
- Thirty-minute sessions billed as one-hour sessions
- Removal of sutures billed as a surgical procedure[2,4]

Up-coding of medical equipment and devices

This scheme is very similar to up-coding of services except here the up-coding involves medical equipment and devices. In this instance, a provider files a claim for a more expensive piece of equipment or device, however, delivers to the patient a cheaper version. For example, a provider delivers to the patient a basic manually propelled wheelchair, then files a claim for a more expensive motorized wheelchair.[2,4]

Substitute providers/misrepresenting the provider of service

Private insurance companies as well as Medicare and Medicaid reimburse claims based on a number of factors, one being the level or status of the provider. The question to be asked is who provided the service? Insurance companies reimburse at different rates based on the level of the provider who performed the service. The reimbursement rate for physicians is higher than mid-level practitioners, nurses, medical assistants, etc. Healthcare fraudsters will often file the claim indicating that a physician performed the service when actually a physician assistant, nurse, or medical assistant performed the service.[3,9]

Unnecessary or excessive tests or services

This scheme is centered on filing claims for tests or services that are not necessary and are in excess of the patient's actual needs. This type of fraud is often seen in cases of excessive diagnostic studies. An example of unnecessary or excessive service may include numerous diagnostic tests to confirm a rather simple illness that one or two tests would easily confirm.[2,4]

Unnecessary surgeries and procedures

It is estimated that 7.5 million unnecessary surgeries and procedures occur each year in the United States and that 12,000 people die each year as a result.[3] One of several factors that help explain the pervasiveness of unnecessary surgeries is the trust factor. Patients place tremendous trust in their physician and if the physician recommends surgery, the patient is likely to agree.[3]

EXAMPLE

In June, 2002, a Chicago cardiologist was sentenced to 12-1/2 years in federal prison and was ordered to pay $16.5 million in fines and restitution after pleading guilty to performing 750 medically unnecessary heart catheterizations, along with unnecessary angioplasties and other tests as part of a 10-year fraud scheme. Three other physicians and a hospital administrator also pleaded guilty and received prison sentences for their part in the scheme, which resulted in the deaths of at least two patients. The physicians and hospital induced hundreds of homeless persons, substance abusers, and elderly men and women to feign symptoms and be admitted to the hospital for the unnecessary procedures. How? By offering them incentives such as food, cash, and cigarettes. "There were seven-hundred-fifty people who had needles stuck into their hearts purely for profit, not because they needed it," said one of the federal prosecutors.[4]

In order to "justify" the need for unnecessary or excessive services or surgeries, the patient's diagnosis must be falsified indicating a diagnosis of a more serious condition necessitating the procedures.[4] As stated above, this not only puts the patient at risk for potential complications, the fraudulent medical record may place the patient at risk when seeing other providers who are making medical care decisions based on inaccurate information.

Unbundling

Unbundling is the practice of filing separate claims for individual components of a procedure that should be billed together at a reduced cost, that is, billing each step of a procedure as if it was a separate procedure.[2,4]

> **EXAMPLE**
>
> The various components of knee replacement surgery should be bundled and the cost of the procedure should be a certain dollar figure for the entire procedure. When unbundled, each component of the knee surgery is billed separately. The surgeon's fee, the anesthesiologist's fee, the surgical assistants' fees, the cost of blood replacement, hardware (the artificial knee itself), medications administered in recovery, physical therapy, etc., are all billed as if separate from the overall procedure itself. This form of unbundling drastically inflates the cost of the overall procedure.

Misrepresenting noncovered treatments as medically necessary

There are many procedures that are not covered by insurance or Medicare or Medicaid such as cosmetic procedures. Often a provider will file a claim indicating that the procedure was medically necessary when in fact the procedure was elective. For example, a patient has a cosmetic procedure on their nose; however, the provider bills the insurer for a deviated septum repair.[4]

Kickbacks

A healthcare provider engages in an illegal kickback scheme when he/she offers, solicits, pays, or accepts money or something of value in exchange for the referral of a patient for healthcare services. Example: A physician and laboratory owner engage in an illegal kickback scheme when the laboratory owner pays the physician $50.00 for each patient the physician sends to the laboratory for testing. Kickbacks are often paid in cash, however, payment may take the form of vacations, jewelry, or other valuable items.[2] When investigating this type of scheme, it is imperative to establish the quid pro quo, or "this for that."[9]

Investigation

The investigation of healthcare fraud will likely involve the efforts of various agencies in that access to certain information and data may be limited to the medical board investigator as may be dictated by federal and state law. Medical board subpoenas may have limited authority when dealing with specific agencies. Many healthcare fraud investigations are often conducted in the criminal arena and at times criminal investigations and administrative investigations encounter difficulties in the sharing of information, data, and patient charts.

Agencies commonly involved in healthcare fraud investigations include:

- US Department of Health and Human Services, Office of Inspector General
  - This federal agency administers the federal Medicare and Medicaid programs.
- Federal Bureau of Investigation
  - The FBI provides national guidance and assistance in support of healthcare fraud investigations. The FBI works closely with other federal, state, local agencies, the Centers for Medicare and Medicaid Services, and privately sponsored programs in the suppression of healthcare fraud.[2]
- State Medicaid Fraud Control Units (MFCU)
  - MFCUs are single identifiable entities of state government and are certified by the U.S. Department of Health and Human Services. They conduct a statewide program for the investigation and prosecution of healthcare providers that defraud the Medicaid program. The majority of MFCUs are housed in the state office of the attorney general. The MFCUs of six states are housed in other state agencies. See appendix 24 for a list of the 49 MFCUs and contact information. North Dakota does not have an MFCU. The units are required to be staffed with attorneys, specialized investigators, and auditors skilled at analyzing benefit claims data and medical records, and analysts skilled in research. MFCUs are also required to be separate and distinct from the state agency that administers the Medicaid program.[10]
- State Office of the Insurance Commissioner
  - State departments of insurance are staffed with investigators skilled in the investigation of insurance fraud to include healthcare fraud. Several of the departments of insurance have investigators with criminal investigative authority. All 50 states and the District of Columbia have a department of insurance. See appendix 25 for a list of departments of insurance and contact information.[11]

- State agency that administers the Medicaid program (not MFCUs)
  - The state agency that administers the Medicaid program typically has a Program Integrity Unit. This unit usually handles contract oversight, recipient investigations, and clinical teams. The unit also handles complaint/case intake and triages cases to determine if the case should be referred to the MFCU. The program integrity unit also maintains claim and payment data.
- State Regulatory Boards
  - Many healthcare professions are regulated by a specific licensing board and investigators for these boards can be of significant assistance when other healthcare providers are identified in the fraud scheme.
- Private insurance companies often have their own internal investigative unit and are excellent sources of information and assistance.

Healthcare fraud investigations are often conducted using a multiagency approach combining the knowledge and expertise of various agencies. As healthcare fraud investigations can be quite complex, tedious, and tax an agency's time and resources, a cooperative coordinated effort will enhance the quality of the investigation and help ensure that the needs of all involved agencies are met.

Complainant interview

Of course, the complainant's background, the nature of the allegations, schemes used, and other factors will impact the direction of the interview. However, the interview should address certain items of information. Following is a brief outline of topics to be covered with the complainant:

- Obtain complete contact information for all complainants
- What is the complainant's relationship to the suspect provider?
  - Current or former employee
  - Patient
  - Other practitioner
- Identify the provider allegedly committing the fraud
- Attempt to determine what scheme(s) the provider is using
  - How is the fraud being perpetrated?
- Identify other witnesses that may have knowledge of the scheme
- Identify the patients whose claims are being used to defraud the program
- Identify what benefit programs are being defrauded
  - Medicare (federal)
  - Medicaid (state and federal)
  - Private insurance program

- Identify other providers that may be involved in the scheme
  - Chiropractors
  - Psychologists
  - Nurses
  - Other physicians
  - Physician Assistants (PAs)
  - Advanced Practice Registered Nurses (APRNs)
- Identify other entities that may be involved
  - Nursing homes
  - Physical therapy/rehab facilities
  - Imaging facilities
  - Other medical specialty groups
- Attempt to identify bank accounts being used

Witness interviews

When interviewing witnesses much of the above information sought from the complainant will also be asked of witnesses. If witnesses include employees of the suspect provider, it is suggested that they be interviewed in a location away from the clinic. In addition to the above information, the following information should be obtained:

- Obtain detailed contact information for all witnesses.
- Confirm what scheme(s) the provider is using.
  - How is the scheme carried out and by whom?
- Identify the patients whose claims are fraudulent.
  - These records will be the focus of search warrants and/or subpoenas.
- Confirm the information provided by the complainant.
- Probe the witness for additional information such as additional witnesses, other involved providers/entities, etc.
- What were the witnesses' observations of fraudulent activity?
  - Conversations overheard.
  - Observations of overt chart falsification or alteration.
- Was the witness coerced into making fraudulent entries, billings, etc.?
  - By whom?
  - How was the witness coerced? What threats were made?

Benefit program data

When the specific patients whose claims have been allegedly defrauded are identified, claim information submitted by the provider(s) to the benefit program(s) should be obtained. A period of time to be examined should be determined; one year, two years, etc. Depending on the number of patient records and claim information to be obtained, the investigation could become overwhelming.

With regard to Medicaid investigations, the state agency that administers the Medicaid program should be contacted. The program integrity unit or a similarly commissioned office will be a good place to start when seeking claim data. The agency will also likely have in-house legal counsel that may be of assistance. With regard to private insurance companies a good starting point will be with the company's claims manager. This individual should be able to route the investigator to the appropriate personnel to assist. Private insurance companies often have in-house legal counsel as well as in-house investigators that may be able to assist.

Health insurance claim forms will vary from program to program, however, they all are similar and require an abundance of information (see sample claim form, Appendix 26). The claim form will contain the date(s) of service, place of service, type of service, procedure/services/or supplies provided, diagnosis, charges, and rendering provider. When the provider indicates what procedure/service/or supplies were provided to the patient, a CPT code will be used. CPT stands for *Current Procedural Terminology*. The CPT code set is maintained by the AMA. A CPT code is a numeric figure that describes the specific procedure/service provided. The term *up-coding* describes a claim using a CPT code that pays a higher reimbursement than the code actually describing the procedure/service. One might also encounter HCPCS codes in conjunction with CPT codes. HCPCS stands for *Healthcare Common Procedure Coding System* and is also maintained by the AMA. HCPCS codes are used for services, products, and supplies not found in the CPT codes.

Claim and payment documents will likely be considered evidence therefore they should be handled and secured accordingly. Make working copies for analysis purposes, mark-ups, etc. An analysis of the claim documents should note:

- Patient identifying data
- Diagnosis or nature of illness or injury
- Dates of service
- CPT codes
- Charges
- Rendering provider
- Any unusual or questionable treatments and coding used
- Unusual patterns of dates of service (1, 2, 3 office visits per week) compared to diagnosis

EXAMPLE

Asthma/respiratory treatments may be more frequent than treatments for other maladies. Dialysis treatments may also be more frequent given the nature of the patient's disease. It would appear suspicious or unusual for a patient to be seen two to three times per week for treatment of strep throat when typically antibiotics are prescribed and perhaps a follow-up office visit in a week or two.

Another interesting anecdote provided by Charles Piper in his article "10 Popular Health Care Provider Fraud Schemes" illustrates this scheme. An allergy specialist prescribed injections for several patients. Upon his review of the patient charts, Piper found that the insurance claim forms indicated that many patients were treated at the clinic four to five days per week (Monday–Friday). These patients were interviewed and they stated that they only received injections twice per week and they only went to the clinic once per month. The patients stated that the staff at the clinic gave them a handful of syringes pre-loaded with medication and instructed them to self-administer the injections at home. Typically home self-injections are not considered reimbursable. The claim forms further indicated that the injections were being given at the clinic. Piper asked the physician how she determined the day of the week the patient self-injected when she prepared the claim form and the physician stated that she just guessed. Interestingly, she always guessed Monday through Friday when the clinic was open and not weekends or holidays when the clinic was closed.[9]

When examining the insurance claim forms, be sure to compare the services rendered to the services noted on the superbills. The superbill is a comprehensive sheet itemizing dozens of common services, to include office visits, office procedures, skin procedures, laboratory, vaccines, medications, and immunizations and their corresponding CPT and HCPCS codes. Medical offices routinely use a form of the superbill when filing insurance claims. Ideally the insurance claim form and the superbill should match and any discrepancies should be further investigated. See appendix 27 for a sample superbill.

As stated earlier, certain office visits and procedures are reimbursed at higher rates. For example, a comprehensive new patient office visit will be reimbursed higher than minimal established patient office visit. The comprehensive new patient visit will take more of the physician's time in terms of taking a medical history, physical examination, and lab work. Therefore, if the physician is consistently billing for comprehensive new patient visits the patients' medical chart should be thoroughly reviewed to determine if the patients are actually new patients or established patients. The procedures and services noted in the chart should also be compared to the superbills and claim forms.

Patient interviews

Interviews with patients may provide the most useful information when questioning dates of service, procedures performed, and other details of office visits. Patient interviews should be conducted away from the provider's clinic. It is also important, as with any witness, to evaluate the patient's competency and credibility especially as it pertains to elderly patients. It is recommended to conduct patient interviews prior to obtaining patient records. Based on the results of the interviews and information obtained, the investigator will then be able to better identify the specific patient charts needed. As with any interview, certain questions will spawn additional questions, however, a basic patient interview outline follows:

- Obtain complete contact information for all patients interviewed.
- What was the reason for the initial visit to the provider (subjective complaint)?
  - Describe initial visit
  - Who did patient see?
    - Nurse, physician assistant (PA), medical assistant (MA)
  - What specifically did that person do?
    - Obtain the patient's medical history, check vital signs, etc.
- Who actually examined and diagnosed the patient's problem?
  - Physician, PA, APRN
  - Describe the encounter with the diagnosing provider.
  - What was discussed, what questions were asked by the provider and what questions were asked by patient?
- Was a physical examination performed?
  - Who performed the examination?
  - Describe the examination.
  - Were any diagnostic tests performed?
    - X-rays or other imaging
    - Blood tests or other lab tests
- Were any procedures performed during any visits?
  - Minor surgical procedures
  - Dermatological procedures
  - Cosmetic procedures billed as therapeutic procedures
- Who performed the procedure(s)?
  - Physician, PA, APRN, RN
- Was the patient actually seen by the physician?
- Describe initial encounter with physician
  - Discussion had with the physician
  - What questions were asked by the physician and what questions were asked by patient?
  - Did the physician perform a physical examination?
    - Describe
  - Did the physician perform or order any diagnostic testing?
    - Describe

- Did the physician render a diagnosis?
  - What was the diagnosis?
  - What treatment was recommended?
  - What medications were prescribed?
    - Directions for use
- Were follow-up visits recommended?
  - For when?
  - Were multiple follow-up visits recommended?
  - How often and for how long?
- Review the claims data with the patient.
  - Did the patient see the provider on each of the dates enumerated in the data?
  - Does the patient have receipts, credit card statements, cancelled checks, etc. indicating the dates they visited the provider?
  - Does the diagnosis in the claims data match the diagnosis told to the patient?
  - Were treatments self-administered at home and billed as office visits?
  - Did anyone refer the patient to this provider?
    - Who?
    - Check for any relationship between the referrer and provider
  - Were any medical devices prescribed?
    - Walker, wheelchair, etc.
    - Examine what was prescribed v. what was billed for.
  - Match who performed any surgical procedures against what was billed on the claim; if mid-level performed the procedure, was it billed as the MD performing the procedure?
  - Match the procedure that as actually performed v. what procedure was billed for
    - 1-2 onabotulinumtoxinA injections v. billing for multiple injections
    - Were routine office visits billed as comprehensive office visits?
    - Were diagnostic images prescribed for unaffected areas of the body?
  - Complaint of injured wrist and x-rays taken of entire body
    - Look for signs of other schemes being used and review with the patient.
    - Does the information provided by the patient match the CPT codes on the claim?
- Once the patient charts are obtained and reviewed, re-interviews with some patients may be necessary to clarify certain information.

Obtain patient charts

After conducting the patient interviews, the investigator should be able to make a clearer determination as to which patient charts need to be obtained. Given that the investigation may be conducted jointly with other agencies, careful planning should be undertaken prior to executing search warrants and subpoenas. You may have only one opportunity to obtain the patient charts. If the charts are to be seized via search warrant by a partner agency, be sure to serve a subpoena on the subject at the same time calling for the same charts. This will enable you to get copies of the seized originals for your administrative board case. Also consider seizing/subpoenaing sign-in logs and appointment logs when patient office visits are questioned.

Review patient charts

The patient charts should be considered evidence and should be handled and secured accordingly. It is highly recommended that a working copy be made in case the investigator needs to make notations or highlight discrepancies that may be uncovered. The charts should be reviewed and matched to the claims data. The CPT codes should be compared to the actual services provided and any discrepancies should be well documented.

Healthcare fraud cases tend to create paper overload and managing "the paper" can be a daunting task. The investigation may involve the claim forms and patient charts for multiple patients and may encompass hundreds of office visits, procedures, and supplies. It is recommended that a separate file folder be created for each patient. Each patient folder should be subdivided with a folder to maintain claim data and a folder to maintain the medical chart. Additional separate folders may be created for additional data that may be pertinent to the specific patient, for example, investigative work product, etc. For example, if there is evidence of fraud as it pertains to patient John Doe, a file should be created to contain copies of the spreadsheet of Mr. Doe's data, copies of claims submitted to Mr. Doe's insurance company or Medicaid, copies of payment data from Mr. Doe's insurance company or Medicaid, a copy of Mr. Doe's patient record obtained from the subject physician and any other documentation pertaining to Mr. Doe that is pertinent.

It may also be helpful to develop a spreadsheet of some form so as to sort and organize the review findings (Appendix 28). This will help keep the data organized and essentially maintains claim data, patient chart information, procedure information, provider information, and coding data in a readily accessible and organized format. Such a spreadsheet will also help when presenting the case to a prosecutor and/or the board as well as during the suspect provider interview.

Interview of suspect provider

Careful planning is encouraged and essential. As with the patient charts, you may only have one chance to conduct the interview. Utilizing the individual patient files as described above will enable the investigator and subject physician to more accurately and efficiently discuss the information developed during the investigation in that all pertinent information pertaining to each patient is in one place and appropriately organized. After a thorough discussion of matters concerning patient Doe, the investigator can move to the next patient, so on and so forth. This process will enable the respondent to more accurately respond to the allegations and will also enable the board to better understand and follow the case when presented. The case would be much more difficult to follow if the respondent and the board were presented with dozens of alleged false claims on multiple patients, with insurance and Medicaid payment information on the same patients, and dozens of medical charts. Such a presentation could be overwhelming in that there is little to no organization to the data to clearly reveal the discrepancies. One of the many aspects of the investigator's job is to organize the information and evidence in such a way that is clear and accurate.

As discussed earlier, healthcare fraud investigations often involve more than one agency. If the interview will involve investigators from multiple agencies, a lead investigator should be agreed upon to lead and conduct the interview. Too many investigators asking questions can make for a disorganized and confusing interview and specific areas of questioning may be overlooked and valuable information lost. Other investigators will be free to closely listen to the provider's responses and take notes. When the lead interviewer is finished, other investigators should be allowed to ask additional questions as necessary in an orderly fashion.

The investigative team should meet and prepare an interview outline to ensure that all pertinent topics and items are thoroughly covered and that specific information needed by each agency represented is addressed. Listen carefully for discrepancies in the suspect's explanations and thoroughly document them. It would be advisable to prepare a detailed memorandum of interview to include the questions asked/topics covered and subject's responses highlighting discrepancies in the subject's explanations as soon as possible to avoid relying on memory and notes resulting in the loss of potentially important details.

References

1. Association of Certified Fraud Examiners, Inc. (ACFE). 2012. Fraud Examiners Manual. Training manual utilized for ACFE certification.
2. Federal Bureau of Investigation. 2011. Financial Crimes Report. Accessed June 15, 2015. https://www.fbi.gov/stats-services/publications/financial-crimes-report-2010-2011

3. Payne, B. K., Ed. *White-Collar Crime: A Text/Reader.* Los Angeles: Sage Publications, Inc., 2012.
4. National Healthcare Anti-Fraud Association. 2012. The Challenge of Health Care Fraud. Accessed March 5, 2015. http://www.nhcaa.org/resources/health-care-anti-fraud-resources/the-challenge-of-health-care-fraud.aspx
5. Law Dictionary. Black's Law Dictionary Free Online Legal Dictionary, 2nd edition. Accessed March 2, 2014. http://www.thelawdictionary.org
6. Legal Information Institute, Cornell Law. 2014. Healthcare Fraud: An Overview. Accessed March 5, 2015. http://www.law.cornell.edu/wex/healthcare_fraud
7. West's Encyclopedia of American Law, 2nd edition. 2008. Accessed March 7, 2015. http://legal-dictionary.thefreedictionary.com/material
8. Blank, S., J. Kaspirin, and A. White. 2009. Health Care Fraud. *American Criminal Law Review* 46:701–759.
9. Piper, C., CFE, CRT. 10 Popular Health Care Fraud Schemes. *Fraud Magazine,* January/February 2013. Accessed January 5, 2015. http://www.fraud-magazine.com/article.aspx?id=4294976280
10. National Association of Medicaid Fraud Control Units. 2014. Medicaid Fraud Control Units. Accessed January 6, 2015. http://www.namfcu/net/about-us/about-mfcu
11. National Association of Insurance Commissioners. 2014. Membership List. Accessed January 6, 2015. http://www.naic.org.

chapter thirteen

Other investigative concerns

Thus far, five primary investigative topics have been addressed. There are, however, other investigative matters facing state medical boards that require some discussion to include:

- Criminal convictions
- Hospital adverse actions
- Disciplinary actions taken by another jurisdiction (another state licensing board, etc.)
- Malpractice settlements/judgments
- Fraud when applying for licensure

It should be noted that an allegation of a violation of any law, rule, or regulation will constitute an investigative concern; however, those discussed in this chapter are perhaps the most common aside from the five primary areas discussed in previous chapters.

Criminal convictions

It is very common for state medical boards to have the authority to sanction a licensee based on evidence of a felony criminal conviction and/or crimes of moral turpitude. Physicians do commit crimes and are often prosecuted. Offenses range from rather benign misdemeanors to egregious felonies. In many states, physicians have a duty to report criminal convictions to their licensing board. When considering a case of this nature, the board is not required to prove the underlying facts. In other words, if the criminal conviction involves vehicular homicide/DUI, the underlying facts of the case have already been investigated by local authorities and the case has been adjudicated by the court. The licensing board is not required to "re-prove" the facts of the case. The board is not necessarily disciplining the physician for committing vehicular homicide; the board is disciplining the physician based on the felony conviction of vehicular homicide.

The board's burden of proof is to prove that a felony conviction was rendered. To meet this burden of proof, the investigation basically consists of obtaining a certified copy of the pertinent records from the court demonstrating that a felony conviction was rendered. The specific court documents used for this purpose are usually the indictment or criminal information, the documented plea or jury verdict, and the judgment or sentencing document. These documents may be referred to by other terminology in various jurisdictions, but essentially what is needed is the charging document formally charging the physician with the specific offense(s), the physician's plea demonstrating responsibility for the offense(s) or the jury's guilty verdict, and the sentence handed down by the court. There are instances whereby other documents from the court may be necessary or beneficial to the board's case such as negotiated plea agreements, documented results of court mandated examinations, special conditions of probation, etc.

It is essential that these documents be properly certified by the clerk of court. As stated earlier, certification of the documents demonstrates that the copies of the documents are authentic and accurate copies of the originals. If the court records are not properly certified by the clerk, they will likely be challenged by the physician or his/her attorney when the board attempts to enter them into evidence. Proper certification will overcome this defense. When communicating with the court clerk's office, simply inform them that the records being requested should be certified and they will oblige. Most court clerk offices will require a written request stating specifically the documents requested. In this written request, be sure to emphasize that the documents must be certified.

Hospital adverse actions

Hospitals grant staff privileges to physicians that work for the hospital and to physicians who admit patients to the hospital. Physicians may have privileges at several hospitals, especially in a large urban setting. Like physicians, hospitals are regulated by their own regulatory body in their specific state and are held to certain standards as well. To comply with regulations and to maintain a high standard of service and care, hospitals are typically governed by by-laws. By-laws are rules and regulations promulgated by an organization, in this case the hospital, to regulate itself. Physicians granted privileges by the hospital must abide by the hospital's by-laws.

If a hospital-privileged physician is suspected of having violated the by-laws, the hospital will initiate an internal investigation. The nature of the investigation will be guided by the nature of the allegations. If the physician is suspected of professional boundary infractions, the investigation will likely involve interviews with victims of the physician's behavior; allegations of disruptive behavior will include interviews with staff and subordinates subjected to the disruptive behavior. Cases involving allegations of substandard care will usually involve a very close review of the treatment records of the affected patients with regard to the physician's

SOC. This may include patient selection for certain surgical procedures, surgical technique, decision-making, and overall care and treatment decisions.

To accomplish such a review, hospitals will often have the treatment records reviewed by a physician in the same or similar specialty of the subject physician. This is often referred to as "peer review." It should be noted that internal hospital peer reviews are protected, to an extent, under federal law.[1] Congress passed the Health Care Quality Improvement Act in 1986 establishing federal guidelines for medical peer review.[2] The law provides immunity for peer review participants under certain circumstances, however, it does not protect peer review documents from disclosure in litigation.[2] A total of 49 states (New Jersey excepted) and the District of Columbia have enacted statutes providing varying degrees of protection of the disclosure of peer review information.[2] Knowledge of the particular statutes in your state will be important as the investigation ensues.

Hospital by-laws provide for a certain measure of due process to include a hearing process. Based on the evidence, the hospital may subsequently enter an action against the privileges of the subject physician. Such action is commonly referred to as an "adverse action." Adverse action may include:

- Revocation of privileges (removal from hospital staff)
- Suspension of privileges subject to certain terms and conditions
- Probation
- Practice restrictions
- Remediation

If the hospital takes an adverse action against the subject physician, such action will likely be reported to the National Practitioner Data Bank (NPDB).[3]

The NPDB was established by Congress in 1987 as part of the Medicare and Medicaid Patient and Program Act. The NPDB is a federal databank that serves as a repository of information about healthcare providers in the United States and is administered by the U.S. Department of Health and Human Services. Certain state medical board actions are also required to be reported to the NPDB and state medical boards have authorized access to query healthcare providers as to reported actions by other entities.

Investigations of this sort usually originate via a report to the board from a hospital that has taken a reportable adverse action against a physician. Some states may have a statute mandating the physician to report an adverse action to the board as well. Usually a good place to start the investigation is making contact with the hospital's chief executive officer (CEO) and scheduling a meeting to discuss the case. The investigator may be referred to the hospital's legal counsel. A copy of the hospital's internal investigation report, witness statements, complainant/victim statements, staff reports, patient complaints, drug screens (if impairment indicated), and any other material contained in the investigative file should be requested. This material is usually not protected by the peer review privilege. Note that some hospitals are less giving than others meaning that some hospitals will more closely screen what is provided to the board than others. If the adverse action was based on patient care issues, a peer review will likely have been conducted and this will fall under the confidentiality privilege. If such is the case, the board investigator should request the names of the patients whose care was questioned. If the hospital will not release the names, they may be willing to provide redacted copies of the patient charts. If the patient charts can be obtained, the board can then seek its own peer review. Again, what information hospitals will provide will vary widely from hospital to hospital.

All witnesses and other key individuals identified in the hospital's internal investigation should be interviewed. It is important to ensure that their accounts are consistent with what was given in the hospital's investigation. The interview also provides an opportunity for the investigator to evaluate the witness and their testimony in terms of competency and credibility. It is also important that the witnesses understand the nature of the board's investigation and that their testimony may be needed at a hearing. Witnesses may not immediately differentiate the board's investigation from the hospital's investigation. It should be made clear to the witness that the board's investigation is entirely separate from the hospital's investigation.

When the investigation is complete, the respondent should be given an opportunity to provide his/her version of the events under scrutiny and provide a statement. The investigator will likely be referred to the physician's attorney which in many cases is a good thing. Most attorneys, from my experience, are fairly prompt in providing the requested information and most work with the board in a professional collegial manner. Most, if not all, of the information needed will likely be possessed by the respondent's attorney. While certified documents from the hospital would be considered the "best" evidence, copies provided by the respondent's attorney will be extremely helpful. Witnesses, patients, and other participants in the hospital's investigation may be identified. If so, the patient charts can then be subpoenaed and witnesses interviewed.

Disciplinary actions taken by another jurisdiction

Many physicians across the country maintain licenses in multiple states. This is common in cities and towns near state borders where the physician operates clinics in both states. Multiple licensure is extremely common with the advent of teleradiology. Teleradiology is the practice of reading and interpreting radiographic images via technology. For example, via technology, an image (x-ray, MRI, etc.) taken in Georgia for a Georgia patient can be read and interpreted by a radiologist in California. Most, if not all, states require the radiologist to be licensed in the state where the patient is. In this scenario, the California radiologist will have to be licensed in Georgia, therefore, it is not uncommon for diagnostic radiologists to hold licensure in many states.

Most, if not all, state medical boards have the authority to take disciplinary action against a licensee if that licensee has been disciplined by another state board. For example, if a physician who is licensed in Georgia, Alabama, and Tennessee receives a disciplinary action from the Tennessee board, the Georgia and Alabama boards would be authorized to take action based on the Tennessee action. The caveat is that the alleged violations in Tennessee would have to be considered violations in Georgia and Alabama had the conduct taken place in those states. For example, if the above-described physician is disciplined by the Tennessee board for sexual boundary violations with a patient then said conduct, had it occurred in Georgia or Alabama, would have to be in violation of Georgia and Alabama laws/rules as well.

In cases such as these, it would not be necessary for the other states to prove the underlying facts of the original case that resulted in the initial disciplinary action. Using the above example, the Georgia and Alabama boards would not have to prove the underlying facts of the Tennessee case. Georgia and Alabama would only have to prove that the Tennessee board took the action. This is commonly achieved by obtaining a certified copy of the documentation of the initial state's action. It varies from state to state as to the names of such documents but one would want to obtain the charging document setting out the allegations and the board's final order of discipline. Many cases are settled prior to hearing and these documents, too, vary by name. Many are referred to as consent agreements or consent orders wherein the licensee consents (agrees) to certain sanctions and the board consents (agrees) to settle the matter and take no further action. A certified copy of this document will also be necessary.

The investigative files of most state medical boards are considered, by law, confidential and not available for release. Many state boards do have authority to release their investigative files to other state boards and to law enforcement. Depending on the specific nature of the case, the investigative file may need to be requested.

A statement from the physician should be requested allowing for an opportunity to respond to the initial state's action. The lack of a statement should not be fatal to your case in that all that is required to be proven is the disciplinary action itself.

Settlements and judgments of malpractice suits

Most state medical boards, via the law or rules, require licensees to report settlements or judgments of malpractice lawsuits. Reports of judgments and settlements also derive from the malpractice carrier and the NPDB, depending on the reporting requirements in each state. It is typically unnecessary for the board to prove the underlying facts of the suit in that such has already been accomplished in the court via settlement between the parties or a judgment ruling by a jury or judge. Many suits are brought based on weak evidence and some are purely frivolous in nature. Often, malpractice insurance carriers may settle such a claim for a relatively small amount of money to alleviate the nuisance and cost of litigating the claim. The mere judgment or settlement of a malpractice claim does not in and of itself prove or demonstrate that the physician practiced below the SOC in the instant case.

The state board's objective in such cases is to attempt to determine if the SOC was breached. To accomplish this, the board will require a certified copy of the patient's medical record(s). When a malpractice lawsuit is filed with the court, the complaint of malpractice is often required to be accompanied by an affidavit from an expert physician who opines that the defendant physician breached the SOC and stating how so. The expert's affidavit should identify the medical records they reviewed and the various entities from which the medical records were obtained. Often the reporting of settlements and judgments contain a copy of the malpractice complaint and accompanying expert affidavit. A thorough review of the complaint and affidavit will provide the nature of the allegations of substandard care and the alleged adverse consequences related thereto.

It would not be uncommon for the patient to have had more than one hospital admission, perhaps at different hospitals; seen by a number of physicians to include specialists, etc. As related to the suit, the patient may also have been seen on multiple occasions at various physicians' private clinic. Certified copies of all identified medical records should be obtained. The subject physician should then be given an opportunity to respond to the allegations of the suit and provide his/her defense as to the care rendered and his/her decision-making process as to diagnosis and treatment.

Upon completion of the investigation, the board may elect to refer the case for an independent peer review discussed in Chapter 8. If the peer review expert opines that the treatment fell below the SOC, the board will then have grounds to move forward with some form of action, whether it is formal public discipline, practice restrictions, or remediation.

Fraud when applying for licensure

When seeking to obtain a medical license, one must make application to the state medical board. (A sample medical licensing application is shown in Appendix 29. Note: The application shown in Appendix 29 is the initial application. It does not include reference forms, malpractice questionnaire, certificate of postgraduate training, NPDB query, or official license verifications from other states.)

Medical board licensing applications require a plethora of information to include:

- Curriculum vitae/resume
- Official medical school transcripts
- Official licensing examination score transcript
- Certificate of postgraduate training to include any probationary status imposed, disciplinary actions, or investigations
- NPDB query results
- Official license verification from all other states in which licensed
- Official military discharge information
- References from licensed physicians
- List of all hospital privileges and status
- Disclosure of all malpractice suits in which named a defendant and result of said suits
- Additional information will be required from foreign-trained physicians

Most of the above items are primary source verified in that the information is required to be submitted to the board directly from the source. For example, medical school transcripts must come directly from the school. These are items that would be extremely difficult for an applicant to alter.

The application will also ask questions regarding the following:

- All treatments for physical, psychiatric, or substance abuse disorders that could impair or place limitations on the ability to practice safely; court ordered treatments or hospitalizations
- All arrests, indictments, or convictions of criminal statutes to include DUI
- Denial of the privilege of taking an examination given by any licensing board or agency
- Prior public or private disciplinary actions or refusal to renew a license by another board or agency
- All surrenders of a medical license or Drug Enforcement Administration (DEA) registration
- Denial of a DEA registration or issued a restricted DEA registration
- All malpractice suits, arbitrations, etc. in which named as a party or defendant
- Hospital staff resignations or adverse actions

- Denial of membership or sanctions by a medical association
- Is the applicant currently the subject of any investigation by any licensing board or agency?
- Applications pending before other licensing boards
- Any Medicaid/Medicare restrictions

As one might see, the sensitive information sought in a medical licensing application may tempt some to either be less than forthcoming or to not disclose the information at all. Falsifying an application is considered unprofessional conduct and may result in a license being denied outright. If the nondisclosure is discovered after the license has been issued, the board may pursue disciplinary action to include revocation. When nondisclosures of this nature are determined, investigation will ensue.

Investigation will follow a course dictated by the specific nondisclosure. For example, if it is discovered that the applicant failed to disclose a criminal conviction, the investigation will seek to confirm that a conviction was entered, for what charges, in what jurisdiction, and the judgment/sentence. The applicant may have a significant history of DUI charges which may indicate a pattern of substance use/abuse. Knowledge of this history will be extremely important to the board when deciding whether or not to issue a license. Based on multiple DUIs, the board may see fit to require the applicant to undergo an evaluation for substance abuse prior to making a decision on granting the license. Many applications contain language in the affidavit section authorizing the board to obtain criminal history information. Many states require the applicant to submit criminal history information as part of the initial application.

If it is discovered that the applicant failed to disclose a hospital adverse action, the investigation should follow the course outlined earlier in the chapter. Given that hospital adverse actions often involve substandard care, the licensing board would need to be cognizant of such information prior to issuing a license. Based on the nature of the adverse action, the applicant may be in need of remediation or perhaps restriction from a specific procedure.

If the applicant fails to disclose licensure in another state or fails to disclose a disciplinary action in another state, a query of the NPDB will help to confirm or refute such in that all public actions are reported to the NPDB by the state medical boards. Malpractice settlements and judgments are also reported to the NPDB by the professional malpractice insurance carriers.

Instances of nondisclosure of medical treatments present a different investigative approach. If the board receives information indicating that the applicant failed to disclose a prior medical or psychiatric treatment, often the most effective approach is to confront the physician/applicant with the information. If the applicant admits to having received prior treatment, HIPAA compliant releases for records should be obtained and subsequently tendered to the treatment facilities. The source of the information provided to the board alleging prior treatment should, of course, be thoroughly interviewed and any leads developed followed up. A less than forthcoming licensee may require the investigator to make contact with officials from the licensee's residency training program, medical school, etc. in an effort to obtain information regarding possible treatments.

A final note with regard to investigations of a fraudulent application; be sure to obtain and secure the original application. The original application will be considered evidence. As with any documentary evidence, do not alter it in any way. Properly store and secure the original and make a copy for work product if necessary.

References

1. 42 U.S.C.§11101-11152. Accessed April 30, 2014. http://uscode.regstoday.com/42USC_CHAPTER117.aspx
2. Modak-Truran, A. 2008. Case law: A fifty state survey of the medical peer review privilege. *Pro Te: Solutio* 1(4): 14–17.
3. U. S. Department of Health and Human Services. 2014. The National Practitioner Databank. Accessed April 30, 2014. http://www.npdb.hrsa.gov/topNavigation/aboutUS.jsp

chapter fourteen

Investigating the unlicensed practice of medicine and complementary and alternative medicine

Consider the following account of the tragic death of Maria Rodriguez:

> One morning, Alexa Garcia drove her mother Maria to a local tile supply store for a "cosmetic procedure." Maria was going to see Gomez Morales (Morales) and his wife Antonella Morales-Perez, ("Perez") both from Colombia, for buttock enhancement injections. Prior to the buttock enhancement procedure, Maria received onabotulinumtoxinA injections in her face and noticed no side-effects, so she scheduled the procedure for buttock enhancement.
>
> Maria arrived with her daughter and was shown to a back room to prepare for the procedure. Morales and Perez first injected her with a local anesthetic, and then began to inject a "gel like" substance into Maria's buttocks. After the first of several injections, Alexa became squeamish and told Maria, Morales, and Perez that she would return in four hours to pick up Maria. Upon leaving, Alexa said, "Take care of her, please." Morales replied, "Everything is going to be fine. Don't worry." Morales continued with the procedure.
>
> Maria began to have complications from the procedure. Alexa returned to find the building empty and no sign of her mother. She called repeatedly with no answer. Maria had not informed her relatives about the procedure because she was afraid they would try and "talk her out of it." After some time, Alexa called the local police and reported her mother as missing. By this time, Maria had walked

> nearly three miles in an unfamiliar part of town, in pain. Witnesses called 911, and an ambulance took her to a local hospital. Maria died from complications from the local anesthetic lidocaine.
>
> The police arrested Morales and Perez at the airport, as they were attempting to board a flight to Colombia. Both were charged with second degree murder and the unlicensed practice of medicine. Prior to trial, the couple pled guilty to involuntary manslaughter, the unlicensed practice of medicine, and conspiracy. The judge sentenced them to the maximum which was four to eight years in prison.[1–4]

In the late nineteenth century, the medical profession began to change. Society was becoming more dependent upon practitioners with higher levels of knowledge, skill, and technique as a result of advancements in science and diagnostic capabilities. Such dependence led to individuals occupying positions of superiority and trust to take advantage of those entrusted to them. As society's dependence increased, so did the need for regulation.[1]

The states began to institute laws and regulations to oversee the practice of medicine to include licensing requirements, competency, and ethical standards. These laws are commonly referred to as *medical practice acts*. By the early 1900s, each state had enacted a medical practice act as a means to protect citizens from potential harm from unqualified and unscrupulous practitioners.[1]

Medical practice acts typically address three core concerns:

- Regulating the quality/competency of practitioners by establishing minimum standards for licensure to include education and training
- Establish standards of professional ethical conduct
- Enforce prescribed standards via designated investigative and disciplinary procedures[1]

A survey of the 65 medical practice acts (50 allopathic medical boards, 14 osteopathic medical boards, and the District of Columbia) revealed that each act contained a statute specifically prohibiting the unlicensed practice of medicine. The survey further revealed that 83% of the acts criminalized the unlicensed practice of medicine (felony 45% and misdemeanor 38%). Seventeen percent of the acts provided for civil remedies only, however, all medical practice acts do provide for civil remedies as well (injunctions, cease & desist orders, etc.). Figure 14.1 shows the percentage of state medical and osteopathic medical boards that criminalize the unlicensed practice of medicine.

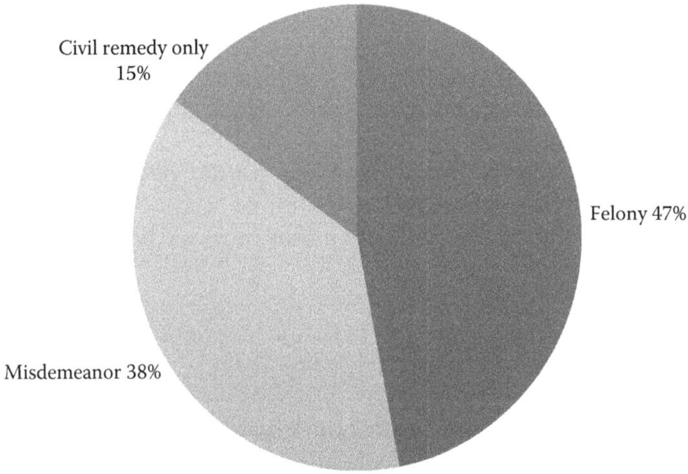

Figure 14.1 Percentage of state boards criminalizing unlicensed practice. (Data from author's survey of U.S. state medical and osteopathic board medical practice acts.)

Given that 83% of medical practice acts criminalize the unlicensed practice of medicine, the seriousness of this offense is appreciated. The mission of regulatory boards is to protect the public and deterring the unlicensed practice of medicine is an important aspect of that mission.

It is interesting to note the California Court of Appeals' comments in its opinion in Hageseth v. Superior Court as they opine the seriousness of this offense:

> The criminalization of these acts represents a reasonable exercise of the state police power, as the statute was designed to prevent the provision of medical treatment to residents of the state by persons who are inadequately trained or otherwise incompetent to provide such treatment, and who have not subjected themselves to the regulatory regime established by the Medical Practice Act.[1,5]

Elements of the offense

As discussed in Chapter 1, the language of the various definitions of the practice of medicine differs from state to state, however, a survey of various medical practice acts reveals three basic core elements:

- Holding oneself out to the public as being engaged in the practice of medicine;
- Diagnose, prescribe or perform any form of treatment, relief, procedure or cure for any human disease, illness, injury or other physical or mental condition;
- Attach the initials "MD," "DO," or similar designation, the designation doctor, surgeon, Dr., doctor of medicine, doctor of osteopathy to one's name indicative that they are licensed to practice medicine.

The unlicensed practice of medicine commonly occurs in three scenarios.

1. A person with some healthcare experience, having no medical license, performing treatments and procedures that fall within the scope of the practice of medicine. An example of this would be a holistic practitioner prescribing topical creams or compounding an elixir for the treatment of a human illness or condition.[1,6] It should be noted that some states license holistic practitioners; therefore, the practice act of the regulatory board regulating holistic practitioners should be examined so as to determine their scope of practice. Another example would include a foreign medical graduate, not yet licensed in the United States, examining, diagnosing, and prescribing forms of treatment.[1,7]
2. A licensed practitioner practicing beyond the scope of their license. An example here would be perhaps a licensed dentist practicing beyond the scope of dentistry. In Kelley v. Texas State Board of Medical Examiners, a dentist, Dr. William Kelley, offered treatments for certain cancers and malignancies.[1,8] Another example would be a licensed chiropractor practicing acupuncture and drawing blood for diagnostic purposes.[1,9] All states have regulatory boards/agencies that regulate many other healthcare providers to include nurses, physician assistants, dentists, chiropractors, and to mention a few. It would be wise for the medical investigator to become familiar with the scopes of practice authorized by the statutes regulating other healthcare professions.
3. Perhaps the most dangerous is the person holding him/herself out to the public as a physician, performing treatments and having no training or experience in healthcare whatsoever. This offender will often prey on unsuspecting and innocent victims causing physical injury, emotional injury as well as financial injury as evidenced by the Maria Rodgriguez case mentioned at the beginning of this chapter.[1,10]

Complementary and alternative medicine

Complementary and alternative medicine (CAM) is a fast-growing trend in the United States and these forms of treatment require discussion as they relate to the unlicensed practice of medicine. *Complementary medicine* refers to using non-mainstream diagnostic and therapeutic approaches together with conventional medicine whereas *alternative medicine* refers to using non-mainstream approaches in place of conventional medicine.[11] CAM is further defined as "diagnosis, treatment and/or prevention which complements mainstream medicine by contributing to a common whole, by satisfying a demand not met by orthodoxy or by diversifying the conceptual frameworks of medicine."[12] While some states do license CAM providers, many states do not. In states that do not license CAM providers at what point does CAM treatment become the unlicensed practice of medicine?

CAM is often associated with the term *holistic medicine*. Holistic medicine is defined as "the art and science of healing that addresses care of the whole person—body, mind, and spirit."[13] If any one of interdependent parts of the body is out of balance, all other parts will be affected. Holistic medicine seeks to restore balance and to integrate conventional and complementary modalities promoting optimum health and to prevent and treat disease by addressing contributing factors.[13]

Complementary and alternative medical approaches are typically not taught in Western medical schools and hospitals. To a large extent CAM has not been adopted by mainstream Western medicine. Some examples of CAM include but are not limited to homeopathy, naturopathy, biofeedback, chelation therapy, aromatherapy, and reflexology. Following are basic definitions of these examples.

- *Homeopathy:* Homeopathy is a system of medical practices based on the theory that any substance that can produce symptoms of disease or illness in a healthy person can cure those symptoms in a sick person. Homeopathic remedies are administered in diluted form and are derived from many natural sources to include plants, minerals, and metals.[14]
- *Naturopathy:* Naturopathy is another alternate medical system that proposes that there is a healing power in the body that establishes, maintains, and restores health. This power is supported through treatments to include nutrition, lifestyle counseling, dietary supplements, plants, exercise, homeopathy, and treatments from traditional Chinese medicine.[14]
- *Biofeedback:* Biofeedback uses electronic devices to teach patients how to consciously regulate bodily functions, such as breathing, heart rate, and blood pressure, in order to improve overall health.

It is commonly used to reduce stress, eliminate headaches, recondition injured muscles, and relieve pain.[14]

- *Chelation therapy:* Chelation therapy is a chemical process whereby a substance is used to bind molecules, such as metals or minerals, and hold them tightly so they can be removed from a system, such as the body. Chelation therapy is used to remove excess toxic metals.[14]
- *Aromatherapy:* Aromatherapy, also referred to as Essential Oil therapy, is defined as the art and science of using naturally extracted aromatic essences from plants to balance, harmonize, and promote the health of body, mind, and spirit. It seeks to unify physiological, psychological, and spiritual processes to enhance an individual's innate healing process.[15]
- *Reflexology:* Reflexology refers to the application of pressure to areas on the feet, hands, and ears. The theory is that these areas correspond to organs and systems of the body and that pressure applied to these areas affects the organs and benefits the person's health.[16]

Prevalence of the use of CAM

Studies suggest that the use of CAM is widespread. CAM is often used by patients suffering from cancer, arthritis, chronic back pain, AIDS, gastrointestinal problems, chronic renal failure, and eating disorders. Based on a 1990 study, 34% of respondents used some form of CAM therapy. Considering the U.S. population at the time, this would amount to approximately 20 million Americans using a form of CAM therapy. CAM use was significantly more common among those from 25–49 years of age (38%) than among those who were younger (33%) or older (28%). Relaxation techniques, chiropractic, and massage were the therapies most often used.[17] Eighty-nine percent of the respondents visited a CAM provider without the recommendation of their physician and 72% did not inform their physician of their use of CAM. Forty-seven percent used some form of CAM therapy with no professional supervision.[17]

A follow-up to the aforementioned study conducted in 1997 revealed an increase in the use of CAM therapies from 34% in 1990 to 42% in 1997. The CAM modalities increasing the most included herbal medicine, massage, megavitamins, self-help groups, folk remedies, energy healing, and homeopathy. The probability of those inclined to see a CAM provider increased from 36% to 46%. When extrapolated to the U.S. population, the study suggests a 47% increase in total visits to CAM providers, 427 million in 1990 to 629 million in 1997. Costs for CAM services increased 45% and were estimated at $21.2 billion in 1997.[18]

Patients seeing a physician for a principal condition and also using CAM therapies increased from 20% in 1990 to 32% in 1997 and patients seeing a physician and also seeing a CAM provider increased from 8.3%

in 1990 to 13.7% in 1997. The study further revealed a 380% increase in the use of herbal remedies and a 130% increase in the use of high-dose megavitamins. Twenty percent of patients taking prescription medication were also using herbs or high-dose vitamins. These results suggest that 15 million patients are at risk for potential adverse interactions.[18]

A 2007 report published by the U.S. Department of Health and Human Services indicates that four out of ten adults used a form of CAM therapy in the past year. The most common used modalities were non-vitamin, non-mineral natural products (17.7%), and deep breathing exercises (12.7%). One in nine children was found to have used a CAM modality in the past year, the most common being natural products, and chiropractic or osteopathic manipulation. Children whose parent(s) used CAM were five times more likely (23.9%) to use CAM as children whose parent(s) did not use CAM (5.1%). From 2002 to 2007, increases in the use of acupuncture, deep breathing exercises, massage, meditation, naturopathy, and yoga were observed.[14]

It is estimated that 30% of Americans aged 65 or older (approximately 10 million) used a form of CAM within the previous year and 19% age 65 or older visited a CAM provider within the past year (approximately 63 million visits). The most common modalities used by this age group were chiropractic, herbal remedies, relaxation techniques, mega-vitamins, and religious or spiritual healing by others.[19]

Additional research suggests several predictors of CAM use to include those with higher education, poorer health status, holistic orientation to health, classification in a cultural group espousing environmentalism, interest in spirituality, and personal growth psychology. Dissatisfaction with conventional medicine was not a predictor of CAM use in that CAM users tend to find alternative therapies more compatible with their own values and beliefs toward health and life.[20]

Ethical issues

There are several distinct differences between conventional medicine and CAM. These differences may foster certain ethical issues and raise questions of efficacy, safety, and cost. [21] Some of the more apparent differences include:

- CAM providers often lack any significant medical training.
    - Untrained CAM providers may lack understanding of anatomy, physiology, pathology, etc. This lack of understanding would likely make it difficult for a CAM provider to effectively communicate with a physician and vice versa. Suboptimal communication between providers could put patients at risk as well as the lack of medical knowledge.[12]

- Nonmedical CAM providers either have their own licensing laws or no regulation whatsoever.
  - Professional regulation exists to establish uniform standards of practice, competent practitioners, and accountability. Many CAM professions are not regulated; therefore, there will likely be nonuniform practice standards, potentially incompetent practitioners and no accountability should an adverse outcome manifest. As such, patients may be placed at risk. Other ethical concerns to consider are to what extent do CAM providers abide by the tenets of informed consent, confidentiality, and appropriate boundaries?[12]
- CAM therapies are relatively under researched as compared to conventional medicine. To what extent are CAM therapies efficacious and safe?
  - Many patients seek out CAM therapies because they assume that because it is "natural" it must be safe and effective. Interactions of herbal and conventional medicines occur but are under-researched and many potential adverse reactions remain unknown. Without sufficient evidence as to the efficacy and safety of many CAM therapies, it is difficult to determine whether more harm than good is being done.[12]
- CAM lacks a tradition or culture of vigorous, modern, scientific research as compared to conventional medicine.
  - The field of CAM has a general lack of research expertise which is primarily due to a lack of funding. As a result, the results of sparse CAM research is methodologically weak and at times flawed.[12]
- CAM is often claimed to be *holistic* and as such, the benefits of CAM therapies are often thought to be mental, psychological, spiritual, and social.
  - These benefits are less tangible and difficult to quantify as opposed to more quantifiable physical variables. The ideology of evidence-based medicine relies on reproducible, quantifiable outcomes.[12]

To further examine some of the ethical issues surrounding CAM, the *four principles approach* discussed in Chapter 2 will be used.[21,22]

The four principles are:

- Respect for autonomy
- Beneficence
- Nonmaleficence
- Justice

Autonomy

The concept of autonomy refers to respecting the decisions of all those involved in the therapeutic process, to include the physician, patient, and the CAM provider. Given that many CAM therapies are unproven and un-researched, conventional medicine physicians may be reluctant to use them and inclined to advise the patient against using them. When patients express to their physician a desire to try CAM therapies, the physician should respect the patient's decision in the spirit of autonomy, however, an ethical dilemma emerges. If the particular CAM therapy in question is not in the patient's best interest, ethically, the physician should refuse cooperation. If evidence exists that the CAM therapy is detrimental, promoting its use would be considered unethical.[21]

Autonomy also requires obtaining agreement from patients before implementing treatment. Most, if not all, medical practice acts require a physician to obtain *informed consent* from the patient prior to initiating treatment, surgery, or other procedures. Informed consent requires the physician to fully inform the patient of all risks and potential benefits of the proposed treatment and the patient must acknowledge having been informed and consenting to the treatment. In the area of CAM, informed consent is extremely difficult in that CAM therapies are under researched and often unproven as to benefits and risks thus making it almost impossible to fully inform the patient.[21]

Autonomy embraces the principle of honesty when communicating with patients and not deceiving them. The promotion of unproven treatments with the intent to benefit financially from desperate patients would clearly be unethical.[21]

Beneficence and maleficence

If a "no harm" principle is applied, therapeutic decisions should be based on an analysis of the potential risks and benefits. No effective therapy comes without potential risk. Does the therapy under consideration have benefits that outweigh the risks or vice versa? Thorough research and clinical trials help to determine the risks and benefits of therapies and medications, however, with CAM, risk/benefit analysis is often unavailable in that potential risks and benefits have not been fully researched. With such scant evidence as it pertains to CAM, therapeutic decisions are often based on opinion rather than evidence.[21]

Another harm potentiated by CAM (and conventional medicine as well) is malpractice and incompetence. Formal training and regulation of CAM providers is extremely lacking and in some instances nonexistent. From an ethical standpoint, it would seem to be fundamentally imperative that professional standards be developed and embraced by nonmedically trained providers. Diagnosing and providing medical treatment presumes that the physician (or CAM provider) possesses a certain level of training and competence.[21]

Justice

As stated in Chapter 2, justice is often considered synonymous with fairness. In the context of health care, justice can be examined from three different perspectives: fair distribution of scarce resources, respect for peoples' rights, and respect for the law.[22] When examining justice as it relates to the allocation of resources, several concerns emerge, to include:

- Providing sufficient health care to meet the needs of all who need it. When this cannot be accomplished, to distribute resources in proportion to the extent of peoples' needs for health care;
- Providing equal access to health care;
- Allowing patients to exercise autonomy in selecting their health care;
- Maximizing the benefits derived from available resources.[22]

When money is spent on adjunct therapies, such as CAM, in addition to customary care, these financial resources will likely not be available in other needed areas. When the cost issues are not fully considered, therapies that are more beneficial could be unavailable and such could be considered inefficient and unethical. Modalities, to include CAM, should be considered on their merit which would require reliable data in terms of prevalence, effectiveness, safety, costs, and cost effectiveness; data that is not currently available.[21]

Legal status of CAM

As stated earlier, 83% of all states criminalize the unlicensed practice of medicine and the various definitions of the practice of medicine are relatively broad. Many states do license and regulate certain CAM professions such as acupuncturists, massage therapists, and naturopaths to list a few. Nonlicensed CAM providers and licensed CAM providers practicing beyond the statutory scope of their profession risk criminal prosecution for the unlicensed practice of medicine.[23]

Under most malpractice regulations, a practitioner is liable for damages resulting from injury or death when their practice deviates from the *standard of care*. CAM by its definition and nature deviates from conventional medicine standards of care. Where licensing and regulation do not exist, CAM providers are often held unaccountable.[23]

Ethnic and cultural practices

Quite often the unlicensed practice of medicine will manifest in communities with various cultural and ethnic populations, for example areas with large concentrations of Hispanic or Asian residents and businesses. In many Asian communities, the practice of Traditional Chinese Medicine (TCM) is widespread. TCM originated in ancient China and has evolved over thousands of years. TCM practitioners use herbal medicines and various mind and body practices, such as acupuncture and tai chi, to treat or prevent health problems. In the United States, people use TCM primarily as a complementary health approach.[24] More often than not, TCM practitioners do not meet the qualifications for licensure as a physician in the United States and often do not understand the concept of licensure due to cultural differences.

In many Hispanic communities, physicians from Hispanic countries immigrate to the United States and provide medical treatment to those of the same ethnicity without becoming licensed. Again, many of these physicians lack the qualifications for licensure in the United States and they typically practice in the close knit Hispanic community. Given the fact that many Hispanics in the United States are illegal aliens, they are reluctant to seek out conventional licensed physicians preferring to be treated by a member of their own background and community so as to avoid attracting the attention of government officials.

It should be noted that the problem of unlicensed medical practice is not exclusively found in Hispanic and Asian communities. Unlicensed practice is common among many other ethnic populations in that many cultures have traditions and remedies that are handed down through generations and are practiced in close knit communities. Investigations of unlicensed practice in ethnic communities can be very difficult due to cultural differences, language barriers, and many immigrants' distrust of government.

Investigation

When preparing to initiate an investigation of unlicensed practice, one should re-familiarize themselves with the basic elements of the offense as it is defined in your state's specific medical practice act. For example, some medical practice acts require that a fee or some form of compensation be made to the unlicensed provider for treatment, whereas other states do not have this requirement. Also, many medical practice acts provide for some exceptions to licensure such as rendering emergency aid or practicing under legitimate religious tenets. As such, a thorough review of your specific state's medical practice act is imperative.

As stated earlier in the chapter, a review of 65 medical practice acts across the United States revealed three common core elements which will be the focus of discussion as to the investigation of unlicensed practice. The core elements once again are:

- Holding oneself out to the public as being engaged in the practice of medicine;
- Diagnose, prescribe, or perform any form of treatment, relief, procedure or for any human disease, illness, injury, or other physical or mental condition;
- Attach the initials "MD," "DO," or similar designation, the designation doctor, surgeon, Dr., doctor of medicine, doctor of osteopathy to one's name indicative that they are licensed to practice medicine.

The conduct of an investigation of unlicensed practice will likely take on one of two approaches, or perhaps both depending on the scope of the investigation. The two approaches are *overt* and *covert*. Overt investigations are those that are not secret or concealed. An overt investigation would involve interviewing complainants, victims, witnesses, issuing subpoenas for documentary evidence, perhaps executing search warrants and partnering with other agencies in the conduct of the investigation.

The covert investigation, often referred to as an "undercover" investigation, is conducted secretly and unknown to the suspect. A covert investigation would include an operative (investigator, informant, etc.) posing as a patient seeking medical treatment from the suspected unlicensed practitioner.

Overt investigation

First, determine the correct identity of the suspect and check the board's records to ensure that he/she does not currently hold a valid medical license or a license in another profession. Once this is accomplished, the initial step in the investigation is to thoroughly review all information provided in the complaint or from the source of the information that initiated the investigation. What are the specific allegations? Does this matter come under the medical board's jurisdiction or the jurisdiction of another regulatory board? Do the alleged activities fall within the definition of the practice of medicine? Is the suspect of a specific ethnicity that may result in language barriers?

Interview of complainant/source of information

The interview of the complainant is necessary to assess their competency and credibility and to evaluate the information provided. The interview should seek to probe for additional details concerning the suspect's activities in an effort to link them with the elements of the offense.

- Is the suspect holding him/herself out to the public as being engaged in the practice of medicine?
  - If so, how so? Is the complainant an employee or former employee, former patient, relative of a patient, etc.?
    - Advertising in local ethnic newspapers or other "underground" publications
    - Running a facility with signage indicating the availability to treat certain maladies
    - Does he/she refer to him/herself as "doctor?" (Many traditional Chinese practitioners refer to themselves as "OMD" or oriental medical doctor.)
- Is the suspect diagnosing and prescribing any form of treatment for any human illness, injury, disease, or any other physical or mental condition?
  - How does the complainant know this?
    - Knows of patients who have been treated by the suspect
- Names and contact information for these witnesses
    - Has personally observed the suspect diagnosing and treating patients
- Where is this practice occurring?
- On what dates were these observations made?
- Days of the week and times of day the "clinic" is open
  - What forms of treatment are being provided?
    - Conventional allopathic, herbal, holistic, etc.?
    - Are any surgical procedures being performed?
- Is the suspect attaching the initials "MD," "DO," or similar designations, referring to him/herself as "doctor," surgeon, Dr., doctor of medicine, doctor of osteopathy indicative that they are licensed to practice medicine?
  - What letters or designations are being used?
  - Are these designations on pamphlets, business cards, stationery? Does the complainant have samples of such?
  - Is the suspect referred to as "doctor" while at the "clinic" by patients and staff?
  - Does the suspect refer to him/herself as "doctor?"

The complainant should be further interviewed regarding additional witnesses and patients. Contact information for these witnesses should be obtained if possible. Has anyone been harmed by the practice? Contact information for this person is necessary as well. If the complainant is or was an employee or patient, have them describe the layout of the facility. Is the facility set up similar to a legitimate medical clinic? How many people work at this facility, what are their roles? Contact information for these people is imperative. If cooperative, they will make potentially strong witnesses. What equipment is maintained at the facility? In some of the worst case scenarios, unlicensed medical practices are conducted out of motel rooms, basements of buildings, back rooms of herb and vitamin shops, and to name a few.

Interview of other witnesses

If other witnesses are identified, they too should be thoroughly interviewed. Again, the goal of these interviews is to establish that the activities of the suspect correlate with the elements of the crime; holding one's self out as lawfully practicing medicine, diagnosing, treating human illnesses, using certain protected designations with their name indicating they are properly licensed.

Interview of patients

Interviews with identified patients may produce a tricky situation. Patients of the suspect may admire and respect him/her in that they may believe that he/she has helped heal or cure their medical problem. Patients of this sort will likely be uncooperative. Former patients who have been harmed in some way by the suspect's practice may be more willing to come forward and provide useful information.

Questions for cooperative patients will largely be dictated by the nature of the illness or condition for which treatment was sought. Basic information to be obtained from cooperative patients should include:

- Nature of the illness or condition bringing them to the suspect
- What happened at the first visit to the facility?
    - Fill out paperwork?
    - Seen by medical assistant or nurse?
    - Any form of physical examination? By nurse, assistant, suspect?
    - What did the physical examination consist of?
    - What did the suspect do or say when he/she came into room?
    - Introduce him/herself as "doctor?"
- In what manner did the suspect diagnose the illness or condition?
    - Were any medical tests performed? Describe.
    - Was blood or urine sample taken?
    - Was the patient told for what purpose this was done? If so, what was the purpose?
- What did the suspect recommend or prescribe to treat the illness or condition?
    - Medication(s)
    - Herbs

    - Tonics or elixirs
    - Exercises
    - Dietary changes or dietary supplements
    - Other forms of holistic therapies
- What was the cost for the visit?
    - How paid? Cash, credit, barter
    - Did the patient receive a receipt for services? If so, a copy should be obtained.
    - If paid by credit or debit, ask patient to provide a copy of the credit/debit card statement showing the charge.
- Did the patient make subsequent visits to the facility?
    - How many? How often?
    - Have patient describe the events of subsequent visits.

Sworn statements or affidavits should be obtained from all witnesses and patients. This form of documentation will be very helpful for board attorneys or criminal prosecutors as they prepare for civil or criminal proceedings.

Obtaining evidence

After all witness, victim, and patient interviews are conducted and based on these interviews, the investigator will then need to determine what physical and/or documentary evidence will need to be obtained, either by subpoena or search warrant, depending on the nature of the medical board's statutory authority. The necessary evidence will include certain documents, and other physical evidence to establish the elements of the offense.

Note that the witnesses interviewed may have in their possession certain documents or physical evidence given them by the provider. Such documents may include receipts for services, business cards, brochures, etc. Physical evidence may include medications, herbal preparations, creams/salves, etc. If the witness possesses any items of potential evidence and is voluntarily willing to turn them over to the investigator, a receipt for evidence should be used. A receipt for evidence will properly document the nature and identity of the evidence, quantity, description, and from whom it was obtained. The receipt for evidence will also begin the chain of custody discussed in Chapter 7.

If the witness is reluctant to voluntarily release the evidence to the investigator, request the witness make photocopies of the evidence or allow the investigator to make photocopies and return the evidence to the witness. Items of physical evidence should be thoroughly documented in detail in the report of investigation as to identity, description, quantity, and who is in possession of the evidence. Photographs of the physical evidence should also be taken. The investigator should ask the witness to maintain the evidence in a secure area in case it is needed at hearing or trial.

If patients were interviewed, the investigator will certainly need to obtain a copy of the patient record maintained by the provider. This may be accomplished in a variety of ways depending on the statutory authority granted to the board. The patient may be willing to sign a HIPAA release authorizing the provider to release the record. The information obtained via patient interviews may also help establish *reasonable cause* (or other legal standard) to enable the investigator to obtain a subpoena to compel the provider to release records. Again, depending on the information obtained, *probable cause* may be established to effect the procurement and execution of a search warrant. Depending on the authority statutorily granted to the board and its investigators, teaming with local law enforcement may be necessary if a search warrant is required.

Covert investigation

As previously stated, the covert investigation is conducted unbeknownst to the suspect unlicensed practitioner. Such an investigation will utilize an "undercover" operative to make a visit to the suspect's location of practice posing as a patient seeking treatment. The operative could be a law enforcement officer, another medical board investigator, or perhaps a patient that has been identified. NOTE: Utilizing a patient or other civilian to act as the undercover operative brings many risks. The medical board could be held liable for any injuries sustained by a civilian working under the auspices of the board. *This text is not intended to provide expert legal guidance therefore the investigator should discuss this matter thoroughly with the board's legal counsel prior to utilizing a civilian in this role. The concept of entrapment should also be thoroughly vetted with legal counsel.*

While at the suspect's office/clinic the undercover operative should be extremely observant for indicators of unlicensed medical practice such as signage, pamphlets, business cards, letterhead, activities of personnel, layout of the office, medical equipment, etc. This information will be very important when the time comes to draft language for subpoenas or a search warrant affidavit. During the visit with the practitioner, the operative should listen attentively and engage the practitioner in conversation related to medical practice.

When the undercover visit is concluded and payment is made, the operative should obtain a receipt for the services rendered. This could be an important piece of evidence. After the operative is away from the office/clinic, all evidence should be accounted for on an evidence receipt/chain of custody form and properly bagged and secured. If the medical board or assisting law enforcement agency has surveillance equipment such as audio and video recording devices that were used during the undercover operation, such recordings also become evidence and should be treated accordingly.

As soon as possible the operative should draft a memo to the case file thoroughly accounting the details of the visit to include his/her observations, discussions by office personnel overheard by the operative, and discussions by the operative with office personnel and the subject practitioner. Was a patient chart or medical record created during the visit? This will be a crucial piece of evidence in that the chart should document the practitioner's diagnosis, any testing that was done, treatment plan, and anything that was prescribed to treat the diagnosed condition.

It would not be unusual to conduct more than one visit. Multiple visits will establish a pattern of conduct by the practitioner and avoid a defense of "I only did this the one time." Multiple visits will strengthen the case as will multiple visits by more than one operative. Certainly available personnel and resources will impact how many visits are made and operatives used.

Upon the conclusion of the investigation, whether overt or covert, the drafting of subpoenas and/or search warrants will be necessary so as to legally obtain the evidence necessary for civil and/or criminal proceedings.

Interview of suspect practitioner

The interview of the unlicensed practitioner is a very important aspect of the investigation. As with any investigation, the interview allows for the investigator to match the information and evidence acquired from the investigation to the suspect. The interview provides the opportunity for the suspect to confess or admit to certain aspects of the case. At a minimum the interview will allow the unlicensed practitioner to explain his/her position and attempt to provide an explanation of their unlicensed activities. Careful questioning and listening may offer a glimpse of the suspect's potential defenses should the case proceed to civil or criminal proceedings. This will provide an opportunity for the investigator to follow up on potential defenses to shore up that aspect of the investigation if necessary.

Telemedicine

Prior to the advent of current technologies, the physician/patient relationship was established via a face-to-face meeting between the physician and patient wherein the patient seeks treatment of a particular malady, the physician agrees to treat the malady, and the patient agrees to the treatment. The advancements and continued development of medical and communications technology have had a profound impact on the practice of medicine. Such advancements offer opportunities for improving the delivery and accessibility of health care, particularly in the area of *telemedicine*.[25]

Telemedicine is the use of medical information exchanged from one site to another via electronic communications to improve a patient's clinical health status.[26] Essentially, telemedicine is the practice of medicine using any number of technological electronic communication devices whereby the physician is in a different location than the patient. Telemedicine is not a separate or distinct medical specialty. Telemedicine includes a growing variety of applications and services using two-way video, email, smart phones, wireless tools, and other forms of telecommunications technology.[26]

The use of telemedicine has spread rapidly and is now becoming integrated into the ongoing operations of hospitals, specialty departments, home health agencies, private physician offices as well as consumer's homes and workplaces.[26] State medical boards, in fulfilling their duty to protect the public, face complex regulatory challenges and patient safety concerns in adapting regulations and standards historically intended for the in-person provision of medical care to new delivery models involving telemedicine technologies, including but not limited to: (1) determining when a physician–patient relationship is established; (2) assuring privacy of patient data; (3) guaranteeing proper evaluation and treatment of the patient; and (4) limiting the prescribing and dispensing of certain medications.[25] A physician using telemedicine technologies in the provision of medical services to a patient must take appropriate steps to establish the physician–patient relationship and conduct all appropriate evaluations and history of the patient consistent with traditional standards of care for the particular patient presentation.[25]

The Federation of State Medical Boards (FSMB) has developed model guidelines for the appropriate use of telemedicine technologies and these guidelines will be presented. *It should be noted that these are merely guidelines and not necessarily adopted by every state that allows the practice of telemedicine.* It should be further noted that the laws and rules in telemedicine states will differ as they pertain to licensure, the establishment of the physician–patient relationship, standard of care, etc. Therefore, the investigator should become very familiar with the laws and rules governing telemedicine in their respective state.

The FSMB guidelines include the following and are used with permission:

Licensure

A physician must be licensed, or under the jurisdiction, of the medical board of the state where the patient is located. The practice of medicine occurs where the patient is located at the time telemedicine technologies are used. Physicians who treat or prescribe through online services sites are practicing medicine and must possess appropriate licensure in all jurisdictions where patients receive care.[25] According to an FSMB study, 48 states require that physicians who engage in telemedicine are licensed in the state in which the patient is located.[27]

Establishment of a physician–patient relationship

Where an existing physician–patient relationship is not present, a physician must take appropriate steps to establish a physician–patient relationship consistent with the guidelines identified in Section Two , and, while each circumstance is unique, such physician–patient relationships may be established using telemedicine technologies provided the standard of care is met.[25]

Evaluation and treatment of the patient

A documented medical evaluation and collection of relevant clinical history commensurate with the presentation of the patient to establish diagnoses and identify underlying conditions and/or contraindications to the treatment recommended/provided must be obtained prior to providing treatment, including issuing prescriptions, electronically or otherwise. Treatment and consultation recommendations made in an online setting, including issuing a prescription via electronic means, will be held to the same standards of appropriate practice as those in traditional (encounter in person) settings. Treatment, including issuing a prescription based solely on an online questionnaire, does not constitute an acceptable standard of care.[25]

Informed consent

Evidence documenting appropriate patient informed consent for the use of telemedicine technologies must be obtained and maintained. Appropriate informed consent should, as a baseline, include the following terms:

- Identification of the patient, the physician, and the physician's credentials;
- Types of transmissions permitted using telemedicine technologies (e.g., prescription refills, appointment scheduling, patient education, etc.);
- The patient agrees that the physician determines whether or not the condition being diagnosed and/or treated is appropriate for a telemedicine encounter;

- Details on security measures taken with the use of telemedicine technologies, such as encrypting data, password protected screen savers and data files, or utilizing other reliable authentication techniques, as well as potential risks to privacy notwithstanding such measures;
- Hold harmless clause for information lost due to technical failures; and
- Requirement for express patient consent to forward patient-identifiable information to a third party.[25]

Continuity of care

Patients should be able to seek, with relative ease, follow-up care or information from the physician (or physician's designee) who conducts an encounter using telemedicine technologies. Physicians solely providing services using telemedicine technologies with no existing physician–patient relationship prior to the encounter must make documentation of the encounter using telemedicine technologies easily available to the patient, and subject to the patient's consent, any identified care provider of the patient immediately after the encounter.[25]

Referrals for emergency services

An emergency plan is required and must be provided by the physician to the patient when the care provided using telemedicine technologies indicates that a referral to an acute care facility or ER for treatment is necessary for the safety of the patient. The emergency plan should include a formal, written protocol appropriate to the services being rendered via telemedicine technologies.[25]

Medical records

The medical record should include, if applicable, copies of all patient-related electronic communications, including patient–physician communication, prescriptions, laboratory and test results, evaluations and consultations, records of past care, and instructions obtained or produced in connection with the utilization of telemedicine technologies. Informed consents obtained in connection with an encounter involving telemedicine technologies should also be filed in the medical record. The patient record established during the use of telemedicine technologies must be accessible and documented for both the physician and the patient, consistent with all established laws and regulations governing patient healthcare records.[25]

Privacy and security of patient records and exchange of information

Physicians should meet or exceed applicable federal and state legal requirements of medical/health information privacy, including compliance with the HIPAA and state privacy, confidentiality, security, and medical retention rules. Physicians are referred to "Standards for Privacy of Individually Identifiable Health Information," issued by the Department of Health and Human Services (HHS).

Written policies and procedures should be maintained at the same standard as traditional face-to-face encounters for documentation, maintenance, and transmission of the records of the encounter using telemedicine technologies. Such policies and procedures should address (1) privacy, (2) healthcare personnel (in addition to the physician addressee) who will process messages, (3) hours of operation, (4) types of transactions that will be permitted electronically, (5) required patient information to be included in the communication, such as patient name, identification number, and type of transaction, (6) archival and retrieval, and (7) quality oversight mechanisms. Policies and procedures should be periodically evaluated for currency and be maintained in an accessible and readily available manner for review.

Sufficient privacy and security measures must be in place and documented to assure confidentiality and integrity of patient-identifiable information. Transmissions, including patient e-mail, prescriptions, and laboratory results, must be secured within existing technology (i.e., password protected, encrypted electronic prescriptions, or other reliable authentication techniques). All patient–physician e-mail, as well as other patient-related electronic communications, should be stored and filed in the patient's medical record, consistent with traditional record-keeping policies and procedures.[25]

Disclosures and functionality on online services making available telemedicine technologies

Online services used by physicians providing medical services using telemedicine technologies should clearly disclose:

- Specific services provided;
- Contact information for physician;
- Licensure and qualifications of physician(s) and associated physicians;
- Fees for services and how payment is to be made;
- Financial interests, other than fees charged, in any information, products, or services provided by a physician;

- Appropriate uses and limitations of the site, including emergency health situations;
- Uses and response times for e-mails, electronic messages, and other communications transmitted via telemedicine technologies;
- To whom patient health information may be disclosed and for what purpose;
- Rights of patients with respect to patient health information; and
- Information collected and any passive tracking mechanisms utilized.[25]

Online services used by physicians providing medical services using telemedicine technologies should provide patients a clear mechanism to:

- Access, supplement, and amend patient-provided personal health information;
- Provide feedback regarding the site and the quality of information and services; and
- Register complaints, including information regarding filing a complaint with the applicable state medical and osteopathic board(s).[25]

Online services must have accurate and transparent information about the website owner/operator, location, and contact information, including a domain name that accurately reflects the identity.[25]

Advertising or promotion of goods or products from which the physician receives direct remuneration, benefits, or incentives (other than the fees for the medical care services) is prohibited. Notwithstanding, online services may provide links to general health information sites to enhance patient education; however, the physician should not benefit financially from providing such links or from the services or products marketed by such links. When providing links to other sites, physicians should be aware of the implied endorsement of the information, services, or products offered from such sites. The maintenance of preferred relationships with any pharmacy is prohibited. Physicians shall not transmit prescriptions to a specific pharmacy, or recommend a pharmacy, in exchange for any type of consideration or benefit from that pharmacy.[25]

Prescribing

Telemedicine technologies, where prescribing may be contemplated, must implement measures to uphold patient safety in the absence of traditional physical examination. Such measures should guarantee that the identity of the patient and provider is clearly established and that detailed documentation for the clinical evaluation and resulting prescription is both enforced and independently kept. Measures to assure informed, accurate, and error prevention prescribing practices (e.g., integration with e-Prescription systems) are encouraged. To further assure patient safety in the absence of physical examination, telemedicine technologies should limit medication formularies to ones that are deemed safe.[25]

Prescribing medications, in-person or via telemedicine, is at the professional discretion of the physician. The indication, appropriateness, and safety considerations for each telemedicine visit prescription must be evaluated by the physician in accordance with current standards of practice and consequently carry the same professional accountability as prescriptions delivered during an encounter in person. However, where such measures are upheld, and the appropriate clinical consideration is carried out and documented, physicians may exercise their judgment and prescribe medications as part of telemedicine encounters.[25]

The following information is taken from the website of the American Telemedicine Association and is used with permission.

What services can be provided by telemedicine?

Sometimes telemedicine is best understood in terms of the services provided and the mechanisms used to provide those services. Here are some examples:

- Primary care and specialist referral services may involve a primary care or allied health professional providing a consultation with a patient or a specialist assisting the primary care physician in rendering a diagnosis. This may involve the use of live interactive video or the use of store and forward transmission of diagnostic images, vital signs and/or video clips along with patient data for later review.[26]
- Remote patient monitoring, including home telehealth, uses devices to remotely collect and send data to a home health agency or a remote diagnostic testing facility (RDTF) for interpretation. Such applications might include a specific vital sign, such as blood glucose or heart ECG or a variety of indicators for homebound patients. Such services can be used to supplement the use of visiting nurses.[26]
- Consumer medical and health information includes the use of the Internet and wireless devices for consumers to obtain specialized health information and on-line discussion groups to provide peer-to-peer support.[26]
- Medical education provides continuing medical education credits for health professionals and special medical education seminars for targeted groups in remote locations.[26]

Benefits of telemedicine

Telemedicine has been growing rapidly because it offers four fundamental benefits:

- Improved Access—For over 40 years, telemedicine has been used to bring healthcare services to patients in distant locations. Not only does telemedicine improve access to patients but it also allows physicians and health facilities to expand their reach, beyond their own offices. Given the provider shortages throughout the world, in both rural and urban areas, telemedicine has a unique capacity to increase service to millions of new patients.[26]
- Cost Efficiencies—Reducing or containing the cost of healthcare is one of the most important reasons for funding and adopting telehealth technologies. Telemedicine has been shown to reduce the cost of healthcare and increase efficiency through better management of chronic diseases, shared health professional staffing, reduced travel times, and fewer or shorter hospital stays.[26]
- Improved Quality—Studies have consistently shown that the quality of healthcare services delivered via telemedicine is as good as those given in traditional in-person consultations. In some specialties, particularly in mental health and ICU care, telemedicine delivers a superior product, with greater outcomes and patient satisfaction.[26]
- Patient Demand—Consumers want telemedicine. The greatest impact of telemedicine is on the patient, their family, and their community. Using telemedicine technologies reduces travel time and related stresses for the patient. Over the past 15 years, study after study has documented patient satisfaction and support for telemedical services. Such services offer patients the access to providers that might not be available otherwise, as well as medical services without the need to travel long distances.[26]

References

1. Bacigalupi, J. *A Uniform Approach to the Unlicensed Practice of Medicine.* Juris Doctor Candidate, William S. Boyd School of Law, University of Nevada, Las Vegas, May 2012.
2. Harasim, P. and M. Blasky. 2011. Backroom surgery death raises questions about 'makeshift' doctors. *Las Vegas Review-Journal,* April 11. Accessed October 21, 2014. www.reviewjournal.com/news/crime-courts/backroom-surgery-death-raises-questions-about-makeshift-doctors.html
3. McCabe, F. 2011. Colombian couple plead guilty in unlicensed surgery death. *Las Vegas Review Journal,* August 4. Accessed October 21, 2014. http://www.reviewjournal.com/news/crime-courts/colombian-couple-plead-guilty-unlicensed-surgery-death.html

4. McCabe, F. 2011. Couple going to prison in woman's death after surgery. *Las Vegas Review Journal*, October 20. Accessed October 21, 2014. http://www.reviewjournal.com/news/crime-courts/couple-going-prison-womans-death-after-surgery.html
5. Hagaseth v. Superior Court, Court of Appeal, First District, California, No. A115390, 2007.
6. *State v. Howard*, 337 S.E.2d 598, 1985. (North Carolina)
7. *People v. Varas*, 487 N.Y.S.2d 577, 1985. (New York)
8. *Kelley v. Texas State Board* of Medical Examiners, 467 S.W.2d 539, 1971. (Texas)
9. *State v. Wilson*, 528 P.2d 279, 1974. (Washington)
10. *People v. Doneski*, 679 N.E.2d 462, 1997. (Illinois)
11. National Institutes of Health, National Center for Complementary and Alternative Medicine. 2013. Complementary, Alternative, or Integrative Health: What's in a Name? Accessed May 28, 2014. http://nccam.nih.gov
12. Ernst, E., H. Cohen, and J. Stone. 2004. Ethical problems arising in evidence based complementary and alternative medicine. *Journal of Medical Ethics*, 30: 156–159.
13. WebMD. 2015. What is holistic medicine? Accessed September 21, 2015. http://www.webmd.com/balance/guide/what-is-holistic-medicine
14. Barnes, P., B. Bloom, and R. Nahin. 2008. Complementary and alternative medicine use among adults and children: United States, 2007. U.S. Department of Health and Human Services, Centers for Disease Control and Prevention, National Center for Health Statistics Reports, No. 12.
15. University of Maryland Medical Center. 2011. Aromatherapy. Accessed September 21, 2015. https://www.umm.edu/health/medical/altmed/treatment/aromatherapy/
16. University of Minnesota. 2013. What is reflexology? Accessed August 19, 2015. http://www.takingcharge.csh.umn.edu/explore-healing-practices/reflexology
17. Eisenberg, D., R. Kessler, C. Foster, F. Norlock, D. Calkins, and T. Delbanco. 1993. Unconventional medicine in the United States—Prevalence, costs, and patterns of use. *New England Journal of Medicine*, 328: 246–252.
18. Eisenberg, D., R. Davis, S. Ettner, S. Appel, S. Wilkey, M. Rompay, and R. Kessler. 1998. Trends in alternative medicine use in the United States, 1990–1997: Results of a follow-up national survey. *Journal of the American Medical Association*, 280(18): 1569–1575.
19. Foster, D., R. Phillips, M. Hamel, and D. Eisenberg. 2000. Alternative medicine use in older Americans. *Journal of the American Geriatrics Society*, 48(12): 1560–1565.
20. Astin, J. 1998. Why patients use alternative medicine: Results of a national study. *Journal of the American Medical Association*, 279(19): 1548–1553.
21. Ernst, E. 1996. The ethics of complimentary medicine. *Journal of Medical Ethics*, 22: 197–198.
22. Gillon, R. 1994. Medical ethics: Four principles plus attention to scope. *British Journal of Medicine*, 309: 184–188.
23. World Health Organization. 2001. Legal Status of Traditional Medicine and Complementary/Alternative Medicine: A Worldwide Review. Accessed May 29, 2014. http://apps.who.int/medicinedocs/pdf/h2943e/h2943e.pdf

24. National Institutes of Health, National Center for Complementary and Alternative Medicine. 2013. Traditional Chinese Medicine: An Introduction. Accessed November 19, 2014. http://nccam.nih.gov
25. Federation of State Medical Boards. 2014. Model Policy for the Appropriate Use of Telemedicine Technologies in the Practice of Medicine. Accessed September 5, 2015. Used with permission. http://www.fsmb.org/Media/Default/PDF/FSMB/Advocacy/FSMB_Telemedicine_Policy/pdf
26. American Telemedicine Association. 2015. What is telemedicine? Accessed October 15, 2015. Used with permission. http://www.americantelemed.org/about-telemedicine/what-is-telemedicine#.Ve8twU2FND8
27. Federation of State Medical Boards. 2015. Telemedicine Policies: Board by Board Overview. Accessed September 5, 2015. Used with permission. http://www.fsmb.org/Media/Default/PDF/FSMB/Advocacy/GRPOL_Telemedicine_Licensure.pdf

chapter fifteen

The report of investigation

Earlier in this text we identified three very broad duties or aspects of the job of an investigator. They *talk* to people, *listen* to people, and *write* about it. This chapter will focus on the writing aspect, the *report of investigation* (ROI). When teaching my course on criminal investigation at Georgia State University, I would assign a writing exercise. When examining the course syllabus, the majority of the students would moan and groan when the writing assignment came up for discussion. I asked why writing was so disliked and many students expressed timidity toward it, while others said that it was too much work. I asked "what do you mean it's too much work?" The responses I often got included "you have to think," "you have to organize your thoughts," "you have to think of what words to use," "writing is not fun," and to name a few.

Writing is work and the ROI is perhaps one of the most important pieces of work in the investigation. Interviewing victims and witnesses, identifying and collecting evidence, and analyzing the evidence are certainly very important aspects of any investigation. All aspects of an investigation may have been conducted with absolute brilliance; however, this brilliance can be diminished by a disorganized, imprecise, and carelessly written report. If an investigation is not properly documented in a well thought out report, the case may face significant defense challenges.

Purpose of the ROI

The ROI has many purposes. First and foremost, it is the official permanent record of the conduct of the investigation and the facts developed during the investigation. It serves as the official memory of the agency and also contributes to performance management of investigative personnel.[1] It is important to be aware of your report's potential audience. The ROI will likely be read by many different individuals throughout the investigative and legal process whether it be a district attorney, medical board attorney, physicians who serve on your medical board, defense attorney, supervisors, agency heads, other agencies to which the report has been released, and to name a few. The content of your report will likely be the only information your board members have when licensure sanctions are being considered.[2] The ROI is not a document intended to entertain, beguile, or amuse the reader. The primary purpose of the ROI is to inform the reader. The report should inform the reader of all facts developed in the investigation.

Characteristics of an effective ROI

Following is a discussion of several characteristics associated with effective investigative reports:

1. *Well organized.* The report should be well organized chronologically as to events, taking the reader from the beginning of the investigation to the end.
2. *Communication of the intended information.* It is essential that the report convey all facts to the reader, as precisely as possible, so that the reader will understand the events that took place during the course of the investigation and its findings.
3. *Write the report in the first person, past tense, and active voice.* First person refers to the use of words such as I, me, my when referring to yourself. Referring to yourself in the third person (this officer, Investigator Doe, etc.) is awkward and can become confusing to the reader.[1] Note: If your agency requires reports to be written in third person then, by all means, do so.
4. *Avoid vulgarisms and slang terms.*[3] The report should be devoid of any vulgarisms unless it is necessary for some reason to quote a vulgar term or phrase. If quoted the reader should be told that the following is a quote and quotation marks should be used.

   Many investigative agencies have a language all their own with esoteric terms and definitions known only to them. Terms such as "perp," (perpetrator), "speed" (amphetamines), and agency acronyms such as DEA (U.S. Drug Enforcement Administration), FDA (US Food and Drug Administration) should be avoided or at least properly explained and defined. Often local law enforcement agencies are referred to by their agency initials such as HCSO (Henry County Sheriff's Office). Be aware that there may other counties whose name begins with the same letter. In Georgia, there are nine counties that begin with the letter H. It would not be uncommon for each of these county sheriff's offices to be referred as HCSO.

   Without properly identifying the specific county agency, the reader will not know what agency is involved in the investigation. In the conduct of medical practice investigations, it is unavoidable to refrain from using very technical medical terms; however, one should be cautious to ensure that the appropriate term is used, in the proper context and spelled correctly.
5. *Correct spelling and grammar* are essential to an effective report. Here are some actual examples of poor spelling and grammar taken from actual investigative reports:
   a. "He was arrested for a *mister meanor.*" (misdemeanor)
   b. "He was a drug *attic.*" (addict)

c. "I called for a *toe* truck." (tow)
d. "The prescription was *past* at the XYZ Pharmacy." (passed)
e. "The suspect was restrained because he was acting *erotically.*" (erratically)

Misspellings such as these can dramatically affect the meaning of the statements and lead to misunderstanding of your intended communication. Your skill and reputation as an investigator may also come into question.

With regard to inaccurate grammar and punctuation, the following examples are offered:

a. "Billy," screamed John, "get out of here!" Who is speaking in this sentence? Billy or John? John is speaking.
b. Billy screamed, "John, get out of here!" Who is speaking in this example? Billy is speaking.
c. Consider the following actual news headline: "Cops shoot dead man while robbing liquor store." Were the cops robbing a liquor store and while doing so shot a dead man? Did the cops shoot a man to death while the man was robbing a liquor store?

As demonstrated, without the proper use of commas, quotation marks, and proper syntax it is easy to confuse the reader. These are obviously elementary examples but they illustrate the point of the importance of proper punctuation and wording.

The 4 Cs of effective report writing

Effective report writing may be broken down into four basic elements and each will be discussed individually:

1. Correct (Accurate)
2. Concise
3. Clear
4. Complete[4]

Correct

It is essential that investigative reports be thoroughly accurate. The report should contain accurate records of times, dates, names of all persons involved, all telephone numbers, addresses, descriptions of evidence, and especially accuracy of the facts of the investigation. To be accurate you must be specific.[3] In other words, rather than saying "During the interview Dr. Doe was impaired," it would be better to describe your observations of Dr. Doe, that is, "I personally observed Dr. Doe slouched in his chair behind his desk, his eyes appeared bloodshot and his speech sounded slurred. He appeared to have difficulty maintaining focus on our conversation and at one point during the interview he laid his head down on his desk." Stating that Dr. Doe was impaired draws a conclusion; one that may not be accurate. Perhaps there was another plausible explanation for Dr. Doe's behavior. The *description* of Dr. Doe's behaviors provides the reader with much more detail and allows the reader to reach their own conclusion without you making conclusionary statements. Describe what you see, not what you think you see.

Conclusionary statements should be avoided. A conclusionary statement is one in which you, the investigator draws a conclusion. For example, in a prescription forgery case you obtain four prescriptions bearing the signature purportedly of Dr. Doe. Your report states that "The four prescriptions were signed *by* Dr. Doe." Unless you personally observed Dr. Doe sign, these prescriptions you cannot make that statement. This is a conclusionary statement. Your report should read, "The four prescriptions were signed 'Dr. Doe'." The use of the word *by* can make a significant difference in how the facts of your report are perceived.[3]

It is interesting to note that the U.S. Internal Revenue Service, Special Agent Manual states in part, "Accuracy is essential; therefore, the facts must be exact. Inaccuracies can be devastating to the value of the report and to the special agent's credibility as a witness."[5]

Concise

Concise means eliminating unnecessary words without omitting important facts. You as an investigator are not evaluated on the length of your reports. An investigative report is not the forum to exhibit your extensive vocabulary. Investigative reports should report all of the facts and pertinent information in as few words as possible. You do not want your reader to have to read 10 pages when only five pages would have been sufficient to state the facts. Be cautious, however, that brevity should not be equated with conciseness. Example:

Brief: I interviewed Dr. Doe.
Concise: I interviewed Dr. Doe on May 5, 2014 at his office.
Wordy: On the above date, time, and place I made contact with Dr. Doe, at which time I interviewed him and he related the following information to me.

When writing your reports, attempt to eliminate superfluous words and phrases without eliminating important facts. Keep it simple and straightforward.

The U.S. Internal Revenue Service, Special Agent Manual states that, "A well written report may lose its effectiveness for lack of a logical presentation. A mass of data indiscriminately presented in the report is confusing and may impair the reader's ability to comprehend the facts relating to the investigation. A well written report requires adherence to the primary purpose of the report. Exclude all material that does not relate to that purpose. Know what you want to communicate and how best to present that information. *Each sentence, paragraph, and section of the report should help develop the primary purpose of the report.*"[5] (Emphasis added by the author)

Clear

An investigative report should have only one interpretation in that two people reading the same report should be able to arrive at the same understanding of the events.[3] Sentences should be written in a manner that is clear and avoids misunderstanding. Examples:

Unclear: Dr. Doe treated the patient with a broken arm. Who had the broken arm, Dr. Doe or the patient?
Clear: Dr. Doe treated the patient who had a broken arm.
Unclear: Forty tablets of oxycodone were reported stolen by the pharmacist. Who stole the oxycodone; the pharmacist, or did the pharmacist report the theft?
Clear: The pharmacist reported that forty tablets of oxycodone were stolen.

Guidelines for clarity

Use specific, concrete facts and details.[3] Example: Dr. Doe wrote the patient a prescription. This sentence, while perhaps accurate, provides no detail. Dr. Doe may have written many prescriptions to many patients. A clearer option may be: On 5/5/2014 Dr. Doe wrote a prescription for oxycodone 30 mg, 40 tablets for patient John Smith.

Keep descriptive words and phrases as close as possible to the words they describe.[3] Example: He put the pills into the bag which he had just stolen. Had he just stolen the pills or the bag? A clearer option may be: He put the pills, which he had just stolen, into the bag.

Avoid the use of industry-specific abbreviations and esoteric terms. In law enforcement, investigative work, and especially in medicine, abbreviations and acronyms abound. Such abbreviations and acronyms should be avoided in that many who will read your report will likely not understand them. Physicians on your medical board will not understand investigative terms and abbreviations and conversely, lay persons will have difficulty understanding medical terms and abbreviations.

Example: I met with Deputy Smith of APD to try to locate Dr. Doe. APD put out a BOLO on Dr. Doe alleging that Dr. Doe was 10-96 and 10-32 (Georgia State Patrol radio codes). What does this mean? This sentence written properly should read: I met with Deputy Smith of Atlanta Police Department. He issued a "be on the lookout" (BOLO) alert on Dr. Doe. The BOLO indicated that Dr. Doe was suicidal and is armed with a firearm.

If one has ever attempted to read a medical chart, they would know immediately that it is very difficult to read and interpret. Medicine is notorious for the use of acronyms and esoteric terms.

Example: The patient was brought to the ER and nonambulatory. He was suffering from SOB and chest pain. He gave no hx. of heart disease. Ordered CXR, O_2, ECG. Dx. is MI and patient admitted. A clearer re-write would be: The patient was brought to the Emergency Room and was unable to walk on his own. The patient was suffering from shortness of breath and chest pain. He gave no history of heart disease. The ER physician ordered a chest x-ray, oxygen, and an electrocardiogram. The patient was diagnosed with myocardial infarction and was admitted to the hospital.

Use short sentences well organized into short paragraphs.[1] Short sentences are easier to read and allow the reader to process and understand the information in small doses. Let's take the above example:

The patient was brought to the Emergency Room and was unable to walk on his own and he was suffering from shortness of breath and chest pain and he gave no history of heart disease at which time the ER physician ordered a chest x-ray, oxygen, and an electrocardiogram then diagnosed myocardial infarction and admitted the patient to the hospital.

That is a large amount of information to process at one time and in one sentence.

Complete

Completeness refers to the *who, what, when, where, why, and how* of your investigation.[1] It is essential that the ROI contain all relevant information pertaining to all witnesses, victims, complainants, and the subject of the investigation. The report should include correct name spellings, all addresses, and telephone numbers associated with the witnesses, victims, complainants, and subject, dates of birth, occupations, and any other information necessary.

Who

Who are the people involved in this investigation? Who is the victim, who is the complainant, who are the witnesses, who is the subject of the investigation? Who discovered the violation, who observed the violation, who reported the violation? To whom was the alleged offense reported (office manager, hospital supervisor, etc.)? Who else may have knowledge pertinent to the case? When writing about the witnesses be sure to clearly identify their role, that is, Dr. Doe's nurse, Dr. Doe's surgical assistant in the operatory, the pharmacist who filled the prescription, etc.

What

What is the alleged offense? What injury or other outcome resulted from the offense? What did the witnesses see or hear? What information do the witnesses know? What evidence should be sought? What evidence is presently available? What actions have already been taken (by the hospital, police, etc.)?

When

When did the alleged offense occur? When was the offense discovered? When was the offense reported? When was the offense reported to the medical board? Document the date, time, and place of all witness, complainant, victim, and subject interviews.

Where

Where did the offense occur? Where is the evidence likely to be located? Where are the witnesses? Where is the complainant? Where is the victim?

How

How was the offense carried out? How was the offense discovered? How does the witness know the information they are providing?

Why

Why was the offense committed? Why were witnesses reluctant to provide information?

The above example questions are not to be considered exhaustive by any means. They are provided for illustrative purposes as each investigation will have its own unique qualities. It is also essential that descriptions of all evidentiary items such as medications, medical equipment, or any other tangible item pertinent to the case be detailed and precise.

The report should present the information and evidence in such a way that it would be clearly understood by a reader unfamiliar with the case.[4] Nothing essential to a complete understanding of the case should be omitted. All statements of fact should be supported by evidence that will establish the veracity of the statement and the source of the evidence should be documented.[3]

Report writing process

The investigative report is the link between what happened and what others know about it. The event occurs, you investigate, you prepare the report, and others learn about it. Remember, the purpose of an investigative report is to *inform*. Investigative reports more effectively communicate information when they are written in *first person*, and *past tense*.[3] Use of *first person* refers to yourself. Words such as *I*, *me*, *my*, *we*, *us*, and *our* are used when writing in the first person.[1] Example: **I** contacted the witness. **I** interviewed Dr. Doe. **I** picked up Investigator Jones and **we** drove to the pharmacy. This tends to be much less confusing than writing in the third person, for example, this investigator contacted the witness. This investigator drove to the pharmacy.

Investigations are typically reactive in that certain events have already happened that triggered the investigation. The investigation is initiated due to some allegation of prior violative actions. Our reports are written in the *past tense* because we are writing about something that has already occurred. Writing in the past tense can also help avoid future problems at trial or hearing. For example, if your report states that Dr. Doe's medical clinic is located at 123 Elm Street and months later at a hearing the defense attorney asks you if Dr. Doe's clinic is at 123 Elm Street your answer would likely have to be "I don't know." Having to repeatedly answer "I don't know" may cast some doubt on the accuracy of your investigation to a trier of fact. "What else does Investigator Smith not know?" It would be better to state that "Dr. Doe practiced at 123 Elm Street" or "at the time of this report Dr. Doe's clinic was located at 123 Elm Street."

The report of investigation reads best when written in chronological order, following the order in which the investigation was conducted. Organization is extremely helpful when preparing to write the report. Organize your investigative notes, interviews, victim/complainant/witness statements, evidence, and subject interview in the order you did them, that is, chronologically. This will make writing the narrative of the report easier.

Many agencies use a specific report format utilizing a template with fill-in-the-blank sections to record routine information such as dates, times, names, addresses, etc. Most report formats that I have encountered over the years also contain a narrative section. The narrative section is simply that… the narrative. Here the investigator takes the reader on his journey of investigation. The narrative should contain at least three primary components which are the introduction, body, and conclusion. Think of it this way; the introduction is the starting line and the conclusion is the finish line. The body of the report is your account of how you got from the starting line to the finish line.

Introduction

The introduction introduces the reader to the matter at hand. Why is the board involved in this case? Who is the subject of the investigation, who is the complainant, who is/are the victim(s), what are the allegations, how was the complaint filed (letter, on-line, telephone, etc.), on what date was the complaint filed, on what date was the case assigned to you, etc.? The introduction should also provide the statutes and/or rules that have allegedly been violated. There should also be a section for identifying information (names, dates of birth, social security numbers) and contact information (telephone numbers, addresses, etc.) for the complainant, subject/respondent, witnesses, victim(s), etc.

Body

The body of the report will contain the chronological account of your investigation. What did you do first? If your first step was to interview the complainant, the facts gleaned from that interview should be discussed. If your next several steps in the investigation were to interview additional witnesses, the results of those interviews should be individually discussed. In other words, if you interviewed three additional witnesses (witnesses A, B, and C) you should discuss the results of your interview with witness A, then the results of your interview with witness B, and then witness C. The reader needs to know what each witness can testify to.

If you next obtained pharmacy prescribing data, a discussion of the findings of the analysis of said data should be undertaken. If you next conducted a review of patient records, the findings of said review should be individually (each patient) discussed, so on and so on. The discussion of each step of your investigation should be contained in a separate paragraph. This will assist the reader and guide them through your investigation.

Conclusion

The conclusion is the point in the report where the investigator attempts to "tie it all together." Based on the investigation, interviews, and evidence discussed in the body of the report, what do we now know? Briefly summarize the information and evidence obtained and how it relates (or does not relate) to the respondent's culpability.

Other than the investigation itself, the report of investigation is perhaps the most important part of the process. The report is the vital link between your hard work and what others know about it. The victim, the subject of the investigation, and the citizens you serve deserve nothing more than a fair, thorough, and well-documented investigation. The last aspect of the preparation of the report is proofreading. Proofreading is crucial for the many reasons that have already been stated. Proofread your report to make sure that it is understandable, avoids misunderstanding, and adheres to the four Cs. A poorly written, sloppy, disorganized report will reflect negatively on your agency and your skill and professionalism.

References

1. Swanson, C., N. Chamelin, L. Territo, and R. Taylor. 2006. *Criminal Investigation*, 9th edition. New York: McGraw-Hill Higher Education.
2. Brandl, S. G. 2004. *Criminal Investigation: An Atypical Perspective*. Boston, MA: Pearson Education, Inc.
3. Bennett, W. W. and K. Hess. 2007. *Criminal Investigation*, 8th edition. Belmont, CA: Thompson Wadsworth.
4. Gilbert, J. N. 2007. *Criminal Investigation*, 7th edition. Upper Saddle River, NJ: Pearson Prentice Hall.
5. United States Internal Revenue Service. Special Agent Manual, Part 9, Chapter 5, Section 8—Investigative Reports. Accessed May 20, 2014. www.irs.gov/irm/part9/irm_09-005-008.html

chapter sixteen

The trial and hearing process and the investigator as a witness

Two amendments to the U.S. Constitution provide for a citizen's right to due process of law. Amendment 5 of the original bill of rights states: "No person shall be held to answer for a capital, or otherwise infamous crime, unless on a presentment or indictment of a Grand Jury, except in cases arising in the land or naval forces, or in the militia, when in actual service in time of war or public danger; nor shall any person be subject for the same offence to be twice put in jeopardy of life or limb; nor shall be compelled in any criminal case to be a witness against himself, *nor be deprived of life, liberty, or property, without due process of law*; nor shall private property be taken for public use, without just compensation."

Amendment 14 states: "All persons born or naturalized in the United States and subject to the jurisdiction thereof, are citizens of the United States and of the State wherein they reside. No State shall make or enforce any law which shall abridge the privileges or immunities of citizens of the United States; *nor shall any State deprive any person of life, liberty, or property, without due process of law*; nor deny to any person within its jurisdiction the equal protection of the laws."

A significant aspect of the 14th amendment is its applicability to the states. Not only the federal government, but the states as well, must provide for due process of law.

The concept of due process of law

Due process of law can be a rather complex concept to define or explain, however, some definitions will be offered. If we look at the two key words, "due" and "process," we can see that the concept includes a *process* or procedure that government must follow prior to it depriving one of life, liberty, or property. It is a process that is *due* (of right) the person whose life, liberty, or property the government seeks to take. In other words, we, as citizens, have a right to expect government to follow a process defined in the law as it seeks to adversely affect one's life, liberty, or property. *Black's Law Dictionary* provides a lengthy narrative on what constitutes due process and excerpts from this narrative follow:

> …There are two aspects of due process: *procedural,* in which a person is guaranteed fair procedures; and *substantive* which protects a person's property from unfair governmental interference or taking…. A course of legal proceedings according to those rules and principles which have been established in our systems of jurisprudence for the enforcement and protection of private rights…. Due process of law implies the right of the person affected thereby to be present before the tribunal which pronounces judgment… to be heard, by testimony or otherwise, and to have the right of controverting, by proof, every material fact which bears on the question of right in the matter involved.[1]

West's Encyclopedia of American Law defines due process of law as:

> A fundamental, constitutional guarantee that all legal proceedings will be fair and that one will be given notice of the proceedings and an opportunity to be heard (have a hearing) before the government acts to take away one's life, liberty, or property.[2]

In essence, government must follow certain established procedures that are fair and protect the rights of those accused of violations of law whether it be criminal, civil, or administrative law.[2] In his article, "Some Kind of Hearing," the late judge Henry Friendly cites 10 elements of a fair hearing:

1. An unbiased tribunal or decision-maker
2. Notice of the proposed action and the grounds asserted for it
3. An opportunity to present reasons why the proposed action should not be taken
4. The right to call witnesses and cross examine opposing witnesses
5. To know the evidence against them
6. To have the decision based solely on the evidence presented
7. The right to have legal counsel
8. The creation of a record of the proceedings
9. A statement of findings of fact and reasons for the decision
10. Judicial review (right to appeal to the courts)[3,4]

The provision of required due process is not only relevant to criminal proceedings but it is equally relevant to administrative proceedings to include actions for licensure sanctions. Procedures that guide administrative government agencies in contested administrative cases (such as a licensure disciplinary matter) are codified in what is commonly referred to as an *administrative procedure act* or *administrative practice act.*

A survey of the administrative procedure acts of all 50 states, the District of Columbia, and the federal administrative procedure act revealed that all contain statutes providing for a right to:

- A hearing presided over by an unbiased decision-maker
- Receive prior notice of the hearing with allegations stated
- Call witnesses
- Cross examine opposing witnesses
- Present evidence
- Have counsel
- Know the evidence to be used by the agency (discovery)
- A written statement of the reasons of the agency's findings
- Judicial review of an adverse decision

The agency seeking an action (in our case the medical board) must serve notice on the accused physician citing the board's authority to sanction the license, the laws and rules allegedly violated, and findings of fact outlining what the physician did to violate the laws and rules. In administrative proceedings, the board is often referred to as the *Petitioner* and the defendant is referred to as the *Respondent.*

Burden of proof

Burden of proof is a duty placed upon the government to prove a disputed fact. The agency bringing the legal action is obligated by law to meet the burden of proof to convince the trier of fact that the respondent is in violation of the laws and rules cited in the notice. The law recognizes two standards of proof; proof *beyond a reasonable doubt* and proof by a *preponderance of the evidence.*

Reasonable doubt

Reasonable doubt is the standard of proof required to convict someone charged with a criminal offense. Proof beyond a reasonable doubt can be described as "proof of such a convincing character that a reasonable person would not hesitate to act upon it in the most important of his affairs." Reasonable doubt is the highest standard of proof in any judicial proceeding in the United States.[2]

Preponderance of the evidence

Preponderance of the evidence is a lower standard of proof than reasonable doubt and is the standard of proof in civil cases. "It is evidence which is of greater weight or more convincing than the evidence offered in opposition to it; that degree of proof which is more probable than not;"[1] "evidence that establishes the truth of a disputed fact by a high probability."[2]

Trial and hearing process

Procedures in civil and criminal trials/hearings will differ in some instances; however, the procedures are essentially the same. The "trier of fact" is an impartial person or other entity overseeing the trial/hearing to ensure that the proper procedures are followed. The trier of fact is often a judge, jury, or other statutorily authorized person or tribunal such as the medical board.

In criminal trials, the contending parties are commonly referred to as the prosecution (the party bringing the case) and the defense or defendant. In civil trials, the parties are often referred to as the plaintiff (the party bringing the case) and the defense or defendant. In licensure hearings, the parties are often referred to as the petitioner (the board) and respondent (the licensee whom the board seeks to sanction).

There are five basic steps in the trial and/or hearing process:

- Opening statements
- Presentation of the prosecution's or petitioner's case
- Presentation of the defense's case
- Rebuttal
- Closing statements[6]

Opening statements

The trial/hearing begins with the opening statement of the attorney representing the agency bringing the case, that is, the medical board (petitioner). The purpose of opening statements is to inform the trier of fact about the case. The opening statement will essentially state the nature of the case, the allegations, and the evidence intended to be produced to prove the allegations. The defense attorney follows with his/her opening statement and will attempt to assert the weaknesses of the petitioner's case. The opening statements must be confined to facts that will be proved by the evidence.[5]

Presentation of evidence by the petitioner

The petitioner's attorney begins the presentation of evidence by calling witnesses. The questions asked of the witnesses are referred to as *direct examination*. Witnesses may be called to testify for several reasons such as factual matters (what they saw, what they heard, what they know) or to identify certain documents or other items intended to be introduced into evidence such as medical records, prescriptions, medications, etc. For example, the medical investigator will be called as a witness by the petitioner to testify as to the overall conduct of the investigation, evidence obtained during the investigation, and properly identify the evidence. In a prescribing case, the pharmacist who filled the prescriptions may be called as a witness to authenticate the prescriptions tendered into evidence.

Opposing counsel may make objections as to the questioning of the witness. Common objections center around questions asked that are beyond the witness' knowledge, questions that call for an answer based on hearsay, and questions as to the relevancy of the testimony.[6] The trier of fact will rule on the objection by either sustaining the objection (agreeing with the objector and stopping the objectionable action) or overruling the objection (disagreeing with the objector allowing the action to continue).[6]

When the petitioner's attorney has finished questioning a witness, the defense attorney may then *cross-examine* the witness. The purpose of cross-examination is to test the credibility and veracity of statements made during direct examination.[7,8] Cross-examination is generally limited to questioning only on matters that were raised during direct examination and matters affecting the credibility of the witness.[1] After the defense has finished cross-examining the witness, the petitioner's attorney may conduct re-direct examination to clear up any issues raised during cross-examination and the defense has the right to re-cross examine.[5]

Presentation of evidence by the defense

After the petitioner has completed calling all of its witnesses and presenting evidence, the defense then presents evidence in the same manner as the petitioner. The petitioner in turn has the right to cross-examine the defense's witnesses. Both sides may then re-direct and re-cross.

Rebuttal

At the conclusion of the defense's case, the petitioner can present rebuttal witnesses or evidence to refute evidence presented by the defendant. Of course, rebuttal witnesses may be cross-examined by the defense.[5]

Closing statements

Closing statements is the last time either attorney will be able to speak to or address the trier of fact. It is their opportunity to summarize the testimony of the witnesses and evidence.[6] The attorneys cannot talk about issues outside the case or about evidence that was not presented.[5] The attorney for the petitioner goes first and summarizes their case commenting on the testimony and evidence. Their effort is to cast their case in such a way as to convince the trier of fact to impose sanctions by demonstrating how the allegations were proved. After the petitioner's attorney has completed his/her closing statement, the defense then presents its closing statement. The defense attorney will often attempt to identify weaknesses in the petitioner's case and try to cast their case in such a way as to convince the trier of fact that there is no basis to impose sanctions. After closing statements, the case is then remanded to the trier of fact for a decision.

The investigator as a witness

Consider the idiom "where the rubber meets the road." How might this idiom apply to the investigator as a witness? Consider an athlete who trains for years to compete in the Olympic Games. When the time arrives for the competition to take place, the rubber is about to meet the road. In other words, the actual competition will tell the athlete how good he/she really is and how well he/she prepared.

The investigator has worked diligently on the case, interviewed all of the witnesses, and followed every lead. Based on the results of the investigation, the medical board has brought formal charges against the respondent. Will the case withstand the oncoming defense? When the investigator takes the witness stand to testify the "rubber is about to meet the road." The investigator, like the athlete, is about to be tested as to the extent of his/her efforts to properly and thoroughly prepare for the "contest."

The quality and effectiveness of the investigator's presentation of evidence can bear heavily on the petitioner's success at the hearing. The effectiveness of the investigator's testimony will also be influenced by his/her appearance and demeanor while on the witness stand and in and around the hearing venue. If you have little or no prior courtroom experience, it would be very useful to attend a hearing and observe the attorneys at work, the witnesses providing testimony, your investigator colleagues being questioned both on direct examination and cross-examination. This will help familiarize you with the hearing venue and the hearing process.[9]

An ill-prepared investigator witness can result in testimony that is disorganized and not well articulated. Being unprepared will also be problematic during cross-examination in that a skilled defense attorney will pick up on the fact that the investigator is not prepared and will take advantage of such. It is crucial that the evidence presented and the testimony given is done in such a way so as to avoid any misunderstanding by the trier of fact. Of course, some of this burden is on the petitioner's attorney as to their strategy, questions asked, and preparation at the prehearing conference, however, the investigator should be well knowledgeable of the case facts and should be able to articulate them effectively.

Credibility

In Chapter 5, the concept of credibility was discussed as it pertained to witnesses. Credibility was defined as having to do with the witnesses' believability. Can the witness be believed? Two seasoned legal and investigative professionals were interviewed regarding the investigator witness' credibility as well as several tips concerning testifying in court and hearings. With regard to credibility, it is important to understand that the investigator is *not entitled* to any more credibility than any other witness. Simply because you occupy a position of authority and public trust, you are not gifted with certain and immediate credibility. Credibility is earned over time through the conduct of quality investigations, professional and ethical interactions with witnesses, suspects, respondents, attorneys, and anyone else involved in the investigation. An investigator's credibility is probably the most important asset he/she possesses. While credibility may take months or even years to earn, it can be lost almost instantly. Never lie, exaggerate, or embellish your testimony. Honesty and truthfulness are essential and anything less is unprofessional, unethical, and potentially criminal. Once your credibility is lost or damaged, it can take years to be reestablished and in some cases, your credibility may never be reestablished.[7,8]

Characteristics of a good investigator witness

Perhaps the most important characteristic of an effective witness is the extent to which he/she has prepared for providing their testimony. Preparation is crucial. It is imperative to know every aspect of your investigation and the case facts. It is certainly permissible to refer to your notes during your testimony, however, too many referrals may indicate a lack of knowledge about the case.[7,8] It is likely that you have investigated many cases since your investigation of specific case at hearing and several of them may have been similar in nature. The lag time between the investigation and hearing could be months and this will affect your ability to recall facts. Review all reports and notes made during the investigation so as to minimize your having to refer to them too often during testimony.[7,8] If you fumble through your notes or read directly from your report, your testimony will be less effective.[9]

Other characteristics of an effective witness include exhibiting confidence, a friendly disposition, transparency, being unbiased, being open and honest, and truthful in all things. Confidence is displayed in the way you approach the witness stand and the way you answer questions. Eye contact is an excellent way to exhibit confidence. When answering questions, look at the person asking the question. Do not offer an opinion unless asked to do so; stick to the facts and answer the question asked.

There are times when a truthful response may be favorable to the defense. Whether the answer is helpful or hurtful, tell the truth. Never construct an answer to a question when you do not know the answer. Be sure to know that this will come back to haunt you during cross-examination and could potentially damage your credibility.[8,9]

Another important step toward providing effective testimony is to have a pre-hearing conference with the board attorney. Get to know the board attorney and their litigation style. The pre-hearing conference provides an opportunity to discuss strategy and anticipated defenses. It is an opportunity to determine what the board attorney expects to ask you and how your testimony will direct the case presentation. Become familiar with the courtroom or hearing room setting and determine who is defending the respondent and their litigation style especially as it pertains to their cross-examination style.[7,8]

During the pre-hearing conference, be sure to share with the attorney all of the case facts to include any damaging information about the case. This will help the board attorney to avoid the unexpected necessity of having to deal with adverse testimony. Sharing all information, good and bad, will allow the board attorney to adequately prepare so as to minimize any potential damage to the case. Attorneys, especially prosecutors, do not want to be surprised by testimony that they were not expecting to hear. Attorneys usually prefer to ask questions to which they already know the answer. You do not want to be surprised by an unexpended question either. The pre-hearing conference helps eliminate surprises which neither the board attorney nor the witness wants.[7,8]

Earlier in the chapter, it was discussed that the respondent is entitled to have the allegations, or charges, provided them in writing by the agency bringing the case. The document setting forth the charges may go by different names from state to state. In Georgia, the document is referred to as the "Matters Asserted." An excellent tip is to review the charging document in which the allegations are presented. This will tell you what the board attorney will be attempting to prove and will allow you to anticipate your role as a witness and what to focus on during your preparation.[7]

Appropriate dress is very important. You make a first impression when you walk into the hearing room or courtroom by the way you are dressed and carry yourself. You only get one chance to make that first impression so make it a good one. Do not be a distraction or controversial based on what you are wearing into the courtroom. One's attire should always be professional and appropriate. Avoid flashy or otherwise flamboyant attire. One should dress in such a way as to show respect for the court and the court/hearing process. A coat and tie for men is recommended and for women, a professional looking suit or dress is recommended. Attire for both men and women should be of a conservative nature. One should be well groomed and clothing should be clean and neat.[7,8]

Be mindful of your demeanor in and about the hearing location. Understand that you are being scrutinized in everything you say and do. Anyone in the hearing venue may possibly be another witness or an attorney for the respondent. You therefore must act professionally at all times both inside and outside of the courtroom or hearing venue. Be courteous to anyone you meet and speak with outside of the courtroom but do not discuss the case facts pertaining to your case prior to taking the witness stand.[8] While sitting in the waiting area, it is suggested to remain isolated so as to avoid any misconceptions as to your relationship with others also waiting to be called to testify. It is advised to refrain from taking or making telephone calls and conducting personal business. Questionable or inappropriate behavior may be called into question and negatively impact your effectiveness as a witness.[7]

Investigators for some state medical boards are considered sworn law enforcement officers and as such carry a firearm. It is recommended to determine if firearms are permitted at the hearing site and if not, act accordingly. If firearms are permitted, it is further recommended to keep them concealed to avoid complaints of unprofessional conduct such as perhaps subjective intimidation and flaunting one's authority.

Testifying on direct examination

As stated earlier, the attorney for the agency bringing the case is referred to as either the prosecuting attorney, plaintiff's attorney, and in licensing board hearings, the attorney for the petitioner (board attorney). Most attorneys will attempt to tell the trier of fact a story and your testimony is a means of telling that story. They will utilize both "yes/no" questions and questions requiring some explanation (narrative method). Most attorneys will guide you to a certain point in the case using "yes/no" questions and will then ask you to elaborate on a certain point. Then they will go back to using "yes/no" questions to get you to another point in the story and will again ask you a question requiring you to explain the evidence further. In this manner, they tell the story.[8]

Example:

Board Attorney: "Investigator Smith did you have an occasion to conduct an investigation of Dr. Jones?"

Investigator Smith: "Yes."

Board Attorney: "Investigator Smith please tell the court the facts of your investigation." At this point, Investigator Smith begins a narrative telling of the investigation in chronological order. A potential risk to this method is that an inexperienced investigator witness may give objectionable or irrelevant information.[7] This is why the pre-hearing conference is so important.

A second method is for the attorney to ask questions that require simple, sometimes *yes/no* answers. Another example:

Board Attorney: "Investigator Smith did you conduct an interview with Dr. Jones?"
Investigator Smith: "Yes."
Board Attorney: "Did you make any observations of Dr. Jones' demeanor during the interview?"
Investigator Smith: "Yes."

At this point in Investigator Smith's testimony, the attorney may switch to the narrative method:

Board Attorney: "Will you please describe your observations of Dr. Jones' demeanor during the interview?"

Investigator Smith will then provide narrative testimony describing his observations.

Investigator Smith: "During the interview I observed Dr. Jones' speech to be slurred, his eyes were red appearing to be blood-shot, he slouched in his chair and his gait was unsteady."

Attorneys typically prefer the witness to keep the explanation response short and to the point. Your answers should be as brief and concise as possible.[8]

When asked a question the witness should hesitate a moment to make sure they fully understand the question. The witness should always look directly at the attorney asking the question or at the trier of fact. If the trier of fact asks the witness a question, then the response should be made directly to the trier of fact. Speak in your own words and speak clearly and loud enough for the attorneys, the trier of fact, and the court reporter to hear you.[10] Answer questions in an unbiased and impartial manner. Remember you are not convicting the accused, you are simply relaying the facts in the case. It is up to the trier of fact to determine guilt or innocence. The job of the investigator is to simply be a means of bringing the evidence (truth) to the trier of fact.[8]

If you do not know the answer to a question respond by stating so, "I do not know the answer to that question." Being honest and open makes you more believable on the responses you do give.

It is also important that the witness be sure that they understand the question before giving an answer. If you do not understand the question, ask the attorney to restate the question or ask the attorney to explain the question. "I am not sure what you are asking" is an appropriate response.

Another good response would be "I want to be clear on what you are asking, would you please explain or restate your question?" If you do not hear the question clearly, ask the attorney to restate the question.[8]

Avoid terms, phrases, slang or any language that may be offensive or not easily understood by the trier of fact. You want the trier of fact to be receptive to your testimony so do not say anything that might be off-putting such as rude, derogatory, or disrespectful language. The law enforcement/investigative profession and the medical profession are rife with very unique and esoteric terms. Your testimony should attempt to avoid such terms as they may not be understood by the trier of fact.[7,8] It is further recommended to avoid using expressions such as "I believe," "as I recall," "I think," as these expressions could raise doubts as to the reliability of your testimony.[8]

Testifying on cross-examination

As stated earlier the purpose of cross-examination is to test the credibility of the witness' testimony, discredit the witness, show that the witness is unreliable, discredit the evidence (facts), and to ensure that the testimony given during direct examination is accurate and truthful.[7,8] The defense attorney does this by attempting to *impeach* the witness' testimony. In other words, the defense will attempt to raise doubt as to the accuracy of your testimony, to show inconsistent testimony on your part.[8,10] If the defense can show that your testimony is inconsistent, incorrect, or untruthful, then they have created an opportunity for reasonable doubt on the part of the trier of fact.[8]

Defense attorneys will attempt to discredit you in several different ways. They will attempt to show that your previous testimony under direct examination is inconsistent with your current testimony under cross-examination. They will also ask the same question over and over and in different ways attempting to elicit inconsistent responses. The defense may also focus on matters that were not covered during direct examination in an effort to draw the trier of fact's attention away from the real facts and evidence.[7,8]

Cross-examination tactics vary. Defense attorneys may come across as friendly and cordial, however, some are more aggressive and combative. It is important to note that licensure hearings are usually carried out before an administrative law judge or the board and there is no jury to "play to." As a result, the combative theatrical attorney would likely not be as effective. According to my interviews on this subject, defense attorneys are generally cordial to the witnesses. Being rude or mean toward a witness, even the investigator, is usually counter-productive.[7,8]

The "friendly" attorney will attempt to draw you into a false sense of security. Once you and the attorney become "friends," the attorney will start leading you down the path he wants by using leading questions or questions that suggest the answer he/she wants. Other tactics may include questioning your skill as an investigator or asking for a simple answer to a complex question. If a complex question is asked, the witness should be allowed to answer as necessary to fully explain and provide correct and accurate testimony. Example: A police officer was effecting an arrest after a traffic stop revealed what was believed to be illicit drugs in the vehicle. During the arrest, the suspect became violent and attempted to take the officer's firearm from its holster. During the struggle, the officer punched the suspect several times in an effort to stop the threat. The suspect was arrested and taken to jail. At trial, the defense attorney wants the jury to know that the officer punched his client in an effort to show the officer as unethical in the "mistreatment" of the defendant.

Defense Attorney: "Officer Smith did you punch my client? Yes or no."
Officer Smith: "Yes but…"
Defense Attorney: "Answer yes or no please."

At this point, the witness should be allowed to complete his testimony and explain the reason for punching the defendant. The prosecuting attorney can also bring the officer back to testify on re-direct to give the officer an opportunity to explain the circumstances to the trier of fact.

Defense tactics can be overcome by remaining confident, professional, calm, polite, unbiased, and respectful. With regard to your dialogue with the defense attorney, be the calmest one in the conversation, then you win.[8] It is important to listen closely to the question being asked and answer only what is asked.[7] Unless the question is complex and requires explanation, a yes/no question should be answered "yes" or "no." Often the investigator witness will answer a yes/no question in a *non-responsive* way. This should be avoided. Example:

Prosecutor: "Did you perform pharmacy surveys of Dr. Jones' prescribing of narcotics?" Investigator Smith: "Yes… I surveyed three pharmacies, Northside Pharmacy, Main Street Pharmacy, and City Pharmacy."

All testimony after "yes" is nonresponsive.[7] Investigator Smith anticipated the next two questions and volunteered the answers. While this may seem harmless, the volunteered information may not have been in keeping with the prosecutor's presentation strategy. Investigator Smith should have limited his answers to the questions asked:

Prosecutor: "Did you perform pharmacy surveys of Dr. Jones' prescribing of narcotics?"
Investigator Smith: "Yes."
Prosecutor: "How many pharmacies did you survey?"
Investigator Smith: "Three."
Prosecutor: "What three pharmacies did you survey?"

Investigator Smith: "Northside Pharmacy, Main Street Pharmacy, and City Pharmacy."

It is also important to guard against questions that call for a conclusion. The defense attorney is asking the witness to *speculate* on a conclusion. Questions of this sort often begin with the following phrases: "Would you assume…" "Do you suppose…" "Couldn't it be that…" "Isn't it possible that…" Some suggested responses to these types of questions may include "My job is to collect evidence, not to assume." "One could assume, however…" "It may be possible, but in this case…" You do not know what someone else saw, heard, or thought. You cannot be expected to testify to something that you do not know to be fact. If this type of question is asked of you, hesitate briefly so as to allow the board attorney an opportunity to object.[8] Regardless of the tactics used by defense attorneys, do not lose your temper and do not fence or argue with them.[9] When the trier of fact interrupts your testimony or when an objection is made by either attorney, stop speaking. Wait for the trier of fact to tell you to continue before answering any further.[10]

In Chapter 5 the subject of nonverbal cues was discussed as to their impact during interviews of witnesses and respondents. The discussion will continue here because nonverbal cues can have significant impact on the quality of your testimony. In his study, Albert Mehrabian concluded that communication is made up of several components to include:

What is said—The actual words spoken make up 7% of the total message communicated.
How it is said—tone of voice, pitch, modulation, etc.—38% of the message.
Nonverbal factors—body language, posture, gestures, etc.—55%.[11]

The investigator should sit up straight and face the defense attorney directly. Answer the questions facing either the defense attorney or the trier of fact. Be aware of your posture, tone of voice, and gestures while on the witness stand. Avoid becoming defensive with your words or with your body language. Stay in control. Allow the defense attorney to rant and rave but you should remain calm. Your demeanor should be consistent during both direct examination and cross-examination. This also includes your posture and facial expressions. For example, shrinking away from the defense attorney or crossing your arms across your chest may signal defensiveness on your part.[8] Do not make the mistake of underestimating the power of nonverbal cues when testifying.

Be wary of the "silent treatment." After you answer a question, the defense attorney will simply stand silent. This is done in an effort to make you feel uncomfortable and cause you to doubt or second guess your answer. A few seconds of silence may feel like an eternity and our inclination as humans is to fill that silence gap. Do not offer additional nonresponsive information to fill the silence gap. If you have answered truthfully, sit quietly and await the next question.

Remember, the hearing is the culmination of your work and effort. Your job is to present the best case that you possibly can and to testify to the truth. If the respondent is found against, the facts and evidence were sufficient leading to the adverse findings. If the matter is found in favor of the respondent, the facts and evidence were not sufficient for an adverse finding. Do your best work; work that begins as your investigation commences and culminating in the courtroom.[8] It is important to remember that no matter how your testimony is attacked, you should be respectful of defense counsel and not view him/her as an enemy. Your role is to speak the facts and tell the truth. Be prepared, know your case. Look good, sound good, and do good.[9]

References

1. Black, H. C. 1990. *Black's Law Dictionary*, 6th edition. St. Paul: West Publishing Company, pp. 500–501.
2. *West's Encyclopedia of American Law*, 2008. 2nd edition. Accessed April 4, 2015. http://legal-dictionary.thefreedictionary.com/burden+of+proof
3. Friendly, H. J. 1975. Some kind of hearing. *University of Pennsylvania Law Review*, 123: 1267.
4. Cornell Law. 2014. Accessed May 5, 2015. http://www.law.cornell.edu/wex/due_process
5. American Bar Association. Division of Public Education. Steps in a Trial. Accessed May 15, 2015. http://www.americanbar.org/groups/public_education/resources/law_related education_network/how_courts_work/steps_in_a_trial2.html
6. Offices of the United States Attorneys, United States Department of Justice. Justice 101. Accessed August 20, 2015. http://www.justice.gov/usao/justice-101/trial
7. Wray, J. B. 2015. Senior Assistant Attorney General, Georgia Department of Law, Regulated Industries and Professions Division. Interview by author. Atlanta, GA, November 10.
8. Kelley, G. R. 2015. Inspector General, Georgia Department of Agriculture; former Deputy Director for Homeland Security, Georgia Emergency Management Agency; former Clayton County, GA police officer, detective, and District Attorney Investigator. Interview by author. Atlanta, GA, December 4.
9. Clark County, Indiana Prosecuting Attorney's Office. Effective Courtroom Performance for Indiana Law Enforcement. Accessed November 15, 2015. http://www.clarkprosecutor.org/html/police/police2.htm
10. United States Department of Justice. Tips for Testifying in Court. Accessed November 15, 2015. http://www.justice.gov/usao-mdpa/victim-witness-assistance/tips-testifying-court
11. Mehrabian, A. 1971. *Silent Messages*, 1st edition. Belmont, CA: Thompson Wadsworth Publishing.

chapter seventeen

Managing your caseload

Chances are that you will, or are handling, a rather extensive caseload. I suspect that across the country complaints to medical boards have risen significantly while the number of investigative personnel has remained stagnant as was experienced in the state of Georgia during the period from 2000 to 2012. As a result, the average caseload per investigator continued to rise each year. I believe that it would be fair to say that the bane of an investigator's existence is his/her burgeoning, oppressive caseload.

To be effective, investigators require the necessary time to conduct their assigned cases and with unwieldy caseloads that cut into this time, several unwanted consequences may become evident. Investigators may feel pressured into taking shortcuts which could result in overlooking details and thoroughness. A situation such as this can create stress resulting in a deterioration of the quality of the investigator's work. Overburdensome caseloads can have a significant negative impact on the unit's motivation and morale.[1]

Managing a caseload requires the ability to effectively manage your time. Many of us are very skilled in managing our time, however, many of us are not. During my tenure as the Director of Investigations for the Georgia Composite Medical Board, I supervised many investigators over the years who were very good "time managers" and several who were not. Once per month I would conduct a case review individually with each investigator. Based on my case management system, I knew when the case was assigned to them. This case review allowed me to discuss with the investigator the progress made on all of their assigned cases, what investigative steps remained, and an estimated time for completion of the investigation. During these case reviews, I observed that some investigators had difficulty managing their time so as to maximize daily accomplishments needed in order to move toward a timely completion of the investigation without compromising the quality of the investigation.

One investigator insisted on handling one case at a time. He would begin and complete his oldest case before starting the next oldest case. With a caseload of over 25 cases, would case number 25 be addressed in a timely manner? This is obviously an example of extreme lack of proper time management. Another of my investigators would have all 25 cases open at once, all in various stages. This, too, can be problematic in that it can become confusing as to what evidence goes with what case and which witness pertains to which case resulting in a sense of inundation. It is important to strike a balance between the two extremes.

One might ask, "What adjustments must be made with regard to my time management?" "Am I using my time effectively?" These questions will be difficult to answer if we do not know how we are actually spending our time. It is suggested to maintain a daily time log of your activities and how much time you spent on those activities. Do this for several days and you should get a pretty clear picture of how you are spending your time. You will realize just how much time certain tasks require and how much time is being wasted.[2] Can improvement be made and what activities can/should be eliminated?

Often we approach our daily activities likened to a shotgun blast… going off in many different directions with little to no planning. We begin a task only to become distracted and begin another task without finishing the first task. Before we know it, we have several unfinished tasks in multiple stages of incompleteness. It is important to set clear goals as to what you wish to accomplish today, this week, this month.[2] There are long-term goals and short-term goals. The short-term goals help us to attain our long-term goals. Once the goals are clearly established, a plan can be developed to attain them.[2]

Just like many other aspects of investigative work, planning is crucial with regard to effective time management. What do you want to accomplish today? Upon establishing what you want to accomplish, you can then develop a plan to achieve that goal.[3] Throughout my career, I often relied on the old fashioned "to-do" list. The to-do list is how you will put your plan into motion. As you develop your to-do list, it is important to prioritize the tasks on the list to ensure that the most important things get done first and expeditiously. At the top of my to-do list are the priority tasks that need to be completed continuing with lesser urgent matters listed in descending order.

Prioritizing also helps to break down large complex tasks into smaller attainable tasks.[2] For example, if you need to review the results of a 10-pharmacy survey of the respondent's prescribing over the past year, you should set a daily goal to review the results of at least three pharmacies per day. This will enable you to make progress on the instant case and still allow time for other tasks pertaining to other cases.

Daily and weekly scheduling of tasks is also a very helpful tool.[2] Many of us are more motivated when we see the tasks written down with a specific day and time set aside to attend to them. A good motivator for me was to scratch the task off of the list when I completed it. An old fashioned desk calendar will work just fine or an electronic calendar found in many office software packages or other electronic devices will work as well. Following is an example of daily scheduling:

Monday, December 1	08:00–09:00:	Review 3 newly assigned cases, prep investigative outlines
	09:00–09:30:	Prep/draft subpoenas for cases 20150000, 20151111, 20152222
	09:30–12:00:	Review and summarize pharmacy data for case 20153333
	13:00–14:30:	Continue review of rx data for case 20153333
	14:30–15:00:	Travel to interview Ms. Doe re-case 20154444
	15:00–16:00:	Interview Ms. Doe
	16:00–16:30:	Travel to XYZ Hospital to serve subpoena on case 20154444
	16:30–17:00:	Meet with XYZ hospital risk manager, serve subpoena
Tuesday, December 2	08:00–09:30:	Make phone calls on cases 20151111, 20152222, 20153333 to set up appointments for interviews
	09:30–10:30:	Write up memo re-interview with Ms. Doe
	10:30–12:00:	Continue review of rx data for case 20153333
	13:00–15:30:	Travel back to XYZ hospital to pick up medical records and interview 4 witnesses, surgical tech, anesthesiologist, and 2 RNs.
	15:30–17:00:	Back to office to write up memos re XYZ hospital interviews

While this example may appear to bore down into minute detail of one's activities, this format can be very helpful to those who struggle mightily with ineffective time management. With practice and the passage of time, such minutiae may no longer be required.

As alluded to earlier, it is helpful to batch-related tasks together. For example, if you have several cases that require subpoenas to be drafted, set aside the appropriate amount of time and draft them all at once. If you have five cases and each case requires three subpoenas (a total of 15 subpoenas) plan to spend the time necessary to draft all 15. If the subpoenas can be served via certified mail, once they have been signed by the appropriate authority, they can be mailed out. While waiting for the information requested by the subpoenas to come in, tasks on other cases can then be undertaken. The batching of related tasks can also apply to geographic organization. State medical boards have statewide jurisdiction and board investigators are required to conduct investigations throughout the state.

It makes sense to organize cases by geographical region. If you have three cases in a certain geographical area, work those cases to the point where you can travel to that geographical area and handle all three cases while you are there, preventing redundant trips.

When juggling many cases, it is easy to forget to follow up on important matters. For example, subpoenas were served to several pharmacies and a hospital, and the three witnesses you interviewed last week promised statements to you within two weeks. Calendar or diary these matters so that you do not forget to follow up on them. Witnesses, attorneys, etc. are all busy and timely follow-up is very important. It was not uncommon for me to follow up with an attorney who promised me a statement from his client only to be told, "Oh my gosh, I have been in trial and forgot to handle this…I will have the statement to you by week's end." If a follow-up call had not been made, the case would have continued to remain incomplete.

Multitasking is one of those skills that we either have or we do not. It is important to recognize if you are an effective multitasker or not. Ineffective multitasking often leads to several tasks being undertaken but never (or at least not timely) completed, disorganized work, and to some extent, a sense of discouragement.[3] For multitaskers, it is important to know when, and when not, to multitask. The ability to multitask is very useful when handling multicase caseloads, however, there are times when multitasking is not necessary or appropriate. For example, you have several cases that are complete and are ready for the report of investigation to be prepared. You have scheduled an entire day to organize and write the reports. Preparing the report of investigation requires good organization and concentration and this is not the time to multitask. Your focus and attention to each case report is essential.

Interruptions are constant when working in a busy, clamoring office of investigators. The telephones are ringing, emails are piling up, and colleagues are talking to you, creating a place where concentration is almost impossible. There are times, however, when interruptions need to be minimized.[3] Conducting a telephonic interview with a party to a case, organizing and drafting a report of investigation are just a couple of examples where the minimization of interruptions is important. It is also important to effectively manage your telephone calls and emails.[2] Not every telephone call has to be answered immediately and not every email requires an immediate response. I can recall many instances in my career when I was busy on an important matter and stopped to answer the telephone only to be tied up for 45 minutes by a disgruntled complainant whose case was closed by the board and needed no further action.

Another important strategy to good time management is to eliminate the unnecessary.[3] What does it mean to eliminate the unnecessary? Let us consider this example: You have set aside a specific amount of time to prepare the report of investigation on a certain case, however, you spend

30 minutes on social media. The time spent on social media was unnecessary and cut into your productivity. Unnecessary activities could be considered those activities that prevent you from reaching your goal, whether they are daily goals or weekly goals.[3]

Essentially effective time management boils down to having good organization systems in place. Having good organization processes in place to file emails, documents, and other case material can save you considerable time when searching for information. Setting up effective organization systems on the front end will save you time on the back end.[2]

The following may seem a bit counterintuitive when we are discussing time management and productivity; however, it is important to take breaks from the work from time to time.[2] While writing this book, I often had to get up and take a walk, stretch my legs and shoulders, and just get away from the manuscript for a while. In doing so, I found that I became refreshed both physically and mentally and was better able to approach my writing with creativity.

The following statement cannot be stressed enough: Know your caseload![4] In other words, know what you have, understand the fundamental aspects of each case. You must know which cases require priority handling and which do not and schedule your time accordingly. Over the years as a supervisor, I occasionally inquired of my investigators the status of a specific case assigned to them. At times, I would get the "deer in the headlights" look from them. They would dig through their file cabinet or their briefcase and finally locate the file and say "I didn't know I had this case." They had become so consumed in other cases that they just forgot they had the one I was inquiring about. I am certain that every medical board has a case management system in place to track the assignment of cases, the progress of cases, and the disposition of cases. Database systems differ in terms of their capabilities to manage data. As an investigator and as a manager, I found it extremely helpful to maintain a simple spreadsheet of cases. The spreadsheet can contain basic information as to the case number, the name of the respondent, the date assigned to you, the date you completed and turned the case in to your supervisor, the type of case it is (SOC, prescribing, sexual boundary, impairment, etc.), the number of man hours expended on the case, and the priority level of the case. This will allow you to readily see all of your assigned cases and their age, priority level, etc. at a single glance.

As we know, investigations vary in complexity and time commitment. Some cases may require only an interview with the complainant, obtaining their patient record from the respondent, and a statement from the respondent. In the simplest of cases, the interview with the complainant may be conducted telephonically and a letter along with the subpoena may be sent to the respondent requesting his/her response to the complaint. When the records and the respondent's statement arrive, write the report of investigation and turn the case file in to your supervisor. If three or four of these simple cases wrap up simultaneously, take some time and write the reports and turn them in. Little "victories" such as this will not only lighten your caseload, but may provide a small psychological lift just knowing that you just moved this work "off of your plate."

Another time management resource sometimes overlooked is the supervisor. Your supervisor can help you prioritize your activities to help maximize your time and productivity.[5] Regular meetings with your supervisor to discuss your caseload will not only help you with time management, it will allow your supervisor to know what obstacles you are facing with certain cases and may be able to provide guidance and determine if additional help is needed. For example, the investigator would tell me that all that was needed to conclude the investigation was a statement from the respondent. The investigator would have documented several nonresponsive telephone calls to the respondent. The investigator would later receive a call from the respondent's attorney stating that they are working on the respondent's statement. Subsequent calls to the attorney go ignored. At this point, the supervisor may step in to make contact with the attorney and overcome this obstacle. A dynamic flow of information between supervisor and investigator will go a long way to improving one's time management and overall case production.

References

1. British Association of Social Workers/College of Social Work. 2010. Workload management and case load management in social work services in England. Accessed December 2, 2015. http://cdn.basw.co.uk/upload/basw_20203–5.pdf
2. Chun, J. 11 Top Tips for Effective Time Management. Accessed December 2, 2015. http://www.careerfaqs.com.au/news/news-and-views/11-top-tips-for-effective-time-management/
3. Bakke, D. 5 Effective Time Management Tips, Techniques, and Skills You Need to Master. Accessed December 2, 2015. http://www.moneycrashers.com/effective-time-management-tips-skills-techniques/
4. Limitless Minds Coaching and Training. 5 Tips to Effectively Manage Your Caseload. Accessed December 2, 2015. http://www.limitlessminds.com.au/managing-your-caseload-article.html
5. Liveston, J. 2014. Top 10 Tips Managing a Busy Caseload. Accessed December 2, 2015. http://locumtoday.co.uk/article.php?s = 2014-08-11-top-10-tips-managing-a-busy-caseload#.VI9AFk2FOpo

Appendix 1: HIPAA privacy authorization form

Authorization for—use or disclosure of Protected Health Information
(Required by the Health Insurance Portability and Accountability Act—45 CFR Parts 160 and 164)

1. I hereby authorize all medical service sources and health care providers to use and/or disclose the protected health information ("PHI") described below to my agent identified in my durable power of attorney for health care named ____.

2. Authorization for release of PHI covering the period of health care (check one)
   a. [ ] from (date) ________________ to (date) ________________ OR
   b. [ ] all past, present, and future periods.

3. I hereby authorize the release of PHI as follows (check one):
   a. [ ] my complete health record including records relating to mental health care, communicable diseases, HIV or AIDS, and treatment of alcohol/drug abuse. OR
   b. [ ] my complete health record *with the exception of the following information* (check as appropriate):
      [ ] Mental health records
      [ ] Communicable diseases (including HIV and AIDS)
      [ ] Alcohol/drug abuse treatment
      [ ] Other (please specify): __________________________________.

4. In addition to the authorization for release of my PHI described in paragraphs 3a and 3b of this authorization, I authorize disclosure of information regarding my billing, condition, treatment, and prognosis to the following individuals:

   Name: ________________________ Relationship: ____________________
   Name: ________________________ Relationship: ____________________
   Name: ________________________ Relationship: ____________________

5. This medical information may be used by the persons I authorize to receive this information for medical treatment or consultation, billing or claims payment, or other purposes as I may direct.

6. This authorization shall be in force and effect until nine (9) months after my death or ___________________ (date or event), at which time this authorization expires.

7. I understand that I have the right to revoke this authorization, in writing, at any time. I understand that a revocation is not effective to the extent that any person or entity has already acted in reliance on my authorization or if my authorization was obtained as a condition of obtaining insurance coverage and the insurer has a legal right to contest a claim.

8. I understand that my treatment, payment, enrollment, or eligibility for benefits will not be conditioned on whether I sign this authorization.

9. I understand that information used or disclosed pursuant to this authorization may be disclosed by the recipient and may no longer be protected by federal or state law.

____________________________________ ____________________________

Signature of Patient Date

Appendix 2: Ambulance call report

ANY COUNTY
FIRE DEPARTMENT
EMS

AMBULANCE CALL REPORT

Incident Date: 00/00/2015 **Call #**: 2015xxxx **Patient Care #**: 1

Patient Information:

Name: *John Q. Patient* **Age**: *81* **DOB**: *00/00/1933* **Gender**: *Male* **SSN**: *xxx-xx-xxxx* **Weight**: *150 lb*
Race: *Caucasian*

Address: *1111 Spruce Street, Anywhere, US 12345* **Phone**: *222-333-4444*

Provider Impression:

Primary Impression: Traumatic injury **Secondary Impression**:

Narrative:

Summary of events: ACFD Medic-1 responded to the incident for an 81 y/o male that fell from ground height and had pain to his right upper leg and right arm skin tear. The patient denied LOC before during or after the fall. He was lying on the floor upon arrival, after assessment he requested transport to XYZ Hospital for further evaluation. No changes in his status during contact. Alert and oriented, airway patent, breathing rate rhythm and depth adequate, crt 2 seconds, skin pink warm and dry. +pms in affected extremity, bruising on mid-shaft right femur with no deformities. Right leg pain, right elbow skin tear. Transport to XYZ Hospital, cardiac monitor, vitals, int, transfer to rn on ems 1 stretcher.

Prior Aid: ______ **Performed By**: ______ **Outcome**: ______

Past Medical History:

Medication Allergies: nkda **Generic Name**: n/a **Description**: n/a

Patient Medications: List left with patient **Generic Name**: n/a **Dosage**: n/a

Medical Surgery History:

Hypertension, hypercholesterolemia

History Primarily Obtained From: Family **Pregnancy**: n/a **Advanced Directives**: none **Practitioner Name**: n/a

Patient Condition:

Chief Complaint: Ground level fall × 5 minutes **Secondary Complaint**: right leg pain × 5 minutes **Alcohol/Drug Use**: None apparent

Injury Onset: 00/00/2015, 18:15 **Injury Cause**: Fall **Injury Mechanism**: Blunt **Injury Intent**: Unintended **Ht. of Fall**: 0

Primary Symptom: Pain **Other Associated Symptoms**: none

Patient Vitals:

Time	B/P	Pulse	Rhythm	Resp	Effort	Sp_{02}	Sp_{02} Qual	$EtCO_2$	GCS	Pain	StrokeSci	PTA	B.G.	RTS	Limb	Patient position
18:37	147/81	80	RR	16	Normal	98	Rm air		15	3			177	12	r/arm	Supine
18:53	141/81	84	RR	13	Normal	99	Rm air		15	3				12	r/arm	Supine

ECG Monitor:

Time: ECG type: ECG lead: ECG interpretation: ECG ectopy: Cause for change:

Procedures and Treatments:

Time: 18:36 Crew: JL Name: Assessment-Adult Location: Head Size of Equipment: N/A Attempts: 1 Response: Unchanged Success: Yes

Intubation Confirmation

Time: Preoxy: Gastric sounds: Lung L/R: Chest L/R: Wave form: $ETCO_2$/color: Verify tube:

EDD draws back: EDD inflates: EDD: Misting: POGO score: Secured: Tube depth:

Depth: Tube size: Verify X-ray: MD/RN verify placement:

Medication Administered:
Time: Crew: Medication: Route: Dosage: Response: PTA: Comments:

Injury Details:

Patient Transport/Positioning:
Patient moved to ambulance: Stretcher Patient's position in transport: Semi-Fowlers Patient moved from ambulance: Stretcher

---

Call type & location: Fall victim Mode: Lights/siren Urgency: Immediate Response: 911 Emergency response (scene) Location: Residence
Call disposition: Treated, transported by EMS Resp. Mode: No lights/siren Destination: Hospital

---

Response Times and Mileage:
Notified: 18:22:42 Call sign: Medic1 Unite dispatch: 18:25:14 Veh#: 1234 En route: 18:25:58 At scene: 18:33:39 At patient: 18:35:00
Depart: 18:51:19 Arrive: 19:01:16 Destination miles 4.2 Destination determination: Patient choice

---

Unit Personnel:
Crew member(s): JDL Advanced EMT; WGM, EMT-paramedic

Billing/Insurance Information: Medicare Relationship to insured: Self

---

Service Defined Question:
Patient received by: Physician signature: Alert: Shift: Helicopter utilized?:
Heavy tool extrication?:

Valuables:

Appendix 3: Emergency department notes

XYZ HEALTHCARE SYSTEM	PATIENT: John Q. Patient
XYZ HOSPITAL	MRN: 0000000
123 Elm Street	DOB: 1/1/1933, Sex: M
Anywhere, US 12345	Adm. 1/3/2015, D/C: 1/7/2015

EMERGENCY DEPARTMENT NOTES

History:
History is provided by the patient. No language interpreter was used.

Time Seen by Physician(s): 19:59, 20:59 __________, MD (name of ED physician seeing patient)

Mode of Arrival: Ambulance

Treatment PTA:
81 y.o. Caucasian male pt with history of hypertension, hyperlipidemia, CAD, presents to ED for evaluation of leg injury. Patient reports a mechanical fall today around 6 PM when he stumbled and fell while turning around too quickly. No head injury or loss of consciousness reported. He now has 3–4/10 pain to the right hip.

PCP: __________________, MD
Specialist(s):

Past Medical History

Diagnoses:	Date
• Hypertension	
• Hyperlipidemia	
• Coronary artery disease	
• Carotid artery occlusion	
• GERD (gastroesophageal reflux disease)	
• H/O of myocardial perfusion scan	09/09/2009
• Fixed inferior perfusion defect consistent with diaphragmatic attenuation, otherwise negative for ischemia.	
• Pigmented basal cell carcinoma	09/11/2008
• Right posterior neck	
• Colon polyp	

Past Surgical History

Procedures:

- Coronary artery bypass graft 11/04/2011
  - LIMA to LAD; SVG to mid-OM
- Esophagus surgery (dysphagia)
- Upper gastrointestinal endoscopy 04/30/2013
- Colonoscopy

Family History

Problem	Relation	Onset
• Heart attack	Brother	
• Heart disease	Brother	
• Diabetes	Neg Hx	
• Celiac disease	Neg Hx	
• Cirrhosis	Neg Hx	
• Colon cancer	Neg Hx	
• Colon polyps	Pos Hx	
• Crohn disease	Neg Hx	
• Cystic fibrosis	Neg Hx	
• Esophageal cancer	Neg Hx	
• Hemochromatosis	Neg Hx	
• Inflammatory bowel disease	Neg Hx	
• Irritable bowel syndrome	Neg Hx	
• Liver cancer	Neg Hx	
• Liver disease	Neg Hx	
• Rectal cancer	Neg Hx	
• Stomach cancer	Neg Hx	

• Ulcerative colitis	Neg Hx	
• Wilson disease	Neg Hx	

Additional Information

History: Substance use topics

• Smoking status	Former smoker—1.0 packs/day for 15 years
• Type	Cigarettes
• Quit date	01/13/1964
• Smokeless tobacco	Not on file
• Alcohol use	No

Review of Systems

Constitutional:	Negative
HENT:	Negative
Eyes:	Negative
Respiratory:	Negative
Cardiovascular:	Negative
Gastrointestinal:	Negative
Genitourinary:	Negative
Musculoskeletal:	Negative
Skin:	Negative
Neurological:	Negative

All other systems reviewed and are negative.

Physical Exam
BP: 149/83 Pulse: 78 Temp: 98.9°F (37.2°C) (Oral) Resp: 17 SpO_2: 98%
Nursing notes and vitals reviewed
Constitutional: He is oriented to person, place, and time. He appears well-developed and well-nourished. No distress.
HENT:
Head: Normocephalic and atraumatic.
Eyes: EOMs are normal. Pupils are equal, round, and reactive to light.
Neck: Normal range of motion. Neck supple.
Cardiovascular: Normal rate, regular rhythm, and normal heart sounds. Exam reveals no gallop and no friction rub. No murmur heard.
Pulmonary/Chest: Effort normal and breath sounds normal. No respiratory distress. He has no wheezes. He has no rales. He exhibits no tenderness.
Abdominal: Soft. Bowel sounds are normal. There is no tenderness.
Musculoskeletal: He exhibits no edema. Left hip: He exhibits decreased range of motion.
Neurological: He is alert and oriented to person, place, and time. No cranial nerve deficit.
Skin: Skin is warm and dry. He is not diaphoretic.
Psychiatric: He has a normal mood and affect. His behavior is normal.

ED Course
Procedures
Screening Assessments
NIH Stroke Assessment Scale
<u>MDM</u>
<u>Number of diagnoses or Management Options</u>
Hip fx:
Intertrochanteric fracture of right femur:
Diagnosis management comments: Differential Diagnoses: Differentials include, but are not limited to:
Fracture vs dislocation vs strain/sprain
Will obtain x-rays

Allergies: No known allergies

Medications
<u>Previous Medications</u>:

Amlodipine 5 mg tablet	Take 1 tablet by mouth once daily
Aspirin 81 mg chewable tablet	Take 1 tablet by mouth once daily
Atorvastatin 40 mg tablet	Take 1 tablet by mouth once daily
Fluoxetine 10 mg	Take 2 tablets by mouth once daily

EMERGENCY DEPARTMENT NOTES, CON'T. 3

Omeprazole 40mg capsule	Take 1 capsule by mouth once daily

Repeat Vitals:
Filed Vitals: 01/03/2015 19:20
BP: 149/83 Pulse: 78 Temp: 98.9°F (37.2°C) (Oral) Resp: 17 SpO_2: 98%

MEDICAL DECISION MAKING
Vital Signs:
Reviewed the patient's vital signs. Pulse oximetry interpretation: 98% on RA, nml at 19:20
Nursing Notes:
Reviewed and utilized the nursing notes

Old Medical Records:
The patient's available past medical records and past encounters were reviewed.
ED Orders (Order placed this encounter):
Procedures:

- X-ray hip right 2 or more views
- X-ray chest 1 view portable
- CBC auto differential
- Comprehensive metabolic panel
- PT and PTT
- Urinalysis complete with reflex cult
- NT-pro bnp
- Troponin
- Manual Differential
- CBC
- Inpatient consult to Orthopedic Surgery
- Admit to inpatient

Laboratory Studies
None

Imaging Studies
Imaging studies were ordered. Independently interpreted by the radiologist, which includes:
XR HIP RIGHT 2 OR MORE VIEWS

Final Result	IMPRESSION: A nondisplaced right femoral intertrochanteric neck fracture is noted. Approved by: (name of radiologist) 01/01/2015, 20:47

XR CHEST 1 VIEW

Final Result	IMPRESSION: The cardiac silhouette is enlarged. Ill-defined sclerotic area is noted in the right humeral neck, a nonemergent right humeral series is recommended as follow-up. Approved by: (name of radiologist) 01/03/2015, 21:45

EKG:
Ordered, reviewed, and independently interpreted the EKG.
Time Interpreted: 23:24
Rate: 76 bpm
Rhythm: NSR
Interpretation: Nml axis, Nml intervals, Nml QRS, NS T wave abnormality.

Medications given in the ED:
None

PROGRESS NOTES

20:59: Initial exam. Patient stable. NAD. Family at bedside. Discussed current results and plan of care with patient and family. They verbalize understanding and consent to treatment.
21:55: Re-evaluation. Updated patient on results and need for hospital admission. He verbalizes understanding and consents to hospital admission.

EMERGENCY DEPARTMENT NOTES, CON'T. 4

22:21: The patient will be admitted to Dr. (attending physician). He is stable for admission. He has been counseled on his results, diagnosis, and treatment plan.

Consultations:
21:48: Discussed case with Dr. (orthopedic surgeon) who will see the patient in the morning.

Appendix 4: Face sheet

XYZ HEALTHCARE SYSTEM XYZ HOSPITAL 123 Elm Street Anywhere, US 12345	PATIENT: John Q. Patient MRN: 0000000 DOB: 1/1/1933, Sex: M Adm. 1/3/2015, D/C: 1/7/2015

PATIENT DEMOGRAPHICS

Name	Patient ID	SSN	Sex/Race	Date of Birth
Patient, John Q.	*0000000*	*123-45-6789*	*M/W*	*0/0/1933 (81 y/o)*

Address	Phone	E-mail	Employer
1111 Spruce Street *Anywhere, US 12345*	*000-111-2222*	*None*	*Retired*

Nearest Relative	Relationship	Phone	Work Phone
Sally Patient	*Spouse*	*222-333-4444*	*N/A*

Nearest Relative Address: *Same as patient*

Emergency Contact

Lucy Patient *Phone: 222-333-4444*

Patient's PCP: ______________, *MD*

VISIT COVERAGE

Payor	Plan	Group Number	Group Name
Medicare	*Medicare A&B*	*987654*	*N/A*

VISIT COVERAGE SUBSCRIBER

Subscriber ID	Subscriber Name	Subscriber SSN	Subscriber Address
123456789A	*Patient, John Q.*	*123-45-6789*	*111 Spruce Street* *Anywhere, US 12345*

ADMISSION INFORMATION

Arrival Date/Time: *1/3/2015/7:09 pm* Admit Date/Time:*1/3/2015/11:59 pm*
IP Admit Date/Time: *None*
Admission Type: *Emergency* Admission Source: *Self Referral* Admit Category: *None*
Means of Arrival: *Ambulance* Primary Service: *Internal Med* Secondary Service: *N/A*
Transfer Source: *None* Service Area: *XYX Healthcare* Unit: *Pfh 4 South*
Admit Provider: ________, *MD* Attending Provider: __________, *MD* Referring Provider: *N/A*
Admit Diagnosis: *Right hip pain; possible right hip fracture*

DISCHARGE INFORMATION

Discharge Date/Time	Discharge Disposition	Discharge Destination	Discharge Provider
1/7/2015	*Skilled Nursing Facility*	*ABC Skilled Nursing, Inc.*	*None*

FINAL DIAGNOSES

Principal	Code	Name	POA	CC	HAC	Affects DRG
[P]	*820-21*	*Closed fracture of intertrochanteric section of femur*	*Yes*	*CC*		*Yes*
	V45.81	*Postsurgical aortocoronary bypass status*	*Exempt*			

ICD PROCEDURES

Code	Name	Date	Performing Provider	PxEvent
79.15	CLOSED RED-INT FEMUR	1/4/2015	____________, MD	
99.04	PACKED CELL TRANSFUSION	1/5/2015	____________, MD	

Appendix 5: Admission note—history and physical

XYZ HEALTHCARE SYSTEM	PATIENT: John Q. Patient
XYZ HOSPITAL	MRN: 0000000
123 Elm Street	DOB: 1/1/1933, Sex: M
Anywhere, US 12345	Adm. 1/3/2015, D/C: 1/7/2015

ADMISSION NOTE—HISTORY AND PHYSICAL

HISTORY AND PHYSICAL
______________, PA-C
______________, MD
Internal Medicine Service, XYZ Hospital
1/3/2015

Patient: John Q. Patient
1/1/1933
81 y.o. male
Current Room Moderate-27/MOD-27

PCP: ____________, MD
CHIEF COMPLAINT:
Patient presents with:

- Leg pain

81 yo male to ED with ACEMS from home with c/o right upper leg pain. Pt c/o 2/10 pain.

HISTORY OF PRESENT ILLNESS:
John Q. Patient is an 81 y.o. male with a past medical history of hypertension, CAD s/p CABG 3 years ago, hyperlipidemia who presented to the ED for evaluation of right leg and hip pain following a fall this evening. Patient states he was trying to turn around but turned too quickly, tripping and falling on his right side. He notes immediate right hip pain. He denies any LOC or hitting his head. He notes the severity of pain is 1–2/10 at this time. He denies any use of blood thinner medications and takes an ASA daily. He denies fevers, chills, chest pain, SOB, abdominal pain, n/v or syncope.

REVIEW OF SYSTEMS:
General: Negative for fever, diaphoresis, chills, appetite changes
Head: Negative for headache or dizziness
Eyes: Negative for visual changes
Cardiovascular: Negative for chest pain or discomfort, orthopnea, or swelling of lower extremities
Pulmonary: Negative for shortness of breath, coughing, or wheezing
GI: Negative for nausea, vomiting, and diarrhea. Negative for abdominal pain, hematochezia, melena, or hematemesis
GU: Negative for dysuria or hematuria
MSS: Positive for right hip pain. Negative for back pain. Negative for joint pain, color changes of extremities, or swelling
Neuro: Negative for confusion and weakness. Negative for tingling or numbness
Skin: Negative for rashes or lesions
Psych: Negative for mood changes

Past Medical History

Diagnosis:	Date:
Hypertension	
Hyperlipidemia	
Coronary artery disease	
Carotid artery occlusion	
GERD (gastroesophageal reflux disease)	
H/O myocardial perfusion scan	9/9/2009

Fixed inferior perfusion defect consistent with diaphragmatic attenuation, otherwise negative for ischemia

Pigmented basal cell carcinoma	9/11/2008
Right posterior neck—Dr. Jones	
Colon polyp	

1

ADMISSION NOTE—HISTORY AND PHYSICAL, CONT. 2

Past Surgical History

Procedure:	Date:
Coronary artery bypass graft	11/4/2011
LIMA to LAD; SVG to mid-OM	
Esophagus surgery	
Dysphagia	
Upper gastrointestinal endoscopy	4/30/2013
Colonoscopy	

No Known Allergies
Prior to Admission Medications:

Medication	Sig	Start date	End date	Authorizing Provider
Amlodipine 5 mg tablet	1 tab by mouth once daily	5/3/14		____________, MD
Aspirin 81 mg chewable Tablet	1 tab by mouth once daily			____________, MD
Atorvastatin 40 mg tablet	0.5 mg by mouth daily	5/3/2014		____________, MD
Fluoxetine 10 mg capsule	20 mg by mouth daily			____________, MD
Omeprazole 40 mg capsule	1 capsule by mouth daily	8/19/2014	8/19/2015	____________, MD

Family history reviewed and negative to this hospitalization.

Problem:	Relation:	Age of onset:
Heart attack	Brother	
Heart disease	Brother	
Diabetes	Neg Hx	
Celiac disease	Neg Hx	
Cirrhosis	Neg Hx	
Colon cancer	Neg Hx	
Colon polyps	Neg Hx	
Crohn disease	Neg Hx	
Cystic fibrosis	Neg Hx	
Esophageal cancer	Neg Hx	
Hemochromatosis	Neg Hx	
Inflammatory bowel disease	Neg Hx	
Irritable bowel syndrome	Neg Hx	
Liver cancer	Neg Hx	
Liver disease	Neg Hx	
Rectal cancer	Neg Hx	
Stomach cancer	Neg Hx	
Ulcerative colitis	Neg Hx	
Wilson disease	Neg Hx	

History

Social History

Marital status: Married

Spouse name: N/A

Number of children: N/A

Years of education: N/A

ADMISSION NOTE—HISTORY AND PHYSICAL, CONT. 3

Social History Main Topics

Smoking status:	Former smoker—1.0 packs/day for 15 years
Types:	Cigarettes
Quit date:	1/13/1964
Smokeless tobacco:	None
Alcohol use:	No
Drug use:	No
Sexually active:	None

Other topics

None

Social history narrative

None

PHYSICAL EXAM

Filed Vitals	1/3/2015 19:20
BP:	149/83
Pulse:	78
Temp:	98.9°F (37.2°C)
TempSRC:	oral
Resp:	17
SpO_2:	98%

There is no height or weight on file to calculate BMI

General Appearance: Alert, awake elderly male, sitting up in bed, NAD
Head: Normocephalic, without obvious abnormality, atraumatic
Eyes: PERRL, conjunctiva/corneas clear
Throat: Lips, mucosa, and tongue normal; teeth and gums normal
Neck: Supple, symmetrical, trachea midline, no adenopathy
Lungs: Clear to auscultation, bilaterally, respirations unlabored
Heart: Regular rate and rhythm, S1 and S2 normal, no murmur or gallop
Abdomen: Soft, nontender, bowel sounds active all four quadrants, nondistended
Extremities: Mild tenderness to right hip region. Restricted ROM. Extremities normal, atraumatic, no cyanosis or edema
Pulses: DP and PT pulses 2+ and symmetric
Skin: Skin color, texture, turgor normal, no rashes or lesions
Neurologic: Alert and conversant. Cooperative. Oriented to person, place, and time. Grossly nonfocal
Psych: Appropriate affect and attitude

LABS:

WBC

Date	Value	Range	Status
1/3/2015	11.2*	3.4–10.8 K/μL	Final
12/9/2014	5.9	3.4–10.8 K/μL	Final

Hemoglobin

Date	Value	Range	Status
1/3/2015	10.3*	14.0–18.0 g/dL	Final
12/9/2014	12.7*	14.0–18.0 g/dL	Final

ADMISSION NOTE—HISTORY AND PHYSICAL, CONT. 4

BUN

Date	Value	Range	Status
1/3/2015	15	9–20 mg/dL	Final
12/9/2014	15	7–25 mg/dL	Final

Creatinine

Date	Value	Range	Status
1/3/2015	0.97	0.66–1.25 mg/dL	Final
12/9/2014	1.14	0.64–1.29 mg/dL	Final

This creatinine method is IDMS traceable.

Labs Reviewed:
CBC WITH AUTO DIFFERENTIAL—Abnormal; Notable for the following:

WBC	11.2 (*)
RBC	3.36 (*)
Hemoglobin	10.3 (*)
Hematocrit	30.0 (*)

All other components within normal limits

* The specific lab value is either above or below the normal range.

COMPREHENSIVE METABOLIC PANEL—Abnormal; Notable for the following:

Glucose	133 (*)
Potassium	3.2 (*)
Total Protein	5.9 (*)
Albumin	3.2 (*)
Alkaline Phosphatase	129 (*)

All other components within normal limits
PT AND PTT—Abnormal; Notable for the following:

PTT	37.9 (*)

All other components within normal limits
URINALYSIS COMPLETE WITH REFLEX CULT
NT-PRO BNP
TROPONIN
MANUAL DIFFERENTIAL

RADIOLOGY:
X-Ray Hip Right 2 or More Views

1/3/2015 XR HIP RIGHT 2 OR MORE VIEWS: HISTORY: pain/T/fall COMPARISON: None. FINDINGS: Narrowing is noted in the right hip joint. Lucencies are noted in the right femoral head and acetabulum. An intertrochanteric femoral neck fracture is noted. A dislocation is not identified. The overlying soft tissue appears unremarkable.

1/3/2015 IMPRESSION: A nondisplaced right femoral intertrochanteric neck fracture is noted. Approved by: Bill Wilson, MD 1/3/2015 20:47

X-Ray Chest 1 View Portable

1/3/2015 XR CHEST 1 VIEW: HISTORY: admission COMPARISON: 1/3/2015 FINDINGS: The heart size is enlarged. Mediastinal structures demonstrate median sternotomy wires. The lungs are symmetrically expanded. The lung fields and costophrenic angles demonstrate no infiltrates or effusions. Ill-defined sclerotic changes are noted in the right humeral neck.

ADMISSION NOTE—HISTORY AND PHYSICAL, CONT. 5

1/3/2015 IMPRESSION: The cardiac silhouette is enlarged. Ill-defined sclerotic area is noted in the right humeral neck, a nonemergent right humeral series is recommended as follow-up. Approved by: __________, MD 1/3/2015 21:45

MEDICATIONS GIVEN IN ED:
Medications: No data to display

ASSESSMENT:
Right femoral intertrochanteric fx

Active:
CAD
HTN

* The specific lab value is either above or below the normal range.

Plan:
Admit to med surg
Diet: Regular, NPO after midnight

Right femoral intertrochanteric fx
Ortho surgery consulted by ED physician—Dr. ___________ to see patient tomorrow a.m. in consultation
Pain management
IVF, hold ASA
EKG ordered
Telemetry

Appendix 6: Radiology note

XYZ HEALTHCARE SYSTEM XYZ HOSPITAL 123 Elm Street Anywhere, US 12345	PATIENT: John Q. Patient MRN: 0000000 DOB: 1/1/1933, Sex: M Adm. 1/3/2015, D/C: 1/7/2015

RADIOLOGY NOTE

X-ray hip right 2 or more views

Ordering Provider:	____________, MD 1/4/15 14:40 Resulted by: __________________, MD
Performed:	1/4/15 15:56–1/4/15 15:57
Specimen Collection:	1/4/15 16:10
Narrative:	HISTORY: FX REPAIR 81 y.o. male patient FINDINGS: There is anatomic alignment of the femoral head neck with separate lesser trochanteric fragment displaced from the body of the femur. Pin is noted centrally within the femoral neck and head. Proximal medullary femoral rod with locking screw also noted.
Impression:	IMPRESSION: Postoperative changes 5 images Approved by ________________, MD 1/4/15 19:11

X-ray chest 1 view

Ordering Provider: ___________, MD 1/3/15 20:41 Resulted by: _________________, MD

Performed: 1/3/15 20:33–1/3/15 20:43

Specimen Collection: 1/3/15 21:22

Narrative: XR CHEST 1 VIEW
HISTORY: Admission
COMPARISON: 1/3/2012

FINDINGS: The heart size is enlarged. Mediastinal structures demonstrate median sternotomy wires. The lungs are symmetrically expanded. The lung fields and costophrenic angles demonstrate no infiltrates or effusions. Ill-defined sclerotic changes are noted in the right humeral neck.

Impression: IMPRESSION: The cardiac silhouette is enlarged. Ill-defined sclerotic area is noted in the right humeral neck, a nonemergent right humeral series is recommended as follow-up.

Approved by ______________, MD 1/3/15 21:11

X-ray hip right 2 or more views

Ordering Provider: ___________, MD 1/3/15 19:58 Resulted by: _________________, MD

Performed: 1/3/15 20:29–1/3/15 20:39

Specimen Collection: 1/3/15 20:56

Narrative: XR HIP RIGHT 2 OR MORE VIEWS
HISTORY: pain/T/fall
COMPARISON: None
FINDINGS: Narrowing is noted in the firth hip joint. Lucencies are noted in the right femoral head and acetabulum. An intertrochanteric femoral neck fracture is noted. A dislocation is not identified. The overlying soft tissue appears unremarkable.

Impression: IMPRESSION: A nondisplaced right femoral intertrochanteric neck fracture is noted.

Approved by ______________, MD 1/3/15 20:47

Appendix 7: Consult note

XYZ HEALTHCARE SYSTEM XYZ HOSPITAL 123 Elm Street Anywhere, US 12345		PATIENT: John Q. Patient MRN: 0000000 DOB: 1/1/1933, Sex: M Adm. 1/3/2015, D/C: 1/7/2015

CONSULT NOTE

Author: ______________, MD (ED Physician)	Service: ED	Author Type: Physician
Filed: 1/4/2015 12:34	Note Time: 12:29	

Consult Orders:

1. Inpatient consult to Orthopedic Surgery ordered by ______________, MD (ED physician) at 1/3/2015 21:06

Chief Complaint: Patient seen today for right hip fx

HPI/Hospital Course Summary:
John Patient is an 81 y.o. male with history of hypertension, CAD s/p CABG 3 years ago, hyperlipidemia who presented to the ED for evaluation of right leg and hip pain following a fall. Right intertrochanteric fx seen on x-ray. Ortho Surgery consulted.

Subjective:
Pertinent Review of Systems:
Patient complains of hip pain. All questions answered.

Objective:
Vital Signs

BP 142/82	Pulse 76	Temp 98.9°F (37.2°C) (Oral)	Resp 14	SpO_2 95%

Physical Exam:
GEN: WNWM NAD
HEENT: anicteric sclerae, some drainage from right eye
Neck supple
GI: soft, N/T ND
MSS: grossly intact but limited due to pain
Neuro: Alert, conversant, and cooperative; well spoken
Sensation, motor, and distal pulses intact b/l LE
Skin: Warm and dry, without visible rash in inspected area

Scheduled Meds:

- Start on 1/5/2015 Cefazolin IV; 2 g, Intravenous — On call to OR
- Morphine 4 g, Intravenous; completed — Once
- Ondansetron 4 g Intravenous; completed — Once
- Potassium chloride 10 mEq Intravenous — Once

Continuous Infusions:

- 0.9% NaCl with KCI 40 mEq

PRN Meds:
Recent Labs:

Lab	1/4/2015 06:07	1/3/2015 21:45
WBC	10.2	11.2*
HGB	10.2*	10.3*
HCT	29.5*	30.0*
PLT	208	219

CONSULT NOTE, CONTINUED 2

Lab	1/4/2015	1/3/2015 21:45
INR		1.02
NA		142
K		3.2*
CL		103
CO_2		25
BUN		15
CREATININE		0.97
GLU		133*
CALCIUM		8.3*
ANIONGAP		7
AST		27
ALT		31
ALKPHOS		129*
BILITOT		0.8

The CrCl is unknown because both a height and weight (above a minimum accepted value) are required for this calculation.

Imaging Studies:
X-ray Hip Right 2 or more views
Right intertrochanteric femur fracture

* The specific lab value is either above or below the normal range.

Assessment:
Principal Problem:
*Hip fx
Active Problems:
Coronary artery disease
Hypertension
Intertrochanteric fracture of right femur

Plan:
*Pt is low risk for surgery. He exercises regularly. No CP/SOB Had neg treadmill stress test in 2012—as per IMS
*HTN—stable
*Modest hypokalemia—on NS c KCI
*Urgent surgery for R hip fracture. Consent obtained, all questions answered from patient and wife.
Cefazolin on call to OR.

Electronically signed by: ________________, MD 1/4/2015 12:34

Appendix 8: Informed consent for invasive, diagnostic, medical, and surgical procedures

XYZ HOSPITAL	Chart No.: Name: Unit No.: (*Patient Imprint Card*)

INFORMED CONSENT FOR INVASIVE, DIAGNOSTIC, MEDICAL, & SURGICAL PROCEDURES

I hereby permit ____________________ (Name of Attending Physician or Authorized Health Care Provider) or his/her Associate Attending Physician of the same service, and assistants as may be selected and supervised by him/her to perform the following medical treatment, operation, or procedure (hereafter called the "procedure"):

REDUCTION OF RIGHT INTERTROCHANTERIC FEMUR FRACTURE

The procedure has been explained to me and I have been told the reasons why I need the procedure. The risks of the procedure have also been explained to me. In addition, I have been told that the procedure may not have the result I expect. I have also been told about other possible treatments for my condition and what might happen if no treatment is received.

I understand that in addition to the risks described to me about this procedure there are risks that may occur with any surgical or medical procedure. I am aware that the practice of medicine and surgery is not an exact science, and that I have not been given any guarantees about the results of this procedure.

I have had enough time to discuss my condition and treatment with my health care providers and all of my questions have been answered to my satisfaction. I believe I have enough information to make an informed decision and I agree to have the procedure. If something unexpected happens and I need additional or different treatment(s) from the treatment I expect, I agree to accept any treatment which is necessary.

I agree to have transfusions of blood and other blood products that may be necessary along with the procedure I am having. The risks, benefits, and alternatives have been explained to me and all of my questions have been answered to my satisfaction. ***If I refuse to have transfusions, I will cross out and initial this section and sign a REFUSAL OF TREATMENT form.***

I agree to allow this facility to keep, use or properly dispose of tissue and parts of organs that are removed during this procedure.

______________________________________ ________________

Signature of Patient or Parent/Legal Guardian Date

If the patient cannot consent for him/herself, the signature of either the health care agent or legal guardian who is acting on behalf of the patient, or the patient's next of kin who is assenting to the treatment for the patient must be obtained.

______________________________________ ________________

Signature of Health Care Agent/Legal Guardian Date

______________________________________ ________________

Signature & Relation of Next of Kin Date

WITNESS:

I, __________________ am a facility employee who is not the patient's physician or authorized health care provider named above and I have witnessed the patient or other appropriate person voluntarily sign this form.

____

Signature and Title of Witness

INTERPRETER/TRANSLATOR: (To be signed by the interpreter/translator if the patient required such assistance)

To the best of my knowledge, the patient understood what was interpreted/translated and voluntarily signed the form.

____

Signature of Interpreter/Translator

Appendix 9: Operative note

XYZ HEALTHCARE SYSTEM
XYZ HOSPITAL
123 Elm Street
Anywhere, US 12345

PATIENT: John Q. Patient
MRN: 0000000
DOB: 1/1/1933, Sex: M
Adm. 1/3/2015, D/C: 1/7/2015

OPERATIVE NOTE

Op Note signed by ____________, MD Service: Orthopedics Author Type: Physician
Filed 1/4/15 15:54 Note Time: 1/4/15 15:53

Preop: Right intertrochanteric femur fracture
Postop: Same
Surgeon: __________________, MD
Assistant: __________________, PA-C
Complication: None
EBL: 250
Anesthesia: General
To PACU in stable condition

Indications: Fall with intertrochanteric fracture. Risk and benefits were discussed. Risks included but not limited to death, stroke, MI, PE, DVT, and nerve and blood vessel damage. Risks also include possible need for further surgery, residual stiffness, and incomplete relief of symptoms, hardware failure, need for removal of hardware. The patient and family understood and wished to proceed with surgery, therefore they were scheduled and consent was signed.

Description of the Procedure:
The patient was identified and procedure was verified as above. A time out was performed to confirm site, side, and surgical procedure as well as adequate antibiotic administration. After adequate anesthesia, the patient was placed in the supine position on the fracture table and operative extremity was prepped and draped in the normal sterile fashion. The fracture was reduced in the AP and lateral planes and verified with intraoperative x-ray.

An incision was then made over the proximal aspect of the lateral hip just above the greater trochanter. The incision was carried down onto the lateral aspect of the proximal femur at the greater trochanter. The guide wires for the IM nail were placed and confirmed to be in adequate position in the AP and lateral planes under fluoroscopy. This was then over reamed and the rod was placed without difficulty and positioned so that the helical blade was in the center–center position on C-arm. The locking screw was placed in adequate position in the AP and lateral planes using the outrigger guide and C-arm. The wounds were irrigated with sterile saline. The wounds were then closed in layers and staples were used for skin. A final x-ray in the AP and lateral planes demonstrated adequate position of all hardware as well as the fracture. Sterile dressing was applied and patient was awoken from anesthesia without difficulty. Transferred to PACU in stable condition.

___________________________, MD

Electronically signed by ________________, MD on 1/4/2015 15:54

Appendix 10: Anesthesia note

XYZ HEALTHCARE SYSTEM	PATIENT: John Q. Patient
XYZ HOSPITAL	MRN: 0000000
123 Elm Street	DOB: 1/1/1933, Sex: M
Anywhere, US 12345	Adm. 1/3/2015, D/C: 1/7/2015

ANESTHESIA NOTE

Patient: John Q. Patient	Male 81 y.o.		
Height: 5'10"	Weight: 155 lb (70.308 kg) (1/5/2015)	BMI: 22.2	NPO Status: Not recorded

Allergies: DILAUDID (PF) ASA Status: 3

Procedure Summary

Date	Anesthesia Start	Anesthesia Stop	Room/Location
1/4/2015	14:43	16:14	XYZH/MAIN OR

Procedure	Diagnosis	Surgeon:	Anesthesiologist:
ORIF TROCHANTERIC/HIP FRACTURE (right hip)	Intertrochanteric fracture of right femur	____________, MD	____________, MD

Staff

Name	Role	Begin	End
___________, MD	Anesthesia MD	14:43	16:14
___________, AA	Anesthetist	14:43	14:55
___________, CRNA	Anesthetist	14:55	16:14

Events

Date	Time	Event
1/4/2015	14:43	Anesthesia start
	14:46	Patient in room
	14:46	Start data collection
	14:57	Induction
	14:58	Intubation

14:59	Induction complete
15:21	Procedure start
15:21	Time out performed
15:24	Upper warm air on
15:57	Upper warm air off
16:00	Procedure end
16:04	Extubation
16:08	Stop data collection
16:14	Handoff
	Handoff report given and RN satisfied with transfer of care
16:14	Anesthesia stop

Lines, Drains, and Airways

Type	Details	Placement	Removal
Peripheral IV	Placement date: 1/4/2015 Present on admit: yes Size: 20G, orientation: left Location: hand	1/4/2015 by ______, RN	1/6/2015 by ______, LPN
LMAs	Placement date: 1/5/15; Placement time: 14:58, Inserted by: Anesthetist; LMA Device:disposable LMA; LMA size 4; Preoxygenation: yes, by mask; Mask ventilation: easy; Insertion Attempts: 2; Placement: atraumatic; Dental trauma: no; Secured by: tape; Humidifier used: yes; Removal -	1/4/15 14:58 by _____, AA	1/4/15 16:04 by__, CRNA

ANESTHESIA NOTE, CON'T. 2

LMAs, con't.	Airway suctioned: airway not suctioned; Removal-respiratory Effort: adequate; Removal of airway device: yes; device removed Intact: yes; Removal LOC: responds to commands; Resp. exchange post removal: good.		
Incision	1/4/15; 16:28; Hip; Right;1/7/15	1/4/15 16:28 by _____,RN	1/7/15 14:33 by____LPN

Positioning

Pre-operative Vitals

No BP, pulse, respiration, SpO_2, or temp. recorded

Ht. 5'10" (1.778 m) (1/5/15)	Wt. 155 lb (70.308 kg) (1/5/15)
BMI: 22.2	IBW: 160 lb 15 oz (73.001 kg)

Anesthesia History

Hypertension	Hyperlipidemia
Coronary artery disease	Carotid artery occlusion
GERD (gastroesophageal disease)	H/O myocardial perfusion scan
Pigmented basal cell carcinoma	Colon polyp

Facility Administered Medications

No medications found

Surgical History

Coronary artery bypass graft	Esophagus surgery
Upper gastrointestinal endoscopy	Colonoscopy

Anesthesia Medications					
Fentanyl injection	25 mcg	Given IV	1/4/15	14:57	____________, AA
	25 mcg	Given IV		15:03	____________, AA
	25 mcg	Given IV		15:23	____________, CRNA
	25 mcg	Given IV		15:27	____________, CRNA
Lidocaine injection 2%	40 mg	Given IV	1/4/15	14:57	____________, AA
Propofol injection	160 mg	Given IV	1/4/15	14:57	____________, AA
Phenylephrine injection	100 mcg	Given IV	1/4/15	15:10	____________, AA
	100 mcg	Given IV		15:15	____________, AA
	100 mcg	Given IV		15:19	____________, CRNA
	100 mcg	Given IV		15:30	____________, CRNA
	100 mcg	Given IV		15:39	____________, CRNA
	100 mcg	Given IV		15:44	____________, CRNA
	100 mcg	Given IV		15:47	____________, CRNA
Ondansetron injection	4 mg	Given IV	1/4/15	15:49	____________, CRNA
Cefazolin in dextrose (iso-os) IVPB 2 g	2 mg	Given IV	1/4/15	15:02	____________, AA
Hydromorphone injection 2mg/mL	0.5 mg	Given IV	1/4/15	15:36	____________, CRNA
Lactated ringers infusion (mL)	800 mL	New IV bag	1/4/15	14:43	____________, CRNA

ANESTHESIA NOTE, CON'T. 3

Preoperative Note: Last edited 1/4/15 16:28 by ____________, CRNA

Anesthesia Evaluation
No history of anesthetic complications

AIRWAY: Mallampati: I; TM distance: >3 FB; Neck ROM: full; (+) patient has adequate range of motion in the cervical spine and no symptoms of cord compression were reported by the patient.

DENTAL: Normal exam

PULMONARY: (+) ex-smoker, 1 pack/day, 15 years; ROS comment: quit smoking 1964

CARDIOVASCULAR: (+) hypertension: CAD; ROS comment: S/p CABG 11/11. LIMA to LAD; SVG to mid-OM; Pt seen by cardiologist 12/16/14 for increased fatigue…patient was scheduled for a stress test 1/5/15.

NEURO/PSYCH: Negative ROS

ENDO/OTHER:

MUSCULAR/SKELETAL:

OBSTETRICS HISTORY:

Anesthesia Plan:

ASA 3
Anesthesia Type: General

Patient is NPO per protocol

Appendix 11: Physician orders

XYZ HEALTHCARE SYSTEM
XYZ HOSPITAL
123 Elm Street
Anywhere, US 12345

PATIENT: John Q. Patient
MRN: 0000000
DOB: 1/1/1933, Sex: M
Adm. 1/3/2015, D/C: 1/7/2015

PHYSICIAN ORDERS

Morphine injection 4 mg
Ordering user: __________, MD 1/3/2015 22:21 Ordering provider: __________, MD
Authorized by: __________, MD Frequency: Q4H PRN 1/5/2015 07:02
Electronically signed by: _________, MD 1/6/2015 22:21, for discontinuing in per protocol: cosign required mode, Communicator: _______, RN. Released by: _________, RN 1/5/2015
Discontinued by: _________, RN 1/5/2015 07:08
PRN reasons: severe pain (7/10)

Ondansetron injection 4 mg
Ordering user: __________, MD 1/3/2015 22:21 Ordering provider: ___________, MD
Authorized by: __________, MD Frequency: Q6H PRN 1/5/2015 07:02
Electronically signed by: ________, MD 1/6/2015 22:21, for discontinuing in per protocol: cosign required mode, Communicator: _______, RN. Released by: _________, RN 1/5/2015
Discontinued by: _________, RN 1/5/2015 07:08
PRN nausea, vomiting

Vital signs every 4 hours for 24 hours
Ordering user: __________, MD 1/4/2015 14:58 Ordering provider: __________, MD
Authorized by: __________, MD Frequency: Q4H PRN 1/4/2015 19:53 Until specified
Electronically signed by: _________, MD 1/4/2015 14:58, for discontinuing in per protocol: cosign required mode, Communicator: _________, RN. Released by: __________, RN 1/4/2015 16:47

Vital signs every 8 hours for 24 hours
Ordering User: ___________, MD 1/4/2015 14:58 Ordering Provider: ___________, MD
Authorized by: ___________, MD Frequency: Q8H PRN 1/5/2015 19:53 Until specified
Electronically signed by: _________, MD 1/4/2015 14:58, for discontinuing in per protocol: cosign required mode, Communicator: __________, RN. Released by: __________, RN 1/4/2015 16:47

Notify the physician of the following

Ordering user: ___________, MD 1/4/2015 14:58 Ordering provider: _____________, MD
Authorized by: ___________, MD Frequency: Until discontinued 1/4/2015 16:48
Electronically signed by: _________, MD 1/4/2015 14:58, for discontinuing in per protocol: cosign required mode, Communicator: _________, RN. Released by: ___________, RN 1/4/2015 16:47

Comments: Urinary output less than 30 mL/kg/hr or no void within 8 hours after Foley removed; Heart rate less than 50 or greater than 120; Systolic BP less than 90 or greater than 160; Respiratory rate less than 10 or greater than 20; Unable to maintain Pulse Oximeter equal or greater than 90.

Up in chair at least twice per day beginning on POD

Ordering user: ___________, MD 1/4/2015 14:58 Ordering provider: _____________, MD
Authorized by: ___________, MD Frequency: BID 1/5/2015 19:53
Electronically signed by: __________, MD 1/4/2015 14:58, for discontinuing in per protocol: cosign required mode, Communicator: ___________, RN. Released by: __________, RN 1/4/2015 16:47

Stand to void or use bedside commode on day of surgery

Ordering user: ___________, MD 1/4/2015 14:58 Ordering provider: _____________, MD
Authorized by: ___________, MD Frequency: Q4H PRN 1/4/2015 19:53
Electronically signed by: _________, MD 1/4/2015 14:58, for discontinuing in per protocol: cosign required mode, Communicator: ____________, RN. Released by: __________, RN 1/4/2015 16:47

Neurovascular checks

Ordering user: ___________, MD 1/4/2015 14:58 Ordering provider: _____________, MD
Authorized by: ___________, MD Frequency: Q2H PRN 1/4/2015 18:00—24 hours
Electronically signed by: _________, MD 1/4/2015 14:58, for discontinuing in per protocol: cosign required mode, Communicator: ___________, RN. Released by: ___________, RN 1/4/2015 16:47

Appendix 12: Progress note

XYZ HEALTHCARE SYSTEM	PATIENT: John Q. Patient
XYZ HOSPITAL	MRN: 0000000
123 Elm Street	DOB: 1/1/1933, Sex: M
Anywhere, US 12345	Adm. 1/3/2015, D/C: 1/7/2015

PROGRESS NOTE

Daily Progress Note—Orthopedics

Subjective:

Postoperative Day: 2 status postproximal IM nail right hip
Systemic or Specific Complaints: appropriate pain

Objective:

Blood pressure 150/77, pulse 79, temperature 97.2°F (36.2°C), temperature source Oral, resp. rate 19, height 5'10" (1.778 m), weight 70.302 kg, SpO_2 100.00

General: Alert, comfortable, and cooperative
Wound: Wound clean and dry, no evidence of infection
DVT Exam: No evidence of DVT seen on physical exam
Vascular Exam: Operative extremity neurovascularly intact

Hemoglobin

Date	**Value**	**Range**	**Status**
1/5/2015	8.2*	14.0–18.0 g/dL	Final
1/4/2015	10.2*	14.0–18.0 g/dL	Final

Hematocrit

Date	**Value**	**Range**	**Status**
1/5/2015	23.9*	38.0–49.0	Final
1/4/2015	29.5*	38.0–49.0	Final

Assessment:

Status postproximal IM nail right hip
Physical therapy progress is good
Complications: None
Acute blood loss anemia—symptomatic—received blood through the night—feels better now

* The specific lab value is either above or below the normal range.

Plan:

Weight bearing status—partial weight bearing (PWB)
Continue current postop. course
OK to transfer to SAR from ortho standpoint—will need to continue current PT and see in office for x-rays at 4 weeks PO
Will need suture removal at 12–14 days PO per SAR staff

Signed:
____________________, MD
1/6/2015
14:58

Appendix 13: Nursing notes

XYZ HEALTHCARE SYSTEM
XYZ HOSPITAL
123 Elm Street
Anywhere, US 12345

PATIENT: John Q. Patient
MRN: 0000000
DOB: 1/1/1933, Sex: M
Adm. 1/3/2015, D/C: 1/7/2015

NURSING NOTES

DATE	TIME	NOTES	INITIALS
1/3/15	2410	Patient resting comfortably; pain scale 4/10; IV intact	aaa
1/3/15	0217	Patient restless; pain scale 6/10; IV intact; 800 mg ibuprofen given	aaa
1/3/15	0622	Vitals: BP 144/76; temp 98.7; resp 15; pulse 71. Surgical dressing checked and wound cleaned and dressing changed; ordered meds given	aaa
1/3/15	0915	Patient resting comfortably; pain scale 4/10; catheter checked intact; voided 20 cc; no breakfast eaten	bbb
1/4/15	1218	Patient repositioned; medications given; no acute distress at this time; vitals stable	bbb
1/4/15	1623	Patient in room post surgery; sleeping; IV intact; on telemetry	bbb
1/4/15	2045	Patient resting comfortably; pain scale 4/10; BP 145/75; temp 98.4; pulse 70; Medications given	bbb
1/5/15	0934	Patient repositioned; breakfast not eaten; pain scale 6/10; 800 mg ibuprofen given	ccc
1/5/15	1324	Patient out of bed sitting in chair; ambulatory; assisted to bathroom; patient declined pain medication	ccc
1/5/15	1530	Patient back in bed; resting comfortably; pain scale 4/10	ccc
1/5/15	2010	Patient ambulatory with increased activity; assisted to bathroom	ccc

1/6/15	1127	Patient to PT; ate minimal breakfast	ddd
1/6/15	1230	Patient in room after PT; states tired, back in bed; complains of pain (5/10) 800 mg ibuprofen given	ddd
1/6/15	1522	Post surgical dressing intact; skin intact on right elbow	ddd
1/7/15	0945	Patient to PT; required minimal assistance; ambulatory with walker	eee
1/7/15	1215	Patient activity limited due to complaints of pain; requires several rest periods during activity; patient limited by fatigue	eee
1/7/15	1637	BP 147/80, temp 98.5, pulse 68; patient out of bed with assistance; unable to complete heel slides	eee
1/7/15	2145	Decreased bed mobility, decreased gait, decreased balance, increased fall risk	fff
1/8/15	0932	Patient discharged to skilled nursing facility	ggg

Appendix 14: Medication administration record

XYZ HEALTHCARE SYSTEM
XYZ HOSPITAL
123 Elm Street
Anywhere, US 12345

PATIENT: John Q. Patient
MRN: 0000000
DOB: 1/1/1933, Sex: M
Adm. 1/3/2015, D/C: 1/7/2015

MEDICATION ADMINISTRATION RECORD

0.9% NaCl Infusion
Ordered on 1/4/15 1314 by ____________, MD
Dose: (Remaining/Total): (–/–)
Route: Intravenous
Admin. Instructions:

Starts/Ends: 1/4/15 1315–1/4/15 1623
Frequency: Continuous
Rate/Duration: 75 mL/hr

Administration	Status	Dose	Route	Site	Given By
1/4/15 1751	Rate 75 mL/hr	500 mL	IV		________________, RN

0.9% NaCl with KCL 20 mEq Infusion
Ordered on 1/4/15 1647 by ____________, MD
Dose: (Remaining/Total): (–/–)
Route: Intravenous
Admin. Instructions:

Starts/Ends: 1/4/15 1700–1/7/15 1953
Frequency: Continuous
Rate/Duration: 75 mL/hr

Administration	Status	Dose	Route	Site	Given By
1/6/15 1238	New bag Rate: 75 mL/hr		IV		_____________, RN
1/5/15 2017	New bag Rate: 75 mL/hr		IV		_____________, RN
1/5/15 0532	New bag Rate: 75 mL/hr		IV		_____________, RN
1/4/15 1730	New bag Rate: 75 mL/hr		IV		_____________, RN

0.9% NaCl with KCL 40 mEq 1000 mL Infusion

Ordered on 1/4/15 0757 by____________, MD
Dose: (Remaining/Total): (–/–)
Route: Intravenous
Admin. Instructions:

Starts/Ends: 1/4/15 0900–1/4/15 1623
Frequency: Continuous
Rate/Duration: 100 mL/hr

Administration	Status	Dose	Route	Site	Given By
1/4/15 0913	New bag Rate: 100 mL/hr	IV			____________, RN

Alprazolam tablet 0.25 mg

Ordered on 1/4/15 1647 by ____________, MD
Dose: (Remaining/Total): (–/–): 0.25 mg
Route: Oral
Admin. Instructions: Hold for sedation

Starts/Ends: 1/4/15 1647–1/7/15 1953
Frequency: Every 6 hours PRN
Rate/Duration:

Administration	Status	Dose	Route	Site	Given By
1/4/15 1700		0.25 mg	Oral		____________, RN
1/5/15 0900		0.25 mg	Oral		____________, RN
1/6/15 0930		0.25 mg	Oral		____________, RN
1/7/15 1010		0.25 mg	Oral		____________, RN

Appendix 15: Lab report

XYZ HEALTHCARE SYSTEM
XYZ HOSPITAL
123 Elm Street
Anywhere, US 12345

PATIENT: John Q. Patient
MRN: 0000000
DOB: 1/1/1933, Sex: M
Adm. 1/3/2015, D/C: 1/7/2015

LAB REPORT

CBC
Ordering Provider: ______________, MD 1/4/15 00:07
Specimen Collection: Blood 1/4/15 06:07

Component	**Value**	**Ref. Range**	**Flag**	**Comment**
WBC	10.2	3.4–10.8 K/μL		
RBC	3.16	4.30–6.10 m/mm^3		
Hemoglobin	10.2	14.0–18.0 g/dL		
Hematocrit	29.5	38.0–49.0%		
MCV	93	80–96 fL		
MCH	32	26–34 pg		
MCHC	35	32–36 g/dL		
RDW	15.2	11.5–15.5%		
MPV	8.5	6.0–9.5 fL		
Platelets	208	150–440 K/μL		

Hemoglobin and hematocrit, blood—daily for 3 days starting on POD 1

Ordering Provider: ______________, MD 1/5/15 00:07
Specimen Collection: Blood 1/5/15 03:35

Component	**Value**	**Ref. Range**	**Flag**	**Comment**
Hemoglobin	8.2	14.0–18.0 g/dL		
Hematocrit	23.9	38.0–49.0%		

BASIC METABOLIC PANEL
Ordering Provider: ______________, MD 1/5/15 00:07
Specimen Collection: Blood 1/4/15 03:35

Component	Value	Ref. Range	Flag	Comment
Glucose	152	82–115 mg/dL		
BUN	24	9–20 mg/dL		
Creatinine	1.40	0.66–1.25 mg/dL		
Sodium	140	137–145 mmol/L		
Potassium	4.3	3.5–5.1 mmol/L		
Chloride	103	98–107 mmol/L		
CO_2	23	22–30 mmol/L		
Calcium	8.0	8.4–10.2 mg/dL		
Anion gap	18	10–20		
BUN/creatinine ratio	17	7–25		
GFR MDRD	49	>60 mL/min/1.73 sqm		

BASIC METABOLIC PANEL
Ordering Provider: ______________, MD 1/7/15 00:06
Specimen Collection: Blood 1/7/15 04:05

Component	Value	Ref. Range	Flag	Comment
Glucose	112	82–115 mg/dL		
BUN	22	9–20 mg/dL		
Creatinine	0.98	0.66–1.25 mg/dL		
Sodium	137	137–145 mmol/L		
Potassium	3.9	3.5–5.1 mmol/L		
Chloride	106	98–107 mmol/L		
CO_2	24	22–30 mmol/L		
Calcium	8.1	8.4–10.2 mg/dL		
Anion gap	12	10–20		
BUN/creatinine ratio	22	7–25		
GFR MDRD	49	>60 mL/min/1.73 sqm		

Appendix 16: Discharge summary

XYZ HEALTHCARE SYSTEM	PATIENT: John Q. Patient
XYZ HOSPITAL	MRN: 0000000
123 Elm Street	DOB: 1/1/1933, Sex: M
Anywhere, US 12345	Adm. 1/3/2015, D/C: 1/7/2015

DISCHARGE SUMMARY

Patient ID: John Q. Patient—81 y.o. male
000-00-0000

Admit Date: 1/3/2015 19:09

Admitting Physician: ________________, MD

Discharge Physician: ________________, MD

Admission Diagnoses: Coronary artery disease, hypertension, hip fracture, intertrochanteric fracture of right femur

Discharge Diagnoses: Principal Problem: *Hip fx
Active Problems: Coronary artery disease, hypertension, intertrochanteric fracture of right femur

Hospital Course:
John Q. Patient is an 81 y.o. male with a past medical history of hypertension, CAD s/p CABG 3 years ago, hyperlipidemia who presented to the ED for evaluation of right leg and hip pain following a fall on 1/3/2015. Patient states that he was trying to turn around but turned too quickly, tripping and falling on his right side. Orthopedics consulted, ORIF 1/4/2015. Transfusion 2 units PRC 1/5/2015. Patient tolerating physical therapy and discharged to SAR for continued therapy. The patient will follow up with Orthopedics in 4 weeks.

Discharge Exam:
GEN: Thin WM NAD
HEENT: Anicteric sclerae, MMM, O/P clear; no thrush, neck supple, without cervical or supraclavicular adenopathy
CVS: RRR, S1 and S2, no LE edema B/L
RESP: CTA B/L
GI: +BS, soft, N/T N/D

MSS: Strength appropriate, right thigh drsg C/D/I
NEURO: Alert, conversant, and cooperative
SKIN: Warm and dry, without visible rash in inspected area

Objective:

Vital Signs: BP 147/77; Pulse 80; Temp 98.4°F (36.9°C) (oral); Resp 20; Ht 5'10" (1.778 m); Wt 70.308 kg; BMI 22.24 kg/m^2; SpO_2 93%

Recent Labs:

Lab	**1/7/15**	**1/5/15**	**1/4/15**	**1/3/15**
WBC	11.9*	—	10.2	11.2*
HGB	8.8*	8.2*	10.2*	10.3*
HCT	24.2*	23.9*	29.5*	30.0*
PLT	186	—	208	219
NEUTROPHILPCT	72	—	—	81*
MONOPCT	3	—	—	3
INR				1.02

Lab	**1/7/15**	**1/5/15**	**1/4/15**	**1/3/15**
NA	137	140	—	142
K	3.9	4.3	—	3.2*
CL	106	103	—	103

Lab	**1/7/15**	**1/5/15**	**1/4/15**	**1/3/15**
CO_2	24	23	—	25
BUN	22*	24*	—	15
CREATININE	0.98	1.40*	—	0.97
GLU	112	152*	—	133*
CALCIUM	8.1*	8.0*	—	8.3*
ANIONGAP	12	18	—	17

Lab	**1/3/15**
AST	27
ALT	31
ALKPHOS	129*
BILITOT	0.8

Discharged Condition: Good

Disposition: SNF

Patient Instructions:

Meds:

Home Medication Instructions:
Aspirin 81 mg chewable tablet; take one by mouth daily
Fluoxetine 10 mg capsule; take 20 mg by mouth daily
Atorvastatin 40 mg tablet; take 0.5 mg by mouth daily

* The specific lab value is either above or below the normal range.

Atorvastatin 20 mg tablet; take 1 tablet by mouth daily
Omeprazole 40 mg capsule; take 1 capsule by mouth daily
Amlodipine 5 mg tablet: take 1 tablet by mouth daily
Cetirizine 10 mg tablet; take 1 tablet by mouth daily as needed for itching
Docusate sodium 100 mg capsule; take 1 capsule by mouth two times daily as needed for constipation
Enoxaparin 40 mg/0.4 mL Syrg; inject 0.4 mL (40 mg total) into the skin daily
Ibuprofen 400 mg tablet; take 1 tablet by mouth every 6 hours as needed
Magnesium hydroxide 400 mg/5 mL suspension; take 30 mL by mouth nightly as needed for constipation
Pantoprazole 40 mg tablet; take one tablet by mouth every morning before breakfast
Zolpidem 5 mg tablet; take 1 tablet by mouth nightly as needed for sleep
Tramadol 50 mg tablet; take 1 tablet by mouth every 6 hours as needed for pain

Patient Instructions:
As per patient discharge instructions

Follow up with Orthopedics in 4 weeks
Activity as tolerated
Regular diet

Suture removal in 10–14 days per SAR staff

Signed: ________________, NP

1/7/2015
14:03

Electronically signed by ________________, MD 1/8/2015, 20:11

Appendix 17: Incident report

XYZ HEALTHCARE SYSTEM

INCIDENT REPORT

Use this form to report any unexpected patient incidents related to patient care or treatment, even if there is no adverse patient outcome (includes errors, safety hazards, injuries, and sentinel events). This form is to be completed by XYZ Hospital personnel.

Identification of person affected by incident:
Name: ____________________
Date of Birth: ____________________
Date/Time of Incident: ____________________

Location:
Hospital: ____________________
Department/Unit: ____________________

Onsite Staff Involved:

Name:	Title:
____________________	____________________
____________________	____________________
____________________	____________________

Nature of Incident: (Check all boxes that apply)

Malfunction Equipment/Monitors	[ ]	Breach of Policies/Protocol	[ ]	Failure to Perform Investigation	[ ]
Lack of Equipment/Monitors	[ ]	Poor Patient Preparation	[ ]	Delay in Urgent Investigation	[ ]
User Error of Equipment/Monitors	[ ]	Inappropriate Request	[ ]	Failure to Interpret Results	[ ]
Medication Prescription Error	[ ]	Inappropriate/No Escort	[ ]	Wrong Dose Radiation	[ ]
Medication Dispensing Error	[ ]	Breach of Confidentiality	[ ]	Wrong Site	[ ]
Medication Administration Error	[ ]	Patient Documentation	[ ]	Wrong Patient	[ ]
Extravasation	[ ]	Patient Positioning	[ ]	Repeat Dose Unnecessarily	[ ]
Infection Control Issue	[ ]	Consent	[ ]	Pregnancy not Considered in Radiation Exposure	[ ]

Patient Outcome: (Check all boxes that apply)

Death	[ ]	Pain/Prolonged Pain	[ ]	Disruption to Services	[ ]
Critical Condition	[ ]	Patient Distress	[ ]	Unable to Assess Outcome	[ ]
Injury	[ ]	Delay in Treatment	[ ]	Near Miss by Chance	[ ]
Ill Health	[ ]	Change to Treatment	[ ]	Near Miss by Intervention	[ ]
Temporary Deterioration of Condition	[ ]	Prolonged Stay in Hospital	[ ]	No Adverse Effect	[ ]
Transfer to Higher Level of Care	[ ]	Radiation Overexposure	[ ]		

Contributory Factors: (Check all boxes that apply)

Knowledge/Training	[ ]	Poor Communication	[ ]	Poor Documentation	[ ]
Staffing Issues	[ ]	Distraction	[ ]	Poor Handwriting	[ ]
Lack of Appropriate Equipment	[ ]	Labeling	[ ]	Use of Abbreviations	[ ]
Breach of Policy/Procedure	[ ]	Supplies	[ ]	Storage	[ ]
Other:					

Narrative Summary of Incident: (State facts only and not opinion—attach separate sheet if necessary—ensure that all necessary steps have been taken to support and treat anyone injured and prevent injury to others—ensure that medical records are factual and current)

Action Taken as a Result of Incident:

Employee Acknowledgment:

Employee Name: ______________________________ Title/Position: ______________________________

I acknowledge that the facts and circumstances reported above are true and accurate to the best of my knowledge:

Employee Signature: ______________________________ Date: ______________________________

Appendix 18: Evidence receipt and chain of custody

AGENCY NAME

EVIDENCE RECEIPT AND CHAIN OF CUSTODY

Case Name: ______________________________ Case No.: ____________

Submitting Officer: (Name/ID#): ____

Date/Time Evidence Obtained: ____________________ Location: ____________

Description of Evidence

Item #	Quantity	Description of Item

Chain of Custody

Item #	Date/Time	Released by	Received by	Purpose

Appendix 19: Peer review report

PEER REVIEW REPORT

Peer Review of: ________________, MD
Date: ________________
Peer Review Conducted By: ________________, MD

Brief description of symptom, diagnosis, and course of treatment:

________________, M.D. is a board-certified pediatrician who practiced in Atlanta, Georgia at XYZ Health Associates. He finished his pediatric residency in 1986. He has no listed ABMS certified pain management boards. He lists himself as a pain management physician.

Review of 12 charts showed that he was seeing patients from Kentucky, Tennessee, and Virginia with no listed insurance. Many had been seen by pain clinics in Florida. No old records from prior treating physicians were in the charts. The patients were not referred by treating physicians. Immunoassay drug testing was done. The results were not followed or commented upon. Interestingly, patients were charged extra if the results were not consistent. Patients were treated with high doses of oxycodone. Oxycodone 30 mg and oxycodone 15 mg were prescribed for all patients. The combination makes no pharmacological sense. All of them were also treated with relatively high doses of alprazolam with no diagnosis. They were given subtherapeutic doses of ibuprofen. MRIs were from out of state in the majority of cases.

1. Patient A. A. is a 20 y/o female from Kentucky who had no listed insurance. She was treated with oxycodone 30 mg 6/day, oxycodone 15 mg 3/day, alprazolam 2 mg 1/day, and ibuprofen 800 mg 1/day. Urine drug screen (UDS) was positive for oxycodone, methadone, and THC. There were no records from her previous pain clinic. THC use was not addressed.
2. Patient B. B. is a 40 y/o male from North Carolina who had no listed insurance. He was treated with oxycodone 30 mg 6/day, oxycodone 15 mg 3/day, alprazolam 2 mg 1.5 1/day, and ibuprofen 800 mg 1/day. MRI was from West Palm Beach, FL. UDS was positive for oxycodone and benzodiazepines. He admitted to being treated by a pain clinic in FL. There were no records from his previous pain clinic.

3. Patient C. C. is a 26 y/o male from Tennessee who had no listed insurance. He was treated with oxycodone 30 mg 5/day, oxycodone 15 mg 3/day, alprazolam 2 mg 1/day, and ibuprofen 800 mg 20/month. MRI was from Boca Raton, FL. UDS was positive for oxycodone and benzodiazepines. He admitted to being treated by a pain clinic in Georgia. There were no records from his previous pain clinic.
4. Patient D. D. is a 49 y/o male from Virginia who had no listed insurance. He was treated with oxycodone 30 mg 6/day, oxycodone 15 mg 3/day, alprazolam 2 mg 1/day, and ibuprofen 800 mg 1/day. MRI was from Bristol, TN. He admitted to being treated by a pain clinic which had been closed. There were no records from his previous pain clinic.
5. Patient E. E. is a 51 y/o female from Virginia who had no listed insurance. She was treated with oxycodone 30 mg 6/day, oxycodone 15 mg 3/day, alprazolam 2 mg 1.5 q day, and ibuprofen 800 mg 1/day. MRI was from Bristol, TN. She admitted to being treated by a pain clinic in Kingsport, TN and FL. There were no records from her previous pain clinic. UDS was negative for all drugs. She was prescribed high doses in the face of negative UDS.
6. Patient F.F. is a 54 y/o male from Ohio who had no listed insurance. He was treated with oxycodone 30 mg 6/day, oxycodone 15 mg 3/day, alprazolam 2 mg 1 q day, and ibuprofen 800 mg 1/day. MRI was from Ashland, KY. He admitted to being treated by a pain clinic in Ashland, KY. There were no records from his previous pain clinic. UDS was positive for oxycodone and benzodiazepines.
7. Patient G. G. is a 23 y/o male from Kentucky who had no listed insurance. He was treated with oxycodone 30 mg 5/day, oxycodone 15 mg 3/day, alprazolam 2 mg q day, Flexeril bid, and ibuprofen 800 mg 20/month. MRI was from Tamarac, FL. UDS was not done. He admitted to being treated by a pain clinic in FL which was closed. There were no records from his previous pain clinic.
8. Patient H. H. is a 30 y/o male from Tennessee who had no listed insurance. He was treated with oxycodone 30 mg 6/day, oxycodone 15 mg 3/day, alprazolam 2 mg 2/day, ibuprofen 800 mg q day, and gabapentin 300 mg q day. MRI was from GA. UDS was positive for oxycodone and benzodiazepines. He admitted to being treated by a pain clinic. There were no records from his previous pain clinic.
9. Patient I. I. is a 30 y/o male from Tennessee who had no listed insurance. He was treated with oxycodone 30 mg 6/day, oxycodone 15 mg 3/day, alprazolam 2 mg 2/day, and ibuprofen 800 mg q day. MRI was from GA. UDS was positive for oxycodone and benzodiazepines once and negative for benzodiazepines (BZO) once. Alprazolam was prescribed in the face of negative UDS. He admitted to being treated by a pain clinic. There were no records from his previous pain clinic.
10. Patient J. J. is a 29 y/o male from Tennessee who had no listed insurance. He was treated with oxycodone 30 mg 6/day, oxycodone 15 mg 3/day, alprazolam 2 mg 2/day, and ibuprofen 800 mg q day. MRI was from Bay View, FL. UDS was positive for oxycodone and opiates while negative for benzodiazepines. No explanation for the UDS was given. He admitted to being treated by a pain clinic in Florida. There were no records from his previous pain clinic.
11. Patient K. K. is a 49 y/o male from Kentucky who had no listed insurance. He was treated with oxycodone 30 mg 6/day, oxycodone 15 mg 3/day, alprazolam 2 mg 2/day, and ibuprofen 800 mg q day. MRI was from Plantation, FL. UDS was positive for oxycodone and BZO. He admitted to being treated by a pain clinic in Florida. There were no records from his previous pain clinic.

12. Patient L. L. is a 44 y/o female from Kentucky who had no listed insurance. She was treated with oxycodone 30 mg 6/day, oxycodone 15 mg 3/day, alprazolam 2 mg/day, and ibuprofen 800 mg q day. MRI was from Plantation, FL. UDS was positive for oxycodone and BZO. She admitted to being treated by a pain clinic in Florida. There were no records from her previous pain clinic.

Can an opinion be formulated?

Based on my background, experience, and review of all information provided, and assuming that the treatment as documented was provided, I can form an opinion as to whether the care rendered by the physician, including diagnosis, treatment, and/or record-keeping, departed from or failed to conform to the minimal standards of acceptable and prevailing medical practice.

Opinion:
A.) *Diagnosis* (evaluation of a medical problem using means such as history, physical examination, laboratory, and radiologic studies, when applicable)

Dr. ____________ failed to conform to the minimal standards of acceptable and prevailing medical practice for the diagnosis of a medical problem. The history and physical fall below minimum standards. There is no appropriate history of the disease. Appropriate history includes at a minimum onset of the disease and the pain symptoms, location, quality, severity, and intensity of the pain. Description of the pain: Description of previous treatments and the success and failure of them. These are not included in the records. Physical exam was unacceptable for the complaint. There was no attempt to get old records. Diagnosis for a chronic pain patient at a minimum requires getting records from previous treating physicians, copies of old test results, and appropriate imaging studies, and blood work if this has not been performed. This was not done. He fell below minimum standards in seeing patients from another state without adequate workup and review of old records. The patients he was seeing from out of state who had seen other pain clinics in another state are presumed drug abusers until proven otherwise. Patients who are self referred who come from another state long distances are presumed drug abusers until proven otherwise. His treatment of patients from Ohio, Virginia, and Kentucky was below minimum standards. There was no response to inappropriate UDS which is below minimum standards.

B.) *Treatment* (use of medications and other modalities based on generally accepted and approved indications, with proper precautions to avoid adverse physical reactions, habituation, or addiction)

Dr. ____________ failed to conform to be minimal standards of acceptable and prevailing medical practice for the treatment of chronic pain. All of the patients were treated with the same combination of medications. Oxycodone and alprazolam were used. The oxycodone combination makes no pharmacologic sense. The ibuprofen dose is subtherapeutic. There was no attempt to use adjuvant medications. There was no attempt to use physical modalities or invasive treatment methods. There was no attempt to use proper precautions to avoid habituation or addiction. Prescriptions for narcotics to patients from Kentucky, Virginia, and Tennessee who had been seen in Florida pain clinics were given without adequate safeguards. Minimal standards require these patients to be treated as drug abusers and/or diverters until proven otherwise. Universal narcotic precautions should have been utilized in these patients. Urine drug screen results should have been responded to.

C.) Records (maintenance of records to furnish documentary evidence of the course of the patient's medical evaluation, treatment, and response)

Dr. ____________ failed to conform to the minimal standards of acceptable and prevailing medical practice in the maintenance of records. The records do not document any evidence of the treatment response and do not contain records from prior treating physicians. Minimal standards require the response to treatment to be documented and old records from prior treating pain clinics to be obtained.

Respectfully Submitted by:

________________________, MD

Appendix 20: Prescription drug monitoring programs and contact information[*]

Alabama
Program Manager
Prescription Drug Monitoring Program
Alabama Department of Public Health
201 Monroe Street, Suite 1010
Montgomery, AL 36130
334-206-3061

Alaska
Program Manager
Alaska Department of Business &
Professional Licensing
550 W. 7th Avenue, Suite 1500
Anchorage, AK 99501
907-269-8109

Arizona
Program Director
Arizona Board of Pharmacy
1616 West Adams Street, Suite 120
Phoenix, AZ 85007
602-7712744

Arkansas
Administrator
Prescription Drug Monitoring Program
Department of Health, Pharmacy Services
4815 W. Markham Street, Slot 25
Little Rock, AR 72205
501-683-3960

California
Manager
Prescription Drug Monitoring Program
Department of Justice—CURES/PDMP
4949 Broadway, Room G-110
Sacramento, CA 95820
916-227-3436

Colorado
Program Director
Prescription Drug Monitoring Program
Board of Pharmacy
1560 Broadway, Suite 1310
Denver, CO 80202
303-894-7751

* (Provided by the National Association of State Controlled Substance Authorities with permission)

Connecticut
Director
Drug Control Division
Department of Consumer Protection
165 Capitol Avenue, Room 145
Hartford, CT 06106
860-713-6079

Delaware
Program Administrator
Prescription Drug Monitoring Program
Board of Pharmacy
861 Silver Lake Blvd.
Cannon Building, Suite 203
Dover, DE 19904
302-744-4518

District of Columbia
Prescription Drug Monitoring Program
Board of Pharmacy
DC Pharmaceutical Control Division
899 North Capitol Street, First Floor
Washington, DC 20002
202-727-9856

Florida
Program Manager
Prescription Drug Monitoring Program
Florida Department of Health
4052 Bald Cypress Way, Bin #C16
Tallahassee, FL 32399
850-245-4797

Georgia
Program Manager
Prescription Drug Monitoring Program
Georgia Drugs & Narcotics Agency
254 Washington Street, SW, Suite G-2000
Atlanta, GA 30334
404-656-5100

Hawaii
Administrator
Narcotics Enforcement Division
Department of Public Safety
3375 Koapaka Street, Suite D-100
Honolulu, HI 96819
808-837-8470

Idaho
Program Information Coordinator
Board of Pharmacy
1199 Shoreline Lane, Suite 303
Boise, ID 83702
208-334-2356

Illinois
Data Manager
Prescription Drug Monitoring Program
Illinois Department of Human Services
401 N. Fourth Street, Room 126
Springfield, IL 62702
217-558-0943

Indiana
Program Manager
INSPECT
Indiana Professional Licensing
402 W. Washington Street, Room W-072
Indianapolis, IN 46202
317-234-1987

Iowa
Executive Director
Iowa Board of Pharmacy
400 S. W. Eighth Street, Suite E
Des Moines, IA 50309
515-281-5944

Kansas
Director
Prescription Drug Monitoring Program
Kansas State Board of Pharmacy
800 S. W. Jackson, Room 1414
Topeka, KS 66612
785-296-8717

Kentucky
KASPAR Program Manager
Kentucky Cabinet for Health & Family Services
275 E. Main Street, 5ED
Frankfort, KY 40621
501-564-2815 ext. 3162

Louisiana
Administrative Assistant
Prescription Drug Monitoring Program
Board of Pharmacy
3388 Brentwood Drive
Baton Rouge, LA 70809
225-925-4767

Maine
Coordinator
Prescription Drug Monitoring Program
Maine Office of Substance Abuse
11 State House Station
41 Anthony Avenue
Augusta, ME 04333
207-287-3363

Maryland
Manager
Prescription Drug Monitoring Program
Department of Health and Mental Hygiene, Behavioral Health
55 Wade Avenue
Catonsville, MD 21228
410-402-8609

Massachusetts
Director
Office of Prescription Monitoring and Drug Control
Department of Public Health
99 Chauncy Street
Boston, MA 02111
617-753-8062

Michigan
Director
Prescription Drug Monitoring Program
Bureau of Health Professions
Health Investigation Division
611 West Ottawa Street, 1st Floor West Side
Lansing, MI 48933
517-335-1769

Minnesota
Manager
Prescription Drug Monitoring Program
Board of Pharmacy
2829 University Avenue, SE-#350
Minneapolis, MN 55414
651-201-2833

Mississippi
Manager
Prescription Drug Monitoring Program
Board of Pharmacy
6360 I-55 North, Suite 400
Jackson, MS 39211

Missouri
Administrator
Bureau of Narcotics and Dangerous Drugs
P.O. Box 570
Jefferson City, MO 65102
573-751-6321

Montana
Program Manager
Prescription Drug Monitoring Program
Board of Pharmacy
301 S. Park Avenue
P.O. Box 200513
Helena, MT 59620
406-439-6015

Nebraska
Administrator
Prescription Drug Monitoring Program
Investigative Services Division
Nebraska State Patrol
P.O. Box 94907
Lincoln, NE 68509
401-499-7860

Nevada
Program Analyst
Prescription Drug Monitoring Program
Controlled Substances Task Force
Board of Pharmacy
550 W. Washington, #3
Carson City, NV 89706
775-687-5694

New Hampshire
Program Manager
Prescription Drug Monitoring Program
121 South Fruit Street
Concord, NH 03301
603-271-2350

New Jersey
Director
Prescription Drug Monitoring Program
Division of Consumer Affairs
124 Halsey Street
Newark, NJ 07101
973-273-8010

New Mexico
Manager
Prescription Drug Monitoring Program
Board of Pharmacy
5200 Oakland, N.E., Suite A
Albuquerque, NM 87113
505-222-9847

New York
Assistant Director
Bureau of Narcotic Enforcement
Riverview Center
150 Broadway
Albany, NY 12204
518-408-0248

North Carolina
Manager
Drug Control Unit
NC Department of Health and Human Services
3008 Mail Service Center
Raleigh, NC 27699
919-733-1765

North Dakota
Program Assistant
Prescription Drug Monitoring Program
1906 E. Broadway Avenue
P.O. Box 1354
Bismarck, ND 58502
701-328-9537

Ohio
Director
Prescription Drug Monitoring Program
Board of Pharmacy
77 S. High Street, Room 1702
Columbus, OH 43215
614-466-4143

Oklahoma
Program Manager
Prescription Drug Monitoring Program
OK Bureau of Narcotics
440 N. E. 39th Street
Oklahoma City, OK 73105
405-530-3140

Oregon
Program Manager
Prescription Drug Monitoring Program
Public Health Division
800 N. E. Oregon Street, Suite 772
Portland, OR 97232
503-5728585

Pennsylvania
Supervisory Narcotics Agent
Office of Attorney General
16th Floor
Strawberry Square
Harrisburg, PA 17120
814-836-4330

Rhode Island
Data Manager
Prescription Drug Monitoring Program
Department of Health
3 Capitol Hill, Room 105
Providence, RI 02908
401-222-1109

South Carolina
Director
Prescription Drug Monitoring Program
Bureau of Drug Control
2600 Bull Street
Columbia, SC 29201
803-896-0630

South Dakota
Director
Prescription Drug Monitoring Program
Board of Pharmacy
4305 S. Louise Avenue, Suite 104
Sioux Falls, SD 57106
605-362-2737

Tennessee
Director
Prescription Drug Monitoring Program
Board of Pharmacy
665 Mainstream Drive
Nashville, TN 37243
615-253-1305

Texas
Manager
Narcotics Regulatory Program
Compliance and Enforcement Section
5805 N. Lamar Blvd.
P.O. Box 4087
Austin, TX 78773
512-424-2458

Utah
Director
Division of Occupational & Professional Licensing
160 E. 300 S.
P.O. Box 146741
Salt Lake City, UT 84114
801-530-6292

Vermont
Program Coordinator
Prescription Drug Monitoring Program
Department of Health
P.O. Box 70
Burlington, VT 05042
802-652-4147

Virginia
Director
Prescription Drug Monitoring Program
Board of Pharmacy
9960 Maryland Drive, Suite 300
Henrico, VA 23233
804-367-4523

Washington
Program Director
Prescription Drug Monitoring Program
Department of Health
P.O. Box 47852
Olympia, WA 98504
360-236-4806

West Virginia
Administrator
Controlled Substance Monitoring Program
Board of Pharmacy
106 Capitol Street, Suite 100
Charleston, WV 25301
304-558-0558

Wisconsin
Director
Prescription Drug Monitoring Program
Department of Safety and Professional Services
P.O. Box 8366
Madison, WI 53708
608-266-0011

Wyoming
Records Analyst
Prescription Drug Monitoring Program
Board of Pharmacy
1712 Carey Avenue, Suite 200
Cheyenne, WY 82002
307-634-9636

Appendix 21: Pharmacy data printout

PHARMACY DATA PRINTOUT

Confidential Patient Information
Prescription Profile
8/1/14 through 2/28/15

Report Date/Time: 2/28/15 1214

Patient Info: John Q. Patient
Gender: Male

Address:
Allergy Conditions:

Phone:
Health Conditions: None on file

Date of Birth: xx/xx/1933

Prescription Number	Medication	NDC	RPh	Prescriber	Date of Rx	Quantity	Price
11111-0999	Amlodipine 5 mg	xxxxxxx	ABC	Doe, John, MD	9/28/14	90	
2222-1234	Simvastatin 20 mg	xxxxxxx	XYZ	Doe, John, MD	9/28/14	90	
11122-0000	Fluoxetine 20 mg	xxxxxxx	JKL	Doe, John, MD	10/22/14	90	
1234-987	Hydrocodone 30 mg	xxxxxxx	JKL	Doe, John, MD	10/22/14	60	
1234-987	Hydrocodone 30 mg	xxxxxxx	ABC	Doe, John, MD	11/22/14	60	
Refill							
2222-1234	Simvastatin 20 mg	xxxxxxx	TUV	Doe, John, MD	11/22/14	90	
Refill							
3332-0000	Oxycodone 80 mg	xxxxxxx	ABC	Doe, John, MD	11/30/14	120	
7654-345	Alprazolam 5 mg	xxxxxxx	XYZ	Doe, John, MD	12/15/14	120	
7654-345	Alprazolam 5 mg	xxxxxxx	XYZ	Doe, John, MD	12/15/14	120	
Refill							
1234-999	Hydrocodone 30 mg	xxxxxxx	ABC	Doe, John, MD	11/22/14	60	

Appendix 22: Patient record review

PATIENT RECORD REVIEW

Case of: John Doe, MD
Case #: 2015-0000

Patient: ______________________

Initial Visit Date: ________________

Complaint: ____

____

Vitals/Hx/Physical/Ht./Wt.: ____

____

Assessment: ____

____

Dx Testing Performed: ____

Recommended Tx/Rx: ____

____

Frequency of Visits: ____

Common Complaints: ____

Medications Prescribed: ____

Dosages/Frequency: ____

____

Contraindications: ____

Specific Commissions and/or Omissions Noted: ___________________________

____

____

*Appendix 23: State physician/ professionals health programs**

Alabama Physician Health Program
19 South Jackson Street
Montgomery, AL 36104
(334) 954-2596
staff@alabamaphp.org
www.alabamaphp.org

Alaska State Medical Association Physician Health Program
4107 Laurel Street
Anchorage, AK 99508
(906) 561-9644 or (907) 903-1848
phcak@alaska.net

Arizona Monitored Aftercare Program
P.O. Box 1420
Scottsdale, AZ 85252
(480) 990-3111
www.greenbergandsucher.com

Arkansas Medical Foundation
Physician Health Committee
10 Corporate Hill Drive, Suite 150
Little Rock, AR 72205
(501) 224-9911
www.arkmedfoundation.org
director@arkmedfoundation.org

Pacific Assistance Group of California
3838 Watt Ave. C300
Sacramento, CA 95821
(916) 480-1277
info@pacificassistancegroup.net

Colorado Physician Health Program
899 Logan Street, Suite 410
Denver, CO 80203
(303) 860-0122
www.cphp.org

HAVEN (Health Assistance Intervention Education Network for Connecticut Health Professionals, Inc.)
835 West Queen Street, 2nd Floor
Southington, CT 06489
(860) 276-9196
www.haven-ct.org

Delaware: No information available

Florida Professionals Resource Network
P.O. Box 16510
Fernandina Beach, FL 32035-3126
(800) 888-8776
www.flprn.org

* Provided by the Federation of State Physician Health Programs with permission.

Georgia Professional Health
Program, Inc.
The Highland Building
675 Seminole Avenue, Suite 108
Atlanta, GA 30307
(678) 825-3764
www.gaphp.org

Hawaii Program for Healthcare Professionals
(HPHP)
320 Ward Avenue, Suite 203
Honolulu, HI 96814
(808) 593-7444
www.hawaiiphp.org

Idaho Physician Recovery Network
Southworth Associates
413 S. Orchard, Boise, ID 83705
(208) 323-9555
www.southworthassociates.net

Illinois Professionals Health Program
701 Lee Street, Suite 100
Des Plaines, IL 60016
(847) 795-2810 or (800) 215-4357
www.advocatehealth.com/IPHP

Indiana State Medical Association
Physician Assistance Program
322 Canal Walk
Indianapolis, IN 46202
(317) 261-2060

Iowa Physician Health Program
Iowa Board of Medicine
400 SW 8th Street, Suite C
Des Moines, IA 50309
(515) 281-6491

Kansas Medical Society
Medical Advocacy Program
623 SW 10th Avenue
Topeka, KS 66612
(800) 332-0156

Kentucky Physicians Health Foundation
9000 Wessex Place, Suite 305
Louisville, KY 40222
(502) 425-7761
www.kyrecovery.org

Louisiana Physicians Health Foundation
4303 Bluebonnet Blvd.
Baton Rouge, LA 70809
(225) 291-5000 and (888) 743-5747
www.phfl.org

Maine Medical Professionals Health Program
Maine Medical Association
P.O. Box 69
Manchester, ME 04351
(207) 623-9266
www.mainemphp.org
mphp@mainemed.com

Maryland Physician Health Program
Maryland Professionals Rehabilitation
Program
1202 Maryland Avenue, 2nd Floor
Baltimore, MD 21201-5512
MPHP—(800) 992-7010 or (410) 962-5580
MPRP—(410) 878-9843

Massachusetts Physician Health Services, Inc.
860 Winter Street
Waltham, MA 02451
(781) 434-7404 or (800) 322-2302, ext. 7404
www.physicianhealth.org

Michigan Health Professional Recovery
Program
P.O. Box 842
Troy, MI 48009
(800) 453-3784
www.hprp.org
hprp@hprp.org

Minnesota Health Professionals Services
Program
Energy Park Place, Suite 202
1380 Energy Lane
St. Paul, MN 55108
(651) 643-2121
www.hpsp.state.mn.us

Mississippi Professionals Health Program
(MPHP)
408 West Parkway Place
P.O. Box 2548
Ridgeland, MS 39158
(601) 420-0240

Missouri Physicians Health Program
680 Craig Road, Suite 308
St. Louis, MO 63141
(800) 958-7124; Hotline (800) 274-0933
www.themphp.org
info@themphp.org

Montana Professional Assistance Program, Inc. (MPAP)
3333 2nd Avenue North, Suite 200
Billings, MT 59101
(406) 245-4300
www.montanaprofessionalassistance.com
mpap@mtphp.net

Nebraska: No information available

Nevada Professionals Assistance Program
9811 W. Charleston Blvd., Suite 2-735
Las Vegas, NV 89117
(702) 257-6727

New Hampshire Professionals Health Program
P.O. Box 6274
Amherst, NH 03031
(603) 491-5036

Professional Assistance Program of New Jersey, Inc.
742 Alexander Road
Princeton, NJ 08540
(609) 919-1660

New Mexico Monitored Treatment Program
11930 Menaul Avenue, NE, Suite110
Albuquerque, NM 87112
www.monitoredtreatment.com
mtp@monitoredtreatment.com

Committee for Physician Health
Medical Society of the State of New York
99 Washington Avenue, Suite 410
Albany, NY 12210
(518) 436-4723
www.cphny.org

North Carolina Physicians Health Program
220 Horizon Drive, Suite 201
Raleigh, NC 27615
(919) 870-4480 or (800) 783-6792 Toll-free

North Dakota Physician Health Program
418 E Broadway Ave, Suite 12
Bismarck, ND 58501
(701)-328-6500

Ohio Physicians Health Program, Inc.
130 E. Chestnut Street, Suite 400
Columbus, OH 43215
(614) 841-9690
www.ophp.org

Oklahoma Health Professionals Program (OHPP)
313 N.E. 50th
Oklahoma City, OK 73105
(405) 601-2536

Oregon Health Professionals' Services Program
1220 SW Morrison
Portland, OR 97205
(888) 802-2843 Toll Free
Rbhhealthpro.com

Pennsylvania Physicians' Health Program
777 East Park Drive
PO Box 8820
Harrisburg, PA 17105
(717) 558-7819
PHP-Foundation@pamedsoc.org

Rhode Island Medical Society
Physician Health Program
235 Promenade Street, Suite 500
Providence, RI 02908
(401) 528-3287

South Carolina Recovering Professionals Program
440 Knox Abbott Drive, Suite 220
Cayce, SC 29033
(803) 896-570

South Carolina Recovering Professionals Program
440 Knox Abbott Drive, Suite 220
Cayce, SC 29033
(803) 896-570

South Dakota
Health Professionals Assistance Program
3130 W. 57th Street, Suite 111
Sioux Falls, SD 57108
(605) 275-4711
www.mwhms.com

Tennessee Medical Foundation
Physicians Health Program
216 Centerview Drive, Suite 304
Brentwood, TN 37027
(615) 467-6411
www.e-tmf.org

Texas Medical Association
Committee on Physician Health and Wellness
401 West 15th Street
Austin, TX 78701
(512) 370-1342
www.texmed.org/phw

Utah Recovery Assistance Program
160 E. 300 South, Box 146741
Salt Lake City, UT 84114
(801) 530-6106

Vermont Practitioner Health Program
P.O. Box 133
Montpelier, VT 05601
(802) 223-0400

Virginia Health Practitioners Monitoring Program
701 East Franklin Street, Suite 1407
Richmond, VA 23219
(804) 828-1551

Washington Physicians Health Program
720 Olive Way, Suite 1010
Seattle, WA 98101
(206) 583-0127
http://www.wphp.org

Medical Society of DC
Physician Health Program
1250 23rd St. NW, Suite 270
Washington, DC 20037
(339) 440-2024

West Virginia Medical Professionals Health Program
680 Genesis Blvd., Suite 201
Bridgeport, WV 26330
(304) 933-1030
http://www.wvmphp.org/

Wisconsin: No information available

Wyoming Professional Assistance Program, Inc.
P.O. Box 1496
Casper, WY 82602
(307) 472-1222

*Appendix 24: List of medicaid fraud control units**

Medicaid Fraud Control Unit of Alabama
Office of the Attorney General
500 Dexter Avenue
Montgomery, AL 36130
Phone:(334) 353-8793
Fax:(334) 353-8796
www.ago.state.al.us

Medicaid Fraud Control Unit of Alaska
Office of the Attorney General
310 K Street
Suite 308
Anchorage, AK 99501
Phone:(907) 269-6292
Fax:(907) 269-6202
http://www.law.state.ak.us

Medicaid Fraud Control Unit of Arizona
Office of the Attorney General
1275 W Washington Street
Phoenix, AZ 85007
Phone:(602) 542-3881
Fax:(602) 364-5997
https://www.azag.gov

Medicaid Fraud Control Unit of Arkansas
Office of the Attorney General
323 Center Street
Suite 200
Little Rock, AR 72201
Phone:(501) 682-8104
Fax:(501) 682-8135
http://www.ag.state.ar.us

Medicaid Fraud Control Unit of California
Office of the Attorney General
1425 River Park Drive
Ste. 300
Sacramento, CA 95815
Phone:(916) 263-1448
Fax:(916) 263-0864
http://www.ag.ca.gov

Medicaid Fraud Control Unit of Colorado
Office of the Attorney General
1300 Broadway
9th Floor
Denver, CO 80203
Phone:(720) 508-6000
Fax:(866) 858-7486
http://www.coloradoattorneygeneral.gov

* Provided by the National Association of Medicaid Fraud Control Units with permission.

Medicaid Fraud Control Unit of Connecticut
Office of the Chief State's Attorney
300 Corporate Place
Rocky Hill, CT 06067
Phone:(860) 258-5845
Fax:(860) 258-5838
http://www.ct.gov

Medicaid Fraud Control Unit of Delaware
Office of the Attorney General
820 N French Street
Wilmington, DE 19801
Phone:(302) 577-8859
Fax:(302) 577-3090
http://attorneygeneral.delaware.gov

Medicaid Fraud Control Unit of D.C.
Office of D.C. Inspector General
717 14th St., N.W.
5th Floor
Washington, DC 20005
Phone:(202) 727-8008
Fax:(202) 727-5937
http://oig.dc.gov

Medicaid Fraud Control Unit of Florida
Office of the Attorney General
The Capitol
PL-01
Tallahassee, FL 32399-1050
Phone:(850) 414-3600
Fax:(850) 921-5194
http://myfloridalegal.com

Medicaid Fraud Control Unit of Georgia
Office of the Attorney General
200 Piedmont Ave SE
West Tower, 19th Floor
Atlanta, GA 30334
Phone:(404) 656-5400
Fax:(404) 657-7441
http://law.ga.gov

Medicaid Fraud Control Unit of Hawaii
Office of the Attorney General
333 Queen Street
10th Floor
Honolulu, HI 96813
Phone:(808) 586-1073
Fax:(808) 586-1077
http://ag.hawaii.gov

Medicaid Fraud Control Unit of Idaho
Office of the Attorney General
P.O. Box 83720
Boise, Idaho 83702-0010
Phone: (208) 334-4100
Fax: (208) 854-8082
http://www.ag.idaho.gov/index.html

Medicaid Fraud Control Unit of Illinois
Illinois State Police
801 South 7th Street, Suite 200-M
P.O. Box 19461
Springfield, IL 62794
Phone:(217) 785-3322
Fax:(217) 524-6405
http://www.isp.state.il.us

Medicaid Fraud Control Unit of Indiana
Office of the Attorney General
8005 Castleway Drive
Indianapolis, IN 46250-1946
Phone:(317) 915-5300, ext 7
Fax:(317) 232-6523
http://www.in.gov/attorneygeneral

Medicaid Fraud Control Unit of Iowa
Department of Inspections and Appeals
3rd Floor, Lucas State Office Building
Des Moines, IA 50319
Phone:(515) 281-0506
Fax:(515) 725-1245
http://www.state.ia.us

Medicaid Fraud Control Unit of Kansas
Office of the Attorney General
120 SW 10th Ave.
2nd Floor
Topeka, KS 66612-1597
Phone: (785) 368-6220
Toll Free: (866) 551-6328
Fax: (785) 368-6223
http://ag.ks.gov

Medicaid Fraud Control Unit of Kentucky
Office of the Attorney General
1024 Capitol Center Drive
Frankfort, KY 40601
Phone:(502) 696-5405
Fax:(502) 573-8316
http://ag.ky.gov

Medicaid Fraud Control Unit of Louisiana
Office of the Attorney General
P.O. Box 94005
Baton Rouge, LA 70804-9005
Phone:(225) 326-6210
Fax:(225) 326-6295
http://www.ag.state.la.us

Medicaid Fraud Control Unit of Maine
Office of the Attorney General
6 State House Station
Augusta, ME 04333-0006
Phone:(207) 626-8555
Fax:(207) 287-3120
http://www.maine.gov/ag

Medicaid Fraud Control Unit of Maryland
Office of the Attorney General
200 St. Paul Place
18th Floor
Baltimore, MD 21202
Phone:(410) 576-6521
Fax:(410) 576-6314
http://www.oag.state.md.us

Medicaid Fraud Control Unit of Massachusetts
Office of the Attorney General
One Ashburton Place
Boston, MA 02108
Phone:(617) 963-2366
Fax:(617) 727-2008
http://www.ago.state.ma.us

Medicaid Fraud Control Unit of Michigan
Office of the Attorney General
2860 Eyde Parkway
East Lansing, MI 48823
Phone:(517) 241-6500
Fax:(517) 241-6515
http://www.michigan.gov/ag

Medicaid Fraud Control Unit of Minnesota
Office of the Attorney General
445 Minnesota St.
900 Bremer Tower
Saint Paul, MN 55101-2219
Phone:(651) 757-1299
Fax:(651) 282-5801
http://www.ag.state.mn.us

Medicaid Fraud Control Unit of Mississippi
Office of the Attorney General
P.O. Box 56
Jackson, MS 39205
Phone:(601) 359-4220
Fax:(601) 359-9681
http://www.ago.state.ms.us

Medicaid Fraud Control Unit of Missouri
Office of the Attorney General
221 West High Street
Jefferson City, MO 65102
Phone:(573) 751-7192
Fax:(573) 751-0207
http://ago.mo.gov

Medicaid Fraud Control Unit of Montana
Division of Criminal Investigation
303 N Roberts Street
Room 367
Helena, MT 59620
Phone:(406) 444-6680
Fax:(406) 444-7913
https://dojmt.gov

Medicaid Fraud Control Unit of Nebraska
Office of the Attorney General
1221 N St.
Suite 500
Lincoln, NE 68508
Phone:(402) 471-3843
Fax:(402) 471-4725
http://ago.nebraska.gov/

Medicaid Fraud Control Unit of Nevada
Office of the Attorney General
100 North Carson St.
Carson City, NV 89701-4717
Phone:(775) 684-1191
Fax:(775) 684-1192
http://ag.nv.gov/

Medicaid Fraud Control Unit of New Hampshire
Office of the Attorney General
33 Capitol Street
Concord, NH 03301-6397
Phone:(603) 271-1246
Fax:(603) 271-2110
http://doj.nh.gov/
http://www.state.nj.us/lps/dcj/njinsurancefraud

Medicaid Fraud Control Unit of New Jersey
Office of the Attorney General
25 Market Street
P.O. Box 094
Trenton, NJ 08625
Phone:(609) 896-8772
Fax:(609) 896-8696

Medicaid Fraud Control Unit of New Mexico
Office of the Attorney General
111 Lomas Blvd. N.E.
Albuquerque, NM 87102
Phone:(505) 222-9079
Fax:(505) 222-9008
www.nmag.gov

Medicaid Fraud Control Unit of New York
Office of the Attorney General
120 Broadway
13th Floor
New York, NY 10271
Phone:(212) 417-5250
Fax:(212) 417-4284
http://www.ag.ny.gov/

Medicaid Fraud Control Unit of North Carolina
Office of the Attorney General
3824 Barrett Drive
Suite 200
Raleigh, NC 27609
Phone:(919) 881-2320
Fax:(919) 571-4837
www.ncdoj.gov

North Dakota does not have an MFCU

Medicaid Fraud Control Unit of Ohio
Office of the Attorney General
150 East Gay Street
17th Floor
Columbus, OH 43215
Phone:(614) 466-0722
Fax:(614) 644-9973
http://www.ag.state.oh.us/

Medicaid Fraud Control Unit of Oklahoma
Office of the Attorney General
313 NE 21st Street
Oklahoma City, OK 73105
Phone:(405) 521-3921
Fax:(405) 522-4875
http://www.ok.gov/oag/

Medicaid Fraud Control Unit of Oregon
Office of the Attorney General
1515 SW 5th Avenue
Suite 410
Portland, OR 97201
Phone:(971) 673-1880
Fax:(971) 673-1890
http://www.doj.state.or.us

Medicaid Fraud Control Unit of Pennsylvania
Office of the Attorney General
1600 Strawberry Square
Harrisburg, PA 17120
Phone:(717) 772-2772
Fax:(717) 705-7247
https://www.attorneygeneral.gov

Medicaid Fraud Control Unit of Rhode Island
Office of the Attorney General
150 S Main Street
Providence, RI 02903
Phone:(401) 274-4400 x 2376
Fax:(401) 222-3014
www.riag.ri.gov

Medicaid Fraud Control Unit of South Carolina
Office of the Attorney General
P.O. Box 11549
Columbia, SC 29211-1549
Phone:(803) 734-3660
Fax:(803) 734-8754
www.scag.gov

Medicaid Fraud Control Unit of South Dakota
Office of the Attorney General
G.S. Mickelson Criminal Justice Center
1302 E. Hwy 14, Suite 4
Pierre, SD 57501
Phone:(605) 773-4102
Fax:(605) 773-6279
http://atg.sd.gov/

Medicaid Fraud Control Unit of Tennessee
Bureau of Investigation
901 R.S. Gass Boulevard
Nashville, TN 37216-2639
Phone:(615) 744-4362
Fax:(615) 744-4659
http://www.tbi.state.tn.us

Medicaid Fraud Control Unit of Texas
Office of the Attorney General
6330 Hwy 290 East
Suite 250
Austin, TX 78723
Phone:(512) 463-2011
Fax:(512) 320-0974
https://www.texasattorneygeneral.gov

Medicaid Fraud Control Unit of Utah
Office of the Attorney General
5272 College Drive
Suite 200
Salt Lake City, UT 84123
Phone:(801) 281-1258
Fax:(801) 281-1250
http://attorneygeneral.utah.gov/

Medicaid Fraud Control Unit of Vermont
Office of the Attorney General
109 State Street
Montpelier, VT 05609-1001
Phone:(802) 828-5511
Fax:(802) 828-3188
http://www.atg.state.vt.us/

Medicaid Fraud Control Unit of Virginia
Office of the Attorney General
900 E Main Street, 5th Floor
Richmond, VA 23219
Phone:(804) 692-0171
Fax:(804) 225-3064
www.ag.virginia.gov

Medicaid Fraud Control Unit of Washington
Office of the Attorney General
P.O. Box 40116
Olympia, WA 98504-0116
Phone:(360) 586-8888
Fax:(360) 586-8877
http://www.atg.wa.gov

Medicaid Fraud Control Unit of West Virginia
WV Office of Inspector General
Capitol Complex
Bldg. 6 Rm. B-848
Charleston, WV 25305
Phone:(304) 558-1858
Fax:(304) 558-3498
http://www.wvdhhr.org/oig/mfcu

Medicaid Fraud Control Unit of Wisconsin
Office of the Attorney General
17 W Main Street
Madison, WI 53703
Phone:(608) 266-9222
Fax:(608) 261-7991
www.doj.state.wi.us/

Medicaid Fraud Control Unit of Wyoming
Office of the Attorney General
2424 Pioneer Avenue
4th Floor
Cheyenne, WY 82002
Phone:(307) 777-3444
Fax:(307) 777-5094
http://ag.wyo.gov/

*Appendix 25: State insurance commissioner offices**

Alabama Department of Insurance
P.O. Box 303351
Montgomery, Alabama 36130-3351
Street Address
201 Monroe Street, Suite 502
Montgomery, Alabama 36104
334-269-3550

Alaska Department of Commerce, Community & Economic Development
Division of Insurance
550 West 7th Avenue, Suite 1560
Anchorage, Alaska 99501-3567
907-269-7900
Juneau Mailing Address
P.O. Box 110805
Juneau, Alaska 99811-0805
Juneau Street Address
333 Willoughby, 9th Floor
Juneau, Alaska 99801
907-465-2515

Arizona Department of Insurance
2910 North 44th Street, Suite 210
Phoenix, Arizona 85018-7269
602-364-3100

Arkansas Insurance Department
1200 West Third Street
Little Rock, Arkansas 72201-1904
501-371-2600

California Department of Insurance
300 Capitol Mall, Suite 1700
Sacramento, California 95814
916-492-3500
San Francisco Office
45 Fremont Street, 23rd Floor
San Francisco, California 94105
415-538-4010
Los Angeles Office
300 South Spring Street, South Tower
Los Angeles, California 90013
213-346-6464

Colorado Department of Regulatory Agencies
Division of Insurance
1560 Broadway, Suite 850
Denver, Colorado 80202
303-894-7499

Connecticut Insurance Department
P.O. Box 816
Hartford, Connecticut 06142-0816
Street Address
153 Market Street, 7th Floor
Hartford, CT 06103
860-297-3800

Delaware Department of Insurance
841 Silver Lake Boulevard
Dover, Delaware 19904
302-674-7300

* Provided by the National Association of Insurance Commissioners with permission.

District of Columbia Department of Insurance, Securities, and Banking
810 First Street, N. E., Suite 701
Washington, DC 20002
202-727-8000

Florida Office of Insurance Regulation
The Larson Building
200 E. Gaines Street, Rm 101A
Tallahassee, Florida 32399-0305
850-413-5914

Georgia Office of Insurance and Safety Fire Commissioner
Two Martin Luther King, Jr. Dr.
West Tower, Suite 704
Atlanta, Georgia 30334
404-656-2070

Hawaii Department of Commerce and Consumer Affairs
Insurance Division
P.O. Box 3614
Honolulu, Hawaii 96811-3614
Street Address
King Kalakaua Building
335 Merchant Street, Room 213
Honolulu, Hawaii 96813
808-586-2790

Idaho Department of Insurance
P.O. Box 83720
Boise, Idaho 83720-0043
Street Address
700 West State Street, 3rd Floor
Boise, Idaho 83720-0043
208-334-4250

Illinois Department of Insurance
320 W. Washington Street
Springfield, Illinois 62767-0001
217-782-4515
122 S. Michigan Avenue, 19th Floor
Chicago, Illinois 60603
312-814-2420

Indiana Department of Insurance
311 W. Washington Street
Suite 103
Indianapolis, Indiana 46204
317-232-2385

Iowa Insurance Division
Two Ruan Center
601 Locust, 4th Floor
Des Moines, Iowa 50309-3438
515-281-5705

Kansas Insurance Department
420 SW 9th Street
Topeka, Kansas 66612-1678
785-296-3071

Kentucky Department of Insurance
P.O. Box 517
Frankfort, Kentucky 40602-0517
Street Address
215 West Main Street
Frankfort, Kentucky 40601
502-564-3630

Louisiana Department of Insurance
P.O. Box 94214
Baton Rouge, Louisiana 70804-9214
Street Address
1702 N 3rd Street
Baton Rouge, Louisiana 70802
225-342-5900

Maine Bureau of Insurance
Department of Professional Financial Regulation
34 State House Station
Augusta, Maine 04333-0034
Street Address
76 Northern Avenue
Gardiner, Maine 04345
207-624-8475

Maryland Insurance Administration
200 St. Paul Place
Suite 2700
Baltimore, Maryland 21202-2272
410-468-2090

Massachusetts Division of Insurance
Office of Consumer Affairs and Business Regulation
1000 Washington Street, 8th Floor
Boston, Massachusetts 02118-6200
617-521-7794

Michigan Department of Insurance & Financial Services
P.O. Box 30220
Lansing, Michigan 48909-7720
Street Address
Ottawa Building, 3rd Floor
611 W Ottawa
Lansing, Michigan 48933-1070
517-373-0220

Minnesota Department of Commerce
85 7th Place East, Suite 500
St. Paul, Minnesota 55101
651-539-1500

Mississippi Insurance Department
P.O. Box 79
Jackson, Mississippi 39205-0079
Street Address
1001 Woolfolk State Office Building
501 N. West Street
Jackson, Mississippi 39201
601-359-3569

Missouri Department of Insurance, Financial Institutions and Professional Registration
P.O. Box 690
Jefferson City, Missouri 65102-0690
Street Address
301 West High Street, Room 530
Jefferson City, Missouri 65101
573-751-4126

Montana Office of the Commissioner of Securities and Insurance
Montana State Auditor
840 Helena Avenue
Helena, Montana 59601
406-444-2040

Nebraska Department of Insurance
P.O. Box 82089
Lincoln, NE 68501-2089
Street Address
941 O Street, Suite 400
Lincoln, Nebraska 68508
402-471-2201

Nevada Department of Business & Industry
Division of Insurance
1818 East College Pkwy, Suite 103
Carson City, Nevada 89706
775-687-0700
Las Vegas Office
2501 E. Sahara Avenue, Suite 302
Las Vegas, Nevada 89104
702-486-4009

New Hampshire Insurance Department
21 South Fruit Street, Suite 14
Concord, New Hampshire 03301
603-271-2261

New Jersey Department of Banking and Insurance
20 West State Street
P.O. Box 325
Trenton, New Jersey 08625-0325
609-292-7272

New Mexico Office of Superintendent of Insurance
P.O. Box 1689
Santa Fe, New Mexico 87504-1689
Street Address
P.E.R.A. Building
1120 Paseo De Peralta
Santa Fe, New Mexico 87501
505-827-4601

New York State Department of Financial Services
One State Street New York, New York 10004-1511
212-709-3500

North Carolina Department of Insurance
1201 Mail Service Center
Raleigh, North Carolina 27699-1201
Street Address
Dobbs Building
430 N. Salisbury Street
Raleigh, North Carolina 27603-5926
919-807-6000

North Dakota Insurance Department
State Capitol, Fifth Floor
600 E. Boulevard Avenue
Bismarck, North Dakota 58505-0320
701-328-2440

Ohio Department of Insurance
50 West Town Street
Third Floor, Suite 300
Columbus, OH 43215
614-644-2658

Oklahoma Department of Insurance
Oklahoma City Office
Five Corporate Plaza
3625 NW 56th Street, Suite 100
Oklahoma City, OK 73112
405-521-2828
Tulsa Office
7645 E. 63rd St., Suite 102 Tulsa, OK 74133
918-295-3700

Oregon Department of Consumer & Business Services
Insurance Division
P.O. Box 14480
Salem, Oregon 97309-0405
Street Address
350 Winter Street NE
Salem, Oregon 97301-3883
503-947-7980

Pennsylvania Insurance Department
1326 Strawberry Square
Harrisburg, Pennsylvania 17120
717-783-0442

Rhode Island Department of Business Regulation
Division of Insurance
1511 Pontiac Avenue, Building 69-2
Cranston, Rhode Island 02920
401-462-9520

South Carolina Department of Insurance
P.O. Box 100105
Columbia, South Carolina 29202-3105
Street Address
Capitol Center
1201 Main Street, Suite 1000
Columbia, South Carolina 29201
803-737-6160

South Dakota Department of Labor & Regulation
Division of Insurance
South Dakota Division of Insurance
124 South Euclid Avenue, 2nd Floor
Pierre, SD 57501
605-773-3563

Tennessee Department of Commerce & Insurance
Davy Crockett Tower Twelfth Floor
500 James Robertson Parkway
Nashville, Tennessee 37243-0565
615-741-6007

Texas Department of Insurance
P.O. Box 149104
Austin, Texas 78714-9104
Street Address
333 Guadalupe Street
Austin, Texas 78701
512-676-6000

Utah Insurance Department
3110 State Office Building
Salt Lake City, Utah 84114-6901
801-538-3800

Vermont Department of Financial Regulation
89 Main Street
Montpelier, Vermont 05620-3101
802-828-3301

Virginia State Corporation Commission
Bureau of Insurance
P.O. Box 1157
Richmond, Virginia 23218
Street Address
1300 East Main Street
Richmond, Virginia 23219
804-371-9741

Washington State Office of the Insurance Commissioner
P.O. Box 40256
Olympia, Washington 98504-0256
Street Address
5000 Capitol Boulevard, SE
Tumwater, Washington 98501
360-725-7000

West Virginia Office of the Insurance Commissioner
P.O. Box 50540
Charleston, West Virginia 25305-0540
Street Address
1124 Smith Street
Charleston, West Virginia 25301
304-558-3354

Wisconsin Office of the Commissioner of Insurance
P.O. Box 7873
Madison, Wisconsin 53707-7873
Street Address
125 South Webster Street
GEF III—Second Floor
Madison, Wisconsin 53703-3474
608-266-3585

Wyoming Insurance Department
106 East 6th Avenue
Cheyenne, Wyoming 82002-0440
307-777-7401

Appendix 26: Health insurance claim form

HEALTH INSURANCE CLAIM FORM

1. MEDICARE [ ] (Medicare No.) · MEDICAID [ ] (Medicaid No.) · TRICARE CHAMPUS [ ] (Sponsor SSN) · CHAMPVA [ ] (Member ID) · GROUP HEALTH PLAN [ ] (SSN/ID) · FECA BLKLUNG [ ] (SSN) · OTHER [ ] (ID)		1a. INSURED'S I.D. NUMBER
2. PATIENT'S NAME (Last Name, First Name, Middle Initial)	3. PATIENT'S DATE OF BIRTH MM DD YY · SEX M [ ] F [ ]	4. INSURED'S NAME
5. PATIENT'S ADDRESS (No., Street) CITY STATE	6. PATIENT'S RELATIONSHIP TO INSURED Self [ ] Spouse [ ] Child [ ] Other [ ] 8. PATIENT STATUS Single [ ] Married [ ] Other [ ] Employed [ ] Full-time Student [ ] Part-time Student [ ]	7. INSURED'S ADDRESS CITY STATE
ZIP CODE TELEPHONE		ZIP CODE TELEPHONE
9. OTHER INSURED'S NAME (LN, FN, MI)	10. PATIENT'S CONDITION RELATED TO:	11. INSURED'S POLICY GROUP NO.
	a. Employment? (Current or Previous) [ ] Yes [ ] No	a. INSURED'S DATE OF BIRTH MM DD YY
a. OTHER INSURED'S POLICY/GROUP NO.	b. Auto Accident? Place: (State) [ ] Yes [ ] No [ ]	b. EMPLOYER'S OR SCHOOL NAME
b. OTHER INSURED'S DATE OF BIRTH MM DD YY	c. Other Accident? [ ] Yes [ ] No	c. INSURANCE PLAN NAME d. IS THERE ANOTHER PLAN? [ ] Yes [ ] No
c. EMPLOYER'S OR SCHOOL NAME		
d. INSURANCE PLAN NAME	10d. RESERVED FOR LOCAL USE	

<table>
<tr><td colspan="2">12. PATIENT'S AUTHORIZED SIGNATURE: I authorize the release of any medical or other information necessary to process this claim. I also request payment of government benefits either to myself or to the party who accepts assignment below.

SIGNED ______________________ DATE:__________</td><td>13. INSURED'S OR AUTHORIZED PERSON'S SIGNATURE: I authorize payment of medical benefits to the undersigned physician or supplier for services described below.

SIGNED ______________</td></tr>
<tr><td>14. DATE OF CURRENT:
MM DD YY
ILLNESS (First symptoms) OR INJURY (Accident) OR PREGNANCY (LMP)</td><td>15. IF PATIENT HAS HAD SAME OR SIMILAR ILLNESS GIVE FIRST DATE
MM DD YY</td><td>16. Dates Patient Unable to Work in Current Occupation
FROM MM/DD/YY TO MM/DD/YY</td></tr>
<tr><td>17. NAME OF REFERRING PROVIDER OR OTHER SOURCE</td><td>17a.
17b. NPI</td><td>18. Hospitalization Dates Related to Current Services
From MM/DD/YY To MM/DD/YY</td></tr>
<tr><td colspan="2" rowspan="3">19. RESERVED FOR LOCAL USE
21. DIAGNOSIS OR NATURE OF ILLNESS OR INJURY
1 ______________ 3 ______________
2 ______________ 4 ______________</td><td>20. OUTSIDE LAB? CHARGES
[ ] Yes [ ] No</td></tr>
<tr><td>22. MEDICAID RESUBMISSION</td></tr>
<tr><td>CODE ORIGINAL REF#</td></tr>
</table>

23. A. Dates of Service	B. Place of Service	C. EMG	D. Procedure, Services or Supplies	E. Diagnosis	F. Charges	G. Days/ Units	H. EPSDT Family Plan	I.ID J.	Rendering Provider ID#
1. FRM:mm/dd/yy TO:mm/dd/yy			CPT/HCPCS MODIFIER						
2. FRM:mm/dd/yy TO:mm/dd/yy			CPT/HCPCS MODIFIER						
3. FRM:mm/dd/yy TO:mm/dd/yy			CPT/HCPCS MODIFIER						
4. FRM:mm/dd/yy TO:mm/dd/yy			CPT/HCPCS MODIFIER						

24. FED TAX ID#:SSN/EIN 25. PATIENT ACCOUNT NO. 26. ACCEPT ASSIGNMENT? | 27. TTL CHG | 28. AMT P | D/BAL DUE

29. SIGNATURE OF PHYSICIAN OR SUPPLIER 30. SVC FACILITY 31. BILLING PROVIDER

X____________________________

Appendix 27: Superbill

Superbill

Date of Service:							Insurance:	Today's Chgs:	
Patient Name:							Subscriber:	Balance Due:	
DOB: Age: Sex:							Copay:		
Phone:							Physician:		
Rank	**Office visit**	**New**	**Est**	**Rank**	**Office procedures**	**CPT**	**Rank**	**Laboratory**	**CPT**
	Minimal		99211		Anoscopy	46600		Venipuncture	36415
	Problem focused	99201	99212		Audiometry	92551		Blood glucose, monitoring dev	82962
	Expanded problem focused	99202	99213		Cerumen removal	69210		Blood glucose, visual dipstk	82948
	Detailed	99203	99214		Colposcopy	57452		CBC w/autodifferential	85025
	Comprehensive	99204	99215		Colposcopy w/ biopsy	57455		CBC w/out autodifferential	85027
	Comprehensive (new patient)	99205			ECG, w/ interpretation	93000		Cholesterol	82465
	Significant, separate service	−25	−25		ECG, rhythm strip	93040		Hemocult, guaiac	82270
	Well visit	**New**	**Est**		Endometrial biopsy	58100		Hemocult, immunoassay	82274
	<1 y	99381	99391		Flexible sigmoidoscopy	45330		Hemoglobin A1C	85018
	1–4 y	99382	99392		Flexible sigmoid w/biopsy	45331		Lipid panel	80061
	5–11 y	99383	99393		Fracture care, cast/splint	29___		Liver panel	80076
	12–17 y	99384	99394		Site:			KOH prep (skin, hair, nails)	87220
	18–39 y	99385	99395		Nebulizer	94640		Metabolic panel, basic	80048
	40–64 y	99386	99396		Nebulizer demo	94664		Metabolic panel, comprehensive	80053
	65 y +	99387	99397		Spirometry	94010		Mononucleosis	86308

	Medicare preventive services				Spirometry, pre and post	94060		Pregnancy, blood	84703
	Pap		Q0091		Tympanometry	92567		Pregnancy, urine	81025
	Pelvic & breast		G0101		Vasectomy	55250		Renal panel	80069
	Prostate/PSA		G0103		**Skin procedures**			Sedimentation rate	85651
	Tobacco counseling/3–10 min		99406		Burn care, initial	16000		Strep, rapid	86403
	Tobacco counseling/ > 10 min		99407		Foreign body, skin, simple	10120		Strep, culture	87081
	Welcome to Medicare exam		G0344		Foreign body, skin, complex	10121		Strep A	87880
	ECG w/welcome to Medicare ex		G0366		I & D abscess	10060		TB	86580
	Flexible sigmoidoscopy		G0104		I & D, hematoma/seroma	10140		UA, complete, nonautomated	81000
	Hemocult, guaiac		G0107		Laceration repair, simple	120__		UA, w/o micro, nonautomated	81002
	Flu shot		G0008		Site:________ Size: ________			UA, w/micro, nonautomated	81003
	Pneumonia shot		G0009		Laceration repair, layered	120__		Urine colony count	87086
	Consultation/preop clearance				Site:________ Size: ________			Urine culture, presumptive	87088
	Expanded problem focused		99242		Lesion, biopsy, one	11100		Wet mount/KOH	87210
	Detailed		99243		Lesion, biopsy, each add'l	11101		**Vaccines**	
	Comprehensive/mod complex		99244		Lesion, destruct, benign 1–14	17110		DT, <7y	90702
	Comprehensive/high complex		99245		Lesion, destruct, premal/sing	17000		DTP	90701
	Other services				Lesion, destruct, premal, ea	17003		DtaP <7y	90700
	After posted hours		99050		Lesion, excision, benign	114		Flu 6–35 months	90657
	Evening/weekend appointment		99051		Site:________ Size: ________			Flu, 3 y +	90658
	Home health certification		G0180		Lesion, excision, malignant	116__		Hep A, adult	90632
	Home health recertification		G0179		Site:________ Size: ________			Hep A, ped/adol, 2 dose	90633
	Postop follow-up		99024		Lesion, paring/cutting, one	11055		Hep B, adult	90746

	Prolonged/30–74 min		99354		Lesion, paring/cutting, 2–4	11056		Hep B, ped/adol, 3 dose	90744
	Special reports/forms		99080		Lesion, shave	113__		Hep B-Hib	90748
	Disability/Workers comp		99455		Site:________ Size: ________			Hib, 4 dose	90645
	Radiology				Nail removal, partial	11730		HPV	90649
					Nail removal, w/matrix	11750		IPV	90713
					Skin tag, 1–15	11200		MMR	90707
	Diagnoses				**Medications**			Pneumonia, >2 y	90732
1					Ampicillin, upto 500 mg	J0290		Pneumonia conjugate, <5y	90669
2					B-12, upto 1000 mcg	J3420		Td, >7y	90718
3					Epinephrine, upto 1 ml	J0170		Varicella	90716
4					Kenalog, 10 mg	J3301		**Immunizations & injections**	
	Next office visit				Lidocaine, 10 mg	J2001		Allergen, one	95115
	Recheck Prev PRN____ D W M Y				Normal saline, 1000 cc	J7030		Allergen, multiple	95117
	Instructions:				Phenergan, upto 50 mg	J2550		Imm admin, one	90471
					Progesterone, 150 mg	J1055		Imm admin, each add'l	90472
	Referral				Rocephin, 250 mg	J0696		Imm admin, intranasal, one	90473
	To:				Testosterone, 200 mg	J1080		Imm admin, intranasal, ea addl	90474
					Tigan, upto 200 mg	J3250		Injection, joint, small	20600
	Instructions:				Toradol, 15 mg	J1885		Injection, joint, intermediate	20605
					Miscellaneous services			Injection, joint, major	20610
	Physician signature							Injection, ther/proph/diag	90772
					Supplies			Injection, trigger point	20552
	______________________								

Appendix 28: Fraud worksheet

John Doe, MD Case # 2015-0031

Fraud Worksheet

CLAIM #	PATIENT NAME	DATE SUBMITTED	SERVICE BILLED FOR	DATE OF SERVICE	CPT CODE USED	ACTUAL SERVICE PROVIDED	CORRECT CPT CODE	AMOUNT PAID ON CLAIM	CORRECT AMT SHOULD HAVE BEEN PAID	DOCUMENTED IN PATIENT RECORD?	WHO PROVIDED SERVICE?	PROVIDER ON CLAIM? MD, PA, RN, ETC.	PATIENT VISIT DOCUMENTED ON SIGN-IN LOG?
123456	Jones, B.	02/16/15	New Patient Comprehensive OV	1/27/15	99205 highest reimburse code	Est. patient routine follow up	99212	$160.00	$120.00	No	PA	MD	Yes
224584	Lewis, A.	02/22/15	Est. patient comprehensive OV	1/29/15	99215 highest reimburse code	Est. patient routine follow up	99212	$160.00	$120.00	Yes	PA	MD	Yes
567234	Johnson, L.	02/22/15	Est. patient comprehensive OV	1/30/15	99215 highest reimburse code	Est. patient routine follow up	99212	$160.00	$120.00	Yes	APRN	MD	No
145378	Allen, M.	02/26/15	Excision of nasal polyps-polypectomy	1/30/15	30410 Rhinoplasty-not covered	Rhinoplasty; cosmetic proc not covered	30115	$12,000.00	$0	Polypectomy was documented	MD	MD	Yes
314977	Smith, N.	02/26/15	Est. patient comprehensive OV	2/1/15	99205 highest reimburse code	Est. patient routine follow up	99212	$160.00	$120.00	No	APRN	MD	Yes
222964	Stevens, E.	02/27/15	Est. patient comprehensive OV	2/2/15	99205 highest reimburse code	No service documented	None	$160.00	$0	No	No one	MD	No
441008	Hughes, L.	02/27/15	Est. patient comprehensive OV	2/2/15	99205 highest reimburse code	Est. patient comprehensive OV	None	$160.00	$0	Yes-Patient interview states out of town this date	No one	MD	No
231567	Evans, M.	02/27/15	Est. patient comprehensive OV	2/3/15	99205 highest reimburse code	Est. patient routine follow up	99212	$160.00	$120.00	Yes	PA	MD	Yes
134956	Jones, B.	03/05/15	Est. patient comprehensive OV	2/17/15	99205 highest reimburse	Est. patient routine	99212	$160.00	$120.00	No	PA	MD	No
774881	Smith, A.	03/05/15	Excision of nasal polyps- polypectomy	2/18/15	30410 Rhinoplasty-not covered	Rhinoplasty; cosmetic proc not covered	30115	$12,000.00	$0	Polypectomy was documented	MD	MD	Yes

Appendix 29: Initial physician application

MEDICAL BOARD USE ONLY	
Temporary #: __________	File #: __________
Date Issued: __________	License #: ______
	Date Issued: _____

STATE OF ______________

[ ] Check this box if you are applying for an Administrative License
(nonclinical practice)

INITIAL PHYSICIAN APPLICATION
All fees are nonrefundable and subject to change.

Name and Personal Detail

This information is authorized to be obtained and disclosed to state and federal agencies by (state statute(s)). This information may also be disclosed to the National Practitioner Data Bank or other state medical boards or regulatory agencies for license tracking purposes.

Social Security No. ________________________________

Last Name (Surname) ________________________________

First Name ________________________________

Middle Name ________________________________

Other Surnames ________________________________

Degree [ ] MD [ ] DO Specialty ________________

Date of Birth (mm/dd/yy) ______/______/______

Contact Detail Summary

General Addresses

Mailing Address: Correspondence from the Board is sent to this address. Email address is utilized by the Board to contact you in case of an emergency situation. This address will not appear on the Internet *unless you **fail** to provide a practice location address*.

____

Street Number Street Name City State Zip Apt

______________________ Email: __________@______________

Area Code Phone Number

Practice Location/Administrative Office Location: Posted on the Internet when the license number is issued. **"Your mailing address will appear on the Internet if you do not provide a practice/office location"**

____

Street Number Street Name City State Zip Suite/Bldg

____

Area Code Phone Number

Applicant Questionnaire

"Yes" responses require a personal explanation and supporting documentation.

	YES	NO
1. During the past 7 years, have you suffered from any physical, psychiatric, or substance use disorder that could impair or require limitations on your functioning as a professional or has resulted in the inability to practice medicine for more than 30 days, or required court-ordered treatment or hospitalization? (If yes, provide treatment history documentation to include diagnosis, treatment regimen, hospitalization, and ongoing treatment/medication to the Board.) **NOTE: If you are currently enrolled in the State PHP, you may check NO.**	[]	[]
2. Have you entered a plea bargain, been arrested, indicted, or convicted for violating any state or federal law including DUI (excluding minor traffic violations)? As used in this question, the term "conviction" shall include a finding or verdict of guilt, or a plea of guilty, or a plea of nolo contendere in a criminal proceeding, regardless of whether the adjudication of guilt or sentence is withheld or not entered.	[]	[]
3. Have you ever been denied the privilege of taking an examination given by any Licensing board or Agency?	[]	[]
4. Has any licensing board or agency ever taken a public or private disciplinary action against you?	[]	[]
5. Has any licensing board or agency ever refused you renewal of a license?	[]	[]
6. Have you ever been denied a DEA registration number?	[]	[]
7. Have you ever been issued a restricted DEA registration?	[]	[]
8. Are you currently registered with the DEA? If yes, provide DEA number ____________ and state of issue ____________	[]	[]

9. Have you ever been named as a party in a malpractice suit, arbitration hearing, State review panel proceeding, or a VA/federal agency review? [ ] [ ]

10. Have you ever resigned from a hospital staff position or training program after a complaint or peer review action has been initiated against you? [ ] [ ]

11. Have you ever been denied membership in, or in any way sanctioned, by any medical or osteopathic association, society, or specialty society? [ ] [ ]

12. Have you ever surrendered a medical license? [ ] [ ]

13. Have you ever surrendered a controlled substance registration? [ ] [ ]

14. Have you ever surrendered a DEA registration? [ ] [ ]

15. Have you ever been, or are you currently, the subject of an investigation by any licensing board or agency? [ ] [ ]

16. Do you have any applications for licensure pending before any other licensing Board or agency? If yes, provide a list. [ ] [ ]

17. Have you ever had any restrictions as a Medicaid provider? [ ] [ ]

18. Are you in default on a state or federally funded and/or guaranteed school loan? [ ] [ ]

19. Are you in default on child support payments? [ ] [ ]

20. Do you intend to practice in (state in which application is made)? [ ] [ ]
Please provide your plans below:

____

____

____

Program Questions

1. What examinations have you taken? [ ] USMLE [ ] NBME [ ] COMLEX [ ] LMCC
[ ] FLEX [ ] NBOME [ ] ______ State Board Structured Examination

2. How long have you lived in the United States? ________ years ______months

3. Have you served in the U.S. Armed Forces? If yes provide a copy of military discharge paperwork. [ ] Yes [ ] No

4. Are you Board certified in your specialty? [ ] Yes [ ] No
If yes, provide specialty ______________________________

5. Will you be using FCVS? [ ] Yes [ ] No

6. Are you a U.S. citizen? [ ] Yes [ ] No

If you are not a U.S. citizen, you must submit documentation that will determine if you have a qualified alien status. **Only those applicants who can provide proof will be granted a license. The Board participates in the DHS-USCIS SAVE** (Systematic Alien Verification for Entitlements or "SAVE") program for the purpose of verifying citizenship and immigration status information of noncitizens. In order to confirm your status with the SAVE program, you need to provide the Board with **legible** copies of **one** of the documents on the enclosed list.

License History

Provide history for each permanent, temporary, training, provisional, or limited license obtained in any state in the United States, Canadian territory or province, or U.S. federal jurisdiction.

State ______________ Country ____________ Status ____________________

Issued From: ______________ (mm/dd/yy) To: ____________________ (mm/dd/yy)

State ______________ Country ____________ Status ____________________

Issued From: ______________ (mm/dd/yy) To: ____________________ (mm/dd/yy)

State ______________ Country ____________ Status ____________________

Issued From: ______________ (mm/dd/yy) To: ____________________ (mm/dd/yy)

State ______________ Country ____________ Status ____________________

Issued From: ______________ (mm/dd/yy) To: ____________________ (mm/dd/yy)

State ______________ Country ____________ Status ____________________

Issued From: ______________ (mm/dd/yy) To: ____________________ (mm/dd/yy)

State ______________ Country ____________ Status ____________________

Issued From: ______________ (mm/dd/yy) To: ____________________ (mm/dd/yy)

State ______________ Country ____________ Status ____________________

Issued From: ______________ (mm/dd/yy) To: ____________________ (mm/dd/yy)

State ______________ Country ____________ Status ____________________

Issued From: ______________ (mm/dd/yy) To: ____________________ (mm/dd/yy)

Medical/Osteopathic Education

Premedical Education

Beginning month and ending year for each year of attendance is required.

College: ____

1st Year From: ________________ (mm/yy) To: ________________ (mm/yy)

2nd Year From: ________________ (mm/yy) To: ________________ (mm/yy)

3rd Year From: ________________ (mm/yy) To: ________________ (mm/yy)

4th Year From: ________________ (mm/yy) To: ________________ (mm/yy)

5th Year From: ________________ (mm/yy) To: ________________ (mm/yy)

6th Year From: ________________ (mm/yy) To: ________________ (mm/yy)

7th Year From: ________________ (mm/yy) To: ________________ (mm/yy)

Medical Education

Beginning month and ending year for each year of attendance is required.

Medical School: ______

1st Year	From: ______	(mm/yy)	To: ______	(mm/yy)
2nd Year	From: ______	(mm/yy)	To: ______	(mm/yy)
3rd Year	From: ______	(mm/yy)	To: ______	(mm/yy)
4th Year	From: ______	(mm/yy)	To: ______	(mm/yy)
5th Year	From: ______	(mm/yy)	To: ______	(mm/yy)
6th Year	From: ______	(mm/yy)	To: ______	(mm/yy)
7th Year	From: ______	(mm/yy)	To: ______	(mm/yy)

Post Graduate Training

Specialty ______
Hospital ______
Address ______

Specialty ______
Hospital ______
Address ______

Hospital Privileges

Have you ever held any hospital privileges? Yes [ ] No [ ]

Hospital ______
Address ______
City/State/Zip ______

Hospital ______
Address ______
City/State/Zip ______

Hospital ______
Address ______
City/State/Zip ______

Hospital ______
Address ______
City/State/Zip ______

Hospital ______
Address ______
City/State/Zip ______

Hospital ____

Address ____

City/State/Zip ____

Hospital ____

Address ____

City/State/Zip ____

Appendix 30: State medical and osteopathic medical boards

Alabama Board of Medical Examiners
P.O. Box 946
Montgomery, AL 36101-0946
(street address: 848 Washington Ave.)
(334) 242-4116/Fax: (334) 242-4155
(800) 227-2606
www.albme.org

Alaska State Medical Board
550 West Seventh Ave., Suite 1500
Anchorage, AK 99501-3567
(907) 269-8163/Fax: (907) 269-8196
www.commerce.state.ak.us/occ/pmed.htm

Arizona Medical Board
9545 East Doubletree Ranch Road
Scottsdale, AZ 85258-5514
(480) 551-2700/Fax: (480) 551-2704
Toll Free: (877) 255-2212
www.azmd.gov

Arizona Board of Osteopathic Examiners in Medicine and Surgery
9535 East Doubletree Ranch Road
Scottsdale, AZ 85258-5539
(480) 657-7703/Fax: (480) 657-7715
www.azdo.gov

Arkansas State Medical Board
Victory Bldg.
1401 West Capitol Avenue, Suite 340
Little Rock, AR 72201-2936
(501) 296-1802/Fax: (501) 296-1805
www.armedicalboard.org

Medical Board of California
2005 Evergreen Street, Suite 1200
Sacramento, CA 95815-5401
(916) 263-2389/Fax: (916) 263-2387
(800) 633-2322
www.mbc.ca.gov

Osteopathic Medical Board of California
1300 National Drive, Suite 150
Sacramento, CA 95834-1991
(916) 928-8390/Fax: (916) 928-8392
www.ombc.ca.gov/

Colorado Medical Board
1560 Broadway, Suite 1300
Denver, CO 80202-5140
(303) 894-7690/Fax: (303) 894-7692
www.dora.state.co.us/medical

Connecticut Medical Examining Board Department of Public Health
P.O. Box 340308
Hartford, CT 06134-0308
(street address 410 Capitol Ave., MS #13PHO)
Licensing/Examinations (860) 509-8374
Administrative (860) 509-7648/Fax: (860) 509-7553
Complaints: (860) 509-7552/Complaint Toll Free: (800) 842-0038
www.dph.state.ct.us

Delaware Board of Medical Licensure and Discipline
861 Silver Lake Blvd., Suite 203,
Cannon Building
Dover, DE 19904
(302) 744-4500/Fax: (302) 739-2711
www.dpr.delaware.gov

District of Columbia Board of Medicine
899 North Capitol St. NE, 1st Flr.
Washington D.C. 20002
(202) 724-4900/Fax: (202) 442-8117
doh.dc.gov/bomed

Florida Board of Medicine
Department of Health
4052 Bald Cypress Way, BIN #C03
Tallahassee, FL 32399-3253
(850) 245-4131/Fax: (850) 488-9325
Complaints Toll Free: (888) 419-3456
www.flboardofmedicine.gov/

Florida Board of Osteopathic Medicine
4052 Bald Cypress Way, BIN C06
Tallahassee, FL 32399-3256
(850) 245-4161/Fax: (850) 921-6184
www.floridasosteopathicmedicine.gov

Georgia Composite Medical Board
2 Peachtree Street, NW, 36th Floor
Atlanta, GA 30303-3141
(404) 656-3913/Fax: (404) 656-9723
www.medicalboard.georgia.gov/

Hawaii Medical Board
Department of Commerce and Consumer Affairs
P.O. Box 3469
Honolulu, HI 96813
(street address: 335 Merchant St., Room 301, 96813)
(808) 586-3000/Fax: (808) 586-2874
www.hawaii.gov/dcca/pvl

Idaho Board of Medicine
1755 Westgate Drive, Suite 140
Boise, ID 83704-7190
(street address: 83704)
(208) 327-7000/Fax: (208) 327-7005
bom.idaho.gov

Illinois Division of Professional Regulation
Medical Disciplinary Unit
100 W. Randolph Street, Suite 9-300
James R. Thompson Center
Chicago, IL 60601
(312) 814-4580/Fax: (312) 814-5392
Complaints: (312) 814-6910
www.idfpr.com

Illinois Division of Professional Regulation
Medical Licensing Unit
320 W. Washington St., 3rd Floor
Springfield, IL 62786
(217) 524-7534/Fax: (217) 524-2169
www.idfpr.com

Medical Licensing Board of Indiana
402 W. Washington St., Room W072
Indianapolis, IN 46204-2298
(317) 234-2060/Fax: (317) 233-4236
www.in.gov/pla/medical.htm

Iowa Board of Medicine
400 SW 8th St., Suite C
Des Moines, IA 50309-4619
(515) 242-3268/Fax: (515) 242-5908
www.medicalboard.iowa.gov

Kansas State Board of Healing Arts
800 SW Jackson, Lower Level-Suite A
Topeka, KS 66612
(785) 296-7413/Fax: (785) 296-0852
www.ksbha.org

Kentucky Board of Medical Licensure
Hurstbourne Office Park
310 Whittington Parkway, Suite 1B
Louisville, KY 40222-4927
(502) 429-7150/Fax: (502) 429-7158
kbml.ky.gov

Louisiana State Board of Medical Examiners
P.O. Box 30250
New Orleans, LA 70190-0250
(street address: 630 Camp St., 70130)
(504) 568-6820/Fax: (504) 568-6880
www.lsbme.louisiana.gov

Maine Board of Licensure in Medicine
137 State House Station (U.S. mail)
161 Capitol Street (delivery service)
Augusta, ME 04333-0137
(207) 287-3601/Fax: (207) 287-6590
www.maine.gov/md

Maine Board of Osteopathic Licensure
142 State House Station
Augusta, ME 04333-0142
(207) 287-2480 (207) 287-3015
www.maine.gov/osteo/

Maryland Board of Physicians
P.O. Box 2571
Baltimore, MD 21215
(street address: 4201 Patterson Ave., fourth floor, 21215)
(410) 764-4777/Fax: (410) 358-2252
(800) 492-6836
www.mbp.state.md.us/

Massachusetts Board of Registration in Medicine
200 Harvard Mill Square, Suite 330,
Wakefield, MA 01880-3238
(781) 876-8200/Fax: (781) 876-8384
(800) 377-0550
www.massmedboard.org

Michigan Board of Medicine
P.O. Box 30670
Lansing, MI 48909-8170
(street address: 611 W. Ottawa St, 1st floor, 48933)
(517) 335-0918/Fax: (517) 241-9416
www.michigan.gov/healthlicense

Michigan Board of Osteopathic Medicine and Surgery
P.O. Box 30670
Lansing, MI 48909-8170
(street address: 611 W. Ottawa St, 1st floor, 48933)
(517) 335-1001/Fax: (517) 373-2179
www.michigan.gov/healthlicense

Minnesota Board of Medical Practice
University Park Plaza
2829 University Ave. SE, Suite 500
Minneapolis, MN 55414-3246
(612) 617-2130/Fax: (612) 617-2166
Hearing impaired 1-800-627-3529
www.bmp.state.mn.us

Mississippi State Board of Medical Licensure
1867 Crane Ridge Drive, Suite 200B
Jackson, MS 39216
(601) 987-3079/Fax: (601) 987-4159
www.msbml.state.ms.us

Missouri Board of Registration for the Healing Arts
3605 Missouri Blvd.
P.O. Box 4
Jefferson City, MO 65109-7111
(street address: 3605 Missouri Blvd., 65109)
(573) 751-0098/Fax: (573) 751-3166
www.pr.mo.gov/healingarts.asp

Montana Board of Medical Examiners
P.O. Box 200513
Helena, MT 59620-0513
(406) 841-2360/Fax: (406) 841-2305
Discovering Montana

Nebraska Board of Medicine and Surgery
Health and Human Services
Regulation and Licensure Credentialing Division
P.O. Box 94986
Lincoln, NE 68509-4986
(402) 471-2118/Fax: (402) 471-8614
dhhs.ne.gov/Pages/default.aspx

Nevada State Board of Medical Examiners
P.O. Box 7238
Reno, NV 89510
(775) 688-2559/Fax: (775) 688-2321
www.medboard.nv.gov

Nevada State Board of Osteopathic Medicine
901 American Pacific Dr., Unit 180
Henderson, NV 89014
(702) 732-2147/Fax: (702) 732-2079
www.bom.nv.gov

New Hampshire Board of Medicine
Philbrook Building
121 S. Fruit Street Suite 301
Concord, NH 03301-2412
(603) 271-1203/Fax: (603) 271-6702
Complaints (800) 780-4757
www.state.nh.us/medicine

New Jersey State Board of Medical Examiners
P.O. Box 183
Trenton, NJ 08625-0183
(609) 826-7100/Fax: (609) 826-7117
www.state.nj.us/lps/ca/medical.htm#bme5

New Mexico Medical Board
2055 S. Pacheco Street Building 400
Santa Fe, NM 87505-0503
(505) 476-7220/Fax: (505) 476-7237
www.nmmb.state.nm.us

New Mexico Board of Osteopathic Medical Examiners
P.O. Box 25101
Santa Fe, NM 87501
(505) 476-4629/Fax: (505) 476-4665
www.rld.state.nm.us/boards/Osteopathy.aspx

New York State Board for Medicine (Licensure)
89 Washington Avenue, 2nd Floor, West Wing
Albany, NY 12234
(518) 474-3817 Ext. 560/Fax: (518) 486-4846
http://usny.nysed.gov/professionals/

New York State Office of Professional Medical Conduct (Discipline)
Riverview Center
150 Broadway Suite 355
Albany, NY 12204
(518) 402-0855/Fax: (518) 402-0866
www.health.state.ny.us/

North Carolina Medical Board
P.O. Box 20007
Raleigh, NC 27619-0007
(919) 326-1100/Fax: (919) 326-1131
www.ncmedboard.org

North Dakota Board of Medical Examiners
City Center Plaza
418 E. Broadway Avenue, Suite 12
Bismarck, ND 58501-4086
(701) 328-6500/Fax: (701) 328-6505
www.ndbomex.org

State Medical Board of Ohio
30 E. Broad St. 3rd Floor
Columbus, OH 43215-6127
(614) 466-3934/Fax: (614) 728-5946
(800) 554-7717
www.med.ohio.gov

Oklahoma Board of Medical Licensure and Supervision
P.O. Box 18256
Oklahoma City, OK 73154-0256
(405) 962-1400/Fax: (405) 962-1499
(800) 381-4519
www.okmedicalboard.org

Oklahoma State Board of Osteopathic Examiners
4848 N. Lincoln Blvd., Suite 100
Oklahoma City, OK 73105-3321
(405) 528-8625/Fax: (405) 557-0653
www.ok.gov/osboe/

Oregon Medical Board
1500 SW 1st Ave., Suite 620
Portland, OR 97201-5815
(971) 673-2700/Fax: (971) 673-2670
www.oregon.gov/OMB

Pennsylvania State Board of Medicine
P.O. Box 2649
Harrisburg, PA 17105-2649
(717) 787-2381/Fax: (717) 787-7769
Pennsylvania State Board

Pennsylvania State Board of Osteopathic Medicine
P.O. Box 2649
Harrisburg, PA 17105-2649
(street address: 124 Pine St., 17101)
(717) 783-4858/Fax: (717) 787-7769
www.dos.state.pa.us

Rhode Island Board of Medical Licensure and Discipline
Department of Health
3 Capitol Hill Room 401
Providence, RI 02908-5097
(401) 222-3855/Fax: (401) 222-2158
http://www.health.ri.gov

South Carolina Board of Medical Examiners
110 Centerview Drive, Suite 202
Columbia, SC 29210-8432
(803) 896-4500/Fax: (803) 896-4515
www.llr.state.sc.us/pol/medical

South Dakota Board of Medical and Osteopathic Examiners
101 N. Main Avenue, Suite 301
Sioux Falls, SD 57104
(605) 367-7781/Fax: (605) 367-7786
www.sdbmoe.gov

Tennessee State Board of Medical Examiners
665 Mainstream Drive
Nashville, TN 37243-0001
(615) 532-4384/Fax: (615) 253-4484
health.state.tn.us

Tennessee Board of Osteopathic Examination
665 Mainstream Drive
Nashville, TN 37243-0001
(615) 532-3202/Fax: (615) 253-4484
health.state.tn.us

Texas Medical Board
P.O. Box 2018
Austin, TX 78701-2018
(512) 305-7010/Fax: (512) 305-7051
Disciplinary Hotline (800) 248-4062
Consumer Complaint Hotline (800) 201-9353
www.tmb.state.tx.us

Utah Physicians & Surgeons Licensing Board
PO Box 146741
Salt Lake City, UT 84114-6741
(801) 530-6628/Fax: (801) 530-6511
www.dopl.utah.gov

Utah Osteopathic Physicians & Surgeons Licensing Board
PO Box 146741
Salt Lake City, UT 84114-6741
(801) 530-6628/Fax: (801) 530-6511
www.dopl.utah.gov

Vermont Board of Medical Practice
108 Cherry Street
P.O. Box 70
Burlington, VT 05402-0070
(802) 657-4220/Fax: (802) 657-4227
www.healthvermont.gov

Vermont Board of Osteopathic Physicians and Surgeons
Office of Professional Regulation
89 Main Street, 3rd Floor
Montpelier, VT 05620-3402
802-828-1502/Fax: (802) 828-2465
www.vtprofessionals.org

Virginia Board of Medicine
Perimeter Center
9960 Mayland Drive, Suite 300
Henrico, VA 23233-1463
Phone: (804) 367-4600
Fax Licensing Unit: (804) 527-4426,
Fax Discipline Unit: (804) 527-4429
www.dhp.virginia.gov

Washington Medical Quality Assurance Commission
Department of Health
PO Box 47866
Olympia, WA 98504-7866
(360) 236-2750/Fax: (360) 236-2795
www.doh.wa.gov

Washington Board of Osteopathic Medicine and Surgery
Department of Health
P.O. Box 47852
Olympia, WA 98504-7852
(360) 236-4700/Fax: (360) 236-4818
www.doh.wa.gov

West Virginia Board of Medicine
101 Dee Drive, Suite 103
Charleston, WV 25301
(304) 558-2921/Fax: (304) 558-2084
www.wvbom.wv.gov

West Virginia Board of Osteopathic Medicine
405 Capitol Street, Suite 402
Charleston, WV 25301
(304) 558-6095/Fax: (304) 558-6096
www.wvbdosteo.org

Wisconsin Medical Examining Board
1400 E. Washington Avenue Room 178
Madison, WI 53703-3041
(608) 266-2112/Fax: (608) 267-3816
Complaints Toll Free: (877) 617-1565
dsps.wi.gov

Wyoming Board of Medicine
130 Hobbs Avenue, Suite A
Cheyenne, WY 82002
(307) 778-7053/Fax: (307) 778-2069
Complaint Toll Free: (877) 617-1565
wyomedboard.state.wy.us

Appendix 31: Miscellaneous agency web addresses

Miscellaneous Agency Web Addresses

Academy of Integrative Health and Medicine	http://aihm.org/
Association of State Criminal Investigative Agencies	https://www.ascia.org/
Administrators in Medicine	http://www.docboard.org/
Alliance of States with Prescription Drug Monitoring Programs	http://www.nascsa.org/
American Board of Medical Specialties	http://www.abms.org/
American Medical Association	http://www.ama-assn.org/
American Psychiatric Association	http://www.psychiatry.org/
Association of Certified Fraud Examiners	http://www.acfe.com/
Centers for Disease Control and Prevention	http://www.cdc.gov/
Centers for Medicare and Medicaid Services	http://www.cms.gov/
Federal Bureau of Investigation	http://www.fbi.gov/
Federation of State Medical Boards	http://www.fsmb.org/
Federation of State Physician Health Programs	http://www.fsphp.org/
National Association of Attorneys General	http://www.naag.org/
National Association of Boards of Pharmacy	http://www.nabp.net/
National Association of Insurance Commissioners	http://www.naic.org/
National Association of Medicaid Fraud Control Units	http://www.namfcu.net/
National Association of Secretaries of State	http://www.nass.org/
National Association of State Controlled Substance Authorities	http://www.nascsa.org
National Healthcare Anti-Fraud Association	http://www.nhcaa.org/
National Institutes of Health	http://www.nih.gov/
National Insurance Crime Bureau	https://www.nicb.org/
National Practitioner Data Bank	http://www.npdb-hipdb.hrsa.gov/
U.S. Drug Enforcement Administration	http://www.dea.gov/
U.S. Food and Drug Administration	http://www.fda.gov/
World Health Organization	http://www.who.int/

Index

R

U

V

W

For Product Safety Concerns and Information please contact our EU representative GPSR@taylorandfrancis.com
Taylor & Francis Verlag GmbH, Kaufingerstraße 24, 80331 München, Germany

www.ingramcontent.com/pod-product-compliance
Ingram Content Group UK Ltd.
Pitfield, Milton Keynes, MK11 3LW, UK
UKHW020022200926
475702UK00014B/2015
9780367596279